CHRIST

The Ideal of the Priest

DOM MARMION, O.S.B.

CHRIST
The Ideal of the Priest

Translated by

Dom Matthew Dillon

IGNATIUS PRESS   SAN FRANCISCO

Original English edition published in 1952 by
B. Herder Book Co., St. Louis, Missouri

Published with ecclesiastical approval
Printed in Great Britain

Reprinted by permission of Glenstal Priory

*Adaptations for the 2005 edition made by
Father Donald L. Toups
St. Vincent de Paul Regional Seminary, Florida*

Cover art: Peter Paul Rubens
Christ Washing the Apostles' Feet
Erich Lessing / Art Resource, NY

Cover design by Riz Boncan Marsella

Published in 2005 by Ignatius Press, San Francisco
Foreword © 2005 by Ignatius Press, San Francisco
All rights reserved
ISBN 978-1-58617-014-1
ISBN 1-58617-014-7
Library of Congress Control Number 2005926535
Printed in the United States of America ∞

CONTENTS

FOREWORD

ON the third of September of the Jubilee Year 2000, Abbot Columba Marmion was beatified by Pope John Paul II, who said in the homily that the new Beatus "will illumine our steps at the dawn of the third millennium". Whenever Blessed Columba Marmion's works are explored, the reader is always edified in spirit. Marmion's classical and organic synthesis of theology, spirituality, and examples of pastoral life is exactly what is needed today to help "post-moderns" find integration in their lives. This contribution is especially true for priests. *Christ—The Ideal of the Priest* offers a combination of dogma and spirituality to help encourage priests of the twenty-first century to be holy and faithful servants of the Lord. Priests are, by virtue of their ordination, eternally and ontologically changed, and this new reality must be incorporated into their priestly life and ministry. Dom Marmion understood well the Thomistic axiom *agere sequitur esse* (doing follows being) and believed that everything the priest does must flow from the grace and character received at ordination. At all times the priest is called to act *in persona Christi capitis* and *in nomine Ecclesiae*. Having a fuller awareness of one's true identity can only help the priest respond to the diverse situations that will inevitably arise in his life. The priest who understands his sacerdotal character will likely be more faithful and joyful in his life of loving service in the Church.

Christ—The Ideal of the Priest, published posthumously in 1952, yet nevertheless "authentic Marmion", is a treasure trove of encouragement for today's parish priest. In this current re-publication, more than fifty years later, several observations need to be made. First of all, the biblical citations of verses have been taken from the Revised Standard Version (RSVCE), thus adjusting some references that were from an earlier Latin Vulgate edition. Secondly, additional translations have been inserted when the Latin quotations (so loved by Marmion) do not appear self-evident. Thirdly, a few editorial notes have been added for the sake of clarity for contemporary readers. Many thanks to the Benedictine monks of Maredsous, Belgium, and Glenstal, Ireland, for allowing this project to move forward, and to Ignatius Press for seeing it through to completion.

It is my desire that this work of Marmion will once again encourage and inspire priests as it did a generation ago. May it be an impetus of renewal within priestly hearts and may it be of assistance to those in need of rekindling the gift of God bestowed on them through the imposition of hands (see 2 Tim 1:6). I wish to close this foreword with an inscription I found in an old edition of the book, which encapsulates what it has to offer to priests today. These words are from a religious sister to a priest friend: "All the wonderful things I'd want to tell you, all the spiritual advice I long to give, you will find within the pages of this book. Read and Do, so that it may be said of you, 'Thou art another Christ!'"

Reverend David L. Toups, S.T.D.

St. Vincent de Paul Regional Seminary
Boynton Beach, Florida
May 1, 2005

PREFACE TO THE 1952 EDITION

On 16 March 1918, a few months after the publication of *Christ, the Life of the Soul*, a work destined to have so great a success, Dom Marmion mentioned to one of his correspondents that the ensemble of his works would comprise four volumes: *Christ, Our Life, The Mysteries of Christ, Benedictine Asceticism,* and *Sacerdos, Alter Christus*.

On 25 September of the same year, he wrote: "I have begun the fourth volume for priests. Here is the plan: (1) The Eternal Priesthood; (2) The Priestly Vocation; (3) The Mass; (4) The Sacrifice of Praise; (5) The Sacrifice of Thanksgiving; (6) Propitiation; (7) Impetration. *Christ in His Mysteries* appeared in 1919, and shortly after the publication (September 1922) of *Christ, the Ideal of the Monk*, on 30 January 1923, the Abbot of Maredsous was called to God. The celebrated trilogy was left without its crown, that part of his message second in importance only to *Christ, the Life of the Soul*, which Dom Marmion had intended for priests.

Pendent opera interrupta

This "interruption" was to be prolonged over many years. Why? As the person solely responsible, the writer of this preface owes his readers an explanation. As is generally known, Dom Marmion wrote nothing himself for publication. The first three volumes treating of Christ were edited by one of his monks, with the help of notes taken at the Abbot's conferences by his disciples. From this mass of documents the editor has succeeded in extracting a systematic exposition of doctrine and of asceticism.

This delicate task was accomplished with the encouragement of Dom Marmion. There is not a single page which was not submitted to him, not a page which was not revised by him,

9

pen in hand, making a correction here and there and adding an occasional text from the Scriptures, the Fathers or the Liturgy, the better to illustrate his thought. This constant and exhaustive revision not only served to guarantee the editor against all danger of error, but enabled Dom Marmion to give his work the hall-mark of absolute authenticity.

After his death, numerous notes written in his own hand on the priesthood and on the sanctity of the priest were found among his papers. They were the notes he had used in the preparation of his conferences. From this material, collected over a period of thirty years, it would have been possible to develop a systematic, homogeneous treatise. Unhappily it would not be possible to submit this work to the control of the true author; there could be no revision, no approval to guarantee its value.

From this fact, as can easily be understood, there arose in the mind of the editor a scruple which gradually became insuperable and until recently paralysed every attempt to carry out the work.

It was only quite recently that the opportunity presented itself to undertake the task under conditions more favourable than could have been hoped for. Dom Ryelandt, who had been a disciple of Dom Marmion from an early date and had attended his conferences for many years, was freed from other important and engrossing duties. With that generosity which is well known to our readers he has given us the invaluable help of his profound knowledge of the teaching of Dom Marmion. His constant and learned collaboration has enabled us to present to the public a synthesis of sacerdotal doctrine worthy of our common Master.

It may be of interest to give some details about the ministry which Dom Marmion exercised among the clergy. He was particularly fond of this branch of the apostolate because it was addressed to the friends of Jesus who had been associated by the divine Master with Himself in His work of Redemption. He often used to say when speaking of these conferences that they were "relayed by loudspeakers".

He had been well prepared by Providence for this noble task. Dom Marmion had an intimate knowledge of seminary life both in Dublin and in the Irish College in Rome where he completed his theological formation. Coming back to Ireland after his ordination in the Eternal City in 1881, he was appointed curate in Dundrum on the outskirts of Dublin. During one year he served there his initiation to the manifold activities of the parochial ministry. His archbishop then appointed him to the chair of philosophy in the seminary of Clonliffe; he occupied it for four years, in the course of which many aspirants to the priesthood came to submit themselves to his direction. At the same time he had charge of two communities of nuns and provided for the spiritual needs of the prisoners, men and women, in the prisons of Dublin.

Through this prolonged intercourse with different types of souls, the most abandoned as well as the most noble, Fr. Marmion familiarized himself gradually with the innermost depths of the human conscience.

He was twenty-eight years old when, already rich in priestly experience, he was able, in 1886, to realize his aspirations to the cloister and enter Maredsous.

After his religious profession he came in touch with the parishes in the neighbourhood of the Abbey and on account of his ardent zeal was in great demand among the parish priests who saw in him a born preacher whose turn of phrase, sometimes imperfect but always original, moved the souls of his hearers. His fame spread little by little. Soon he inaugurated at Dinant sur Meuse his real apostolate among priests by a series of monthly recollections to the clergy of the town. This series lasted over two years, 1897–1898.

But it was in Louvain, whither he was sent in 1899 and where he remained ten years, that this ministry was to find its full development. In the Collège du Saint Esprit, which comprises professors of the faculties of Theology and young priests studying for degrees, as well as in the seminary Léon XIII and the American seminary, he gave forth his doctrine in the course of many retreats and series of conferences. A new voice was heard in this university milieu; the dogmatic character of his preaching and the profound conviction and vitality which inspired it made a vivid impression. Dom Marmion rapidly won the respect of these priests, many of whom chose him as their director.

The most illustrious of these was Msgr. Mercier. When he later became Archbishop and then Cardinal, Mercier entrusted to Dom Marmion the spiritual conferences for eighty priests of the parishes and colleges of Brussels (1907–1908). But already England had made her claim on him. Cardinal Bourne, Archbishop of Westminster, and Msgr. Amigo, Bishop of Southwark, frequently invoked his zeal on behalf of their clergy.

This apostolate, which was especially fruitful during these years, continued until his death. The seminaries of Tournai and Nottingham (August and September 1922) were the last to profit by this teaching which was at the same time so supernatural and so human.

As we have said, Dom Marmion has left a very large accumulation of notes written in his own hand for conferences.[1] Sometimes the whole conference has been summarily sketched out but, more frequently, these notes are fragmentary, without order, incomplete, jotted down in pen or pencil, or consisting merely of a few lines scribbled on the leaf of a note-book. Nevertheless, they are elevated in matter and rich in doctrine. They are the principal and the most authentic element of our documentation; we have relied especially on the notes of the Louvain period (1899–1909) which give evidence of an ever increasing mastery of his subject.

From 1909 the documentation is less extensive. This is due to the fact that from this date Dom Marmion, having been elected Abbot of Maredsous, was more and more occupied with the duties of his office. Moreover at this time he was in the full maturity of his talent and had a complete command of his doctrine. Being endowed with a remarkable memory, he lived

---

[1] It is noteworthy that when preaching Dom Marmion never used his notes; always, even during retreats comprising a large number of conferences, he spoke from the abundance of his heart, not confining himself to the notes which he had prepared.

on the riches of his store. For this last period we have another source to rely on: the notes taken by his attentive audiences during his spiritual conferences. Especially noteworthy among these are the complete texts of two retreats: one given in 1919 to the religious who had come back from the war; and one given to the seminarists of Tournai, both of which manifest a great elevation of thought and a rich experience.

From this variety of documents, of different dates and of varying values, in which inevitably there is much repetition, it was necessary to construct by careful and judicious selection a composite whole at once coherent and complete.

The plan given by Dom Marmion in his letter of 25 September 1918 is so summary that it can only be regarded as a very general idea of the book, although the place it gives to the sacrifice of the Mass is significant of his line of thought. The richness of the documentation and our anxiety to omit nothing of such treasures has led us to divide up the whole doctrine in a simple, logical framework well adapted to the amplitude of the priestly life. Any other plan would have prevented us from grouping in a single synthesis all the numerous and precious elements which Dom Marmion has left us. He would himself without doubt have approved of this course which recalls the plans of *Christ, the Life of the Soul* and *Christ, the Ideal of the Monk*, which had been approved by him. The constant aim of our common effort has been, and we have always had it in mind, to give the substance of the Marmion doctrine in all its purity and entirety, while preserving the essential unity and variety of his approach.

Let us try to identify what is characteristic in the doctrine of Dom Marmion. In his thought, which is the echo of the thought of St. Paul, the priestly life, like the Christian life itself, must be envisaged as dominated by Christ and in constant dependence on His merits, His grace and His activity. It is in this revealing perspective that the dignity of the priesthood and the work of his sanctification must be understood: the priest holds his supernatural powers in virtue of a priesthood which is far above him: the priesthood of the Incarnate Word: and he only

exercises these powers in complete subordination to the supreme Pontiff. It follows that the virtues proper to the priest
shall be a reproduction of those of his divine model; they will
be a reflection among men of the virtues of Jesus Christ. In all
his actions, in the sacred acts of worship, in the administration
of the sacraments, in his apostolic zeal, in his private devotions
and in his daily occupations, the priest must always regard himself as the minister of the Saviour, *Alter Christus*. Accordingly
for him even more than for the simple Christian, sanctification
can only be conceived as the reflection of Christ. For him
Christ will be everything: *the Alpha and the Omega*.

As regards the work itself, it has been carried out, it need
hardly be said, with the greatest respect for the depth and
preciousness of the thought of the venerable Abbot, manifesting at once the learning of the doctor of theology and the skill
of the director of conscience. We were at all times careful to
preserve his direct style, his clear, simple form with that personal, informal turn of phrase and even his favourite expressions. Those who have already been in touch with the teaching
of Dom Marmion will meet here subjects which have been
treated already in his earlier works: Christ, model and source of
all sanctity, faith, charity, the Mass, prayer. Should we, in this
volume, have passed over these subjects, merely giving the
reference to earlier writings? Such a course would not only
have proved a distraction for the reader but would have involved a mutilation of the teachings of the master. In fact, the
sanctification of the priest cannot be accomplished apart from
Christ and His grace, apart from the virtues, especially the
Christian virtues of faith, humility and zeal, apart from the
eucharistic offering and apart from prayer. It is for this reason
that we decided to deal with these subjects once more, but this
time from a point of view peculiarly adapted to the clergy,
embracing on the one hand the indispensable review of the
fundamental ideas, while avoiding on the other hand their
fuller but more general development which is to be found in
the earlier writings. This solution, safeguarding as it did the full
plenitude of Dom Marmion's teaching and the homogeneity of

the book, seemed the obvious one. We are confident that it will meet with the approval of our readers.

When Dom Marmion was preaching a priests' retreat it was not his aim to establish a particular line of theological teaching or to inculcate a number of pastoral directions or to inaugurate detailed examinations of conscience: he was trying, we shall not say solely, but principally, to introduce his listeners into that atmosphere of faith at once lively, brilliant, and contemplative, in which his own soul dwelt. By the warmth of his own convictions and his infectious enthusiasm he inspired in the priests a new certainty of those spiritual realities in the midst of which their ministry is exercised: he gave them a spiritual impulse which emancipated them from routine and mediocrity: he aroused in them a generous desire to unite themselves more and more to Christ and to give first place to the interior life. In this, as always, he goes straight to the essential, that essential point which Our Holy Father, Pius XII, the Supreme Pastor, has recalled with such emphasis on many occasions and especially in his exhortation *Menti Nostrae* of 23 September 1950.*

Christ—The Ideal of the Priest is simply a continuation of this apostolate. Every one of its chapters is calculated to raise the reader to this same supernatural atmosphere, to give him a better understanding of the sovereign importance of the life of union with God through Christ. Here you will find again Dom Marmion with all his qualities: his perfect knowledge of

* It should be noted that Dom Marmion's works were greatly respected by Pope Paul VI and John Paul II. Marmion's writings have had a direct influence on several popes of the twentieth century: Benedict XV, Pius XI, Pius XII, Paul VI, and John Paul II. Pope Pius XII stated that the words of Marmion were "outstanding in the accuracy of their doctrine, the clarity of their style, and the depth and richness of their thought". While working at the Vatican Secretariat of State, Msgr. Giovanni Battista Montini (the future Paul VI) wrote a beautiful letter of approbation for *Christ, the Ideal of the Priest* in 1952. As a young priest finishing his doctorate at the Angelicum in Rome and living at the Belgian College, Fr. Karol Wojtyla (the future John Paul II) was known to have taken and read all of the writings of Marmion from the college library. It was remembered fondly by his classmate Fr. Léon-Joseph Suenens, the future archbishop of Mechlin-Brussels, Belgium, that Wojtyla not only read all the works of Marmion, but also in all of the available translations. Not long after his election to the pontificate, Pope John Paul II said to a group of priests and seminarians at the Irish College in Rome that Marmion has left "to the whole Church extensive writings of deep insight and great value on this mystery of the divine sonship and on the centrality of Jesus Christ in God's plan of sanctification".

dogma, his clear doctrine—"the pure doctrine of the Church", as Benedict XV has described it—his wide knowledge of the Scriptures, especially of St. John and St. Paul, his vast experience of souls, his approach which is so penetrating and so profitable to souls. One can feel in it the throb of an intensive priestly life,[2] of an ardent love of Christ, eager to communicate itself to others.

On all these grounds, but especially on account of the abundance, the richness and the originality of the varying aspects hitherto unedited, this volume will take its place inevitably by the side of its three forerunners; it is their completion, their crown; it forms with them a unity and constitutes a worthy completion of the *corpus asceticum* of Dom Marmion centred on Christ. The message of the master of the spiritual life with all its spontaneity and life is now communicated to the world in its entirety.

Many souls in the retirement of the cloister dedicate themselves by a life of prayer and silent immolation to the sanctification of the clergy. May these pages, by revealing to them the grandeur of the priesthood and its great need of sanctity, help them to realize their own mission—a mission hidden but most fruitful—in the service of the Church of Christ.

May we close this preface with a quotation which has a peculiar value as coming from the pen of Cardinal Suhard. The late Archbishop of Paris was well known for his deep appreciation of the needs of souls, those of the clergy and of the laity. We have only to recall *The Priest in the City*.

A fervent admirer of Dom Marmion and his teaching, the Cardinal, with all the authority of his pen, expressed a keen desire for the publication of this work, foreseeing the good it would do and the influence it would have. In a long tribute to the memory of the former Abbot of Maredsous on the occasion of the twenty-fifth anniversary of his death which he addressed to the writer of these lines, the prince of the Church was good enough to write: "The spiritual teaching of Dom Marmion

---

[2] See the personal notes of Dom Marmion, pp. 380ff.

furnishes a Catholic synthesis at once profoundly human and supernatural which is perfectly adapted to the needs of our times and to the present orientation of Catholic piety. But Dom Marmion has not yet completed his work, or rather, if he has completed it, it has not yet been given to the public. *Christ, the Ideal of the Priest* is the work which we are awaiting from your hands. If you will open up (for the benefit of those priests of whom we are thinking) the treasures of life and light which the venerable deceased has left as a legacy to the Benedictine family, all the pastors of the Church, including the Archbishop of Paris, will be indebted to the Abbey of Maredsous both for themselves and for the sake of their clergy."

We now present with all confidence to the ministers of Christ this book so sincerely desired by the eminent prelate. May the reading of it help priests to maintain the daily effort towards sanctity which the sublimity of their vocation requires of them.

* * *

All the footnotes (whatever their motive: bibliographical or intended to illustrate the thought of Dom Marmion) are our own. In his conferences Dom Marmion almost invariably quoted scripture in Latin: sometimes he referred to the Greek text. For the sake of those readers who do not know Latin we have either replaced the Latin quotation by a translation or, where the Latin text seemed more expressive, we have given the meaning. We have given no references to the texts of the Ordinary of the Mass which are so familiar. We would like to thank all those who have helped in this publication; they have their share in the good that it will do to souls.

Part I

CHRIST, AUTHOR OF OUR PRIESTHOOD AND OF OUR SANCTITY

I.

THE PRIESTHOOD OF CHRIST

I. THE GLORY OF GOD

St. Paul has revealed to us that the absolute dependence of all creatures on the sovereignty of God imposes on man the obligation to give glory to the divine majesty. *Ex Ipso et per Ipsum et in Ipso sunt omnia: Ipsi gloria in saecula. Amen* (Rom 11:36). All glory to the Holy Trinity.

God renders to Himself a praise that is perfect and infinite. All the canticles of the angels and of the whole universe can add nothing to it.

However, God requires of His creatures that they should associate themselves with this glorification which is a part of His intimate life. According to the divine plan, the glory which man must render to the Lord is outside the scope of natural religion; it ascends to the Holy Trinity through the priesthood of Christ, the official mediator between heaven and earth.

This is the splendid prerogative of the priesthood of Christ and His priests: to offer to the Holy Trinity in the name of man and of the universe a homage of praise agreeable to God. It is the privilege of this priesthood to ensure the return of creation in its entirety to the Master of all things. With all the respect of a lively faith let us begin by fixing our eyes on the mystery of this glorification in the bosom of the Trinity; it has existed before all ages like God Himself; and will last for ever, *sicut erat in principio et nunc et semper*. It is the perfect model of all praise, human or angelic. We are called to unite ourselves to it on earth and in heaven. This is our sublime destiny.

What is this glory which the Divine Persons render to each other?

In His essence God is not only great, *magnus*, but also "the object of all praise", *laudabilis nimis* (Ps 47[48]:1). It is preeminently fitting that He should receive the glory due to His majesty; it is fitting that He should be glorified in Himself by a praise corresponding to the immensity of power, of wisdom and of love which are in Him. God could have refrained from creation; He could have remained without us in the ineffable and blessed society of light and of love of the Divine Persons.

The Father engenders the Son: from all eternity He communicates to Him that supreme gift: the life and the perfections of the divinity; He communicates to Him all that He is Himself excepting that which is "proper" to Him: His paternity.

Being His perfect substantial image, the Word is "the splendour of the glory of the Father", *Splendor gloriae et figura substantiae eius* (Heb 1:3). Born of the focus of all light, His brilliance is reflected back like an unbroken canticle towards Him from Whom He comes. "All things are Thine and Thine are Mine" (Jn 17:10).

Thus, by the natural impulse of His filiation, the Son reciprocates to the Father all that He has from Him.

The Holy Spirit, Who is charity, has His exclusive source of origin in the love of the Father and the Son. This union of infinite love between the three Persons effects the eternal communication of life in the bosom of the Trinity. Such is the glory which God renders to Himself in the sacred intimacy of His eternal life.

II. THE SACERDOTAL CONSECRATION OF CHRIST

What is the essence of the priesthood? The Epistle to the Hebrews gives us a celebrated definition. "Every high-priest taken from among men is ordained for men in the things that appertain to God, that he may offer up gifts and sacrifices for sins", *Omnis pontifex ex hominibus assumptus pro hominibus constituitur in iis quae sunt ad Deum, ut offerat dona et sacrificia pro peccatis* (Heb 5:1).

The priest is the mediator who offers to God oblations and sacrifices in the name of the people. In return God chooses him to communicate to men His gifts of grace, of mercy and of pardon. The special excellence of the priesthood springs from this mediation.

From what source does Christ hold His priesthood? St. Paul gives us the answer. The priesthood, he tells us, is of such grandeur that no one, not even Christ in His humanity, has been able to assume for Himself this dignity. *Nec quisquam sumit sibi honorem sed qui vocatur a Deo—sic et Christus non semetipsum clarificavit, ut pontifex fieret.* Then he continues: "The Father Himself has established His Son as eternal priest; He has said to Him: *Filius meus es tu, ego hodie genui te—Tu es sacerdos in aeternum* (Heb 5:4–6).

Thus the priesthood is a gift bestowed on the humanity of Jesus by the Father. As soon as the Word was made flesh the eternal Father looked on His Son with infinite complacency. He acknowledged Him as the one mediator between heaven and earth, a pontiff for ever.

As Man-God Christ was to have the privilege of uniting in Himself the whole of humanity to purify it, to sanctify it and to bring it back to the bosom of the divinity. By this He was to render to the Lord a perfect glory in time and in eternity.

He did not need to be consecrated by an external anointing like other priests. The soul of Jesus Christ was not stamped with the ineffaceable priestly character as was ours on the day of our ordination. Why? We touch here on the very heart of the mystery. By virtue of the hypostatic union the Word enters into and takes possession of the soul and the body of Jesus; He consecrates them. When the Son of God became flesh He took complete possession of this humanity. The moment of the priestly consecration of Christ was the moment of His Incarnation; at that moment Christ was marked for ever as the one eternal mediator between man and God. "He was anointed with the oil of gladness," says St. Paul (Heb 1:9), for the Word Himself was this anointing of infinite sanctity. Jesus is the priest par excellence. "For it was fitting that we should have such a high priest, holy, innocent, undefiled and made higher than the heavens" (Heb 7:26). Until the end of time the priests of this earth will receive no power which is not part of His; He is the one source of the whole priesthood which glorifies God in the manner conceived by Him.

In order to enter more deeply into the mystery of this marvellous priestly consecration, let us consider the coming of the angel to Nazareth. Mary is in prayer, she is full of grace. The angel, who has been sent as an ambassador, delivers a message to her. What is the message? That the Word has chosen her womb as the nuptial chamber in which to espouse humanity: "The Holy Spirit will descend upon you," and Mary replies: "Be it done unto me according to thy word" (Lk 1:33–38). At this sacred moment the first priest is consecrated and the voice of the Father resounds in heaven: "Thou art a priest for ever according to the order of Melchizedek" (Ps 110[109]:4).

Mary thus becomes in all truth the House of Gold, the Ark of the Covenant, the tabernacle in which human nature was united to the Word, and by this very union Jesus was established for ever in His role as mediator.

III. THE UNIQUE PREROGATIVE OF THE PRIESTHOOD OF CHRIST: TO BE THE PRIEST AND VICTIM

In the Old Testament, as you know, the priest and the victim were distinct. In the sacrifice of expiation, for example, he who offered the sacrifice immolated a living being which represented the people; he extended his hands over the offering, and by this gesture imposed upon it the sins of all the people. You had therefore, on the one hand the priest, on the other the victim presented to God.

In the sacrifice offered by Jesus it is not so. By an astonishing and admirable prerogative of His priesthood, on Calvary as on our altars, His sacrifice is divine by virtue both of the dignity of the pontiff and the excellence of the victim which is immolated. Priest and victim are united in the one person, and this sacrifice constitutes the perfect homage which gives glory to God, makes the Lord propitious to men, and obtains for them all the grace of eternal life.

The *consummatum est* pronounced by the dying Christ was at once the last sigh of love of the Victim who has made full expiation, and the solemn attestation of the Pontiff completing the supreme act of His priesthood.

Let us meditate for a few moments on the mystery of the interior dispositions of Jesus as priest and as victim. The attitude of Christ, the Sovereign Priest, was essentially one of profound reverence and adoration. And what was the source of this attitude? The vision of His Father, *Patrem immensae maiestatis*. He knew Him as no other creature can ever know Him: "Just Father, the world hath not known Thee; but I have known Thee" (Jn 17:25).

The full depth of the divine perfections were open to His sight: the absolute sanctity of the Father, His sovereign justice, His infinite goodness. This sight filled Him with that reverential fear and that spirit of religion which must animate the offerer of a sacrifice.

What was the fundamental attitude of Jesus the Victim? It was likewise adoration, but here it finds expression in the acceptance of destruction and death. Jesus knew that He was destined to the Cross for the remission of the sins of the world; before the divine justice He felt Himself burdened with the crushing weight of all the sins of the world. He gave His full consent to this role of Victim. He had not, however, contrition like a penitent who mourns for his own personal faults. But on many occasions He experienced a sadness unto death at seeing Himself overwhelmed by the burden of so much iniquity. Did He not say in the Garden of Olives: "My soul is sorrowful even unto death." We can see that the attitude of the victim is in perfect conformity with that of the priest.

We must not consider the eternal designs from our short-sighted human point of view; let us envisage them as God has conceived them and revealed them to us. Let us not enquire what the Lord in His absolute power could have accomplished but see rather what He willed to do. He could have pardoned sin without requiring an expiation proportioned to the greatness of the offence, but, in His wisdom, He decreed the salvation of the world by the death of Christ. "Without the shedding of the blood of Jesus Christ there is no remission of sin for us": *Sine sanguinis effusione non fit remissio* (Heb 9:22).

So, coming into the world, the Son of God assumed a "sacrificial body" suited for enduring suffering and death. He was truly a member of the human race, like us, and it is in the name of His brethren that He is to offer Himself as victim to reconcile them with their Father in heaven. Tertullian has given us this penetrating thought: "No one is so supremely a Father as God, no goodness can approach His goodness": *Tam Pater nemo, tam Pius nemo.*[1] We may also say: "No one is so supremely a brother as Jesus: *Nemo ita frater ac ille.* According to St. Paul, in the eternal predestination, Christ is the "first born among many brethren" (Rom 8:29) and again, "He is not ashamed to call them brethren" (Heb 2:11). What did Christ Himself say to Mary Magdalen after His resurrection? "Go to My brethren and say to them: I ascend to My Father and to your Father" (Jn 20:17). And what a brother Jesus was! He was a God who willed to share our infirmities, to experience our sorrows and our pains. By personal experience He learned to sympathize with our troubles. "Our high priest is not incapable of having compassion on our infirmities, having willed to experience them all like us, excepting sin" (Heb 4:15).

IV. THE ACTS OF THE PRIESTHOOD OF CHRIST

A. Ecce Venio

The whole life of Jesus was that of a supreme pontiff dedicated to the glory of the Father and to the salvation of man. This priesthood attained its climax at the Last Supper and on Calvary. But the whole existence of the Saviour is stamped with the priestly character. The first movement of His most sacred soul at the time of the Incarnation was a sovereign act of religion. The evangelists have not revealed to us the secret of this

[1] *De poenitentia,* 8; PL 1, 1353.

priestly oblation of the Saviour; St. Paul, whose role it was to make known to us the mysteries of God and of His Christ, had knowledge of it: "Wherefore when He cometh into the world," writes the apostle, "Christ said, 'sacrifice and oblation Thou wouldst not: but a body Thou hast fitted to Me. Holocaust nor sacrifice for sin did not please Thee. Then said I: Here I am—for it is written of Me in the head of the Book—I come to do Thy will, O God'" (Heb 10:5–7). In recognition of the supreme dominion of the Father, Christ offered Himself to Him without reserve. This ineffable offering was His reply to the unparalleled grace of the hypostatic union; it was a priestly act, the precursor of the redemptive sacrifice and of all the acts of the heavenly priesthood. We cannot insist too strongly on this text which gives us a glimpse of the interior priestly life of Jesus.

Ingrediens mundum. On His entry into the world, His soul, brilliant with the light of the Word, contemplated the divinity and, in this august vision, it was given Him to know the infinite majesty of the Father. Jesus saw at the same time the immense injury done to God by sin and the inadequacy of the victims offered until then. He understood that God, in giving Him His human nature, had consecrated it so that it might be offered as a victim and that He was Himself the priest of this sacrifice. What did Christ do then? Turning to His Father in an outburst of inexpressible love, He abandoned Himself absolutely to His good pleasure.

At this sacred moment, as we may believe, all the activity of heaven was suspended in contemplation of this initial dedication of itself by the human nature of Jesus.

Although itself without spot, the human nature of Jesus belonged to the race of sinners: *in similitudinem carnis peccati* (Rom 8:3), and in accepting the task of bearing the sins of the world, the Saviour accepted at the same time the conditions of His immolation. That is why Jesus said: "O Father, the sacrifices of the Mosaic law were in themselves unworthy of You": *Hostiam et oblationem noluisti: holocautomata pro peccato non tibi placuerunt.* "Here I am." *Ecce venio*: accept Me as a victim [Heb 10:8

Vulgate]. You have given Me a body in which I can sacrifice Myself; grind it, break it, overwhelm it with sufferings, crucify it, I accept it all: "I come to do Your will."

Note these words: "You have formed for Me a body." Christ wishes us to understand that His flesh is not glorious and impassible as it was after His resurrection, not even transfigured as it was on Mount Tabor, but that He accepts from the Father a body subject to fatigue, to suffering, to death, capable like ours of enduring every kind of maltreatment, every kind of suffering: "O Father, I accept this body as You have chosen it for Me."

Jesus knows that at the head of His book of life there is inscribed for Him the divine decree of His immolation. He resigns Himself unreservedly to it: *In capite libri scriptum est de me ut faciam, Deus, voluntatem tuam* [Heb 10:7 Vulgate].

His will to glorify the Father, to satisfy divine justice, and to offer Himself for our salvation, has never wavered. It remains fixed for ever in the centre of His heart.

The whole existence of Jesus from this moment until the sacred hour when He offered Himself as a victim on the Cross will be a continuous manifestation of that deep-seated desire. It extends over His whole life. The shadow of Calvary projects itself continuously over His thoughts. He lived in advance all the varied incidents of the great drama: the ingratitude of Judas, the mockery of Herod, the cowardice of Pilate, the flagellation, the affronts of the Crucifixion.

One day, as Our Lord was going up to Jerusalem, He spoke to His disciples about the Son of Man. And what did He say: "He shall be delivered to the gentiles and shall be mocked, and scourged and spit upon" (Lk 18:32). Again, on Mount Tabor, Christ shows Himself to His dazzled apostles in all the glory of His sacred humanity radiating the splendour of the divinity. Elijah and Moses appeared, speaking with Jesus. And what was the subject matter of the conversation? St. Luke reveals it to us: they were speaking of His approaching Passion in Jerusalem (Lk 9:31). The Passion is in truth the climax of the whole earthly life of Jesus.

At His death Christ represented the whole of mankind, and in the unique sacrifice of the Cross which He accepted freely and the first movement of which dates from the Incarnation, He saved and sanctified us all. This is the significance of the teaching of St. Paul when to the text already quoted he adds: "In the which will, we are sanctified by the oblation of the body of Jesus Christ once" (Heb 10:10).

B. *The Last Supper*

The offering of Jesus as He pronounces His *Ecce Venio* is certainly irrevocable and worthy of all admiration, but it is at the Last Supper and on the Cross, and only then, that the Saviour is to accomplish the supreme sacerdotal act. There, while He presents His sacrifice to the Father, He reveals Himself to us in all the majesty and power of His supreme pontificate.

Let us transport ourselves in spirit to the Cenacle and assist at this farewell repast of immense love at which Jesus consecrates the bread and the wine. Before the Passion, He offered His body and blood under a new rite, a figure of the impending sacrificial oblation. The words pronounced by Him over the bread and wine leave no room for doubt as to the meaning which He attached to this gesture. Beyond all doubt it was "His own body which was to be offered up" and "His own blood. The blood of the New Testament—which shall be shed unto the remission of sins". This oblation was made to the Father. The Council of Trent asserts it: "At the Last Supper, declaring Himself to be a priest established for ever according to the order of Melchizedek, He offered to the Father His body and blood under the appearance of bread and wine" (Sess. 22, c. 1). On our altars, as at the Last Supper, Christ is priest and victim: it is still He who gives Himself as food; but in the Mass, Christ makes use of the ministry of His priests; at the Last Supper He employed no minister. As sovereign priest by His own immediate authority, He instituted three supernatural prodigies which He bequeathed to His Church: the sacrifice of the Mass, the sacrament of the Eucharist, intimately united to the Mass, and our priesthood, derived from His own and destined to perpetuate till the end of time His gesture of power and mercy.

The liturgy of the Mass therefore springs spontaneously from the heart of Christ. Taking bread and wine, "He gave thanks" to His Father, *gratias egit* (Mt 26:27). The giving of thanks was admittedly a part of the ritual of the Passover, but may we not legitimately believe that Jesus, at this solemn moment, thanked His Father, not only for His past bounties towards the chosen people, but also for all those of the New Testament. He saw the innumerable multitude of Christians who would refresh themselves at the holy table, who would feed on His adorable flesh and drink of His precious blood. He thanked the Father for all the help which he had destined for His members and especially for His priests until the end of time. Let us not forget that the bosom of the Father is the source from which flows, through Jesus, all mercies and all gifts: *Omne datum optimum . . . descendens a Patre luminum*: "Every good gift . . . coming down from the Father of lights" (Jas 1:17). It was, above all, for the glorious gift of the priesthood and the Eucharist that Jesus gave thanks. This incomparable act of gratitude accomplished by the Saviour in His own name and in that of all His members gave to the Father immeasurable glory.

C. The Supreme Sacrifice of the Cross

Let us ascend to Calvary and assist together at the bloody sacrifice of the Cross.

What do you see? Jesus is there surrounded by a crowd of callous soldiers, of blasphemous Pharisees, of hateful executioners. There was present also the little group of faithful disciples gathered around the Virgin Mary. "Behold the great Pontiff of our faith": *Aspicientes in auctorem fidei* (Heb 12:2). This crucified one is true God, our God: *Crucifixus etiam pro nobis.*

As I shall frequently remind you, the foundation of our spiritual life is faith in the divinity of Jesus Christ: "He that believeth in the Son hath life everlasting" (Jn 3:36). The man fixed with nails to the wood of the Cross is the equal of the Father: "Consubstantial with the Father . . . light of light." But clothed in our human nature, He has become our brother.

What then is He doing on this gibbet of suffering? What action is He accomplishing?

As you know, all the actions of the Man-God are divine in the broad sense of the word; they emanate at once from God and from man. The dignity of the person of the Word confers on the human acts of Christ a divine value: *Actio est suppositi,*[2] and, here, the *suppositum* is divine. His every sigh, every drop of His blood has sufficient expiatory value to compensate for the sins of the world. But according to the desires of the eternal wisdom, the Father has willed that the Son should redeem us by the most noble of all acts of religion: sacrifice. That is why, the Apostle says: "He has delivered Himself for us, an oblation and a sacrifice to God for an odour of sweetness" (Eph 5:2).

This sacrifice was preeminently propitiatory. By virtue of the infinite dignity of His divine person and the immensity of His human love, Jesus presented to the Father an act of homage more pleasing than the iniquities of the world had been displeasing. In the eyes of God, the value of the immolation of His Son exceeded beyond all measure His aversion for our wrongdoing. According to the bold expression of St. Paul, Jesus has "snatched from the justice of the Father the decree which condemned us": *Chirographum decreti quod est contrarium nobis*; "He has destroyed it, fastening it to the Cross": *affigens illud Cruci* (Col 2:14). The attitude of God towards us has been transformed: we were "children of wrath": *filii irae* (Eph 2:3) but now the Lord has become for us "rich in mercy": *dives in misericordia* (Eph 2:3–4).

This is what Jesus, our brother, has done for us. And if we understood the greatness of this love, how readily we would unite ourselves to this sacrifice, saying, like the Apostle: "He hath loved me, and delivered Himself up for me" (Gal 2:20). He

---

[2] The act belongs to the person.

does not say: *Dilexit nos* but *Dilexit me*: it was "for me". All this concerns me personally.

We must appreciate clearly that what God asked of Jesus, and what gave the sacrifice all its value, was not the mere shedding of His blood in itself, but the shedding of it animated by the spirit of love and of obedience.

In His divine plan God wished to adapt Himself to our human ways. Now, for us human beings, the supreme act of love is the gift of one's life, the gift of one's self unto death: *Maiorem hac dilectionem nemo habet, ut animam suam ponat quis pro amicis suis* (Jn 15:13). Jesus Himself asserts the importance of love in His Passion when He says: "That the world may know that I love the Father . . . and as the Father hath given Me commandment so do I" (Jn 14:31).

He was determined also that we should appreciate that His sacrifice was accomplished in obedience. In the Garden of Olives, during His agony, three times Jesus asked that the chalice be removed from Him. And in the face of the inexorable silence of heaven, freely, by an act of supreme submission and in an impulse of love the Saviour conforms His human will to the will of the Father: "Not My will, but Thy will be done" (Lk 22:42). St. Paul can say of Jesus: "He made Himself obedient unto death, even unto the death of the Cross" (Phil 2:8). Isaiah had foretold this free acceptance of His suffering by the Saviour: "He was offered because it was His own will," *quia ipse voluit* (Is 53:7). And so, whatever may be the number and the enormity of the sins of the world, the reparation offered by our divine Master will always be superabundant. The words of the Apostle, throbbing with admiration at the mystery, express it admirably: "Where sin abounded grace did more abound" (Rom 5:20).

When Christ—in His capacity of redeemer and head of the mystical body—offers His Passion to the Father, the meritorious value of this action extends beyond the person of Jesus to the universality of men redeemed by Him, and to all those of whom He is the head. His merits belong to us so that in Him we have become "rich with all spiritual blessings" (Eph 1:3; cf.

1 Cor 1:5). Our "riches in Jesus Christ" are so great that we cannot grasp their immensity; that is why St. Paul declares them to be "unsearchable": *Investigabiles divitiae Christi* (Eph 3:8). Let our hearts be filled with a lively faith, with unlimited confidence. Has not Jesus Himself said: "I come that they may have life and may have it more abundantly" (Jn 10:10).

The sacrifice of Jesus is the light-giving centre of the divine graces and the divine pardons. All the supernatural help granted to men springs from the supreme sacerdotal immolation of Golgotha. All the goodness of God towards us, all the depths of His mercy for us are His replies to the unceasing invocation of the merits of Christ. If the whole human race raised to heaven its cries of distress it would all be of no avail without Jesus: it is the cry of the Son of God which alone gives value to our supplication.*

But the drama of Calvary is perpetuated in the bosom of the Church. At the consecration, under the veil of the sacrament, the cry of the blood of Jesus sounds forth anew, for at that moment all the love, all the obedience, all the sufferings of His oblation on the Cross are presented to the Father. The liturgy proclaims that "every time the commemoration of this sacrifice is celebrated the work of our redemption is accomplished anew." [3]

Although the eucharistic sacrifice is fundamentally dependent on the priesthood of Christ, we shall not deal with it *ex professo* now. We shall do so later. Nevertheless we must keep in mind this fundamental truth: when God, through the Mass, grants graces to men, He glorifies His Son because He recognizes the all-powerful intercession of the redeeming blood. I shall go even further: it is to His Son that He shows His mercy, for Jesus can certainly say to His Father: "O Father, these men are My members; when dying I bore them all in Myself; they are Mine as they are Yours: all the mercies which You shower on them are in fact granted to Me."

---

* Cf. St. Anselm, "Cur Deus Homo"—answering the question "Why the God-man?"
[3] Secret of the Mass of the Ninth Sunday after Pentecost (in the Missal of St. Pius V).

D. The Heavenly Priesthood

Jesus, ascending into heaven, sits at the right hand of the Father, but in the eternal splendour, St. Paul tells us, His priesthood remains in its full vigour: *Sempiternum habet sacerdotium* (Heb 7:24). Admittedly the sacrifice of the Cross will always be "the one oblation by which He hath perfected for ever them that are sanctified" (Heb 10:14). And so, in order to understand fully the sacerdotal life of Christ in heaven, we must distinguish, according to St. Thomas,[4] between the offering of the sacrifice and its consummation. When the sacrifice has been accomplished, it still remains to communicate its fruits to those assisting at it. This communication of the divine gifts is carried out in virtue of the oblation already made and constitutes its consummation or completion. Although a secondary exercise of the sacerdotal power, it is therefore an act essentially sacerdotal.

How, according to the divine plan, does Jesus exercise His priesthood eternally?

The Epistle to the Hebrews gives us the answer. It reminds us that the high priest of the Old Testament, going within the veil, represented Christ. This pontiff entered into the Holy of Holies only once a year, after having immolated the victim and sprinkled himself with its blood. He wore on his heart twelve precious stones symbolizing the twelve tribes of Israel. In this manner the whole people entered mystically with him into the sanctuary.

This solemn entry of the pontiff into the Holy of Holies was only a figure of a sacerdotal act infinitely more noble. Jesus is the true pontiff who, after having been immolated and after shedding His blood, entered on the glorious day of His Ascension into the true tabernacle in the highest seat of heaven: *Introivit semel in sancta*. "He entered there for ever and once for all" (Heb 9:12).

When the high priest penetrated into the sanctuary, he did not gain access for the people who accompanied him, but

---

[4] *Summa* III, q. 22, a. 5.

Christ, our Pontiff, leads us after Him into heaven. Never forget this marvellous doctrine of our faith: we cannot enter except through Him. No man, no creature can attain the eternal tabernacles, can enjoy the beatific vision except after and by the power of Jesus: this is the triumphant reward of His sacrifice.

All the elect contemplate God, but whence comes this light by which they see the divinity? The Apocalypse of St. John gives us the answer again and again: In the Heavenly Jerusalem it is the Lamb who will be the light: *Lucerna eius est Agnus* (Rev 21:23). All the inhabitants of the holy city will realize always that it is only the graces springing from the sacrifice of Jesus which have gained for them access to the Father and given them the power to praise Him. They will chant without ceasing: "You have redeemed us by Your blood from every tribe and every nation and You have made of us the kingdom of God."

As man, the Saviour has certainly the right to penetrate into the secret of the divinity, for His humanity is the humanity of the Word Itself. But Christ is also "pontiff", *Pontem faciens*, mediator, head of the mystical body: by these titles and by virtue of His Passion, He introduces us with Himself into the bosom of the Father.

Thus, we are justified in deducing from the Scriptures that a majestic liturgy is celebrated in Heaven. Christ offers Himself in all His splendour and this glorious oblation is, as it were, the completion, the consummation of the redemption.

In this celestial liturgy we shall be united to Jesus and to each other. We shall be the trophy of His glory. We shall take part in the adoration, the love, and the thanksgiving which He and all His members send up to the supreme majesty of the Holy Trinity. The word-pictures of Revelation give us a glimpse of the realities. The Epistle to the Ephesians proclaims it: "at the end of time in His kingdom the Father will accomplish His design: to bring all things to Himself, uniting them all under one chief: *recapitulare omnia in Christo*. This is certainly the sense intended by St. Paul. The expression of the Vulgate *Instaurare omnia in Christo* (Eph 1:10) has not the same vigour.

Everything shall be "subject to Jesus Christ", says St. Paul again, *Oportet illum regnare* (1 Cor 15:25) and the Son Himself with all His elect will do homage to Him who has made all things subject to Him so that God may be "all in all": *Cum autem subiecta fuerint illi omnia, tunc et ipse Filius subiectus erit ei qui subiecit sibi omnia, ut sit Deus omnia in omnibus* (1 Cor 15:28).

For all eternity it shall be our joy to realize that our beatitude comes to us from Jesus, that His priesthood is the source of all graces which we shall have received during our sorrowful earthly pilgrimage. Is it not to Him that we owe our divine adoption, our priesthood, and the look of pardon, of tenderness and of love from Him whom at the Mass we call *Clementissime Pater*?

When we celebrate the Holy Sacrifice, we must believe that we enter into this magnificent torrent of praise, that we participate in this liturgy of heaven. Let us realize at the moment when we receive the Blessed Sacrament that for us, as for the blessed, it is the sacred humanity of Jesus alone which puts us in contact with the divinity. As we await the vision and the full clarity of the city of God let it be our joy to repeat: O Jesus, for Your elect You are everything! for us also be everything while we march on in the spirit of faith towards the eternal Jerusalem; "so that they who live may not now live to themselves but unto Him Who died and rose again for them": *Ut et qui vivunt iam non sibi vivant, sed ei qui pro ipsis mortuus est et resurrexit* (2 Cor 5:15).

II.

CHRIST THE MODEL AND THE SOURCE
OF PRIESTLY SANCTITY

THE heavenly Father has Himself undertaken the task of establishing for us, ministers of Christ, our ideal of sanctity. He has predestined us to become like, not to some creature, not to an angel, but to His Son, Whom the Incarnation has consecrated priest in His human nature. St. Paul reveals to us this thought of the Father when he says: *Praedestinavit nos conformes fieri imaginis Filii sui* (Rom 8:29). God provides for us a divine model of perfection. He wishes to see reproduced in us the characteristics of His incarnate Son and by that very fact to see our soul resplendent with the reflection of His sanctity.

If it is true that the grandeur of every human life depends on the ideal which it pursues, to what heights must the sincere desire to make ourselves like to Jesus Christ elevate the whole existence of us priests? With the Word the Father is well pleased; and thus our assimilation with Christ is for us an abundant source of benedictions and graces.

Let us pause and contemplate this mystery with profound reverence.

I. THE SUPERNATURAL

Though God, that ocean of perfection, is incomprehensible for every created intelligence, He Himself, in His infinity, grasps in one glance the fullness of His grandeur; He expresses His knowledge in one thought, in one single expression, His Word. To this Word He communicates all His divine life, all His light, all that He is. This generation in the bosom of the Father, being the very life of God, had no beginning and will have no end. At this moment as I write, the Father, with an exultation which is

infinite, says to His Son: "Thou art My Son; today"—that is, in
an eternal present—"have I begotten Thee" (Ps 2:7).

The Father has given us this Son as a model and as the source
of all sanctity. "In Him are hid all the treasures of wisdom and
knowledge" (Col 2:3). An eternity of contemplation would not
suffice to exhaust the depths of this mystery and to thank God
for this benefit.

Before going more deeply into this question I would like to
draw your attention to the error of those who do not base their
lives sufficiently on faith in the divine plan, and who wish to
constitute themselves the architects of their own sanctity.

The sanctification of the soul is a supernatural work. What is
the true concept of the supernatural? It is the realization in
time of the eternal designs of the Father. God, in His goodness, has destined man to find His final beatitude in the vision
of the divinity face to face, a vision which is natural to God
alone. Revelation, the Incarnation, the Redemption, the
Church, faith, the sacraments, grace, and sanctity, all belong
to the munificence of this plan of which Christ and our adoption in Him form the centre. This communication is absolutely
gratuitous; it exceeds the needs and the requirements of all
created nature, whether angelic or human: that is why it is
supernatural. We have here a glorious ensemble, a world of
graces to which is connected the whole activity of the man
destined to celestial beatitude. For nature, left to its own de-
vices, has not the capacity to tend efficaciously towards its
supernatural end.

One meets, even among priests, persons who are marking
time in the spiritual life in spite of a more or less exact fidelity
to their religious exercises: all their application does not succeed
in making them live the interior life of Christ. They make an
effort without knowing exactly towards what ideal they should
direct that effort; they are in doubt as to the best manner of
going towards God. In contrast to this we have St. Paul who
said: "I therefore so run, not as at an uncertainty: I so fight, not
as one beating the air" (1 Cor 9:26). It is of the utmost importance for us and for those whom we direct to have a clear idea

of the nature of the sanctity to which we aspire so that we may not "beat the air".

When we study the Acts of the Apostles and the history of the early Christians to whom St. Paul addressed his epistles, we can see that they were truly abounding in the gifts of the Holy Spirit. These Christians found the inspiration of their life in Jesus Christ, in the grace of their baptism, in the expectation of the heavenly kingdom, in the doctrine of the divine plan as the apostles taught it to them. I do not blame those who, for their sanctification, have recourse to such means of supererogation as may appeal to them, because they feel the need of the stimulation which they afford: it is better to walk on crutches than not to move at all. But I should like to reassert most emphatically for your benefit the immense riches which we possess in Jesus Christ. Men are too much inclined to want to substitute their ideas for those of God, to want to attain perfection according to their own short-sighted point of view, rather than according to the divine point of view. St. Paul draws attention to this tendency in his day: "Beware lest any man cheat you by philosophy and vain deceit; according to the traditions of men, according to the traditions of the world, and not according to Christ" (Col 2:8).

In our days naturalism reigns in the world; it infiltrates even among those who wish to live by faith. Do not we ourselves ignore the strictly supernatural character of our interior life? To conform ourselves to the designs of God in the work of our sanctification is, therefore, to seek, above all, to sanctify ourselves in the manner foreseen and determined by the Lord Himself according to His will.

II. THE DIVINE PLAN OF SANCTIFICATION

Let us see how the Father has prepared for His priests an ideal and a never-failing source of sanctification.

The gifts of God are irrevocable: when God gives, He does not take back, it is a gift for ever.

By an eternal and free predestination of love, God has willed to give His Son to the world: *Sic Deus dilexit mundum ut Filium suum unigenitum daret* (Jn 3:16). Christ belongs to each one of us unreservedly, totally, as our precious personal possession. "Christ Jesus, Who of God, is made unto us wisdom, and justice and sanctification and redemption": *Factus est nobis sapientia a Deo, et justitia et sanctificatio et redemptio* (1 Cor 1:30). All the sanctity destined for man has been, as it were, entrusted to Him. Let us try to appreciate fully this design of the wisdom and the love of God in our regard.

God wills to communicate Himself to us to be our supernatural beatitude, but He wills to do so exclusively through Christ, with Him, in Him, *Per Christum, cum ipso, in ipso.* To gather all things to Himself, but purified, sanctified, reunited under Christ as under a single head: *instaurare omnia in Christo* (Eph 1:10): such is the majestic and merciful design of the Father. St. Paul liked to preach of "this mystery hidden in the divine thought from eternity": *Illuminare omnes quae sit dispensatio sacramenti absconditi a saeculis in Deo* (Eph 3:9).

The sanctity which God expects from His priests, which He has prepared for them in His eternal prevision, is not therefore a mere morality based on self-control and on rectitude in the exercise of the natural virtues. The sanctity which God wishes to find in them includes certainly human uprightness, but it is in its essence supernatural.

The redemptive Incarnation is the centre of this divine plan. It is revealed to us as a sublime gift of God and of His sanctity. This communication was made first, in all its fullness, to the humanity of Jesus and then, through it, to every Christian. According to the divine intention all the treasures destined to sanctify man are in Jesus Christ: *In omnibus divites facti estis in illo* (1 Cor 1:5).

His merits belong to us, they are at our disposition. In the matter of sanctity there is nothing that we may not hope to obtain by them, provided our faith is up to the level of that hope.

By this communication, Christ is already for us the source of all grace. But this is not all: by His death on the Cross He has acquired, in accordance with the divine decrees, a unique prerogative: the whole work of the sanctification of man is confided to His hands. That is why, as the instrument of the divinity, Jesus Himself, by means of the sacraments, and even apart from them, is the universal efficient cause of every infusion of grace. While dominating His mystical body by the causality of His merits and of His sanctifying action, Christ is besides the exemplary cause or perfect model of all sanctity: because, for adoptive sons, perfection consists in resembling as far as possible the Son according to nature. It is according to these three kinds of causality that we must understand how, in accordance with the eternal designs, Christ is for us everything in the work of our sanctification. We can thus better understand the truth of the emphatic declaration of St. Paul: "for other foundation no man can lay but that which is laid: which is Christ Jesus" (1 Cor 3:11). "Thanks be to God for His unspeakable gift" (2 Cor 9:15).

III. CONFORMITY WITH THE IMAGE OF THE SON OF GOD

Let us now consider this same mystery from the human side. Sanctity may be defined as: "a divine life, communicated and received". This life is communicated from above, by God, by Christ. It is received by man, from the moment of his baptism.[1] This sacrament confers the grace of adoption and thus sanctifies the soul; it brings to it, as it were, the dawn of the divine life, but this brightness is intended to increase steadily to the glory of a noon that will not fade. Baptismal or sanctifying grace implants in the soul a capacity to share in the very nature of God, by knowledge, by love, and by the possession of the divinity in an intuitive manner which is natural to God alone. This divine gift establishes in man a wonderful and supernatural participation in the divine life. *Quaedam participata similitudo divinae naturae*, says St. Thomas.[2]

---

[1] Cf. *Christ, the Life of the Soul*, chapter on baptism, the sacrament of divine adoption and Christian initiation. (This is Marmion's first work, published in 1918. Marmion is referred to by some scholars as the "Doctor of Divine Adoption".)

[2] A certain participation by way of resemblance in the divine nature, *Summa* III, q. 62, a. 1.

It is a new life which springs up in the soul, and its coming constitutes for the baptized person a second, spiritual birth.

Jesus has said it: *Oportet vos nasci denuo* (Jn 3:7). God alone can give to His creatures the seed of this supernatural life; that is why in all truth it is He alone who begets them to this life: *qui . . . ex Deo nati sunt* (Jn 1:13). From this moment, an adoptive sonship, modelled on the eternal filiation of the Son of God, is established in the soul of the person baptized.

In face of these splendours St. Leo exclaims: "O Christian, learn to appreciate your dignity": *Agnosce, O Christiane, dignitatem tuam.* And again: "Since we participate in the generation of Christ, let us renounce the works of the flesh": *Adepti participationem generationis Christi, carnis renuntiemus operibus.*[3] If, as St. Thomas says, the natural and eternal filiation of the Word in the bosom of the Father is the sublime model of our adoptive filiation: *Filiatio adoptiva est quaedam similitudo filiationis aeternae,*[4] the sanctity proper to the humanity of the one true Son of God must likewise be the model for the sanctity of the adoptive sons. In what does the sanctity of Jesus consist?

First of all we must recognize in Jesus a primary sanctity, of the divine order, which is to be found in Him alone, and which is the fruit of the hypostatic union. This "assumption" of a body and soul by the Word communicated to the whole human nature of Jesus an incomparable sanctity, that of the second Person of the Blessed Trinity. It is with good reason that we say: "the sacred humanity", and the Church in the liturgy of the Mass celebrates with exultation this unique sanctity: *Tu solus sanctus . . . Jesu Christe, cum Sancto Spiritu, in gloria Dei Patris.**

In the second place, sanctifying grace of unequalled fullness, *et vidimus eum plenum gratiae* (Jn 1:14), ennobled the soul of Jesus, and the Holy Spirit guided all His activities in a perfect manner, conforming them admirably to the supreme dignity of the Son of God.

---

[3] *Sermo* 31, 3; PL 54, 192.

[4] *Summa* III, q. 23, a. 2.

* This is taken from the Gloria of the Mass: "You alone are the holy one . . . Jesus Christ, with the Holy Spirit, in the glory of God the Father."

In the Holy Trinity, the Persons are themselves the relations to each other. As the theologians express it, they are subsisting relations. It is, therefore, by His whole essence that the Son is Son, and is related to the Father. By the action of the Holy Spirit the soul of Jesus Christ is completely united to this life of the Word. As a human being, by immense charity, it was *tota ad Patrem*[5]: it made known His name, accomplished His will and glorified Him unceasingly. All the interior movements of Jesus corresponded fully to His divine filiation; they were preeminently acts of religion and of love.

By sanctifying grace the Christian participates in the sanctity of Christ. This grace is, as it were, a reflection of the divine light which enters into the soul, establishes it in a state of justice, and makes it resemble the Son by nature. This initial sanctification, which is destined to increase, is given at the moment of baptism. When by their good actions, the sons of adoption imitate the virtues of Christ, they contribute to the perfecting in themselves of the life of Christ.

At the Last Supper, after having washed the feet of His disciples, Jesus pronounced these solemn words: *Exemplum enim dedi vobis ut quemadmodum ego feci vobis, ita vos faciatis.* "For I have given you an example that as I have done to you, so you do also" (Jn 13:15). Whether it be a matter of religion, of humility, of patience, indulgence, or charity, all the virtues of Christ must be the inspiration of our virtues: they are the model, especially for His priests. If the essence of our priestly perfection consists in acting always as adoptive sons of the Father and as ministers of Christ, we must, like Him, the Son of God and the supreme Pontiff, constantly relate all our activity to the love and the glory of the Father in imitation of the virtues of which He provides the model.

This resemblance to Christ will appear especially in the ever-increasing domination of charity over all our conduct. Love will orient every deliberate action towards our supernatural end; its rays will extend to the whole of our life, and by virtue of its

---

[5] Entirely oriented towards the Father.

ever-widening sphere of dominion, it will take firmer root in our hearts, and control them in all things. In this manner the kingdom of God becomes more and more firmly established in the Christian soul. Is this soul therefore confirmed in grace? No; it remains exposed to temptation and to sin; but God, Christ, and their rule become the sole motive power of its actions. The Lord is in full possession of this soul, *Dominus regit me*: "The Lord leads me" (Ps 23[22]:1), for, in all truth, by reason of the absolute supremacy of charity, it only lives through Him, by Him and for Him. From this moment the saying of the Apostle begins to be fully realized in this member of Christ: "And I live now, not I, but Christ liveth in me" (Gal 2:20). It is then that the soul attains sanctity. Certainly, there are many degrees of sanctity. Generosity in self-sacrifice, heroism in the practice of the virtues, can assume many forms, and are capable of almost infinite development. We must not be too quick to believe we have attained it. Here, as elsewhere, time must play its part. The fidelity required of true servants of God is generally of long duration and there are many trials to increase its strength and its merit. The gifts of contemplative prayer have also their special influence on the elevation of the faithful and on the perseverance of the elect.

In practice, for you, priests, apart altogether from the mystery of predestination and of grace, it is essential to develop a very sincere desire for priestly perfection. You cannot remain indifferent to the divine invitation. If my words do not find in you a profound desire to respond to the greatness of your vocation, they will be of no effect. I do not say to you: "Aspire straightaway to the highest sanctity." But I do recommend you strongly—for it is of the utmost importance—to try to walk in the way of sanctity which God has chosen for you. He alone knows your weakness: *ipse cognovit figmentum nostrum* (Ps 103[102]:14), and, in His wisdom, He has measured exactly what you are capable of, and what is the power of the graces destined to support your progress. It is from this desire of sanctity that all true spiritual life proceeds: by it the soul prepares itself to receive the gift from on high; in its acknowledgement of its powerlessness and in its expectation of the help of grace, it lays itself open to the influence of the Lord, and increases its capacity for the divine. The pursuit of sanctity is like an interior flame, a sacred fire which we bear within us. At times this fire seems to be only a spark, but, believe me, it can be revived and become bright again. If we wish the Father, when He looks at us, to be able to say, as He said of Jesus: "This is my beloved Son," let all our efforts and all our aspirations tend towards the establishment of the reign of charity in our hearts.[6]

IV. HAVING BECOME LIKE CHRIST, THE PRIEST REPRODUCES IN HIMSELF THE SANCTITY OF THE FATHER

The Gospel records for us an astonishing sentence which fell from the lips of Jesus: "Be ye perfect as your heavenly Father is perfect" (Mt 5:48).

Why must our perfection and our sanctity reproduce the divine sanctity, so infinitely removed from our human weakness? Are we given the power to know the mystery of this divine life? The answer to this double question is contained in these words: We must resemble the heavenly Father because we are His children by adoption. And to know the perfection of this Father, it suffices to turn to Jesus Christ. St. John tells us, "No one has ever seen God": *Deum nemo vidit unquam* (Jn 1:18). Must we, then, despair of ever knowing Him? No, because the disciple adds immediately the glorious truth: "His only Son, Who is in the bosom of the Father, He hath declared Him." St. Paul, inspired by this same revelation, declares: "God inhabits light inaccessible," *Deus lucem inhabitat inaccessabilem* (1 Tim 6:16), but "He Who by His word commanded the light to shine out of the darkness hath shined in our hearts . . . by the resplendent

---

[6] We cannot consider here whether there exists for the priest as such a form of sanctity specifically distinct from that of other Christians. By baptism and sanctifying grace, the same essential sanctity is communicated to all. But we must recognize the fact that in the minister of Christ, sanctity connotes a very special and supernatural elevation of soul. This is proper to him by reason of the character imprinted on his soul by ordination, by reason of his mission in the Church, and by reason of the means of sanctification proper to the eminent dignity of his state. But these are accidental circumstances which do not affect the essence of sanctity.

brilliance of the face of Jesus Christ" (2 Cor 4:6). The liturgy of Christmas repeats it to us each year: "Knowing God visibly, let us be transported by Him into the love of things invisible." Christ is God adapted to our capacity, in human form. After the Last Supper, Philip said to Jesus: "Lord, show us the Father," *Domine ostende nobis Patrem* (Jn 14:8). And Our Lord replied in solemn words which contain, as it were, the key to the mystery: "Philip, he that seeth Me seeth the Father also" (Jn 14:9). Everything in Jesus Christ is therefore a revelation of God. Saint Augustine proclaims it: *Factum verbi verbum nobis est.*[7] At the feet of Jesus we shall learn to know the perfection of God; it is by meditating on His words, on His actions, on His sufferings and on His death that we shall penetrate the secrets of the infinite mercy.

This is realized in the case of the priest more fully than in that of the simple faithful. To a much greater extent than they can, he contemplates Jesus Christ in reading the Scriptures, in following the course of the liturgical year and in celebrating the sacrifice of the Mass.

In what does this sublime divine attribute called sanctity consist according to the teaching of theology?

God possesses a sovereign transcendence; He is infinitely distant from all His creation, from all imperfection, from all our world; this is the first aspect, and rather a negative one, of His sanctity. Moreover, according to our human manner of speaking, it may be said that God's sanctity consists in the love which He bears His own essence, His own goodness. This adherence of love is wise and supremely justified, for it is in conformity with the absolute excellence of the divine nature. In other words, in the contemplation of His essence God loves Himself and wills for Himself all that is in accord with the perfection of His own being. It is in this love and in this will that we can say that sanctity exists in God. In Him, this will and this love are not only in conformity with His infinite goodness but are identified with it. From this springs their immovable strength.

---

[7] *Tractatus in Joannem* 24, PL 35, 1593.

In His work of creation and of sanctification God wishes to see His creatures act in accordance with the order and the subordination which becomes them. It is by this that they give glory to God. When man recognizes his absolute dependence in regard to his Creator, he is acting in complete conformity with the law of his nature, and God approves this submission and this glorification; just as, for the same reason, God must necessarily disapprove of any attitude of insubordination or revolt, and condemn sin. This is not from egoism or from pride, but on account of His sanctity which desires that all things should be accomplished in accordance with rectitude, wisdom, and truth. It is in this sense that we must understand that "God is holy in all His works": *Sanctus in omnibus operibus suis* (Ps 145[144]:13), and that "He made all things for Himself": *Universa propter semetipsum operatus est Dominus* (Prov 16:4).

This divine perfection dazzles the heavenly spirits. When Isaiah and St. John saw for an instant heaven opened, what did they behold? The angels singing without ceasing: *Sanctus, Sanctus, Sanctus* (Is 6:3; Rev 4:8).

Sanctity in God is therefore the love which He bears to His own supreme goodness, a love which is supremely wise and of the most absolute rectitude.

In its full perfection sanctity exists in God alone, for He alone has a perfect love of His infinite goodness. The three divine Persons possess this essential attribute but each in His own personal "relation".

It will always be beyond our powers of understanding to have an exact idea of divine sanctity in itself. On the other hand, when we contemplate it in Jesus, divine sanctity reveals itself to us and commands our admiration. Man recognizes it as something which is accessible, close to him.

Jesus, in His human nature, participates in the sanctity of the Word: He is far removed from all sin, from all imperfection; everything in Him is a reflection of the life of the Word: by a perfect love of the infinite goodness He refers Himself always and entirely to the Father Whom He glorifies in all His actions.

This is the model to which we make bold to raise our eyes,

especially we who are invested with all the powers of Jesus Christ: "As the Father hath sent Me, I also send you" (Jn 20:21).

If the Word—Who by His simple and infinite activity expresses all that the Father is—has revealed the secrets of the divine life in human language, and by examples adapted to our weak intelligence, is it not the height of folly on the part of men to be inattentive to His message, and to think of becoming holy in their own way without making Jesus Christ the object of their aspirations, of their confidence, and of their life?

V. CHRIST, THE LIVING SOURCE OF SANCTITY

Christ, the transcendent and yet most accessible model of sanctity, by His omnipotent grace gives us an active participation in it.

Some souls imagine, more or less subconsciously, that they can resemble Christ by imitating His virtues by their own efforts. This is a great illusion.

In England, among educated people, one finds sometimes an astounding infatuation for this or that great man. They want to imitate him at all costs. They read only his books, they enter into everything that he says or does, and they try to copy him—they might even be said to ape him. These admirers are called hero-worshippers. We have had thus Gladstonians and Newmanists; for Newman especially this kind of imitation was very much the fashion at certain times.

If anyone adopted this exterior and factitious practice to unite himself to Jesus Christ and to conform to His likeness he would be making a mistake. One might pass one's whole life in efforts of this kind: it would be a mere human affectation and, when the eternal Father considered the results of this work, the aspirant would appear to Him as one who was not born of His grace; one might almost say that He would regard him as an illegitimate child.

Yes, Our Lord is the model of all sanctity, but this exemplary cause is divine and divinely active. It is He who impresses on the soul His own resemblance.

How is this marvel of grace accomplished? Christ has revealed the secret to us: "I am the way and the truth and the life" (Jn 14:6).

"I am the way"

Between every creature and God there is an infinite distance. The angels, apart from their supernatural preferment, are at an immeasurable distance from the divinity. God alone, by His own nature, sees Himself as He is; He alone has the right to contemplate the depths of His own perfections. Men know God only by His works: "Clouds and darkness are round about Him" (Ps 97[96]:2). And still, we are called to see God as He sees Himself, to love Him as He loves Himself, and to live by the divine life. Such is our supernatural destiny. Now, between this preferment and the capacities of our nature there is an impassable chasm. Through Christ, at once God and Man, and through the grace of adoption, we are enabled to triumph over this separation. Christ is, as it were, the bridge thrown over these fathomless depths: through His sacred humanity He is the way by which we can come to the Trinity. Did not Jesus Himself say: "No man cometh to the Father but through Me," *Nemo venit ad Patrem nisi per me* (Jn 14:6). This way does not lead us astray; he who follows it will arrive infallibly at the goal; "he shall have the light of life": *Qui sequitur me, non ambulat in tenebris sed habebit lumen vitae* (Jn 8:12). For, as Word, Jesus is one with the Father, and His humanity of necessity makes us attain to the divinity. When He incorporates us into His mystical body, in all truth He takes us to Himself, so that we may live there where He is Himself, that is to say, be united to the Word and to the Holy Spirit in the bosom of the Father: "I will come again and take you to Myself, that where I am you also may be" (Jn 14:3).

Rely, then, in everything on the merits of our dear Saviour. Your hope of arriving at the divine union cannot be based on the poverty of your own merits but rather on the immensity of

His. The more completely you find your riches in Him, the more will Your search for God be blessed and the more fruitful will your ministry be. Efface yourself, put Christ first, attach yourself to Him, like St. Paul, who said: "But God forbid that I should glory save in the Cross of Our Lord Jesus Christ" (Gal 6:14) and again: "I regard all but as dung, that I may gain Christ" (Phil 3:8).

"I am the truth"

According to our natural state, we walk, here on earth, in the darkness: *In tenebris et in umbra mortis* (Lk 1:79). In order to raise ourselves towards God we must be supernaturally enlightened.

It is Christ alone who makes manifest religious truth: He is "the light of the world": *Ego sum lux mundi* (Jn 8:12). His teaching, while it does not dissipate all the shadows, allows us to recognize Him as the envoy of the Father and to adhere to Him as to the supreme, infallible truth. "God is my light" (Ps 27[26]:1).

The Gospel gives to the world the revelation of all the great religious truths: the Trinity, the Incarnation, the Redemption and the sanctions of the world to come. It unveils to men also the mystery of the divine paternity. When Jesus speaks to us of God, He represents Him always as our Father: "I ascend to My Father and to your Father" (Jn 20:17). It is a characteristic of the New Testament that it has taught us to call God our Father, to act towards Him as His children: *Pater noster, qui es in caelis* (Mt 6:9), "For the Spirit Himself giveth testimony to our spirit that we are the sons of God" (Rom 8:16). Along with the divine paternity, Jesus also reveals to us our adoption, our blessed heavenly destiny and all the attitudes of charity and of virtue proper to the Christian.

Let us receive these doctrines from His sacred lips, let us realize that they come from Truth itself; let us attach ourselves to them by an unshakable faith.

Furthermore, Christ brings us truth by a grace of illumination of our souls which is personal to each one of us. This personal illumination is essential to the progress of the life of

Christ in us. Thanks to it, the priest enters into the divine paths of sanctification. He "walks in truth": *Ambulare in veritate* (2 Jn 1:4), as St. John so admirably puts it. We must therefore consider the paths of this world by the light of our faith in Christ. Let us place it as a divine lamp in the centre of our hearts. Let us cast at the feet of Jesus our ideas, our judgements, our desires, so that we may see the world, people and events through His eyes. Then we shall appreciate at their proper value the things of time and the things of eternity.

"I am the life"

To attain the goal it is not enough to keep to the right road and to be illuminated on the journey; we must also have the vital force: it is it alone which permits us to advance. In the work of sanctification, Christ is also the life: "I am the resurrection and the life. I am come that they may have life and have it more abundantly": *Ego sum resurectio et vita . . . Ego veni ut vitam habeant et abundantius habeant* (Jn 11:25; 10:10).

By His divine virtue or by the gift of the Holy Spirit He is the efficient and universal cause of all grace. His humanity is the instrument of the divinity. It effects in souls that increase of the supernatural life which transforms them and enables them to present to the eyes of the Father the true image of His incarnate Son. Christ acts through the sacraments, but He acts also apart from them; prayer, the contemplation of His mysteries, humility, and love in all its forms, prepare the soul for His action upon it.

According to the mind of the Church, the Holy Spirit—the supreme gift of the Father and the Son—traces in our innermost hearts this authentic resemblance to the Son of God. He is the finger of the right hand of the Father: *Dextrae Dei tu digitus.*[8] How does He realize in our souls this work of our adoption? By making us exclaim "Abba, Father" (Gal 4:6). You see the action of the Holy Spirit, like that of the Word Incarnate, leads us to the Father. Everything proceeds from this source of all goodness and, in a sublime transport of gratitude, everything

---

[8] Hymn *Veni Creator*, Monastic Breviary.

refers itself back to it. We are thus associated with the divine Persons and imitate Their movement of eternal love.

Jesus Himself has willed to confirm by a comparison our faith in His sanctifying influence: "I am the vine," He said, "you are the branches" (Jn 15:5). The branches have life, but they do not themselves provide the sap which nourishes them. They are constantly drawing their vitality from the sap which comes from the parent stem. Coming itself from another source, it is this sap which gives them life. And so it is for the members of Christ: their good actions, their practice of the virtues, their spiritual progress, their sanctity, belong to them certainly; but it is the sap of grace coming from Christ which produces these wonders in them: "As the branch cannot bear fruit of itself, unless it abide in the vine, so neither can you unless you abide in Me" (Jn 15:4).

In Jesus Christ, everything radiates life: His words, His actions, the different phases of His life. All the mysteries of His life on earth, those of His childhood, as well as those of His death, possess an ever efficacious power of sanctification. In Him the past is not effaced: "Christ dieth no more: death shall no more have dominion over Him" (Rom 6:9). Jesus Christ yesterday and today and the same for ever (Heb 13:8). He never ceases to pour into our souls His supernatural life.

But too often our inattention or our lack of faith paralyses the effect of His action on our souls. For us, to live is to possess sanctifying grace, and by our intention inspired by faith and love, to make our thoughts, our affections and all our activity emanate from Christ. If anyone should say to you: "To aspire to such elevation of soul is beyond my capacity, I must give up the idea," you should reply firmly: "Yes, it is impossible for you if you must rely on your natural strength and without allowing the necessary length of time." But so powerful is the action of Christ, so sanctifying the influence of a Mass well celebrated, of Holy Communion, of the atmosphere of prayer and of noble generosity in which the priestly life is normally lived, that you must fill your heart with unlimited confidence. If you show even a little fidelity to Him, Christ, by His grace, will raise you up.

Even if your life as a priest appears mediocre in the eyes of some—the world often judges thus—you may be sure that, in the eyes of God, it is great and agreeable because the Father sees in it the image of the life of His Son. "For you are dead: and your life is hid in Christ with God" (Col 3:3).

III.

SACERDOS ALTER CHRISTUS

I. THE SACRAMENTAL CHARACTER

Quod est Christus, erimus Christiani: "That which Christ is we Christians shall become," said a Father of the Church,[1] to remind the faithful of their eminent dignity. In fact, the whole effect of the sacraments, beginning with baptism, is to assimilate us to the Saviour: "You also . . . being baptized in Christ, have put on Christ" (Gal 3:27). For everyone, "to put on Christ" is to become like Him in His quality of Son of God; for us priests, it is, in addition, to be invested with His priesthood. This assimilation to Christ, which is the effect of the sacraments, is full of mystery. Sanctifying grace and the special characters of baptism, confirmation, and holy orders co-operate, each in its own way, to perfect in the soul of the priest this supernatural resemblance.

The grace of adoption, as you know, is a seed of life endowed with activity, subject to a law of growth and destined by all its forces to make man participate in the divine beatitude. By this grace we are psychologically disposed to know, love and possess God as He knows and loves Himself. We enter into the intimacy of the divine life.

The three sacramental characters contribute also, though in quite a different way, to produce in the soul a resemblance to Christ. This resemblance is subject to no vital growth, is not capable of change. It is fixed once for all in the soul and is indelible.

What, in fact, is this character? It is a sacred imprint, a spiritual seal impressed on the soul to consecrate the recipient to

---

[1] St. Cyprian, *De idolorum vanitate* 15; PL 4, 603.

Christ as a disciple, as a soldier or as a minister. It marks us for ever with the sign of the Redeemer and thus makes us already, in a certain manner, like to Him.

By its very presence, the sacramental character claims, calls for, requires, in the soul, and as a permanent quality, sanctifying grace. Would it not be inconsistent with the condition of a disciple, of a soldier and, above all, of a minister associated with His divine Master to offer sacrifice and to dispense the sacraments, not to live in friendship with Him whose ineffaceable mark he bears in the depths of his being.

"Consecration", "indelible seal", "claim to grace"—these terms do not exhaust the idea of character as the Church understands it. We must, besides, see in it a spiritual power, *spiritualis potestas.*

The character conferred in baptism gives to every Christian, as well as the capacity to receive the other sacraments, a real though inchoate power to participate in the priesthood of Christ. At the Mass he may associate himself in all truth with the celebrant and offer, with the priest, the body and blood of Christ; he can add to the immolation of the Saviour the spiritual "sacrifice" of his actions and his sufferings.[2] Admittedly he does not effect the sacramental immolation with the priest: the baptismal character does not connote such a power. Yet, restricted as it may be, this priesthood of the layman has a great dignity. That is why St. Peter gave the Christian assembly the splendid title of "kingly priesthood", *regale sacerdotium* (1 Pet 2:9).

Confirmation, by virtue of its character and of its special graces, adds new features to this resemblance of the baptized soul to Christ and its assimilation to Him. The sacrament imprints its mark on the disciple to make of him a Christian who will proclaim the faith, will bear testimony to it, will defend it, propagate it, and fight for it as a soldier of Christ, strong in the gifts and in the grace of the Holy Spirit. This assimilation is achieved in its highest degree in the sacrament of holy orders.

[2] St. Thomas, *Summa* III, q. 82, a. 1, ad 2.

By the imposition of hands by the bishop the candidate for ordination receives the Holy Spirit Who communicates to him a signal power over the physical body and over the mystical body of Our Lord. The priests of this earth are thus associated with the eternal Pontiff and become mediators between man and the divinity.

The principal effect of this sacrament is its character.[3] Just as, in Jesus, the hypostatic union is the reason for His fullness of grace, so, in the priest, the sacerdotal character is the source of all those gifts which raise him above the simple Christian.

You have been endowed with a supernatural power, a power which enables you, as ministers of Christ, to offer the eucharistic sacrifice and to pardon sins. This character is also a focus from which springs abundant grace which is the force and the light of your whole life. Moreover, it marks your soul with an imprint which cannot be effaced: it will remain in you for all eternity, as a cause of immense glory in heaven or of unspeakable shame in hell.

You understand, therefore, how close is the union between Christ and His priest. In the eyes of early Christendom the priest was simply one with Jesus Christ. He is the living image, the accredited representative of the supreme Pontiff: *Sacerdos Christi figura expressaque forma.*[4] The familiar saying *Sacerdos alter Christus* expresses perfectly the belief of the Church.

Remember what happens on the day of ordination. On that blessed morning, a young levite, overwhelmed by the sentiment of his own unworthiness and weakness, prostrates himself before the bishop who represents the heavenly Pontiff; he bows his head under the imposition of hands by the consecrating prelate. At this moment the Holy Spirit descends upon him and the eternal Father is able to contemplate with ineffable complacency this new priest, a living reproduction of His beloved Son: *Hic est Filius meus dilectus.* While the bishop holds his hand extended and the whole assembly of priests imitate his gesture, the words of the angel addressed to the Virgin Mary are accom-

---

[3] St. Thomas, *Summa* III, suppl., q. 34, a. 2.
[4] St. Cyril of Alexandria, *De ordinatione in Spiritu Sancto*, PG 68, 882.

plished anew: "The Holy Spirit shall come upon thee and the power of the Most High shall overshadow thee" (Lk 1:35). At this moment, full of mystery, the Holy Spirit takes possession of this chosen one of the Lord, and effects between Christ and him an eternal resemblance; when he rises, he is a man transformed: "Thou art a priest for ever, according to the order of Melchizedek" (Ps 110[109]:4).

You have received then a divine imprint which marks your whole being, and by it, you have been consecrated to God, body and soul, like a vessel of the altar which it would be a sacrilege to profane.

II. THREE ASPECTS OF THE ASSIMILATION OF THE PRIEST TO JESUS CHRIST

There could be no more fatal error for the priest than to underestimate the sacerdotal dignity. He must, on the contrary, have a very high conception of it.

The first aspect of our resemblance to Christ in the priesthood is expressed by the words of Jesus to His apostles: "You have not chosen Me, but I have chosen you" (Jn 15:16).

No one may presume on his own authority to assume the dignity of the priesthood. He must be called to it by God like Aaron (Heb 5:4). Why is this necessary? Because no one has the right to raise himself to so eminent a state. In Jesus Christ, the priesthood is a gift of the Father; Christ, says St. Paul, did not raise Himself to the supreme pontificate; He received it from Him who said to Him: "Thou art My Son . . . a priest for ever, according to the order of Melchizedek." The priest likewise must be chosen by the Almighty. We must at all times maintain a lively and grateful faith in the choice which Providence has made of us for the priesthood. "The divine oil has been poured on thee above thy fellows" (Ps 54[44]:7). This choice supposes that God regards us with a very special love. It often happens that from childhood or adolescence Our Lord extends to us His special protection and guides us on the way of life. The gift of the priesthood is like a golden ring which is the beginning of a new chain of special graces, reserved for the ministers of the altar. We must learn to find in this great thought a constant stimulus for our fidelity.

Admittedly none of us can penetrate the mystery of the decrees of predestination hidden in God. But revealing indications may permit us to form in all prudence a practical personal conviction regarding the divine plan for a soul. It is for the bishop alone, as the accredited representative of God, to pass judgement in the last resort on the signs of a vocation and, by a canonical call, to manifest the will of the Most High.

It is a most grave offence to attempt to receive the Holy Spirit and the priestly anointing without this heavenly call. This offence will bring its own punishment.

On the other hand, when, in obedience to the voice of his bishop, the deacon receives the imposition of hands, he must regard it as certain that God, in His infinite mercy, has really chosen him. That is why the happiness he experiences at being a priest is so pure, and the pride which he feels so legitimate.

Henceforward, the priest identifies himself with Christ by reason of the power with which he is clothed.

The essential function of the priesthood is to establish sacred intermediaries between heaven and earth to offer to the Lord the gifts of men and to communicate to them in exchange the graces of God. The priest is divinely appointed to supply the religious needs of the people: *Pro hominibus constituitur in iis quae sunt ad Deum*, "chosen from among men is appointed to act on behalf of men in relation to God" (Heb 5:1).

Before ascending to heaven, Jesus wished to leave behind Him men whose role it would be to continue, by renewing them, His own actions of power and of love. The priest takes the place of Christ: *Sacerdos vice Christi vere fungitur qui, id quod (Christus) fecit, imitatur.*[5] It is thus that St. Cyprian expresses it in accordance with all Christian tradition.

Christ communicates to His priests something more than a simple delegation. He clothes them with His own power; He

---

[5] The priest truly takes the place of Christ as he reproduces that which Christ did before him.

operates efficaciously through their ministry. That is why their priesthood is so entirely subordinated to that of Christ, but it is from this subordination that its supreme dignity is born; it is the reflection of the priesthood of Christ among us. The priest is entrusted with sacred gifts: *sacra dans*. And this is so in a double sense: to the Father, he offers Jesus sacramentally immolated; this is the supreme gift which the Church on earth presents to God; to men he distributes the fruits of the redemption, that is to say he imparts to them the divine graces and pardons. The priest is associated with the whole work of the Cross, as the authorized dispenser of the treasures and the mercies of Christ: *Sic nos existimet homo ut ministros Christi et dispensatores mysteriorum Dei.*[6]

Jacob once clothed himself in the garments of his brother Esau in order to present himself before Isaac, and he drew down upon himself all the blessings reserved for his elder brother. In like manner, the priest, being invested, by virtue of his priestly character, with the power of Jesus Christ Himself, can say to the Lord with more truth than Jacob: "I am Thy first-born son" (Gen 27:32).

So complete is his identification with the eternal Pontiff that, in the Mass, the priest does not say: "This is the body . . . the blood of Christ"; but "This is *my* body . . . this is *my* blood." And in the confessional when he forgives sins, what words does he use? *Ego te absolvo*: "I absolve you." He does not appeal to God; on the contrary, he speaks and commands with authority. Why? Because the Church, in prescribing for him these sacred formulas, knows with absolute certainty that, in the exercise of his ministry, he is one with Christ Who operates in him and by him: *Agit in persona Christi*, "He acts in the person of Christ."

The priesthood is a sublime prerogative bestowed on the priest by the Father just as He granted it to His Son. It is the closest resemblance that man can have to the Incarnate Word. Here on earth nothing can exceed the excellence of the priesthood.

[6] "Let a man so account of us as the ministers of Christ and the dispensers of the mysteries of God" (1 Cor 4:1).

In the third place, as Jesus Christ is true God and true man, so the priest bears in his person a divine element and a human element.

During the days of his His mortal life, Christ hid His divinity under the veil of His humanity. In the eyes of the world He was the son of a working man: *Nonne hic est fabri filius* (Mt 13:55). To the Sandredrin and the Roman soldiers He appeared as a malefactor worthy of the severest punishment. And yet, in spite of appearances, He was the Word of God, the supreme Master of the universe, the source of all blessings.

Under the exterior of a man subject to the trials and miseries of this world, the priest conceals within himself the invisible grandeur of the priesthood. The unbeliever often regards him as a being dangerous to society; he will hardly concede to him the respect or the rights which are recognized as the due of the least of citizens.

And yet, what superhuman power there is in these fragile hands! In this man of ordinary appearance there resides a power which is truly divine. He speaks, and Christ descends on the altar to be immolated. The penitent, overwhelmed with the weight of his faults, kneels before him and, in the name of God, the priest says: "Go in peace." This sinner who, a minute ago, would perhaps have been condemned to eternal punishment, rises pardoned, justified, with his soul illuminated with heavenly grace.

Jesus Himself continues in this way to sanctify His faithful; from their birth until the last agony of death He intervenes, through the intermediary of His priests, at every stage of the lives of His elect. We can understand the reverence and love with which Christ's ministers have always been surrounded in every Christian society. In the belief of the Church they are, as it were, identified with their divine Master.

On one ordination day St. Francis de Sales noticed a young priest. When the ceremony was over, he remarked that at the door of the church the newly ordained stopped as though he were disputing with some invisible person as to who should pass first. "What is it?" the Saint asked. The young levite confessed that he had the privilege of seeing his guardian angel. "Before I was a priest," he said, "he always went in front of me, but now he will no longer pass before me."[7] The angels are not priests, but they reverence in us that dignity which they adore in Christ.

III. THE CALL TO SANCTITY

Jesus regards His priests as His intimate friends. After their elevation to the priesthood, He addressed these words to the apostles: "I will not now call you servants; for the servant knoweth not what his lord doeth. But I have called you friends: because all things whatsoever I have heard of My Father I have made known to you" (Jn 15:15). After your ordination the same words were said to you in the name of Jesus.

As a consequence of the dignity of your calling, there is a grave obligation of conscience and, as it were, a constant invitation to tend towards the perfection of your state.

Everything about the priesthood is supernatural. We cannot measure or appreciate the divine gift according to the maxims of this world: "The world does not know God; nor the things of God": *Pater juste, mundus te non cognovit* (Jn 17:25). From his seminary days the priest must be convinced of the real sanctity to which he is called. As time goes on, he will maintain and develop this conviction by a life of prayer and of devotion. It is impossible to exaggerate the value of the grace received on one's ordination day: *Noli negligere gratiam quae in te est*: "Do not neglect the gift you have" (1 Tim 4:14).

To pretend that it is sufficient to avoid sin, without aiming higher, that is to say, without living a life of faith and of love, is to run a great risk of losing one's soul. Even if one does not come to this ultimate disaster, it means passing one's life without experiencing those profound joys which God reserves for His faithful priests, and without having accomplished, in all its fullness, the priestly work which is expected of us.

[7] Msgr. Trochu, *Saint Francis de Sales*, I:25.

Even in the Old Testament, God required sanctity from His ministers; and yet their sacrifices of goats and heifers were only a figure of the sacrifice of the New Testament. How much more, therefore, will the Lord require a great purity of life from us? There are three motives which should constantly remind every priest of his duty to aspire to this sanctity: (1) His power over the body and blood of the Son of God; (2) His function as dispenser of grace: in this capacity, should he not be the first to be sanctified by it? Finally, (3) the Christian people look to him for a lesson by example; if he preaches to others the law of Christ, can he by his conduct deny the truth of what he teaches?

St. Thomas, summing up the traditional doctrine on this subject, extols priestly sanctity. This is how he puts it: "He who receives holy orders is made capable of exercising the most excellent functions by which homage is paid to Christ in the sacrament of the altar."[8] "Being raised to so exalted a ministry," the great doctor adds, "priests cannot be satisfied with a mediocre moral goodness; eminent virtue is required of them."[9]

Are we sufficiently conscious of the fact that we are the intimate friends of Jesus Christ, the ministers of His sacrifice? This proximity of the Saviour should be a constant stimulus to us. Even those laymen who are most pleasing to God cannot enjoy the same facility of access to Him that we do. A St. Gertrude, a St. Teresa, overwhelmed as they were with graces, intimately united as they were to Our Lord, could never have consecrated the bread and wine, could never have taken the sacred Host in their hands, never have distributed Holy Communion.*

The Host is so completely the possession of the priest that his power over it is limited only by the laws and prescriptions of the Church. Jesus has entrusted Himself to His priest, just as He entrusted Himself to Mary, and it is the priest alone, except in the case of extreme necessity, who has the right to touch Him,

---

[8] *Summa* II-II, q. 184, a. 8.

[9] *Summa*, suppl. q. 35, a. 1, ad 3.

* This was written well before permitted use of Extraordinary Ministers of Holy Communion.

to distribute Him to others. It is he who keeps the key of the tabernacle; he who takes Jesus to give Holy Communion to the sick, to bless the people; and he who carries Him in procession through the streets.

Let us try to say to Jesus in all truth: "O Christ, You have given Yourself to me, You have entrusted to me Your body and Your blood, You have confided to me the care of those souls which belong to You; I now wish to entrust myself to You; use me as You see fit."

When Jesus was working in Nazareth, when He was walking on the roads of Galilee, in conversation with His apostles, in prayer on the mountain, He always knew that He was a priest. It must be the same with us. We do not cease to be priests when we leave the altar; we are priests everywhere and always. Like Jesus, let us live with our minds intent on the interests of God: *In his quae Patris mei sunt, oportet me esse*: "Did you not know that I must be about my Father's business? " (Lk 2:49 Douay-Rheims).

You remember the parable of the talents: we are of those who received five. Reflect on it. Do we carry out the duties of our priesthood in the most worthy spirit possible? Just as Mary, the mother of Jesus, was possessed of a surpassing sanctity, so the priest, on account of his intimacy with Him Who is sanctity itself: *Tu solus sanctus, Jesu Christe*, must aim throughout his whole life at a great purity and a constant elevation of soul.

In order not to lose courage in this uphill journey we must continuously renew in our hearts the desire for perfection, and the memory of the words of the Pontifical addressed by the bishop to the candidate for the priesthood: "God is powerful enough to increase His grace in you," *Potens est Deus ut augeat in te gratiam suam.*

IV. IMITAMINI QUOD TRACTATIS *

The priest is *alter Christus* and, like his divine Master, he must be a victim immolated to the glory of God, and delivered up for

---

* These words are from the ordination rite: "Imitate the mystery you celebrate. . . ."

the salvation of souls. He may be a scholar, a social reformer or an organizer of genius, but if he is only that, he does not correspond to God's expectation of him.

To what heights in the moral life does the Church actually expect her priests to ascend?

The Pontifical indicates concisely but clearly the ensemble of virtues which are fitting for a minister of Christ: there can be no more authoritative teaching.

Before the rite of the imposition of hands, the bishop says these words: "May the candidates recommend themselves by a constant 'fidelity to justice': *diuturna iustitiae observatio*; may their conduct express their 'chastity and purity of life'." He asks again that "they may preach by example no less than by doctrine, and that the sweet odour of their virtue may be the joy of the Church of God": *Sit odor vitae vestrae delectamentum Ecclesiae Christi.*

There is one exhortation of the pontiff which must claim our special attention: "Consider well what you do: imitate the mystery of which you are the minister, that is the mystery of the death of our Lord": *Agnoscite quod agitis; imitamini quod tractatis: quatenus mortis dominicae mysterium celebrantes, mortificare membra vestra a vitiis et concupiscentiis omnibus procuretis.*

This is our true programme of sanctity. If we wish to rise to the heights of our priesthood, if we wish it to give its perfume to our whole life and to inflame us with love and zeal for the conquest of souls—and is not this our most noble ambition—we must, in accordance with the words of the consecrating bishop, imitate and reproduce Christ, the Priest and the Victim. If we share in His priestly dignity, is it not right that we should take part in His oblation?

We can contemplate Jesus in the different phases of His life and in the variety of His virtues. He is the ideal for all men. The child can find his model in Him as can the simple Christian, the worker, the consecrated virgin, and the religious. But there exists in Him a holy of holies, a tabernacle which is closed, where the soul of the priest must be eager to enter, because it is there that the whole interior life of Jesus finds its source. From the moment of the Incarnation, the Saviour devoted Himself entirely to the accomplishment of the will of the Father; He gave Himself in a transport of perfect love: *Ecce venio . . . ut faciam, Deus, tuam voluntatem* (Heb 10:7), and this desire was His for ever. These, then, are our orders of the day: to follow Jesus in the absolute consecration of His life to the glory of the Father and to the salvation of the world. This is perfection for the priest; it is a vocation higher than that of the angels.

Obedience to this invitation to imitate the mystery of which you are the ministers, means not merely to celebrate the sacrifice itself piously, but also to unite to the offering of Jesus the absolute donation of our own life. Let it be clearly understood that the whole existence of Jesus on this earth was a preparation for His death on the Cross. It was *for us* that He came down from heaven, as the Credo says: *Propter nos homines et propter nostram salutem.** In Nazareth, in the modest workshop of Joseph, He knew that He was the Victim destined for this supreme immolation. He had accepted in advance the whole plan of His life with all its affronts and all its sufferings. When His hour had come, Jesus, in a transport of immense love, offered Himself for our redemption: *Crucifixus etiam pro nobis.*

This whole-hearted acceptance of all the designs of God must serve us as a model. *Imitamini. . . .* We also at the altar present to God the whole course of our life, accepting it, loving it, dedicating it in the spirit of love to the cause of God and to the salvation of souls.

Thus, by daily imitation of the offering of Jesus, it will be granted us to enter, little by little, into the mysterious intimacy of the soul of the divine Master.

V. THE EXAMPLE OF ST. PAUL

Of all those upon whom Christ conferred the signal honour of associating them with His priesthood no one has appreciated better than St. Paul the amplitude and the depth of this vocation.

---

* For us men and for our salvation.

From the moment that Christ revealed Himself to the apostle, the world and public opinion no longer meant anything to him: *Continuo non acquievi carni et sanguini*: "I did not confer with flesh and blood" (Gal 1:16). He knew that he was the minister, the priest, the apostle, of Christ, "predestined as such from the womb of his mother": *Me segregavit ex utero matris meae* ["He set me apart before I was born"] (Gal 1:15). He writes to the Corinthians telling them of his life, and how does he describe it? As an unbroken sequence, a wondrous chain of sufferings endured for Christ, and of labours undertaken to make known the riches of His grace: "Thrice was I beaten with rods, once I was stoned." . . . Perils of every kind marked his days: "Perils in the cities . . . perils in the wilderness . . . perils from false brethren." Hunger and cold and all kinds of other miseries were his common lot. Besides all this he bore in his heart grave solicitude for the newly founded churches: *Sollicitudo omnium ecclesiarum*; the personal difficulties of his converts found their echo in his heart: "Who is weak and I am not weak? Who is scandalized and I am not on fire?" (2 Cor 11:25ff.).

Despite these many tribulations, St. Paul was not overwhelmed. How was it that he maintained his courage? He gives us the explanation: "Gladly therefore will I glory in my infirmities, that the power of Christ may dwell in me" (2 Cor 12:9). Elsewhere he says: "But in all these things we overcome because of Him that hath loved us" (Rom 8:37). He had attained such a degree of Union with the Saviour that he could exclaim: "For to me, to live is Christ" (Phil 1:21); and again: "I live in the faith of the Son of God Who loved me and delivered Himself up for me" (Gal 2:20). If ever a priest understood the depths of the significance of the Passion and death of Jesus and the immensity of the divine mercy, it was the great St. Paul. He spoke of himself as "nailed to the Cross": *Christo confixus sum cruci* (Gal 2:19). Now, he who is attached to the Cross is in very truth a victim.

What was the consequence of all this? He was able to say: *Vivo ego iam non ego, vivit vero in me Christus*: "I live, yet not I, Christ is living in me" (Gal 2:20). Christ is in me; you see me act, but this zeal, these words are not from me; they are from Christ, Who inspires my whole life, because I have renounced all that I am in order to be completely His minister. By the grace of God I live by the love of Him Who has given His life for me.

If we wish to maintain the nobility and the sanctity of our priestly life instead of seeing it reduced to a hasty recitation of the breviary and a routine celebration of the Mass, we must attach ourselves in a very true sense to the Cross of Christ; we must have it in our heart so that Jesus may associate us with His holocaust. St. Paulinus de Nola expresses this admirably: *Ipse Dominus hostia omnium sacerdotum est . . . ipsique sunt hostiae sacerdotes.*[10]

We meet many people in the world who think that they are victims, but they are victims only in their own imagination, in their own emotions, and they protest at the slightest pinprick. The souls which are really given to God are faithful to their dedication in every detail of their day; their acts of devotion and their sufferings rise unceasingly and silently like a perfume before the throne of God. Women hidden in obscure cloisters or even living in the world have sometimes dedicated themselves entirely to this ideal. Why should not we, the priests of Jesus, live for it, too?

To return to St. Paul: his doctrine throws light on the challenge: "I fill up in my flesh those things that are wanting of the sufferings of Christ" (Col 1:24). What a mysterious saying! Can there be anything wanting in the infinite merits of Jesus Christ? Has He not carried out to the last iota, and with perfect love, the programme of His Father? And yet St. Paul writes: "I fill up." Here is the explanation: by a decree of His adorable wisdom, God has reserved for His Church a part of the satisfaction required for the sins of the world. Souls who, in this spirit, unite themselves with Christ, render great glory to God: they "fill up" by their offering the total expiation which infinite justice requires of humanity. Nothing can be more realistic therefore

---

[10] "The Lord Himself is the victim Whom all the priests offer . . . and the priests must themselves be victims in their turn" (*Epist.* 11; PL 61, 196).

than to place yourself upon the altar and to ask the Father to accept you as an oblation in union with the oblation of Jesus Christ.

Why did the Apostle speak in this way? Because he was a priest in every sense of the word, a priest who joined to the immolation of Christ the offering of an existence of self-denial and of zeal for the good of souls: "that they also who live, may not now live to themselves but unto Him Who died for them and rose again" (2 Cor 5:15).

St. Paul did not merely celebrate the holy sacrifice; he united himself to it, he lived it, he regarded himself as priest and victim with Christ.

If you want to be holy priests, as I hope you do, follow this example of the Apostle. Has he not written: "Be ye followers of me, as I also am of Christ": *Imitatores mei estote sicut et ego Christi* (1 Cor 4:16).

VI. THE PRIEST, SOURCE OF GRACE FOR SOULS

The eternal priesthood of Christ is the source of all the graces which men receive here on earth and of the beatitude which they will enjoy for eternity: *De plentitudine eius nos omnes accepimus*: "From his fulness we have all received" (Jn 1:16).

Because it continues Christ's work on earth and acts by virtue of His power, the Christian priesthood is in practice the ordinary conduit of all the supernatural gifts which God grants to the world.

If we consider our dignity as priests from this aspect we shall see in it an incomparable grandeur.

God could, assuredly, in His sovereign liberty and liberality, share out all grace independently of our ministry. Yet, according to the plan of the eternal wisdom, it is by the intervention of men invested with power from on high that the divine adoption, the pardon of sins, the heavenly help and all the teaching of revealed truth comes to us.

This order of things is a continuation of the dispensation of the Incarnation. Just as the world has been redeemed by the sacrifice of one man, the new Adam, but of infinite merit, so it is through the intermediary of men replacing Christ that the graces of redemption are communicated.

By this dispensation, in conformity with the will of the Father, the Son is glorified unceasingly. In fact, when the faithful have recourse to the priest for enlightenment and strength they give practical recognition to the fact that, in the work of salvation and sanctification, all spiritual good is derived from Christ. By this practical act of faith, the members of the mystical body contribute to the universal exaltation of the Saviour; in their own way they enter into the spirit of the Father when He said: "I have glorified Him and will glorify Him again" (Jn 12:28). The object of the Incarnation is to elevate creatures to the supernatural order. This was accomplished radically in Jesus Christ, but it is still necessary that each soul should realize in itself this divine exaltation by means of the graces distributed by the Church.

By the gifts which he has in himself, every Christian is capable, at least by means of example, of attracting his neighbour to virtue. But the priest must be a focus radiating divine life. It is for him to communicate the divine gifts, especially the gift par excellence: Jesus Christ. By virtue of his office he is a director: it is for him to guide the religious and the simple faithful alike in the ways of perfection. It is for him also to make the message of the Gospel heard in every heart: *Praedicate evangelium omni creaturae* (Mk 16:15).

The great mission of the priest is to give Jesus Christ to the world.

We read in the Mass of Doctors: "You are the salt of the earth": *Vos estis sal terrae* (Mt 5:13). These are the words of Jesus Christ to His apostles. The priest must offer this germ of incorruptibility to all those who come in contact with him. It must be said of him in all truth: "a healing virtue goes out from him" (Lk 6:19). But this depends, to a great extent, on his personal sanctity.

When the salt has lost its savour it is good for nothing any more; it is cast out as useless. So it is with the priest: any weakening of the fervour of his priestly dedication will tend to diminish his spiritual influence over souls. On the other hand; when he is full of the love of God and devotedly united to Jesus Christ, he does good even when he is not performing any act of his sacred ministry. You have often remarked it: a professor of philosophy, of science, or of arts, or a dean of discipline, if he is a true priest, will infallibly exercise a beneficent influence on his pupils, without perhaps realizing it himself. No layman, however good or edifying he may be, can have so profound an influence for good, because a priest by his very vocation is the "salt of the earth".

Never forget it: we are instrumental causes in the hands of Jesus Christ for the sanctification of the world. The instrumental cause must be closely united to the agent who uses it: it can only produce its effect by virtue of his activity. Let us accept our status as humble and docile instruments in the hands of God and never attribute to ourselves what the Lord accomplishes through us. The validity of our administration of the sacraments depends on our ordination and on the jurisdiction which we receive from the bishop, but the fruitfulness of our words in the confessional, in the pulpit and in all our relations with the faithful depends principally on our union with Christ.

How admirable is the wisdom of the divine economy! In His merciful designs the Father has not willed the Incarnation for the salvation of the world alone; it was His will also that we should find in the divine Mediator a heart like to our own, a heart full of tenderness and compassion which has experience of our sufferings and our miseries, excepting only sin. The priest continues, here on earth, the mission of Christ. That is why Our Lord did not choose the dispensers of His grace from among the angels, pure and full of love as they are, but from among men. These, from their personal experience of the burden of our earthly weakness and from the realization of their own poverty, are the better able to have compassion on the weakness and ignorance of sinners: *qui condolere possit iis qui ignorant et errant, quoniam et ipse circumdatus est infirmitate*: "He can deal gently with the ignorant and wayward, since he himself is beset with weakness" (Heb 5:2).

While we are filled with admiration and reverence for the divinity of Christ Jesus, it is His goodness and mercy which strengthen us and conquer us. In like manner the sublimity of the priesthood is revered among Christian peoples, but the qualities in the priest which attract, which make him the beloved minister of God, are above all his goodness, his compassion for every kind of weakness and trouble, his devotion in the service of all, like St. Paul, who was proud to write to the Romans: "I am a debtor to all, to the wise and to the unwise": *Sapientibus et insipientibus debitor sum* (Rom 1:14). In my country, which has passed through three centuries of religious persecution, not only has the priest preserved the faith in its integrity in the hearts of the people, but in every family and for every individual he is the counsellor whose advice is always listened to, he is the comforter and the most trusted friend.

To this great spirit of kindness which finds its source in the kindness of Jesus, the priest must add a lively faith in the efficacy of the grace which he dispenses. Whatever weaknesses or sins he may meet with, the minister of Christ must believe firmly in the power of grace to aid every individual in his need. As an early author puts it: "Jesus transforms every man of goodwill. He meets a publican and makes him an evangelist; He promises heaven to the penitent thief—a sinner comes to Him, He raises her to the rank of the virgins." [11]

Sometimes the priest, although he is putting his whole heart into his mission, feels that he is not living up to his ideal. This feeling must not discourage him. Indeed, this sentiment of humility is admirably calculated to draw down the blessing of God on him and on his ministry.

But this conviction of his own littleness, if it is to be pleasing to the Lord, must always be accompanied by unlimited confidence in the merits of Jesus: "In all things you are made rich in Him," says St. Paul, "in all utterance and in all knowledge so that nothing is wanting to you in any grace" (1 Cor 1:5–7). If it is important for us to recognize our own poverty; it is still more

---

[11] St. John Chrysostom, PG 52, 803 (Monastic Breviary, Tuesday after Pentecost).

important for us to say, like the Apostle: "I can do all things in Him who comforts me" (Phil 4:13).

In order that He might accomplish this mission of salvation, Christ received of the divine life from the Father; we also receive grace from on high in our work for souls.

We meet Jesus every morning: His flesh and blood give new life to our souls. All that we have to do is to receive Him with faith so that we may "put on the Lord Jesus Christ": *Induimini Dominum Jesum Christum* (Rom 8:1). Then our hearts will be filled with love and compassion for sinners, for the ignorant, for the souls undergoing trials, for those who are in trouble or in suffering. And, following the example of Jesus, we shall desire that "all shall come to us to be comforted": *Venite ad Me omnes qui laboratis et onerati estis, et ego reficiam vos*: "Come to me, all who labor and are heavy laden, and I will give you rest" (Mt 11:28).

Part II

_____

THE PATH
TO PRIESTLY SANCTITY

A. *The Priestly Virtues*

IV.

EX FIDE VIVIT

WE have seen what ideal of sanctity should inspire all the actions of a priest's life: his priesthood is a participation in the priesthood of the Word Incarnate.

We shall never realize our ideal fully. It is important to remind ourselves of this so that we may not be discouraged. Nevertheless, we must maintain a great desire to advance towards this ideal, however unattainable it may seem. It is this desire which inspires our enthusiasm and keeps our mind fixed on the divine Master.

Are we not, moreover, at all times supported by His merits and by the abundance of divine grace?

In order to throw further light on this work of sanctification, let us consider the principal virtues which we must love and cultivate. They are required of every Christian, but the priest must practise them in a special manner, appropriate to his sacred function, to his mission to souls, and to the supernatural sanctity which the heavenly Father expects of him.

I. FAITH, THE ATMOSPHERE OF THE LIFE OF THE PRIEST

All the value of our life springs from faith: *sine fide impossibile est placere Deo* (Heb 11:6). "If our faith is vain," says St. Paul again, "we are the most miserable of men": *Miserabiliores sumus omnibus hominibus* (1 Cor 15:19). This is supremely true for the priest: without faith his whole existence is an offence against truth. In the first place, is not his own priesthood an object of faith? There is no outward sign of his eminent dignity. Our God is a hidden God (Is 45:15) His whole being is light, brilliant and unwaning, but we do not see it. He Himself and all that He effects in us and through our ministry are matters of faith.

What is the priest in the eyes of an unbeliever? A man like any other who abuses the confidence of good people, and has nothing special about him except his clothes. Often, indeed, they hate him because of Christ. The priest, therefore, can be known only by faith. Now, of all those who must believe in the priest, it is the priest himself who is most strictly bound to this act of faith. His faith must keep ever present to his mind the infinite condescension of God in calling him to such a dignity. More even than the deacons to whom St. Paul was speaking, the priest must "hold the mystery of faith in a pure conscience": *Habentes mysterium fidei in conscientia pura* (1 Tim 3:9).

We priests live in constant contact with the Eucharist; we must continually renew in our hearts the liveliness of our faith.

It is possible to lose this precious gift entirely. I remember a poor priest whose bishop asked me to visit him. He was dying. When I recalled to him the great Christian truths, he answered: "All that is mere legend and fantasy." I did not succeed in reviving his faith. Without straying as far as this, any minister of Christ may come to realize that his faith has lost something of its freshness, its spontaneity and its unction.

In the evening of life it is an immense satisfaction to be able to say to God, with St. Paul: *Fidem servavi* (2 Tim 4:7). In all things I have preserved the faith and the point of view of eternity. What is the origin of your priestly vocation? Was it not your faith as a boy or as a young man? When our faith is fervent it makes us "live unto God": *Viventes Deo* (Rom 6:2). Without it we are nothing, and, when it weakens, all the virtues are weakened with it.

In every sphere of life the atmosphere in which our thoughts habitually move is of great importance.

What is the atmosphere best suited to the soul of a priest? Is it the atmosphere of lay society? Of village gossip? Of the latest news in the paper or some book of profane literature? Certainly not. I do not suggest that a priest may not keep in touch with many things, but, first of all, he must have a true interior life, and that can only be nourished and maintained with the food of faith.

We must remember the favours of God and the glorious supernatural realities which the Church dispenses to her children. It is our special mission to communicate Jesus Christ to men: God has so loved the world: *sic Deus dilexit mundum* (Jn 3:16). Having entrusted to us the riches of salvation, God will require a reckoning of the way we have used them.

We must have ever present to our minds a sense of our responsibilities. Our whole conscious life must be based on the habitual conviction that we are not our own. We must say with St. Paul: "I am of Christ" (1 Cor 1:12) and again with him: "To the wise and to the unwise I am a debtor": *sapientibus et insipientibus debitor sum* (Rom 1:14). Can we be in peace before God if we know that a soul which is in our charge is in distress, and neglect to go to its aid?

The priest's outlook on the world must bear the stamp of benevolence. It must not, however, be like that of the young man who is dazzled by the glitter of things, and does not consider the dullness of the reverse side. The minister of Christ may not find his joy in the goods of this world; he must consider them with the eyes of Jesus Christ, that is to say, as his faith reveals to him their value and their vanity.

It is of the utmost importance that the faithful should appreciate this supernatural point of view in the priest: the fruitfulness of our ministry will depend in great measure on it.

II. THE ROLE OF FAITH

Faith is a fundamental virtue. Without it, charity, religion, and indeed every virtue is impossible. Faith is the basis of all our supernatural relations with God. According to the divine plan, it is by its light that we are to be guided during our time of trial here on earth: our approach to God, the use of the necessary means to ensure our union with Him, our merit, all involve a certain obscurity. The angels also were tested in their faith, for, whatever the precise nature of their trial may have been, they underwent it in full liberty, before being admitted to the beatific vision.

The Council of Trent sums up the essential role of faith as follows: "The salvation of man begins by faith; it is the foundation and the root of all justification: without faith it is impossible to please God and to share in the lot of His children."[1] Faith is, for us, the beginning, the basis, the root of our life as children of God. Let us consider these words of the Council.

To whom does God give the power to become His children? St. John tells us: this grace is reserved for believers alone. *His qui credunt in nomine eius*: "for those who believe in His name" (Jn 1:12). St. Paul gives us the same message: A life-giving approach to God presupposes faith: *Credere enim oportet accedentem ad Deum*: "for whoever would draw near to God must believe that He exists" (Heb 11:6).

If faith is necessary to awaken the divine life, it is still more necessary to ensure its growth and development. Faith is in a very real sense the foundation and the root of the interior life. What is the purpose of the foundations in a building? Not only do they permit the construction to begin, but the stability, the equilibrium, the very life of the building are constantly dependent on them.

Faith has the same relation to our whole spiritual existence. It is only the firm basis of our belief that can strengthen our hope, give free scope to our charity, and enable our prayers to ascend to God.

In moments of trials as well as in the course of our normal life, it is from faith that we receive constant support, and faith which provides the most efficacious incentive for our actions. That is why St. Paul urges the Colossians to remain "founded in faith": *In fide fundati* (Col 1:23).

The role of faith may be compared also to that of the root which fixes the tree to the ground, and by its imperceptible but unceasing work maintains its strength. All the growth of the tree, its whole development, depends on this secret nourishment. Cut the roots, and the tree, however splendid and full of life it may be, will perish miserably.

---

[1] Sess. 6:8.

The certitudes of faith are thus of primary importance. Their influence is constant: they ennoble our existence and strengthen our souls; thanks to them, the Christian, and above all the priest, before the onslaught of the powers of evil, has no doubt of the ultimate victory: *Haec est victoria quae vincit mundum, fides nostra* (1 Jn 5:4).

St. Paul has succeeded in summing up in a very short formula the whole of this doctrine which was so dear to him: "The just man liveth *by* faith": *Justus ex fide vivit* (Gal 3:11; Rom 1:17; Heb 10:38). We must grasp the very practical significance of this doctrine, for the stronger our faith is, the more our whole life will be regenerated, and through it, the bonds of our divine adoption will be drawn tighter.

III. THE CONCEPT OF FAITH

What exactly is this faith by which we must live? The Vatican Council[2] tells us in an illuminating definition: "Faith is a supernatural virtue by which, under the inspiration, and with the help of the grace of God, we accept as true what He has revealed: not that we grasp the intrinsic truth of the supernatural verities by the natural light of reason, but we accept them on account of the authority of God Himself Who reveals them and Who cannot deceive or be deceived."

Faith is the homage of our intellect to the divine veracity. God has spoken to us mainly through the lips of Jesus and by the teaching of the apostles. When man accepts the divine revelation with all its splendour and all its obscurity, he prostrates his whole being before God; he surrenders himself to the sovereign and infallible Truth, and thus renders glory to God. For, in this complete acquiescence, the intellect leads the whole man to the most complete submission before the supreme authority of God.

This submission of the intelligence, in its adherence to the supreme Truth revealing the divine mystery and the ways of salvation, constitutes the essence of faith.

[2] Sess. 3, cap. 1. This is evidently a reference to what we now call the First Vatican Council.

Faith is a communion of the intellect, not with the views of a man, however learned, but with the thought of God Himself. By faith we make this thought our own; we share in the knowledge which God has of Himself and of the designs of His eternal predestination. We must accept with the most profound respect divine revelation, both in its ensemble and in each item of truth which the Church, sole final judge in these matters, proposes for our belief. "That which we believe concerning Your glory, we believe on the faith of Your revelation": *quod enim de tua gloria, revelante te, credimus.*[3]

Far from subjugating human reason, faith elevates it; it extends its frontiers enormously and puts it in possession of the essential truths concerning the meaning of its destiny.

Faith connotes essentially three elements: adherence of the intelligence, a movement of the will, and the inspiration of grace, embracing the whole activity of the believer. It is not a conclusion based on reasoning, that is, a conviction produced in the intelligence by the force of arguments. No, it is a submission of the intellect, at once voluntary, confident and complete, to the authority of God Who reveals. Why does faith involve a movement of the will? As you know, it is only by an abstract and difficult effort that we manage to form a concept of those things which are outside our human experience. That is why the supernatural truths must always remain for us shrouded in much darkness. By accepting revelation and its teaching, our intelligence adapts itself to divine truth; it receives it and acquiesces in it, but it could not do this without the impulse of the will desiring to find God and to communicate with Him. Grace embraces all the complexities of these steps, without, however, necessarily making itself felt.

The part played by the free will in the act of faith makes it meritorious in the eyes of God. In all this, God has willed to leave so much obscurity that believing may be an act of profound confidence in Him, and so much light that the act of faith may appear to be in conformity with reason.

[3] Preface of the Trinity.

Finally, in order that we may believe, the action of grace on the intellect and on the will is necessary. Read the Gospels. The contemporaries of Jesus were able to touch Him, to hear Him: they could apprehend Him with their senses; their reason told them that He was an eminent man, a man of outstanding virtue. But in order to penetrate to the holy of holies of His divine being, and to believe that He was the true Son of God, over and above miracles and prophecies, the gift of grace was necessary. Jesus Himself has said it: "Flesh and blood hath not revealed it to thee, but My Father who is in heaven": *Caro et sanguis non revelavit tibi sed Pater meus* (Mt 16:17). And again He says: "No man can come to Me except the Father . . . draw him": *Nemo potest venire ad me, nisi Pater . . . traxerit eum* (Jn 6:44).

Faith comes to us from on high. The unbeliever must humbly implore the grace of its coming, and we, who are in possession of this gift of God, must ask for its increase: *Credo, Domine, adjuva incredulitatem meam*: "Lord, I believe; help my unbelief" (Mk 9:24).

Temptations against faith are always possible, but they will become for us a stimulus for prayer; in this way they will make our faith more lively and make us appreciate better its supernatural and gratuitous character. While we should not expose ourselves rashly by dangerous conversations or readings to doubts concerning divine revelation, we must learn to put our hesitations to good use; we must adhere the more deliberately and the more firmly to Christ and to His message.

IV. PRIVILEGE OF FAITH: THE DAWN OF THE BEATIFIC VISION

All this teaching of the Councils of Trent and of the Vatican is to be found implicitly in the definition of faith given us by St. Paul: "Faith is the substance of things to be hoped for, the evidence of things that appear not": *Est autem fides sperandarum substantia rerum, argumentum non apparentium* (Heb 11:1).

These words mean that faith is the vital support of all our supernatural hopes; it is our conviction of the existence of this heavenly world which we do not see and of which the whole

Epistle to the Hebrews treats. This inspired text reveals the most marvellous prerogative of faith: to be the dawn of the light of heaven. There is no break of continuity between faith and the beatific vision. In practice there exist for us three distinct orders of reality: that of the material world, that of intellectual truths, and the higher sphere of the supernatural. We attain to each of these worlds by the aid of the appropriate light.

Material nature with its immensity and its beauty is revealed to our eyes by its own splendour. Our mind contemplates the same universe but on a higher plane because it ascends from the phenomena to their causes; it sees in things the signs of the creative Omnipotence and Wisdom, and arrives thus at a knowledge of Christ and His perfections. The light which enables our eyes to see is certainly different from that by which the intelligence apprehends, reasons, and judges. The one is not a development of the other; they belong to different orders.

Above the world attained by the senses and by reason, there is a third sphere which is transcendent, inaccessible, divine. "God inhabiteth light inaccessible Whom no man hath seen nor can see ever": *Lucem inhabitat inaccessibilem quem nullus hominum videt nec videre potest* (1 Tim 6:16). It is our destiny, by our supernatural elevation, to penetrate these depths of God, *profunda Dei* (1 Cor 2:10). In heaven, in order that we may contemplate God intuitively, we shall receive a communication of this divine light. "In thy light we shall see light": *In lumine tuo videbimus lumen* (Ps 36[35]:9). However, already here on earth the Lord graciously permits His chosen children of adoption to make contact with this superterrestrial world. How is this wonder effected? By the gift of faith. Faith is the dawn of the beatific vision.

Let us consider what happens in the heavenly Jerusalem. The light of glory strengthens in a marvellous manner the intellectual capacity of the saints and adapts it to the contemplation of God. At the same time, this light sheds its rays on the totality of acts of knowledge, love and joy which make up eternal life and eternal beatitude. Faith plays the same role for us in this life. In the hour of darkness, of effort, or of trial, it makes God present to us; it enables us to adhere to Him; it puts within our grasp all the invisible realities which are the object of our hopes. But at the same time, it illuminates all the acts which are required of a Christian in his ascent towards heaven; all the supernatural activity which prepares the children of God to receive one day the light of glory and permits them to merit, must spring from faith as from an ever-living fountain. "We see now through a glass in a dark manner, but then face to face": *Videmus nunc per speculum in enigmate, tunc autem facie ad faciem* (1 Cor 13:12).

Not only does faith belong to the supernatural order; it finds in the beatific vision its final development and glory. The same life which we receive in baptism is evolved and transformed. Faith is in all truth the first light, the dawn of the eternal vision: St. Thomas sums up this elevated doctrine in terms at once clear and concise: Faith is a "virtue of the intellect by which eternal life is begun in us": *Fides est habitus mentis quo inchoatur vita aeterna in nobis.*[4]

V. FAITH IN CHRIST, THE WORD INCARNATE [5]

God presents Himself to us as an object of faith, especially in the person of Jesus Christ. He desires that we believe firmly that the infant born of Mary, the tradesman of Nazareth, the Master disputing with the Pharisees, the man who was crucified on Calvary, is truly His Son, His equal and that we adore Him as such. The great work which God had appointed to Himself in the economy of salvation is to establish among men faith in the Word Incarnate: *Hoc est opus Dei ut credatis in eum quem misit ille* (Jn 6:29).

Nothing can take the place of this faith in Jesus Christ, true God, consubstantial with the Father, Whose envoy He is. It is the synthesis of all our belief because Christ is the synthesis of all revelation.

This is true for Christians in general, but it is especially true

[4] *Summa* II-II, q. 14, a. 1.

[5] We deal here with a fundamental point which is characteristic of the teaching of Dom Marmion. It is to be found in all his writings. Note especially *Christ, the Life of the Soul*, pp. 167–82; in the volume on the *Mysteries*, pp. 37–60, 221–38; in *Christ, the Ideal of the Monk*, the chapter *Haec est victoria—fides nostra.*

for the priest. For the *raison d'être* of the priest is to communicate to the world the salvation of Christ, the Son of God, made flesh for love of us. The whole life of the great Apostle is summed up in these words: "I live in the faith of the Son of God who loved me and delivered Himself for me": *In fide vivo Filii Dei qui dilexit me et tradidit semetipsum pro me* (Gal 2:20), and our whole existence as priests should bear testimony to the same firm conviction.

The life of the Church supposes always and in all things the adoration of her divine Spouse. In face of the world which denies Him and disowns Him, she repeats unceasingly with St. Peter: "Thou art Christ, the Son of the living God": *Tu es Christus, Filii Dei vivi* (Mt 16:16).

The penetrating vision of faith, which pierces the veil of the humanity of Christ and reaches the depths of His divinity, is wanting to many intellects. They see Jesus, they reach Him, but, like the crowds of Galilee, they see only the externals; their approach is superficial and their souls are not transformed. For others, on the contrary, Jesus is transfigured; grace gives added light to their faith in His divinity. For them Jesus is the sun of justice; He surpasses all the beauties of the earth, and the vision of Him so entrances their heart that no other attraction can detach them from His love. They are able to say with St. Paul: "For I am sure that neither death nor life . . . nor any other thing shall be able to separate me from the love of God which is in Christ Jesus, Our Lord" (Rom 8:38).

A faith such as this fixes Jesus Christ definitely in our hearts. It is not a simple adherence of the intellect; it includes love, hope, and the total consecration of oneself to Christ to live of His life, to participate in His mysteries and to imitate His virtues. Some Christians, and even some priests, have never established Christ as the inspiration of their spiritual life. They believe that Christ is God, but without any personal living conviction, and their faith is not for them the root and foundation of their religion. They have no practical appreciation of the saying of St. Paul: "For other foundation no man can lay, but that which is laid, which is Christ Jesus": *Fundamentum aliud nemo ponere potest, praeter id quod positum est, Jesus Christus* (1 Cor 3:11). That is why their work is often unfruitful.

We must deliberately cast ourselves at the feet of Jesus Christ and offer Him the homage of a very lively faith: "O Christ, without seeing you in all the glory of Your divinity, I confess that You are the Son of the living God": *Deum de Deo, lumen de lumine, Deum verum de Deo vero.* In the spiritual life it is of the utmost importance to base our impulse towards Christ on this foundation of faith in the Word Incarnate.

But it is not sufficient to have formed this intention. Our strength must be restored and our generosity revived every day by virtue of this faith. The more perfect this faith is, the more Christ will share with us His quality of Son of God. This quality is the most excellent thing that Christ has—and He gives it to us. The whole grandeur of this doctrine is derived from this glorious thought: to believe is to participate in the knowledge which God has of Himself and of all things in Himself. By the exercise of this virtue our life becomes, as it were, a reflection of His life. When the soul is filled with faith, it sees, so to speak, with the eyes of God.

Now what is it that the Father is eternally contemplating? His Son. He knows, He loves everything in Him. This contemplation and this love are an essential part of Him. As I speak to you at this moment, what is He looking at? The Word, His equal, Who became man through love.

The Father appreciates His Son infinitely, divinely, as He alone can; that is why He is completely wrapped up in Him; everything that He does is ordained for His glory: "I have glorified Him and will glorify Him again": *Et clarificavi et iterum clarificabo* (Jn 12:28). He wishes His Son to be recognized by His rational creatures with all the reverence due to His divinity. When He introduced Him into this world, He willed that all the angels should adore Him: *Et adorent eum omnes angeli Dei* (Heb 1:6). He claims the same homage from men. The Father wishes that "all men honour the Son as they honour Himself": *ut omnes honorificent Filium sicut honorificant Patrem* (Jn 5:23). And on Mount Tabor did He not require all to believe the words of

Jesus because they were the words of His well-beloved Son? *Hic est Filius . . . ipsum audite* (Mt 17:5). If we could see Christ through the eyes of the Father we would attach an unlimited value to the dignity of His person, to the amplitude of His merits and to the potency of His grace. However great the multitude of our faults, however great our poverty, we possess in Christ an inexhaustible resource of mercy. In our wretchedness, we are "rich in Christ": *In omnibus divites facti estis in illo* (1 Cor 1:5). The superabundance of the merits of a God is for the Church which possesses them an ever fruitful Source of gratitude, of praise, of peace and of joy unspeakable.

For us priests, especially, who are in such frequent contact with the eucharistic mystery, this faith in His divinity commands the most profound respect for Christ. *Veneremur cernui.* If Jesus hides His splendour we must adore all the more the mysterious reality of His presence. We shall love this *mysterium fidei* more and more according as we live it. *Caeleste munus diligere quod frequentant.*[6] It is out of consideration for us that Christ hides His glory from our eyes, so that in our weakness we may not fear to approach Him. Encouraged by this kindness, our faith should pierce the veil and prostrate us in adoration at the feet of the Son of God.

Let us think of this when we genuflect before the tabernacle, or at the last Gospel; when we pronounce the *Filius Patris* of the Gloria, the *Incarnatus est* of the Credo and many other scriptural or liturgical texts. Let us turn to Jesus Christ and say to Him: "As a child in the crib, as a tradesman in Nazareth, on the wood of the Cross, under the appearance of bread and wine, I adore You, O Christ, as my God; I love You, and I accept You with all that You are and all that You prescribe for me."

VI. THREE QUALITIES OF PRIESTLY FAITH

The faith of a priest should be much more perfect than that of the faithful. As he is called to communicate the mysteries of

---

[6] *Oratio super populum*, Thursday of the first week in Lent.

religion to souls, it is necessary for him to hold these mysteries in high esteem: *ut sciatis quae sit spes vocationis eius et quae divitiae gloriae hereditatis eius*: "that you may know what is the hope to which he has called you, what are the riches of his glorious inheritance" (Eph 1:18). Three qualities are especially necessary in the faith of a priest: it must be firm; it must be enlightened, embracing the whole deposit of faith of the Church; finally, it must be practical, that is to say, its influence must appear in all the actions of his life.

If faith is the assent of the intellect to the truths which are revealed by God Himself, if it is man's reply to the divine communication, this assent will be firm, unchanging and unhesitating.

When St. Peter, on the lake of Gennesaret, felt himself almost overwhelmed by the waves, he cried out: "Lord, save me": *Domine, salvum me fac* (Mt 14:30). He still believed in Jesus, since he invoked Him, but his faith was wavering; did not our Lord reproach him on this account? But when he said to our divine Master on Mount Tabor: "It is good for us to be here" (Mt 17:4), and after the promise of the Eucharist: "To whom shall we go? Thou hast the words of eternal life" (Jn 6:69), the strength of his faith was great. Our Lady, on Calvary, believed with her whole soul. She was, in the fullest sense of the word, the faithful Virgin. Did she not bear in her heart the living faith of the whole Church? *Virgo fidelis . . . continens fidem vivam totius Ecclesiae in corde suo.*[7]

In order to grasp fully what constitutes a strong faith, let us consider some other examples drawn from the Scriptures; scriptural examples are always the best. When St. Paul speaks of Abraham, he seems to be filled with a holy enthusiasm. So great was the faith of the father of believers that, against all human probability, with absolute firmness and without any hesitation, he accepted the divine promise: "Against hope believing in hope that he might be made the father of many nations . . . and

---

[7] Perhaps quoted from a sermon on St. Albert preached in London (n.d.). St. Albert the Great writes of the Blessed Virgin: *Fidem habuit in excellentissimo, quae . . . etiam discipulis dubitantibus, non dubitavit* (in Luke 1: *Gratia plena*).

he was not weak in faith: neither did he consider his own body now dead, whereas he was almost a hundred years old" (Rom 4:18–19).

When the centurion of the Gospel affirms that Jesus has authority over physical ills, just as he himself has authority over his soldiers, Jesus is moved to admiration: "Amen, I say to you, I have not found so great faith in Israel" (Mt 8:10). When the woman of Canaan persisted in her appeal to His goodness and power, in spite of His refusals and the apparent obduracy with which He treated her, Jesus seems to be, as it were, overcome, as though the tenacity of the woman's faith had for Him an attraction which was irresistible: "O woman, great is thy faith, be it done as thou wilt" (Mt 15:28). In the Epistle to the Hebrews, the Apostle demonstrates with marked satisfaction how all the patriarchs and the just of the Old Testament were able to accomplish great enterprises for God by faith: "who by faith conquered kingdoms, wrought justice, obtained promises" (Heb 11:33).

When we, priests, with the same noble resolution, try on all occasions to live by faith, we attach ourselves to this line of saints, who, in the Old Testament and in the New, drew their supernatural strength from an unshakable adherence to the revealed word.

In the second place, to be perfect, our faith must be enlightened. For it is possible that, though vigorous, it may remain rudimentary. So was it with the man born blind who was cured by Jesus: when Christ asked him if he believed in the Son of God, he replied by an intense act of faith in which he laid his whole being at the feet of the Saviour: "I believe, Lord, and prostrating himself, he adored Him": *Credo, Domine, et procidens, adoravit eum* (Jn 9:38).

This faith is perfect in its quality of absolute assent; all the same it is very elementary: it does not yet know all that plenitude of truth and of doctrine which the Word Incarnate has come to communicate to the world. It accepts certainly all the revealed truths, but implicitly, en bloc, without any preliminary detailed knowledge. Such a faith, excellent and rich in possibilities as it may be, is implicit and cannot suffice when the individual or society begins to reflect. Our reason wants to apprehend the object of faith, to perceive it clearly, to specify it. From this need, in the course of time, theology was born. This science applies itself to understanding, analysing and coordinating, according to the possibilities of the intellect, the contents of revelation. The true idea of theology will always be that consecrated in the formula of St. Anselm: *Fides quaerens intellectum*.[8]

For us priests this development of our faith is all the more necessary because it is our duty to enlighten the belief of the faithful, and to defend it against the attacks of heresy and impiety. Remember the saying of Scripture: "because thou hast rejected knowledge (of holy things) I will reject thee that thou shalt not do the office of priesthood to me" (Hos 4:6).

Sometimes his sacred studies are dissociated from the priest's interior life. This is regrettable. It is important to fructify the work of the intellect by pious reading, by reflection in the presence of God and by prayer. It is thus that there is formed in the heart of the priest that living theology which is the soul of priestly sanctity.

By study of theology I do not mean, as you will understand, a study of the subtleties nor yet a study of the manuals in everyday use for obtaining the necessary knowledge to pass an examination. I mean a study of the Fathers of the Church, of the principal masters of doctrine, and above all, of St. Thomas. I mean especially the deeper study of the Scriptures. This is the treasure of the Spouse of Christ. The doctors of the Church and the greatest theologians have been formed in this way, and until the end of time, these books will remain the true sources of sacred learning. Does one not often meet priests who are in frequent contact with the mysteries of faith without thinking of them, without even trying to know them better? They pass their lives in the midst of the divine realities; at the altar, in the confessional, in the pulpit, they are in constant relation with the

---

[8] "Faith seeking understanding." *Proslogion*, PL 158, 225.

supernatural powers. For want of an enlightened faith and a theological piety they miss many graces to the detriment of their ministry; many lights shine out destined never to inspire their souls, which remain famished in the midst of abundance. The priest must like to have as complete a knowledge as possible of the revelation brought to us by Jesus Christ. Is not Christ the eternal wisdom?

In our days[9] there is a danger for those who devote themselves to higher studies of losing something of the purity and freshness of their faith. An over-critical spirit has invaded all the domains of study: history, theology, and Scripture. If they are not on their guard, some may run the risk of feeling their faith grow weak, or even of losing it. As a precaution against these dangers I advise you to cultivate a respect for traditional doctrine.

This does not exclude progress, nor the study of the different aspects of modern thought, but it is well to judge these from the heights on which we are established by a deep knowledge of theology.[10]

We must also reject heresy in all its forms; it is the enemy of revealed truth, of the thought of Jesus Christ. We must, however, have the greatest consideration for our brothers who have fallen victims to error.[11] We must be careful to supernaturalize our work. Never begin your studies without having prayed. Try to watch over your intention: see that it is for God and for truth. You meet some people who show great zeal in acquiring the sacred sciences in order to be known as renowned scholars: *ut sciantur ipsi*, says St. Bernard, "and this is shameful vanity": *et turpis vanitas est.*[12] For those who work in this spirit, study does not become a source of sanctity. It is of learning such as this that the Holy Spirit has written: "Knowledge puffeth up" (1 Cor 8:1) and again: "the wisdom of this world is foolishness with

---

[9] Dom Marmion was alluding here to Modernism.

[10] Among the notes of Dom Marmion we found the following quotation from the eighteenth-century English poet Alexander Pope: "Be not the first by whom the new are tried,/ Nor yet the last to lay the old aside" [*An Essay on Criticism*, lines 335–36].

[11] See *Dom Marmion and the Protestants* in *Presence of Dom Marmion* (Paris: Desclée, 1948).

[12] *In Cantic.*, Sermo 36, 1–3.

God" (1 Cor 3:19). One might add "and with men" for there is nothing more displeasing than a priest dazzled by success, and full of the idea of the respect due to his intellectual superiority. Never become the dupes of your own learning: in this life our knowledge will always be imperfect.

We must apply ourselves to study with the intention of working for the kingdom of God and His glory; for the Church; in order to defend the deposit of faith against all attacks, in order to preserve the faith of the people in all its purity and in all its vigour and, finally, in order to fill our own minds with the knowledge of Jesus Christ and of His incomparable mysteries.

This is what our theology must be: a living theology, the soul of our priestly sanctity.

Spiritual reading is also of great importance in the life of a priest. There is for him a real danger of being too much occupied with worldly affairs or of being captivated by reading which contains nothing of the supernatural. Those who devote themselves constantly to the study of the Classics need some antidote to safeguard the vigour of their faith. A professor, or a priest taken up with his ministry, has not much time at his disposal for supplementary study, but could he not apply himself every day to spiritual reading, to the *lectio divina*, as St. Benedict calls it? He will be astonished when he realizes after some time how much this daily application, even in small doses, can do to fill the intelligence with great thoughts, to warm the heart, and to maintain the soul in precious contact with the divine mysteries.

Holy Scripture, carefully read, and even learned by heart, will always be like a living fountain in the heart of the priest.

In the Eucharist the divine Word hides Himself under the sacred species, clothed in majestic silence; in the Scriptures He communicates Himself to us under the form of human speech, which expresses itself according to the manner of our expression.

The Word of God in Himself is incomprehensible. Is He not infinite? In His Son the Father gives expression to all that He is and all that He knows. In the Scriptures we read only one small syllable of that incommunicable Word pronounced by the immensity of the Father. In heaven we shall contemplate this living Word, we shall be introduced into its secret, but even here on earth we must keep our intellect in a state of respectful attention to what has been revealed and to that portion of divine wisdom which has been made known by the holy Writings.

During the life of Jesus Christ—I have said it already, but one cannot insist on it too much—there were many who saw only the externals; they did not suspect that under the appearances of a man was present among them the divinity; for them the Word Incarnate remained hidden. In like manner, there are some minds which do not go beyond the human element in the Scriptures and fail to discover the divine revelation which it enshrines.

The approach of faith is in no way prejudicial to critical study, but in the course of these studies, in order that the divine Word present in these texts may become for us a means of salvation, we must constantly remind ourselves that here is contained the eternal word, the message of God Himself.

If you want to touch the hearts of your people, and do good, I cannot repeat to you too often the advice of St. Paul: "Let the word of Christ dwell in you abundantly": *Verbum Christi habitet in vobis abundanter* (Col 3:16).[13]

Finally, in the soul of the priest, faith must be practical. If it be the foundation of the whole spiritual structure and the root on which depends the growth of our life as children of God, it cannot remain idle and sterile, but must enter into and dominate our whole existence: it must inspire our judgements, control our actions, stimulate our zeal, and be, in accordance with the idea of the Apostle, "a faith that worketh by charity" (Gal 5:6).

In people, practical faith sees in the first place a soul redeemed by the love and the blood of Christ, and destined to

[13] In this matter Dom Marmion may be taken as an example. The salutary unction which is generally acknowledged in his writings springs from his frequent and apt use of Holy Scripture. See *Dom Marmion and the Bible*, by D. Rousseau; "St. Paul and Dom Marmion", by P. Bězy in *La Vie spirituelle*, January 1948.

eternal life. This faith becomes the motive of every act of charity to one's neighbour.

In events, it puts the same value on things that Christ would have done. The ways of God are as profound as is His being, but the priest, living by faith, knows that "God is love": *Deus caritas est* (1 Jn 4:6). By suffering, the Lord wishes to purify, detach, strengthen, and elevate those whom He loves. Just as the Passion of Christ makes the fountain of grace gush forth, so likewise, the pains and trials of the Christian, and a fortiori, those of the priest, count for much in the eyes of God.

In our days the general weakening of religious beliefs may have its effect on the ministers of Christ. Some of them are inclined to believe that, in order to win souls and to extend the kingdom of Jesus Christ, activity and exterior works are the principal and almost the exclusive requisite. It appears to them that the personal sanctity of the priest and prayer are of little avail for the salvation of the world, but that bold enterprises, new methods and intense activity will accomplish the task. And yet, as we know well, the salvation of souls and their sanctification are matters which are essentially supernatural. All the human activity in the world, if it is not made fruitful by grace and the divine blessing, is powerless to convert or sanctify a single soul. Is it not God who holds the hearts of men in His hands? That is why, if we wish to expend our zeal generously in works, it is necessary that the viewpoint of faith should prevail, and that we place our confidence above all in prayer, obedience, and the help of God.

In the saints, faith is like a burning brazier which gives heat and light. The secret of this faith, contagious and all-conquering, is that power to sway others which is a property of strong convictions. To the saints, the supernatural world, though veiled from our eyes, appears as tangible as the realities of this life; that is why the most overwhelming and long drawn-out difficulties do not dishearten them; they do not falter in their advance but, with eyes fixed on the eternal truths, they go forward to ultimate triumph: *Haec est victoria quae vincit mundum, fides nostra* (1 Jn 5:4). When St. Paul exclaims: "I live in the faith of the Son of God":

In fide vivo Filii Dei (Gal 2:20), can you not feel in his words the magnificent pride of his faith in the mystery of Christ, and the heart of the Apostle dilating with a noble and holy joy? The happiness of believing exalts his soul, and makes his faith more radiant. For us also, our unqualified assent to the message of Jesus, the Son of God, the envoy of the Father, the source of all sanctity, should produce the same ennobling effect, the same pride, the same happiness, the same irresistible force.

The revealed truths, as we have said, form, as it were, a superior world which dominates the miseries of this life; the priest must be at home there as in his own proper atmosphere. By regulating its life in accordance with the dictates of faith, the soul of the priest may be said to inhabit this supernatural world. The constant support which he draws from the word of God makes his faith intensely practical; it dominates events and sheds its rays, for the glory of Christ, on all his priestly activity.

Two priests may have the same exterior occupations. But one, filled with love, has a profound influence on souls, his ministry is pleasing to God and fruitful for the Church; the other, lacking fire in his personal interior life, has no lasting effect on souls. What is the explanation of the difference? The quality of their faith.

Faith is the one root of charity in the human heart.[14]

---

[14] See pp. 355ff., the virtue of faith in the priestly life of Dom Marmion.

V.

"DEATH TO SIN"

FOR the priest, as for every Christian, the Gospel has established clearly the two fundamental conditions for salvation: an act of faith and the reception of baptism: *qui crediderit et baptizatus fuerit salvus erit* (Mk 16:16).

Having discussed faith, I shall now speak to you of the life of grace which we receive in baptism. This grace is like a seed which needs to grow, and which every Christian must develop constantly during his whole life.

Here is how St. Paul describes the secret, supernatural force of baptism: "For we are buried together with Him by baptism unto death; that as Christ is risen from the dead by the glory of the Father, so we also may walk in newness of life" (Rom 6:4). These words give us a comprehensive view of the essential elements of our sanctification and the direction we must give to our efforts towards virtue.

God's ways and views are not ours. He has said it Himself: "My thoughts are not your thoughts, nor your ways My ways . . . as the heavens are exalted above the earth, so are My ways exalted above your ways" (Is 55:8–9). In order to sanctify the world, He has chosen what St. Paul calls the "folly of the cross": *stultitia crucis* (1 Cor 1:18). Which of us would ever have imagined that for the salvation of men, it would be necessary for God to deliver up His only Son to the opprobrium of Calvary and the death of the Cross? And yet, that which seemed folly to the eyes of men is the plan ordained by the divine wisdom: "But the foolish things of the world hath God chosen that He may confound the wise" (1 Cor 1:27).

The world has been renewed by the death and resurrection of Jesus Christ, and every Christian, in order to achieve his own salvation and sanctification, must be in spiritual communion with the mystery of this death and this life restored. The whole

essence of perfection for the follower of the Gospel and for the
priest lies in participation in this double mystery.

I. NECESSITY OF DEATH TO SIN

The soul can only be united to God in proportion to its likeness
to Him. In order that God may draw it to Himself and elevate
it, He must be able in some way to identify Himself with it; that
is why, from the beginning, He had created it to His own image
and likeness.

According to the divine plan, man is the link between the
pure spirituality of the angels and corporeal matter; he is destined to reflect, more perfectly than material creation, the
perfections of God: "Thou hast made him a little less than the
angels, Thou hast crowned him with honour and glory" (Ps
8:5). In this canticle the Psalmist contemplates in ecstasy the
divine work in its primitive beauty; he chants the glory of God
as it is revealed in the universe: "O Lord, our Lord, how admirable is Thy name in the whole world" (Ps 8:1). This august
plan was thwarted by the fault of Adam. Sin destroyed in mankind the splendour of the divine image and rendered man incapable of uniting himself henceforth to God. But, in His infinite
goodness, the Lord decided to repair in a wondrous manner the
evil of sin: *Mirabilius reformasti.* And how was this to be accomplished? You know the answer: by the coming of the second
Adam, Jesus Christ, Whose merciful grace makes us sons of
God, like to His image and fitted for the divine union: *Et sicut
in Adam omnes moriuntur, ita et in Christo omnes vivificabuntur*
(1 Cor 15:22).

Baptism is the sacred means established by God to cleanse the
soul of original sin and place in it the seed of eternal life. By
what secret power does the sacrament effect this prodigy? By
the ever active power of the death and resurrection of Christ.
This power engenders in the soul a state of death and a state of
life derived in their entirety from Jesus Christ. As He Himself
entered into His glory only by the immolation of the Cross:
Oportuit pati Christum et ita intrari in gloriam suam (Lk 24:26), so

every Christian must be spiritually associated with this death in order to receive the divine life.

It is in this way that Christ is the archetype and the source of our sanctification: "For if we have been planted together in the likeness of His death, we shall be also in the likeness of His resurrection" (Rom 6:6).

In what sense are we to understand this spiritual death which the grace of baptism inaugurates in us?

It is, first of all, in the voluntary order; by the infusion of sanctifying grace and charity, baptism orients the soul and its affections towards the possession of God. By original sin man was radically averted from God, his one supernatural end. The gift of charity transforms this fundamental disposition of the soul; it destroys in it the active domination of sin and lays open for it access to the divine life.

It must, however, be noted that it is not sufficient to be in the state of grace to be fully dead to the melancholy capacity to commit sin. Baptismal grace leaves many evil roots alive in us; from them arise what St. Paul calls the "works of the flesh": *opera carnis* (Gal 5:19).

Like baptism, the sacrament of penance, although it destroys the actual reign of sin, does not effect in us a complete dying to sin. Attachments, deeply-rooted habits, inclinations which are more or less voluntary, combine with our natural tendencies to keep alive in us the sources of sin.

Death to sin, which begins with the justification of baptism and is maintained by virtue of the sacrament of penance, is only consummated by our personal efforts assisted by grace; these must achieve in the soul a voluntary and ever more active revulsion from everything which constitutes in us an obstacle to the supernatural life.

This idea of the absolute necessity of renouncing everything which is an obstacle to the justice of God in our souls is proclaimed frequently in the Epistles. St. Peter echoes the thought of St. Paul: *Ut peccatis mortui justitiae vivamus*: "that we might die to sin and live to righteousness" (1 Pet 2:24). These words are merely a commentary on those of the Master: *Nisi granum frumenti cadens in terram mortuum fuerit, ipsum solum manet*: "unless a grain of wheat falls into the earth and dies, it remains alone" (Jn 12:24). This death is required, not as an end in itself, but as an essential condition of the new life. Thus "the grain of wheat" dies in the ground; this is essential; but by its destruction it gives birth to a new life more beautiful, more perfect and more fruitful.

We must understand clearly the language of St. Paul. To live means to retain the power of acting for oneself. We attribute life to a being when it possesses in itself its own motive power and directs it towards its own perfection, while we attribute death to any being which has lost this power. The Apostle is fond of using this metaphor when he speaks of sin and its reign in our souls. Sin—according to him—"lives" in us when it dominates us to the point of becoming the effective inspiration of our actions: *Non ergo regnet peccatum in vestro mortali corpore ut obediatis concupiscentiis eius*: "Let not sin therefore reign in your mortal bodies, to make you obey their passions" (Rom 6:12). When sin, therefore, is the inspiration of our activities, its reign is established in us. "We are its slaves," *qui facit peccatum, servus est peccati* (Jn 8:34), and, as it is impossible to serve two masters at the same time (Mt 6:24), by living for sin we separate ourselves from God; we die to Him.

Now it is precisely the contrary result towards which we must strive: we must "die to sin" in order to "live to God". We achieve this death of our own volition when we oppose and break in ourselves this domination of sin, when we prevent it from being the moving spirit in our actions. By refusing to obey the maxims of the world, the desires of the flesh and the suggestions of the demon, the baptized soul frees itself more and more from sin. In this manner it "dies to sin". This interior liberation, according as it is established in the soul, permits the Christian to submit himself ever more fully to Christ, to His example, to His grace, and to His will. Thenceforth the source of all his actions is Christ, Whose life replaces in him the reign of sin: "So do you also reckon," says the Apostle, "that you are dead to sin but alive unto God, in Christ Jesus Our Lord", *Viventes Deo in Christo Jesu* (Rom 6:11).

II. DEGREES OF DEATH TO SIN

The first degree is, manifestly, a complete renouncement of mortal sin. Unless there is a categorical decision to make this break, divine charity cannot live in us.

Next comes a firm renouncement of venial sin. Deliberately to transgress the divine law, even when the matter is not grave, is to offend the Lord. We must never admit such a disorder in the course of our day on any pretext whatever.

As you know, venial sins, while they do not destroy the union established by sanctifying grace, are none the less a cause of great harm to the soul. Every venial sin is an act of infidelity to our heavenly Father, and is an obstacle to our relations of friendship with the divine Master. These relations are of the utmost importance for the sanctification of the priest and for the fruitfulness of his ministry.

I am speaking now of venial sins committed with full consent. Many falls in the course of the day are due to inadvertence, to negligence, or indeed to human frailty, and do not involve any deliberate intention of offending God. Absolute freedom from sin will be ours only in heaven. Here on earth it is a gift which is quite exceptional: even the saints, excepting only the Blessed Virgin, are liable to falls either by surprise or from weakness.

When deliberate venial sins are multiplied, they lessen our fear of displeasing God, they diminish our powers of resistance, and thus predispose us to grave falls. By consenting to live in an habitual state of infidelity to grace and to duty, the soul is established in a state of existence which is called spiritual tepidity.

There are many degrees of this disease. Its characteristics are not, as is sometimes thought, interior dryness, and want of devotion in exercises of piety. The most serious element is that the soul accustoms itself to its state, accepts the deplorable situation, fails to make any effort to emerge from it, and ceases to aspire to serve God in full and sincere fidelity. If a real collapse takes place, the sinner's capacity to react is paralysed by the rut into which he has fallen. Nevertheless, by returning to all the habits of the priestly life, by applying himself to work, to spiritual reading, and, above all, to prayer, he may, with the help of grace, triumph over these obstacles.

Quite a different effect is sometimes caused by a grave fault which arises, not from tepidity, but from a sudden gust of passion. Such a fall may make the sinner look into the depths of his conscience: far from discouraging him, this realization of his state throws him back into the arms of divine mercy: the shame and repentance which he experiences arouse in him a generous ardour which is a source of fidelity. According to the teaching of St. Ambrose, "the memory of his fault becomes a stimulus which provokes new effort and maintains his impulse towards God": *Acriores ad currendum resurgunt, pudoris stimulo maiora reparantes certamina.*[1]

Finally, we must pursue this extirpation of sin to the inmost depths of our soul; we must extend it to those deeply rooted tendencies which predispose us to actual faults. These vicious tendencies are, above all, pride, egoism and sensuality. We must be on our guard not to yield to the interior movements which they suggest; we must emancipate ourselves more and more from our own self-love, our own judgement, our own will, and from all that slovenliness which disfigures our souls and prevents them from resembling Jesus Christ. Until we have made up our minds to fight against any tendency which we know to be contrary to the will of God, sin still reigns in us to a certain degree.

We must not, then, fetter, no matter how slightly, the grace of our baptism. How can we, who are dead to sin, live on in sin: *Qui mortui sumus peccato, quomodo adhuc vivemus in illo* (Rom 6:2).

There are three considerations which will afford us great encouragement in this work of complete liberation.

First of all, according to the divine intentions, time is a factor with which we must reckon. We must die to all that is displeasing to God, not once for all, but every day. To these acts of generosity there correspond in our hearts "those spiritual ascents" of which the Psalmist speaks: *Ascensiones in corde suo dis-*

---

[1] *De Apologia prophetae David* I, 1, c. 2; PL 14, 854.

posuit (Ps 84[83]:5). God does not ask us to advance by forced marches. In the order of grace, as in the order of nature, growth is not accomplished in a day. When the farmer sows, does he not wait many months before reaping? Without any sacrifice of fidelity we must know how to be patient with ourselves in the spiritual life, how to endure reverses and always maintain our confidence. As the Apostle says: "In due time we shall reap, provided we do not fail": *Tempore suo metemus, non deficientes* (Gal 6:9).

And this all the more because we are not alone in the struggle: we can count on the help of Him who has called us. We have the assurance of St. Paul for it: "We are buried together with Christ": *Consepulti sumus cum Christo* (Rom 6:4). Our mystical death can only be realized in union with Jesus Christ and by His power. His Passion and His sufferings have merited for us all the graces of which we have need to die to the flesh, to the world, and to ourselves. And our Mass and our Communion communicate these graces to us each day in abundance.

Furthermore, consider what a joy it is to the heart of a priest to feel that the tyranny of sin is no longer within him, to feel himself free from the constraints of self-interest and self-love, to be no longer the dupe of the attractions and illusions of the world. How much more capable does the priest become on this account of responding to his sublime vocation! The more complete this death, the more receptive his soul will be to grace and the more his ministry will be blessed. We must not bargain with the Lord. As soon as He asks a sacrifice of us, though it be our heart's blood, we must answer like Abraham: *Adsum*, "Here I am, O Lord." Let us say this prayer also: "O my Jesus, may sin never reign over me" even in the smallest measure: *Non regnet in corde meo peccatum* (Rom 6:12). And let us add: "Reign Thou in me, Jesus . . . Deign, Lord, to direct and sanctify our hearts and bodies today . . . in conformity with Thy law." [2] Then the words of St. Paul will begin to be verified in us: "For you are dead,

---

[2] Office of Prime [the first hour of the Divine Office following Morning Prayer—suppressed at Vatican II (cf. *Sacrosanctum Concilium*, 89)].

and your life is hid with Christ in God": *Mortui enim estis, et vita vestra abscondita est cum Christo in Deo* (Col 3:3).

III. THE GRAVITY OF SIN

In the world of souls we meet peaks of sanctity; we praise God for being "admirable in His Saints": *Mirabilis Deus in sanctus suis* (Ps 68[67]:35).

But sometimes one meets also depths of iniquity—happily this is rare. What is the primary reason of these falls? It is the fact that, for these souls who fall, the ascent towards God was not founded on a real death to sin. There should have been a more absolute renouncement in response to the privileged supernatural elevation.

Such a falling-away does not occur all at once: it presupposes lamentable negligences in the employment of the means of sanctification; it supposes also occasions of sin which have been accepted, unlawful thoughts which have not been rejected. Before the collapse, the cracks appeared gradually in the edifice.

In order to make sure of the solidity of the structure of our spiritual dwelling, let us consider firstly the disorder and the enormity of sin in itself; we shall then meditate on the last things; the consideration of these great truths is one of the most efficacious ways of triumphing over our tendencies to evil.

Sin is the "evil of God": *Malum Dei*. We shall never be able to form an adequate idea of the gravity of an offence against God. That is why the Psalmist says: "Who can understand sins?": *Delicta quis intelligit?* (Ps 19[18]:12). God sees Himself, in full light, as worthy of all love and all submission. Being sanctity itself, He wills to ordain all things to His glory. He wills this with a fidelity which is unchangeable because such is the essential order of things. Moreover, by a love which knows no limit, God gives Himself in the Incarnation, in the Eucharist and in heaven. So great is His goodness, His beauty and His splendour that we could not behold God here on earth and live.

And yet by sin man, in so far as it is in his power, sets himself up in revolt against the divine sovereignty: he refuses to recognize his dependence, to obey God, to tend towards Him as towards his last end. By this he outrages the infinite sanctity, he offends Love itself.

Remember also that every sin, even a venial sin, deliberately committed, involves a comparison, a choice, at least an implicit choice. We consider on the one side God and His will and on the other some pleasure, sometimes a very base pleasure: a triumph of self-love, the satisfaction of a hatred or a passion. We choose this passing satisfaction in preference to the eternal goodness. As the Jews before Pilate compared Jesus and Barabbas, so the sinner, following their example, cries, by his action if not with his lips: *Non hunc, sed Barabbam* (Jn 18:40). Admittedly, as I have said before, venial sin is not as grave as mortal sin: it does not sever our friendship with God; but, all the same, it involves a choice and this choice violates a divine law and offends God.

Sin is therefore truly an evil of God, not that the Lord can suffer any loss by it, but because it is an insult addressed to His supreme majesty and a challenge, as it were, to His sovereign dominion.

So great is this insult and so real this offence that in order to expiate it the Father has delivered up His own Son to death: *Proprio Filio suo non pepercit Deus, sed pro nobis omnibus tradidit illum* (Rom 8:32).

It is at the foot of the Cross that one can best discern the gravity of sin. Contemplate, in union with Mary, John and Magdalen, this suffering God. Why is He dying in indescribable torment? To blot out the iniquities of the world: *Traditus est propter delicta nostra* (Rom 4:25). The crucifix is the most vivid revelation of sin. Looking at it, each of us can say: "There is my work, there is what I have done . . . I have offended God."

Sin is also the great evil, the only evil, of man. What is it that man does when, knowingly and willingly, he commits a grave fault? He renounces the eternal heritage prepared for him by the Father. Like Esau, he abandons a patrimony of infinite value for a mess of pottage. Through our adoption in Christ we are heirs to heaven. No creature, however eminent, has a right to enjoy the divine happiness; this joy is natural to God alone. By sanctifying grace the Lord has made it possible for us to participate one day in this beatitude. This grace is a treasure the value of which we shall never appreciate sufficiently. Now, by sin, not only do we lose it, but we become the object of the divine aversion. To be rejected by a God of infinite goodness! This thought is, to my mind, one of the most powerful motives for detesting sin. God, Who can neither err in His judgements nor be betrayed into any exaggeration, Who is much more inclined to exercise mercy than to give free rein to His justice, condemns to eternal reprobation the man who was created for happiness. It seems to me that we can realize from this fact how inconceivable is the disorder of sin. God's point of view is always the true one. Though the divine mercy is ever ready to welcome the repentant sinner, God's attitude to sin itself does not change: the Gospel bears witness to it: it is aversion.

These different considerations assume a special gravity when there is question of the reign of sin in the conscience of a priest. Hardness of heart, spiritual blindness and the progressive loss of faith are most often the terrifying consequences of prolonged infidelity on the part of the minister of Christ. Some time ago a priest who had gone astray was on the point of death. He had been guilty of grave abuse of grace. A friend at his bedside, eager to recall the dying man to hope and pardon, spoke to him of the all-powerful blood of Jesus Christ. The unhappy man replied in these words of despair: "In the time when I used to celebrate Mass, I have drunk it . . . it had no effect on me then; do you think that it can save me now?"

We meet souls who have never offended God gravely. One can observe in them an instinctive fear of displeasing the Lord; the mere thought of sin fills them with apprehension. We must preserve jealously in our souls a holy aversion for evil, even for the least deliberate venial sin. If we should have the misfortune to feel that we are losing this fear of offending God, we must force ourselves by a fervent return to our pious exercises to win back this interior disposition which is so eminently in harmony with our high vocation.

IV. DEATH THE DIVINE PUNISHMENT FOR SIN

In the seventeenth century Quietism succeeded in diverting a Christian elite from meditation on the last things. Certainly their consideration is disturbing; it troubles the serenity and care-free spirit of certain souls. Nevertheless all early spirituality, and especially that of St. Benedict, directs us to keep these great truths constantly before our eyes. The patriarch of monks says to us: "Fear the day of judgement. Dread hell. Desire eternal life with all your soul. Keep the memory of death daily before your eyes." [3]

This spirituality of our fathers is solid and serious; it fills the heart with a salutary fear and with reverence for the sanctity of God; it helps the soul to keep sin at bay and to avoid all compromise with it.

In the first place, how salutary is the thought of death for our whole lives!

The perspective of death keeps man in the way of truth; it enables him to appreciate better the nothingness of transient things and the all-importance of God. On one occasion I was at the bedside of a dying confrère, a zealous observer of the rule and a man of cheerful disposition. Suddenly he said to me: "Eternity is a terrible thing." And he added: "Father, when you do anything which is not for God, you are wasting your time; nothing matters but God and what is done for Him; all other things are trifles, trifles, trifles."

To help you to meditate on death here are three aspects which you should carefully consider: death is certain for every one of us; the time of its coming cannot be foretold; our separation from the world will be final.

Death is certain; it is the divine punishment for sin. "Wherefore as by one man sin entered into this world, and by sin death; and so death passed upon all men, in whom all have sinned" (Rom 5:12). And it is decreed that men shall die only once: *Statutum est hominibus semel mori* (Heb 9:27). This is an infallible

[3] Rule, chap. 4.

truth; nothing can save you from death: neither fortune, nor love, nor science, nor remedies. When the hour comes no creature can intervene between God and the soul. That hour is getting closer every day.

We cannot foretell the exact moment of our death. Jesus Himself warns us: "I shall come like a thief . . . in the middle of the night . . . at that hour you think not" (Mt 24:43–44). To some of His great saints God revealed the moment when they would leave this world, but for us, the hour will remain unknown until the end. It is a trap which the demon lays for priests, when he persuades them to think, although they are old or very ill, that the time of their passing to eternity is still far distant. In more than one diocese we can call to mind this or that priest, even among those who were virtuous and full of merits, who by his obstinacy has deprived himself of the last sacraments. Let us make a resolution to be grateful to those who warn us of our approaching end and to submit to their judgement. The pious reception of the last help which the Church offers us is an immense source of peace and serenity.

For each one of us death is a final departure. When the fatal hour approaches, a complete separation is effected between the soul and the things of this world. One by one all the avenues of the senses which keep us in contact with the exterior world are closed, and the conscience finds itself alone with God. In this absolute solitude none of the friends whom we are leaving can come to our aid. However, for many souls the bitterness of death arises, not so much from the separation from beings who are dear to them, as from the anguish of entering into an unknown world in which the only realities which count are entirely outside all their past experience.

For many also death appears terrible only because it is followed by the judgement: *Post hoc autem, judicium* (Heb 9:27). The way in which God will evaluate the personal conduct of each one of us is, for every man who believes and reflects, a consideration of the utmost gravity. This thought is at times terrifying. As soon as his last breath is drawn, man will find himself in the presence of his Judge to Whom he must render an account of his thoughts, his words, his actions and especially, of the graces which he has received.

This judgement is more to be feared by the priest than by any other on account of the importance of his sacred functions and his responsibilities: more will be required of those to whom more has been given.

We have all known colleagues whom death has called suddenly as they slept. Allow me to give you an important piece of advice: when evening comes, never lie down to rest without the intimate conviction that you are ready to appear before God. Remind yourself that if death were to come that night, the sovereign Judge would give His verdict, from which there is no appeal, on your conduct and on your whole life.

It is important to love this sovereign Judge as your friend. The loyal, faithful friend who will never fail you is Jesus. May He be everything for you during life so that He may be everything at the moment of death: "For though I should walk in the midst of the shadow of death," says the Psalmist, "I will fear no evil for thou art with me": *Etsi ambulavero in medio umbrae mortis non timebo mala quoniam tu mecum es* (Ps 23[22]:4).

V. THE ETERNAL PUNISHMENT DUE TO SIN

Listen to the word of Jesus. All through His preaching He speaks to us of hell—not that it is His principal subject or even His subject of preference—but He deals with it sufficiently often and with such clarity as to leave no room for doubt. "If thy eye scandalize thee, pluck it out. It is better for thee with one eye to enter into the kingdom of God, than having two eyes to be cast into the hell of fire" (Mk 9:46). "After the judgement, the good will go into life everlasting, the wicked into everlasting punishment" (Mt 25:6). Why does our divine Master speak to us so clearly in this way? The reason is that He is truth itself. His soul contemplates unceasingly the immeasurable majesty and the infinite sanctity of the Father; it knows what is required by this justice which cannot permit evil to go unreproved:

"Fear ye Him Who hath power to cast the body and the soul into hell" (Lk 12:5).

And is it not remarkable that He makes this recommendation to His chosen disciples? It is on account of the love He bears them: *Dico vobis, amicis meis*: "I tell you, my friends . . ." (Luke 12:4). It is because the apostles are His friends and His intimates that He gives them this grave warning; He desires ardently that they should escape this dread severity of the justice to come. *Amicis meis*: this form of address in itself should make us listen to Jesus when He is moved by His love for us to warn us against sin and the punishment it entails.

I do not suggest that this belief in eternal punishment should be the normal incentive of our actions; it is love which must inspire us on the road to perfection. But the appreciation of this truth will be most useful to us all through life and especially in times of temptation and struggle. We all experience such times; they can be very difficult; passion obscures everything and the will seems on the point of capitulating. In these moments, the thought of eternity may be the most potent instrument to preserve us from falling.

I shall not attempt to stir up your imagination to picture the physical pains of hell; I shall only recall to you the teaching of faith and of theology on the basic suffering of this home of despair.

In considering this account, we must never forget the Church's teaching on the following points: (1) God does not predestine anyone to damnation; (2) Jesus Christ died for the redemption of all men; (3) The graces necessary for salvation are given to all; (4) Damnation is the work of man alone who refuses obstinately to accept the divine dispensation and prefers to turn away from God for ever, rather than submit himself to Him in the spirit of hope and love. It is a horrible blasphemy to say that God, Who is Justice itself, could condemn a soul without its having merited that condemnation. In the light of these truths we shall understand more clearly the part which the personal responsibility of the individual plays in the loss of his soul.

There are two elements in sin: aversion from the Creator and adherence to creatures: *Aversio a Creatore et conversio ad creaturam.* When man, at the hour of death, in spite of all the divine invitations to repentance, remains obstinate in his voluntary opposition to the Lord, He, in His turn, abandons him. The soul, then, left to itself, and separated from God, experiences the indescribable pain of loss: *separatio a Deo et dolor inde proveniens.*

St. Paul says of heaven: "Eye hath not seen nor ear heard, neither hath it entered into the heart of man what things God hath prepared for them that love Him" (1 Cor 2:9). We must, alas, recognize that it is likewise impossible to conceive the torment of this eternal prison which is hell. To understand it we would have to know what a supreme good it is to possess God and we would need to have experienced the anguish of an existence estranged for ever from its true end, and enlightened by no single ray of hope.

The essential pain of hell lies in being rejected by God: "Depart from me, you cursed": *Recedite a Me, maledicti* (Mt 25:41).

There is inherent in our nature an immense need of happiness: our intelligence, our will, all the many elements of our nature, are seeking constantly their own satisfaction. During our sojourn here on earth, this thirst is partially assuaged by the worldly goods with which we are surrounded. On this depends the imperfect, relative, happiness of this life. Our existence includes enough pleasure to be tolerable, although the hunger for the infinite remains always alive in the depths of our being. St. Augustine expresses it excellently: "You have created us for Yourself, my God, and our heart is not at rest until it finds its repose in You": *Fecisti nos ad Te, Deus, et irrequietum est cor nostrum donec requiecscat in Te.*[4]

Once we have arrived at the end, once we have entered into eternity, the Absolute, which is God, the sole last end of man, is manifested to us as an unalterable necessity, as also is the nothingness of all that is not God. The soul is tortured by an

---

[4] *Confessions,* I, 1; PL 32, 661.

insatiable hunger for happiness; its whole nature craves desperately for the joy which it has lost for ever.

Moreover, the damned soul is fixed in his revolt against God, and this fixation deprives him of all the moral good that he possessed. Even in the worst of men there remains some tendency to good, some reserves: he is capable of reacting, of repenting and rising again. But the heart of the lost soul is the abode of hate; his will, fixed in evil without the possibility of change, becomes essentially perverse like that of the devil; he hates God, he hates his fellowmen, he abhors himself; no movement of pity, no thought of love can ever pass through his soul. Just as charity reigns in God and in the saints, the spirit of revolt holds sway in him. It is not God Who condemns him; it is the damned soul itself which, by its final choice of rebellion, persists for all eternity in its impotent resistance to its Creator.

The damned soul is torn by two forces: its nature tends, with irresistible passion, towards God, the last end for which it was created, and on the other side, its will, fixed in opposition, rejects God, blasphemes Him and finds its satisfaction in this aversion.

Who can describe the torture of this despair? The *conversio ad creaturam* of the damned means that they are in contact only with the nothingness of their own souls stripped of love and deprived for ever of their supreme good. In their interior revolt each bears within him his own hell.

Sometimes, in the silence of the cloister when I am alone with God and face to face with eternity, I think of this separation from the absolute Good and of this overwhelming malediction which men, and even priests, can call down upon themselves: "Depart from Me, you cursed" (Mt 25:41), and I feel then that one should accept all the suffering, all the contempt of this world rather than risk incurring such a torment, and that in our capacity as apostles of Christ we should consecrate all our talents, all our strength and all our zeal, to save these poor blind souls who are rushing into the abyss of eternal misery.

There is another terrifying aspect of the pains of hell: the lost soul is given over to the power of the demons. The nature of these spirits, which is absolutely simple, has been irrevocably deformed. They are entirely evil; their only occupation is to hate and to injure. Although, here on earth, their power is restricted, Holy Scripture describes them none the less as beings to be feared "like lions seeking whom they may devour": *tamquam leo rugiens quaerens quem devoret* (1 Pet 5:8). But, in hell, where the damned, abandoned by God, are given entirely into their power, into this exterior darkness, *in tenebras exteriores* (Mt 12:13), the devils have free play. They cast themselves upon their prey to plague them without respite, to inflict upon them indescribable evils.

Their implacable fury is concentrated especially on the Christian, for in him they see the image of the Man-God. And if the damned soul be that of a priest, its torments will be augmented beyond all description. In the priest, Satan sees one who formerly, in the name of Jesus Christ, had the mission of thwarting his reign among men. Formerly he was obliged to respect him on account of the priestly character imprinted on his soul. Now that the priest is fallen, rejected by God and deprived of all his power, the devil makes him his plaything. The mere thought of being thus abandoned without any protection and for all eternity to the rage of the devil is sufficient to chill us with fear. From the bottom of my heart I appeal to you in the name of Jesus Christ: *Vigilate*: Be vigilant!

We must not deceive ourselves. Reprobation is a possibility for each one of us and for every soul committed to our care. Note the attitude of the Church under the guidance of the Holy Spirit in the formulas of her official prayer. She makes us implore of God the supreme grace of being "snatched from eternal damnation": so it is in the solemn litany of the saints; in like manner also, at the most solemn part of the sacrifice we priests are made to utter the same supplication: *ab aeterna damnatione nos eripi*. And at the moment of Communion she makes us ask Christ never to let us be separated from Him: *A te numquam separari permittas*.

We must therefore shun all negligence and all imprudence. "He that thinketh himself to stand let him take heed lest he fall" (1 Cor 10:12). The same apostle speaks to us of the terror which seizes the sinful soul when, in the hour of eternity, it "falls into the hands of the living God": *Horrendum est* . . . (Heb 10:31). And so he "brings his body into subjection lest perhaps when he has preached to others he should himself become a castaway" (1 Cor 9:27). We must shun also all presumption. It was only a few hours after his ordination to the priesthood that Peter, who had promised Our Lord not to abandon Him, heard Christ say to him: "Watch and pray, for the spirit is willing but the flesh is weak" (Mt 26:41).

It is an invaluable grace to have the experience of the fear of damnation. The great St. Teresa tells us that one day, during prayer, she found herself transported into hell: "I understood that the Lord wished to show me the place which the devils had prepared for me. I was terrified; although about six years have passed since then, my terror is so great as I write these lines that my blood seems to freeze in my veins, here where I am at the moment. I am not afraid to repeat that this is one of the most exceptional graces that the Lord has granted to me. It has been of the utmost profit to me." [5] Zeal for the conversion of sinners, patience in enduring the greatest trials, gratitude towards God for having delivered her, fidelity in the service of the Lord: these, according to the saint, were the precious fruits of this vision.

A lively faith in the eternity of punishment is, for us also, a most salutary grace. It inspires in the priest, in the words of the saint, impetuous desires to snatch souls from the gulf of hell. This form of zeal is eminently suited to the minister of Christ. He is responsible for souls, for those souls for whom Jesus shed His blood. Will he not have to answer for each one of them before God?

[5] Teresa of Avila, *Life*, chap. 32.

VI

THE SACRAMENT OF PENANCE AND
THE SPIRIT OF COMPUNCTION

THE divine Wisdom has appointed a special means to help us to die to sin: the sacrament of penance. If we use this gift well, the reign of sin will be progressively weakened in our souls and we shall triumph over all disordered attachment to creatures.

The Church, the faithful interpreter of the will of Christ, recommends frequent confession even for the Christian who lives normally in a state of friendship with God. Many great saints, like Charles Borromeo, who were in no way given to scruples, practised frequent confession. The broadminded St. Francis de Sales confessed every day before celebrating his Mass. In face of the divine purity their hearts felt the constant need of being washed in the blood of the Lamb: *Amplius lava me ab iniquitate mea* (Ps 51[50]:2). I do not propose to recommend such frequent confession to you; without an inspiration from on high or some special reason it would be an exaggeration. But, on the other hand, I am convinced that priests who make it a practice to confess only at intervals of many weeks, or even many months, are wanting in supernatural prudence. I am not speaking here of strict obligation, but of what a sensitive priestly conscience should dictate. By confessing only at rare intervals a priest sacrifices precious graces of sanctification and exposes himself to grave danger of falling into a state of tepidity.

I. THE IMPORTANCE OF THE ACTS OF THE PENITENT

The sacrament of penance always applies to the soul, *ex opere operato*, the expiation and the merits of the Saviour: "The blood of Jesus Christ cleanseth us from sin" (1 Jn 1:7).

If a Christian has lost supernatural life by a grave sin, sanctifying grace and charity are restored to him by the pardon of the offence. If his friendship with God has not been broken off, he receives an increase of sanctifying grace from the Lord at the same time as the venial sin is remitted.

This pardon and this infusion of grace, which are the fruits of the merits of Jesus Christ, are effected by the gift of the Holy Spirit; they give glory to God in His mercy and outweigh the offence which our sins have caused to His majesty.

The inward dispositions of the Christian play an essential role in this communication of supernatural life.

And why? Because, in accordance with the will of Christ and the nature of the sacrament, grace, in regenerating and sanctifying the soul, is grafted on to the acts of the sinner himself, that is to say, to his confession of his faults, made in the hope of pardon; to his detestation of sin with a firm purpose of amendment; and to his willingness to carry out the penitential exercises imposed by the Church.

These acts are called confession, contrition and satisfaction. The Council of Trent describes them as quasi-matter and constituent parts of penance.[1] United to the absolution of the priest, they are, according to the Thomistic school, elevated by virtue of the sacrament, and made efficacious to destroy sin in us and to confer grace. They belong, therefore, to the very essence of the sacrament.

Not infrequently, unfortunately, these acts are carried out in an imperfect manner with the result that the sacrament does not communicate to the soul that abundance of fruits which might be expected. This is the sad lesson of experience. The explanation why so little profit is often drawn from the frequentation of this sacrament lies in the defect of our dispositions.

There are two causes, it seems to me, which explain the unfruitfulness, in greater or lesser degree, of the confessions of all those who approach the tribunal of penance with only venial sins on their conscience. Firstly, there is a defect in the confession of their faults. This confession has not enough of the character of a sorrowful accusation, united to the humiliations

---

[1] Sess. 14, cap. 3, and canon 4.

of Christ. Secondly, after the confession, the firm purpose of amendment is not maintained in the conscience in sufficient vigour.

As regards the first point, it is certain that the sacrament of penance, by virtue of its institution, applies to our souls the expiation offered by Christ to the justice and the sanctity of God. But we also have our part of expiation to play. At Golgotha, Christ presented Himself before the Father clothed with all our sins: "The Lord hath laid on Him the iniquity of us all" (Is 53:6). He was "the Lamb of God Who taketh away the sins of the world" (Jn 1:29). Christ saw each of our sins, He measured the offence caused by them to the infinite sanctity of God and, in order to save us, He took upon Himself all the opprobrium, all the shame, all the pain which our iniquities had merited.

In the sacrament of penance He leaves to us a part of the expiation: this is necessary in order that His merits may be applied to us. We must feel, therefore, at the tribunal of mercy, that we are burdened with our sins, our ingratitudes and our miseries. The baseness, the indelicacy of our sins and our infidelities must weigh on our conscience and our confession must be sorrowful.

As members of Christ we must unite the humiliation of our voluntary confession with the affronts and outrages of every kind endured by Christ in His Passion. We must share the sentiments of His heart so that the immensity of His expiation may purify our souls to their utmost depths. We must be careful to avoid the use of formulas which veil the ugliness of our offences and spare our self-love. Without going to the length of making a false confession we are sometimes inclined to seek pardon on easy terms.

It is important also to accept whole-heartedly the sacramental penance imposed by the priest and to offer all the actions of our lives for this intention: *quidquid boni feceris vel mali sustinueris*. By receiving the sacrament with these dispositions we gradually bring about a true spiritual death to sin in ourselves by virtue of the sacrifice of satisfaction of Jesus Christ. This should be the way in which we priests habitually confess.

In the second place, confession may bear little fruit, because the purpose of amendment is not maintained in sufficient vigour in our daily life.

When we have acknowledged our guilt, even though our sins be only venial, it is of the utmost importance for our interior life to maintain in the soul an efficacious desire not to give way any more to these negligences or to anything which is displeasing to God.

Admittedly, provided there is no *obex*, the sacrament of itself produces its essential effect. But, as I have already said, if we really wish—and are we not bound to wish?—our confessions to contribute to our progress in perfection, we must try to utilize all the riches of grace contained in the sacrament. To achieve this we must keep present to our mind the firm resolution not to fall again into those faults, even though they be only venial, of which we have accused ourselves. For example, we may have confessed impatience with people in our immediate circle, or uncharitable conversation, or it may be negligence in the carrying out of this or that duty, or egoism in leaving the odd jobs to somebody else and, as soon as the confession is over, we forget about contrition and purpose of amendment, and continue to act as though we had never confessed.

We must maintain a very lively desire to correct our faults for the love of Christ, so that, when the occasion of sin presents itself again, we may be quick to react.

There are many people who remain always weak in the service of God. In confession, they do not face up to their faults with a genuine desire to rid themselves of them. They know certainly that every step in the spiritual life is an elevation of the soul and a source of joy, but they lose sight of the fact that these are the fruits of an interior liberation, and involve therefore a more complete abnegation of self and a more profound renouncement. Nothing great can be accomplished in this world without sacrifice.

Here is another piece of advice to help you make your confessions more profitable. During your Mass on the day of your confession, ask God for the *gratia* and the *donum poenitentiae*; this salutary practice is based on the official doctrine of the Church as it has been promulgated by the Council of Trent.[2] Then, in the course of your daily occupations, try to excite yourself to sorrow for your faults.

II. COMPUNCTION OF HEART

Our consecration to God by baptism and ordination involves, necessarily, a complete and irrevocable break with sin: *quod mortuus est peccato, mortuus est semel* (Rom 6:10). According to the thought of St. Paul, this death to sin means not so much a passing act as a definite state: *mortui enim estis*: "for you have died" (Col 3:3).

Experience teaches us that in certain souls this death to even venial sins is far from complete; their life consists of a series of retreats and advances; sin still reigns in them to too great a degree.

Outside the sacrament of penance there is a means which is very efficacious to help us to gain our spiritual freedom: it is the spirit of compunction. As I advance in life, I see ever more clearly that our lack of stability and of progress in virtue is most often the consequence of a lack of compunction.[3]

What do we mean by compunction of heart?

It is an habitual feeling of regret for having offended the divine goodness. This feeling finds its source principally in perfect contrition, in repentant love. It produces in the soul an aversion for sin on account of the displeasure which it causes to God and on account of the evil which it produces in us. While an act of contrition which is transitory and imperfect disposes the soul to receive grace in the sacrament of penance and fortifies it against another fall, a feeling of sorrow inspired by love and maintained in full vigour in the soul will produce in it a state of irreconcilable opposition to all consent to sin.

You can understand that there is an absolute incompatibility between wanting to drive out sin and continuing to commit it.

[2] Sess. 22, cap. 2.
[3] See *A Master of the Spiritual Life*, chap. 7.

Such an habitual disposition is the best remedy against tepidity. This constant sorrow for our past faults: "My sin is always before me" (Ps 51[50]:3), must be based, not on the circumstances of each sin, but on the fact of having offended God. We must not call to mind the specific details, the recollection of which may sometimes be dangerous, but rather repent of having opposed our human will to God's will, of having outraged His sovereignty, repudiated His love, of having neglected, wasted, or even lost, the great treasure of grace.

We can understand, then, that those holy souls who had a clear vision of the divine majesty, of the grandeur of His supernatural gifts to us and of the gravity of every offence against God, were filled with this spirit of compunction. What was the prayer which St. Teresa of Avila had written out in her own hand and kept always on her work-table? You would find it hard to guess: one would think that she might have chosen one of those elevated expressions of divine charity which used to spring naturally from her heart. No, it was a verse of a Psalm; the greatest of sinners might have chosen it: "Lord, enter not into judgement with Thy servant": *Non intres in judicium cum servo tuo, Domine*[4] (Ps 143[142]:2). This profound compunction was necessary for her. Any other foundation would have crumbled under the weight of her admirable perfection. On her death-bed, St. Catherine of Siena, faithful to the habit of her whole life, repeated constantly these. words: "I have sinned, Lord, have pity on me."[5]

Perhaps you feel that these are pious exaggerations. But consider the words of St. John: "If we say that we have no sin, we deceive ourselves and the truth is not in us; we make God a liar and His word is not in us" (1 Jn 1:8–10). And, in fact, are we not all, in varying degrees, prodigal sons who, by sin or by simple dissipation of spirit, have strayed from the Father? When we recall our failures and our ingratitudes, must we not all say: "Father, I have sinned against Thee, I am not now worthy to be called Thy son" (Lk 15:21). To have offended the Lord, to have

---

[4] *Life of St. Teresa according to the Bollandists*, 2:27.

[5] Drane, O.P., *Life of St. Catherine of Siena*, pp. 54–55.

contributed to the Passion of Jesus, even if it be only once, is a burden on the conscience of the soul who loves Him. Although he may never have sinned gravely, the priest who is eager to live in truth before God will be the more keenly conscious of his faults because he has been the more fully protected by grace.

Has not the Father waited for us as the father in the parable waited for his son? Has He not opened wide to us the arms of His mercy? Has He not forgotten our sins as soon as we came back, and readmitted us to His friendship?

While making us conscious of our offences, compunction gives us also a keen realization of the divine pardon. It is thus a source of peace and confidence—a source likewise of joy, humble but profound. It banishes the satisfaction of sin and those indulgences which lead up to it, spiritual levity and carelessness; it fills the heart with the joy of the Father: the soul feels that the wish of the Psalmist has been realized in it: "Restore unto me the joy of Thy salvation": *Redde mihi laetitiam salutaris tui* (Ps 51[50]:12).

III. THE IMPORTANCE OF COMPUNCTION FOR THE PRIEST

The spirit of compunction confirms the soul in its desire to please God, preserving it from many temptations and helping it to triumph over those which do assail it. This is one of its most precious fruits.

This is especially true for the priest because he is called to sanctity; he lives in the midst of the corruption of this world, where he must face up to three enemies: the flesh, the world and the devil. These enemies pursue him from his ordination to his tomb and conspire to deprive him of his true life, the life which he possesses in Jesus Christ.

The lust of the flesh—Man was created to found a family. If he is to pass his life in virginal solitude, he must do so by rising above himself, with the help of grace. This renouncement will be very hard for some, because the adversary against whom they must fight is their own nature. Neither age nor dignity nor position can render them immune to its assaults. Even the most austere saints have had to endure at times the assaults of this domestic foe. It is told of St. Joseph of Cupertino that, after being rapt in angelic ecstasies, he experienced this humiliating revolt of the passions.[6]

Vigilance is always necessary in this matter, however chaste our past life may have been. We must never think that we are invulnerable. Presumption is always dangerous, whatever its object. No state of intimacy with God, no degree of sanctity can dispense us from the duty of humble watchfulness.

Our second enemy is the world. We live in the midst of ideas, of maxims and aspirations which are radically opposed to the ideas of Christ: "They are not of the world as I also am not of the world" (Jn 17:16). Jesus said this twice to His apostles when He had just ordained them priests. These words should apply to us also.

If our hearts are not filled with the spirit of the Gospel, the spirit of the world will make its way into our souls, and will bring us down little by little to its level; we shall no longer be interested in what is holy, but only in worldly knowledge and worldly well-being. We speak of this earth sometimes as a valley of tears. Fundamentally nothing could be more true; but there are days when the satisfactions of this world make a very strong appeal to our poor nature. The world seems to offer happiness. Its joys, its laughter, its beauty, its comforts and all the thousand trifles which flatter the senses and arouse the passions seem much more agreeable than prayer and the austerities of continence. Some of the great saints have felt the power of this bewitchment: *Fascinatio . . . nugacitatis obscurat*: "fascination . . . obscures" (Wis 4:12). When in contact with the world even in the course of legitimate duties, they confess to having experienced the temptation of the triple concupiscence which reigns there: the concupiscence of the flesh, the concupiscence of the eyes, and the pride of life (1 Jn 2:16). The dust of the world can easily darken the eye of faith and prevent it from keeping itself fixed on God and His love alone. When St. Charles Borromeo,

[6] *Acta Sanctorum*, September 5: 1019.

that model of manly strength and virtue, found himself in his family house with its baronial splendour, he felt that the temper of his spiritual life was weakened.[7] We are neither holier nor stronger than the great bishop, and if we do not watch over ourselves during the visits and the exchanges which are imposed upon us by our ministry, we are in danger of being carried away.

Finally, there is the devil—Even in the worst of men, as we have already remarked, hate is not present without some admixture of sentiments of humanity; it is rarely that the human heart loses all capacity to be touched by the sight of another's misery. Diabolic hate, on the contrary, is pitiless. The nature of the fallen spirits, being immaterial, knows no tiredness, needs no rest. They are always ready to do harm. The devil hates God, but as he cannot reach Him in Himself, he turns against His creatures, and especially against His privileged creature, the priest, the living image of Christ.

By our vocation, by the mission and the duties which it prescribes for us, we, priests, are especially exposed to the attacks and the cunning of these enemies.

When we consider their strength and our weakness, we instinctively recall the words addressed to Jesus by His apostles: "Who then can be saved?": *Quis ergo poterit salvus esse?* (Mt 19:25). The divine Master replies to us as He did to His disciples: "With men this is impossible, but with God all things are possible" (Mt 19:26). These words should be graven in our hearts. It is impossible by our own natural resources to triumph over the temptations of the flesh, the intoxication of worldly success, over the self-satisfaction of pride. But, in the spirit of holy compunction, let us recognize our own fragility and, in accordance with the recommendation of the Lord, let us watch and pray (Mt 26:41).

Vigilate. "Be vigilant." Every thoughtful man realizes by his personal experience and by that of his fellow-men what circumstances lead to moral falls. The priest, above all others, should be able to recognize what negligences in his state of life

---

[7] Juissano: *Vie de saint Charles* (Lyon, 1685), p. 737.

prepare the way for sin. The occasions are different for each individual, according to his tendencies, his weaknesses and his environment, but the possibility of falling exists for us all. You may take it as certain that there was never a sin committed by one man of which another man is not capable.

To vigilance we must unite prayer, recourse to Him to Whom all things are possible, to our divine Master in person.

It is He who has chosen us; for us, as for the apostles, He asks the Father not to take us out of the world, but to keep us from evil (Jn 17:15). Hear St. Paul as he asks: "Who shall deliver me from the body of this death?" and he answers: "The grace of God by Jesus Christ our Lord" (Rom 7:24). Was not this the reply which Jesus Christ Himself had given when the Apostle, buffeted by Satan, had three times implored Christ to deliver him? "My grace is sufficient for thee, for power is made perfect in infirmity" (2 Cor 12:9). It will be the same for us. Read Psalm 91[90] which we recite every evening*; it is the great Psalm of confidence in the struggle; the different kinds of temptations are described in it in expressive metaphors, but God promises that prayer will prevail. "A thousand shall fall at thy side and ten thousand at thy right hand; but it shall not come nigh thee . . . he shall cry to me and I shall hear him; I am with him in tribulation. . . . I will fill him with length of days and I will show him my salvation." [8]

IV. COMPUNCTION IN THE LITURGY OF THE MASS

The Church is the Bride of Christ: she knows better than any-one how her Spouse should be honoured and homage paid to God; moreover in establishing her liturgy she is directed by the Holy Spirit. We can never be so sure that we are in the way of truth as when we conform to her prayer: *lex orandi, lex credendi*.[9]

---

* In the pre-Vatican II breviary (and still in many monastic communities), Psalm 91 is recited daily at Night Prayer.

[8] See the development of these thoughts by Dom Marmion in the chapter "The Temptation of Christ", in *Christ in His Mysteries*.

[9] An abridgement of the well-known saying: *Ut legem credendi statuat lex supplicandi*, Denzinger, no. 139.

Now what are the formulas which the Church puts on our lips in the holy sacrifice of the Mass which is the supreme act of our priesthood? What attitudes does she prescribe for us? What sentiments does she seek to arouse in us?

The priest who celebrates Mass is presumed to be living in friendship with God. And yet when he comes to the altar, he begins by humbling himself, by striking his breast like the publican in the Gospel. In the presence of God, of the saints in heaven and the faithful on earth, he acknowledges himself a sinner: *Peccavi nimis . . . mea maxima culpa* [*Confiteor* of the Mass]. However great his sanctity, he cannot approach the Lord without making this humble confession. The people then accuse themselves in their turn in the person of the acolyte and then the divine pardon descends on the whole Christian family: *Indulgentiam absolutionem et remissionem peccatorum nostrorum.** As the priest ascends the steps of the altar the Church makes him pray: *Aufer a nobis, Domine . . . iniquitates nostras.* One must be purified of every fault to enter into the holy of holies.

By kissing the altar stone the priest signifies his union with Jesus, of Whom the altar is the figure, and also his union with the Church in the person of her martyrs whose relics are encased in the stone. Through their merits he asks pardon for all his sins: *ut indulgere digneris omnia peccata mea.* After the *Introit* the celebrant invokes the Lord nine times; he implores the divine pity on all human miseries, of which the most grievous is sin: *Kyrie eleison.* If we wish to be accepted by God, it must be by appealing to His mercy that we approach Him.

The *Gloria in excelsis* is the echo of the chant of the angels; but on our lips this canticle is continued on a note of supplication: "Thou Who takest away the sins of the world . . . Who sittest at the right hand of the Father . . . have mercy on us."

We may not read the Gospel until we have asked God to purify our lips.

Till now we are only at the preliminaries of the sacrifice, and we can understand that the Church, the better to prepare us to

---

* The prayer of Absolution following the *Confiteor*, in the Missal of St. Pius V.

make the oblation, suggests these sentiments to us with such insistence. But this is not all: according as we enter more deeply into the "action" of the sacrifice she quickens in us this spirit of compunction.

Now we come to the offertory. We take into our hands the host which is to become the holy Victim. Here is the formula with which we present it to the Father: "Receive . . . this spotless host which I, Thine unworthy servant, offer . . . for my innumerable sins, offences and negligences." We thus conform to the recommendation of St. Paul: "And therefore he ought as for the people so also for himself, to offer for sins" (Heb 5:3). Do you realize that this is one of the great consolations of a minister of Christ: to be able every day to offer the divine Victim in satisfaction for his personal faults, for his discourtesies towards God?

After the offering of the elements of the sacrifice, the rubrics prescribe that the priest bow down in an attitude of humility and contrition: *In spiritu humilitatis et in animo contrito suscipiamur a te, Domine*: "Lord, we ask You to receive us and be pleased with the sacrifice we offer You with humble and contrite hearts." He makes to God the offering of his work, of his troubles, of his whole life so that, through Jesus, they may be accepted by the Father. Contrition is already a sacrifice in itself: *Sacrificium Deo spiritus contribulatus* (Ps 51:17[50:19]), but when we present the sacred Victim in this spirit and in union with Christ, the iniquities and ingratitudes of our past life, whatever they may have been, are forgotten by God.

The Canon* is made up of prayers which are sublime. Full of respect, the priest approaches God, Who is all-high but all-clement: *Te igitur, clementissime Pater*. It is through His Son, Jesus, that he can come to the Father in all confidence: *per Jesum Christum Filium tuum*. And what is his attitude as he prays? He bows, kisses the altar and continues: *supplices, rogamus ac petimus*.

Before the consecration, the priest extends his hands over the oblation as, in the Old Testament, the priest extended his hands

---

* Referring to the Roman Canon, also known now as Eucharistic Prayer I. This was the only Eucharistic Prayer in use in the Roman Rite from the Council of Trent to Vatican II.

over the victim which represented the people in their guilt.[10] The prayer which accompanies this gesture implies that the guilty ones are the sinners, who have deserved to be struck by the hand of the Lord. Accept in their stead, O Lord, a holy, immaculate Victim; receive with favour this Victim Whom You love, for it is Christ Himself. And what does the priest ask in virtue of Christ's merits? To be preserved from eternal damnation and numbered among the elect. At this solemn moment he is not absorbed in ecstasy nor carried away in rapture. No, he is filled with sentiments of the most profound compunction.

At the consecration it is no longer the minister who is the chief actor. Now we see only Christ in him. He does not say: "This is the body . . . the blood of the Saviour," but rather: "This is My body . . . this is My blood which shall be shed . . . unto the remission of sins." Here we find expressed the propitiatory force of the sacrifice. These words invite us to dilate our hearts in an immense hope of pardon for all our sins by virtue of the immolation of Jesus.

Shortly afterwards the priest breaks the mysterious silence of the Canon: *Nobis quoque peccatoribus*, he says, striking his breast, and he begs of the Lord that he may be admitted into the society of the martyrs and the saints, not in consideration of his own merits, but by the divine indulgence. Here again the attitude required by the sacred formula is one of profound but confident compunction.

All those great pontiffs whom we venerate—St. Ambrose, St. Leo and St. Gregory—have employed these formulas in part or in whole.[11] They have been used also by the saints of modern times such as St. Francis de Sales, St. Alphonsus Ligouri, the Curé d'Ars and many others.

Now we come to the communion. Under what title does the priest invoke Christ as he unites himself to Him? As Lamb of God . . . Who takest away the sins of the world. Consider the

[10] This is the most common interpretation, although the rite of extending the hands was introduced into the Canon at a comparatively recent date—fifteenth century [now viewed as the Epiclesis, or sending of the Holy Spirit].

[11] During the first centuries the text of the Canon underwent certain modifications and additions. It was firmly stabilized only in the time of St. Gregory.

words: Regard not my sins, but the faith of Thy Church. . . .
Deliver me from all my iniquities. Finally, meditate on the great
truth expressed by the *Domine non sum dignus* which is repeated
three times.* Such is the spirit of the Church. All through the
sacred "action" the Church maintains the spirit of humility in
the souls of her priests by means of the clearest formulas and the
most expressive rites. Through the essential gestures of adoration, of praise and of thanksgiving she constantly intersperses a
note of lively compunction so that we may make it our own. In
His infinite condescension the Lord admits us to His presence
and accepts our supplications, but His justice requires that we
should recognize our condition as sinners.

The angels chant unceasingly: *Sanctus, sanctus, sanctus* before
the throne of God; it is their act of homage to the immeasurable divine sovereignty. During our time of exile, our way of
glorifying the supreme majesty consists principally in celebrating, by a humble confession of our misery and of our sins, the
immensity of the eternal mercy.

Every prayer can serve to stimulate our spirit of compunction. Not only in offering the Holy Sacrifice but also in reciting
the breviary we can find many formulas expressive of a holy
contrition.

How many of the Psalms pour out before God our regrets at
having offended His goodness! To the mourning of a contrite
heart these canticles unite always an expression of confidence
and of faith in the divine forgiveness: "Have mercy on me . . .
according to the multitude of Thy mercies" (Ps 51:1[50:2]).
"Have mercy on me . . . for my soul trusteth in Thee" (Ps
57:1[56:2]). The great desire of the Psalmist is to have a pure
heart: *Cor mundum crea in me, Deus*; to feel himself strengthened
with a perfect spirit: *Spiritu principali confirma me.*

If we recite the canonical hours with devotion, the Holy
Spirit will make us appreciate these verses of the Psalms, so that
by meditating on them we may make the sentiments which
they express become a part of our interior life.

* In the Novus Ordo it is said only once by all: "Lord, I am not worthy. . . ."

V. THE WAY OF THE CROSS: A SOURCE OF COMPUNCTION

The way of the Cross, as I know by long experience, is one of the most fruitful devotions for keeping alive in us the spirit of compunction.[12]

What is it that gives the way of the Cross its special value as a medium of sanctification? It is the fact that in it, in a very special way, Christ is portrayed to us as the exemplary, the meritorious and the efficient cause of sanctity. In His Passion, Jesus is revealed to us as the perfect model of all the virtues. More than elsewhere, He displays to us in it His love for the Father, His love of souls, His patience, His gentleness, His magnanimity in granting pardon. His obedience, a source of immense strength, supports Him and makes Him pursue His sorrowful journey until the *consummatum est.*

By meditating on the interior sufferings of Jesus we learn to share His hatred for sin and we offer with Him His sacrifice to make good the abyss of the iniquities of the world. This is a privilege beyond price.

We must not regard Jesus merely as a model to copy from afar, without any participation in His life. At every stage of the Passion He merited the reproduction in us by His grace of those virtues which we contemplate in Him: "Virtue went out from Him" (Lk 6:19). One day, a poor sick woman touched Christ and was cured. We also, says St. Augustine, can touch Christ by the contact of faith in His divinity: *Tangit Christum qui credit in Christum. . . . Vis bene tangere? Intellige Christum ubi est Patri coaeternus et tetigisti.*[13] Let us look on Christ as He travels the way of the Cross; He gives Himself up, He suffers for us; let us believe that He is God and that He loves us. In this way we can prepare our souls to receive His sanctifying influence.[14]

---

[12] Devotion to the Passion of Christ under the form of the Stations of the Cross was suggested to Dom Marmion in his seminary days by his spiritual director, Fr. Gowan, a saintly Vincentian. Dom Marmion remained faithful to this devotion all his life. See *Abbot Columba Marmion, a Master of the Spiritual Life*, p. 17.

[13] "He touches Christ who believes in Christ. Do you wish to touch Christ as you should? Believe in Christ as being coeternal with the Father and you have touched him" (*Sermo* 243, 2; PL 38, 1144).

[14] Dom Marmion has developed these ideas in the chapter "From the Pretorium to

Our sensibility plays no part in this communication of grace. It can never serve as a basis or as a motive for our piety nor is it a reliable touchstone. Still, when our devotion has a solid foundation of faith, sensibility may be of real use by helping us to be less distracted and to concentrate our thoughts on God.

The Church urges all Christians to meditate on the Passion of Jesus Christ; but for her priests there is a special invitation. In this way she would have us compassionate the sufferings of our Saviour and draw example from His virtues. She wishes also that we should obtain through these mysteries an abundant application of the divine merits for ourselves and for those for whom we pray.

As priests, you are the special dispensers of the fruits of the Passion: *Dispensatores mysteriorum Dei* (1 Cor 4:1). It is by your ministry that the death of Our Lord is announced every day on our altars, as St. Paul puts it. On the altar you are in contact with the source of all graces since they all come from the Cross. The priest therefore must be the first to know the value of the blood of Christ and to hope in His merits,

Now it happens sometimes that we remain spiritually poor in the midst of these riches, famished in the midst of this abundance. Devotion to the way of the Cross may be of great utility as a remedy for our lack of fervour and may become for us a "fountain of water springing up into life everlasting" (Jn 4:14). At each of the fourteen stations we unite ourselves to
* Jesus by a movement of love and we refresh our soul at the fountain of grace which springs from the heart of Jesus.

We can make the way of the Cross at any time, but, when it is possible, there can be no more appropriate moment than during our thanksgiving after Mass. While the divine presence is still within us we make this journey in union with Him Who was the first to make it. To follow the way of Calvary step by step with Jesus present within us is an excellent method of professing our faith in the infinite value of His sufferings, the

---

Calvary" in the volume *Christ in His Mysteries*. He has added a meditation on each station. This chapter has been published separately as a booklet: *Le Chemin de la Croix.*

oblation of which is constantly renewed in the sacrifice of the altar.

No vocal prayer is required for this devotion; it is sufficient to meditate on it piously with mind and heart.

Priests have said to me sometimes: "I do not practise meditation any more; it has become too difficult for me; I have no interior life." My reply is: "Have you tried making the way of the Cross as a form of meditation?"

How are we to recognize the existence of compunction in our heart? I shall give you an infallible test.

Compunction casts a veil over the faults of others because the realization of our unworthiness predominates in us.

Are you severe and exacting for others? Are you inclined to be ironical about the defects and the failings of your neighbour? Do you draw attention to them without any legitimate reason? Are you quick to take scandal at them? If so, it is a sign that your heart has not been touched or penetrated by the realization of your own wretchedness and of the offences for which God has pardoned you.

There is a parable in the Gospel which illustrates this truth excellently. There are two characters, the pharisee and the publican. We see them in the act of praying in the Temple. The pharisee dwells on the faults of others; for these his eyes are fully open; but while he observes his neighbours and judges them with severity, he does not consider his own guilt. He has lost sight of every aspect of his own conduct—the wretchedness of which is known to God—except for the fasting and the almsgiving. He has no thought for his sins. He almost says to God: "You can be proud of me." His prayer is a cry of self-satisfaction. And when he says: "Lord, I give Thee thanks that I am not like this other man" this thanksgiving, though it has a certain speciousness, does not justify him. Why? Because his soul is not moved by compunction. There is a complete lack of humility.

The publican, on the other hand, does not look at the pharisee. He is conscious of his own wretchedness and is not concerned with that of his neighbour. He strikes his breast and groans: "O God, be merciful to me, a sinner" (Lk 18:13). The heart which gives vent to this prayer is filled with compunction. And this compunction, as Jesus tells us, justifies the sinner before God.

VII.

HUMILIAVIT SEMETIPSUM FACTUS OBEDIENS

COMPUNCTION is always accompanied by humility. The importance of humility for our sanctification is so great that we must pause to consider it.

We are all very much inclined to base our concept of God on human standards. For example, we find it hard to form an idea of a being who can give without becoming poor; every time a man exercises his generosity he diminishes to some extent his own possessions. Only God can give without in any way impoverishing Himself. As He is goodness itself and infinite love, His natural inclination is to communicate His riches, to distribute His beatitude, to give Himself: *Bonum est diffusivum sui.* That is why it has pleased God to make man share in His own life, to appoint him His heir and co-heir with Christ (Rom 8:17). The Incarnation, the Redemption, the gift of the Eucharist, the foundation of the Church, all the benefits constantly renewed which He has showered upon us, are a revelation of His goodness, which knows no limits.

Then, you will say perhaps, if God is really anxious to sanctify men, why have they so much difficulty in living the supernatural life? How is it that, although they live among the very sources of grace, the ministers who dispense it are sometimes so divorced from all contact with God? What is it which closes, so to speak, the divine hand?

The answer is—Pride. If we were perfectly humble there would be no limits to the gifts from on high. What is the lesson which the Gospel teaches? It is explicit: "Everyone that exalteth himself shall be humbled, and he that humbleth himself shall be exalted": *Omnis qui se exaltat humiliabitur et qui se humiliat exaltabitur* (Lk 18:14).

The teaching of the Epistles is no less categorical. In two places we read this astonishing sentence: "God resisteth the proud, but to the humble He giveth grace": *Deus resistit superbis, humilibus autem dat gratiam* (1 Pet 5:5; Jas 4:6).

How illuminating these words are in their simplicity! One thing is necessary in order to be raised up to God. We must humble ourselves.

I. THE CREATURE BEFORE GOD

Christian humility is, above all, an attitude of soul, not towards our fellow-men nor towards ourselves, but towards God. Certainly humility does involve a certain deference towards our neighbour and even in certain cases submission, while in that intimate judgement which man makes of himself it will suggest maintaining a healthy modesty. But these are merely the consequences of a disposition which goes deeper. The fundamental attitude of the humble soul is the desire to abase itself before God and live always in accordance with the state of life which God has appointed for it: it is the desire always to think and act in accordance with what the Lord expects of it. Humility therefore presents the soul before God in its misery and in its nothingness, just as it is. It may be defined thus: "the virtue which inclines man to accept the status which is proper to him in relation to the divinity." What are men here on earth? Beings on their way to eternity; they are merely passing through the world.

In the order of creation, and still more in the supernatural order, man possesses nothing which he has not received: *quid habes quod non accepisti.* And the Apostle adds: "Why dost thou glory as if thou hadst not received it" (1 Cor 4:7). Humility does not consist in a theoretical acceptance of this dependence but rather in a voluntary proclamation of it by a practical submission of ourselves to God and to the whole divine order of things. In his attempt to live according to his proper status the humble man will repress all those inordinate desires which impel him to seek his own advantage outside the laws appointed by nature and by God.

Humility, as St. Thomas says, is certainly a virtue of the will.

But it is regulated by knowledge: *Normam habet in cognitione.*[1] What knowledge? The knowledge of the sovereignty of God on the one hand and of the nothingness of man on the other.

These are two abysses, in complete opposition to each other which the soul has before its eyes. We can never completely comprehend the one or the other.

It is, above all, in the silence of prayer that this comparison between man and the Absolute must be made. The Scripture says: *Deus noster ignus consumens est*: "Our God is a consuming fire" (Heb 12:29).

The closer we approach to Him in the spirit of faith the more powerful does His domination of the soul appear. The same light which gives us a glimpse of the grandeur of God reveals to man his own poverty.

Humility is an attitude of truth. As St. Augustine puts it: "We have every right to say that humility is on the side of truth and not on the side of error."[2]

Pride, on the other hand, involves always and primarily an error of judgement. By pride, man takes an inordinate satisfaction in his own excellence to the point of losing sight of, refusing to acknowledge, or even repudiating, the sovereign dominion of God over him. Pride is, of all the inclinations to sin, the most tenacious, the most deep-rooted, and the most dangerous.

Admittedly, there are many varieties and many degrees of this vice, but the intimate disposition of the proud man tends to make the soul live without blessing the hand which dispenses all favours. He regards these divine favours of the natural and even of the supernatural order as quite normal things to be taken for granted. When dominated by pride, man goes his way in life forgetful of the rights of God and of the gestures of His love. That is why the Lord, Who lavishes His goodness on the humble heart, abandons the proud man to the autonomy which he claims: *et divites dimisit inanes.**

[1] *Summa* II-II, q. 161, a. 2 and 6.
[2] *De natura et gratia* 34; PL 44, 265.
* From the Magnificat: "and the rich he has sent away empty" (Lk 1:53).

The gravest forms of pride are not generally found among priests; but they, too, can lose sight of their total dependence on the Lord, and take satisfaction in the exercise of authority and in the good which they accomplish as if it all came solely from themselves. Humility is necessary for all men but it is more vitally necessary for the ministers of Christ.

We must not think that humility paralyses the spirit of initiative or devotion to duty. On the contrary, it is a source of moral strength. When the humble soul acknowledges its weakness and poverty, this does not mean that it gives up the fight, but rather that it finds in God and in the accomplishment of His will a powerful restorative for its energy. This is the way of the saints. Consider the great Apostle of the Gentiles; what was the secret of his indefatigable ardour? He tells us himself: "When I am weak, then am I powerful" (2 Cor 12:10). And why is this? Because: "I can do all things in Him who comforts me" (Phil 4:13). True humility is always accompanied by greatness of heart and confidence in the Lord.

II. HUMILITY AND SPIRITUAL PROGRESS

All that we have said on the subject, while of capital importance, is not sufficient in itself to give us a full understanding of the vital necessity of humility for the interior life. We must try, therefore, to see what exactly is the role of humility in the state in which we find ourselves as a result of sin, a state in which we are naturally inclined to evil, but in which the power of God heals, elevates, and perfects each individual soul.

Its function is, firstly, to prepare the way for the action of grace on the soul and, secondly, to dispose men to give glory to God in the manner which He has preordained, and which is especially dear to Him, that is, by extolling the divine mercy.

From this two-fold aspect of the effect of humility on the soul we can deduce a supplementary definition: "humility is the virtue which inclines the soul to a continuous practical acknowledgement of its own wretchedness before God." What is this wretchedness of which we speak?

First of all, as you know quite well, every creature is weighed down by the sorrowful realization of its own fundamental incapacity to rise to the supernatural plane by its own resources or to remain there when it has risen: "not that we are sufficient to think anything of ourselves, as of ourselves; but our sufficiency is from God": *Sufficientia nostra ex Deo est* (2 Cor 3:5). These are the words of St. Paul. It is only gradually and by the effect of grace that man arrives at a realization of this incapacity.

Secondly, we can all feel that the attraction of the baser pleasures and of the satisfaction of pride and of sin are still there, dormant in the depths of our souls.

Moreover, the duties of our state and our work constitute grave obligations; however noble and courageous our application to the daily task, it requires an effort, and an effort constantly renewed seems to many people a veritable burden.

Add to all this our physical ills: sickness, old age, death. As for moral sufferings, what anxieties, frustrations, disillusionments and sorrows of all kinds overwhelm the human heart! And the bitterness of these is often aggravated by the indifference, ingratitude, and even the ill-will of our neighbours. It was with good reason that Job said: "Man born of a woman, living for a short time, is filled with many miseries" (Job 14:1).

Energy and moral qualities alone are not sufficient to triumph over these evils and to make them a means of sanctification. The heart must turn to God and, by the confession of its own powerlessness, invoke His grace. This orientation of the heart, which by the very admission of its need adapts itself to the supernatural, is the fundamental attitude of Christian humility. It makes man capable of receiving the divine gift without the danger of his attributing it to himself. It purifies the heart by humbling it to its proper station and prepares it to be acted upon by God.

There are souls who do not appreciate their own poverty; because they do not raise their supplications to the Lord from the bottom of their souls, they do not dispose themselves to receive grace.

It was in this spirit of humility that St. Paul exclaimed:

"Gladly therefore will I glory in my infirmities, that the power of Christ may dwell in me" (1 Cor 12: 9). These words are very well known, but their full meaning is not always appreciated. What is it that the Apostle says? "I am not a perfect being, like the angels; I am a man full of infirmities, but I glory in them, because by them I touch the heart of Jesus, and the more keenly I feel my weakness, the more completely do I abandon my soul to the strength of Christ Who lives in me."

We must not, however, confound those human weaknesses, the recognition of which is so important to our spiritual advancement, with our infidelities. These, far from being favourable to the supernatural life, hinder the divine action; they cannot be presented before God as constituting a claim to grace. But repentance and the firm purpose of amendment which these faults provoke certainly involve an admission of our misery which is pleasing to God.

Humility has another function which makes it indispensable for the equilibrium of the whole spiritual life: it is humility alone which enables man to glorify God in accordance with the immensity of His mercy.

This divine perfection is simply infinite charity itself, providing a remedy for sin and bringing aid to human wretchedness.

The Incarnation of the Son of God "in the likeness of sinful flesh", *in similitudinem carnis peccati* (Rom 8:3), His death for our Redemption, our divine adoption, the ever-repeated pardon of sins, constitute a stupefying revelation of the depths of this immeasurable charity. St. Paul teaches expressly that every work of Christ tends to manifest the abundance and the gratuitousness of this divine goodness: "God, Who is rich in mercy for His exceeding charity wherewith He loved us even when we were dead in sins, hath quickened us together in Christ . . . that He might show in the ages to come the abundant riches of His grace" (Eph 2:4, 5, 7). And again: "God hath included all in unbelief." Why? "That He may have mercy on all": *Deus inclusit omnia in incredulitate ut omnium misereatur* (Rom 11:32). How shall we appear in heaven before God? As vessels of mercy: *Vasa misericordiae* (Rom 9:23). We are destined to proclaim eternally in the heavenly city the triumph of grace over our weakness and over sin. We can sum up the whole mission of Jesus in this world in a few words: "Jesus is the herald of infinite mercy to human misery."[3]

If, then, there is one divine perfection which we should extol above all others, it is certainly mercy. All the ways of the Lord in regard to us are simply the condescension of love. In the economy of the Redemption in which we live, God has compassionated our distress to raise us to the power of participating in His life.

What attitude can man adopt in face of these marvels except one of profound humility? By acknowledging his many miseries, man admits that he has no right in justice to become the object of the divine bounty: his sole title to grace is the constant admission of his unworthiness united to his desire to glorify the eternal mercy which has given him all things in Jesus Christ: "*Cum ipso omnia nobis donavit*" (Rom 8:32). This is the splendour of man's predestination, "to show forth the glory of the grace in which God hath graced us in His beloved Son" (Eph 1:6). It is when, in full knowledge of our wretchedness, we persist in hoping in His love that we really give glory to God.

III. HUMILITY AND OBEDIENCE IN JESUS

Humility was a fundamental attitude in Jesus. His soul, illuminated with the light of glory, realized that it was created but realized at the same same time that it had been assumed in a prodigious manner into the unity of the person of the Word. This realization caused in it a complete submission, a perfect acceptance of its dependence both as to its own essence and as to its mission of redemption. This profound humility before the Father produces in Christ an ensemble of virtues. From it spring this gentleness in His relations with others, His patience

---

[3] Dom Marmion has stressed this idea especially in his spiritual letters; see *L'Union à Dieu*, pp. 131–56, and in English, *Union with God*, pp. 125–48. This book, a compilation of letters of spiritual direction, was known to be the favourite book of Blessed Teresa of Calcutta.

and forgiveness in face of injury and, above all, His filial obedience to the divine will. These qualities are a manifestation of the fundamental attitude of dependence which was ever-present in the soul of our Blessed Saviour. Every page of the Gospel reveals to us this meekness of Our Lord, and He wishes us to take example from it: "Learn of me for I am meek and humble of heart" (Mt 11:29). Why did He come into the world? Not to be served but to serve, to belong to each one to the point of giving His life in ransom for him (Mk 10:45). Such a giving of self is an expression of the most absolute humility. And Christ wishes that everyone, but especially His priests, should be inspired by the same outlook: "And whosoever will be first among you shall be the servant of all" (Mk 10:44). At the Last Supper Christ washed the feet of His disciples. This is assuredly an act of sincere humility, and there can be no doubt that He intended thereby to give us an example: "If then, I, being your Lord and Master, have washed your feet, you also ought to wash one another's feet. For I have given you an example" (Jn 13:14–15). This gesture is in the fullest accord with all the preaching of Jesus. The beatitudes, which sum up that teaching, constitute the most admirable code in opposition to all the suggestions of human pride. Blessed are the poor—the meek—the peacemakers—the merciful—the persecuted (Mt 5:3–12).

One incident, among many others, serves as a further revelation of the humility hidden in the sanctuary of the soul of the divine Master. He was passing through Samaria, on the way to Jerusalem, surrounded by His apostles. The people of one city refused to receive the pilgrims. John and James, in their indignation, went so far as to wish that the fire of heaven might come down on the Samaritans and consume them by way of reprisal. But the thought of Our Saviour was on entirely different lines. His reply manifests the condescension and the meekness of the Redeemer of the world: "You know not of what spirit you are; the Son of man came not to destroy souls, but to save" (Lk 9:55–56). Note especially the meekness of Jesus in His Passion: *Saturabitur opprobriis. . . .* "He shall be filled with reproaches" (Lam 3:30). What do these words mean? Christ wished to pay His Father the homage of His humiliations in reparation for our own pride. He is the adorable Word and yet He stands there as one accused appearing before His judges. And what judges? Caiaphas, Pilate, Herod. The last-named, a wretched voluptuary, has only contempt for Him: *Sprevit illum* (Lk 23:11). "So this prophet," said he, "is seeking public honour. Put the white robe upon him and mock him." And what was the attitude of Christ? He accepted everything. Can any of us imagine such humiliation? The infinite Wisdom treated as a madman! And all this series of events was foreseen and planned in advance in the eternal designs. Then the Lord was compared to Barabbas and handed over to the Roman soldiers. These were heartless men who were glad to amuse themselves at the expense of one condemned to death, glad to press a crown of thorns on His forehead, to put a sceptre in His hand and to mock Him: *Illudebant ei dicentes: Ave, Rex Judaeorum* (Mt 27:29). They ridiculed Him as though He were an impostor worthy of all contempt; if ever a man was humiliated, it was indeed He. He wished to humble Himself even unto the death of the Cross. Is it not right that the priest who perpetuates on the altar the sacrifice of Calvary should enter into these sentiments of humility of Jesus? There is nothing more painful to the Christian heart than to see a priest who is proud and forgetful of the humiliations of the Saviour which he commemorates in the divine mysteries. What a contrast between such a man, pretentious, arrogant, impatient, lacking in all consideration for his neighbour, and the goodness and meekness of Christ!

Be on your guard, therefore, against allowing pride—even under its mitigated form of vain self-satisfaction—to enter into your souls. Exterior humility is necessary for a priest for the very reason that he is a person of authority. He is, in the public view, a candle placed upon the candlestick: *positus super candelabrum* (Mt 5:15), his words, his gestures, his attitudes are all the object of notice. If these are open to criticism, if they allow petty preoccupations of self-love to appear, this is a betrayal of the faithful, who like to find in their priest, combined with that perfect dignity befitting the minister of the Lord, something of the profound humility of the divine Master.[4]

The humility in which the soul of Jesus lived under the constant influence of the divinity produced in Him also a complete acceptance of the will of the Father, that is to say, perfect obedience. St. Paul says it: "He humbled Himself, becoming obedient": *humiliavit semetipsum factus obediens* (Phil 2:8). Jesus declares frequently that this submission to the divine will sums up and explains all His conduct. "I came down from heaven, not to do My own will, but the will of Him Who sent Me." . . . "My meat is to do the will of Him that sent Me" (Jn 6:38 and 4:34).

From the moment of the Incarnation, He abandons Himself to all the decrees of the Father in a spirit of the fullest acceptance, of absolute surrender: *Ecce venio . . . ut faciam, Deus, voluntatem tuam*: "Behold I come . . . that I should do Thy will, O Lord" (Heb 10:7). In one glance He sees the succession of sacrifices, of sufferings and of oblations which are to make up His life. He embraces them all; He places them in the midst of His heart: *In medio cordis mei* (Ps 40[39]:8). We may say that this idea of accomplishing at every moment what was written about Him: *ut impleantur scripturae* (Mk 14:49), pursued Our Lord during His entire existence.

In spite of His consideration for His apostles, Jesus did not permit them to remain in any doubt on this point. On one occasion when He spoke to them of His impending Passion and death, Peter, carried away by his natural impetuosity, cried out: "Lord be it far from Thee, this shall not be unto Thee": *Absit a te, Domine; non erit tibi hoc.* And what does Our Lord reply? "Go behind Me, Satan; thou art a scandal unto Me, because thou savourest not the things that are of God, but of men" (Mt 16:22–23). These are severe words, distressing the Apostle, but as He had come into the world at the will of the Father, Christ could not allow His own disciples not to understand that the succession of all the events of His life was the realization of a

---

[4] Compare what Dom Marmion has to say on charity to one's neighbour, pp. 193–94.

programme which had been planned in heaven. Again, remember the words which He addressed to Peter when he wanted to defend Him, on the night of His Passion as His enemies were in the act of seizing Him: "The chalice which My Father hath given Me, shall I not drink it?" (Jn 18:11). This chalice had been prepared in advance. The Father knew that He could count on the submission of His Son to drain it to the last drop. There was not a single suffering, not an anguish or a humiliation of those with which Jesus was overwhelmed which had not been foreseen in the divine decrees. And Jesus was obedient in all things. We shall realize all this in heaven. It is noteworthy that St. Paul, when he speaks of the redemptive sacrifice, likes to recall that it was marked by one particular characteristic— obedience: "As by the disobedience of one man many were made sinners, so also by the obedience of one many shall be made just" (Rom 5:19). This striking parallel was willed by the divine wisdom. Adam, although he had been raised from the beginning to the supernatural plane, scorned the first duty of children, obedience to their parents. To make reparation for this offence, Jesus accepted whole-heartedly the will of the Father: *Non mea voluntas sed tua fiat* (Lk 22:42). "But that the world may know that I love the Father, and as the Father hath given the commandment so do I" (Jn 14:31).

This is the sublime example of filial obedience which Jesus gives us: Not only has His submission made reparation for the transgression of Adam, but through it: "where sin abounded grace did more abound": *Ubi abundavit delictum superabundavit gratia* (Rom 5:20).

The Apostle considers also another aspect of Jesus in His work of redemption on the Cross. He considers Him, humble in obedience, surrendering Himself, not by any ordinary act of submission but "becoming obedient unto death, even to the death of the Cross" (Phil 2:8). Of all the commands which Christ might have received from His Father the most terrible was that of dying on the Cross. Why? Because, according to the thought of St. Paul, it is the climax of obedience to become like one accursed to save the others from the curse: *quia scriptum est:*

maledictus homo qui pendit in ligno (Gal 3:13). As He died, Jesus
looked on the face of the Father. This was the secret of His
strength: during those hours of agony He remained supremely
united in love, and He abandoned Himself entirely to obedience until the *consummatum est* (Jn 19:30). Every time that we
celebrate the Holy Sacrifice we reproduce sacramentally before
God this obedience unto death of His Son and we bring again
before our own eyes this transcendent model of humility and
love: *quotiescumque . . . mortem Domini annuntiabitis*: "For as often . . . you proclaim the Lord's death" (1 Cor 11:26). At the
offertory, let us offer with the host our entire existence; united
to the oblation of Christ, it, too, will become a sacrifice of
submission and of love pleasing to God: *Hostiam . . . Deo
placentem* (Rom 12:1).

IV. PRIESTLY OBEDIENCE

Just as the humility of Christ was expressed during His whole
life by obedience, so must it be with us, His priests. It is in this,
above all, that we must take Him as our model.

In general, to obey is to submit one's activity to a superior
authority. Obedience may be rendered in two ways: the one
purely human, the other supernatural.

The worker obeys the foreman; this is necessary for the running of the workshop or factory; without obedience there
would be disorder. If he does his work, he is playing his part and
has a right to his salary, even though he may feel internally
rebellious against his employer. The soldier submits to discipline
to avoid being imprisoned or shot. He may, if he is of more
noble character, obey from love of his profession and of his
country. But he reserves the right to criticize and blame his
leaders and to regard them as incompetent or unjust. This disci-
plined obedience is certainly useful and praiseworthy, but it is
merely human. Your priestly obedience must be essentially supernatural, based on faith and charity. It must come from the
bottom of your heart and be eager and joyous, given because of
the love you have for Christ and for souls. By supernatural obe-

dience we submit ourselves to the will of God and to the orders of those who represent Him. By this, we render homage to the sovereign majesty.

After your ordination you promised obedience to your bishop. This promise was made to the ordaining pontiff at the most memorable moment of your life. You bound yourself in the presence of God and before the altar, where you had just offered the Holy Sacrifice for the first time in union with the bishop who had ordained you. Admittedly you did not bind yourself by this promise in the same way as do religious when they make their vows of perpetual obedience to a superior according to a rule duly approved. The Church regards their action as a means of sanctification freely chosen so that, by a complete renunciation of their liberty, they may consecrate their persons and their activities for ever to God.

Your promise of obedience is of a different character. The Church requires this promise of you principally in order to ensure the common good of the diocese. The reason for it is that the bishop, the legitimate pastor of souls, must be able to count on the complete submission of his collaborators to his orders and directions, when he has occasion to call upon them. This willing sacrifice on your part is in the highest degree meritorious and pleasing to God, for the most fundamental thing in man is his liberty, his autonomy, the capacity to act as he likes. God Himself in His relations with souls respects this right: the most powerful graces leave intact our human liberty. You have made, therefore, as it were, a contract with the Heavenly Father, "My God", you have said, "for love of You and the good of the Church, I place in the hands of my bishop my talents and my activities. Through him You will tell me what You wish me to do": *Domine, quid me vis facere* (Acts 9:6). "I shall accept as coming from You, the function and tasks which my bishop shall entrust to me. I am confident that in this way I shall have Your blessing for my ministry and for my priestly life." This point of view is entirely supernatural. A priest who surrenders himself in this way, in the spirit of faith, will always be in peace, even in the midst of the greatest difficulties, for he is in the situation which God has willed for him and God is with him, "If God be for us, who is against us?" says St. Paul (Rom 8:31). When the Lord sent Moses to Pharaoh to deliver the Hebrew people from his yoke, Moses was frightened by the mission. And the Lord said to him: "I shall be with you" (Ex 3:12). We know by what wonders God rewarded the obedience of His envoy. The religious who, with full deliberation, tries to take his future into his own hands and impose his views on his superiors will not sanctify himself. The same is true in a great measure of the priest who disregards the importance of his promise.

I do not exclude the right in certain cases to make respectful representations, but they must be made at the opportune time and there must never be a refusal to obey. And what are we to do if the order which displeases us is persisted in? Accept it in a supernatural spirit: "Let the subordinate persuade himself that the thing ordered is for his advantage and let him obey from love, putting his confidence in the help of God." This direction which St. Benedict gives to his sons is assuredly excellent for all.[5]

If God appeared to us and said: "It is My wish that you do this or that," obedience would be easy. Or if God had put angels or perfect beings over us would not everything go magnificently? This is not so certain. However, God chose another way: *Imposuisti homines super capita nostra*: "thou didst let men ride over our heads" (Ps 66[65]:12). It is men that we must obey, men limited in their views and who are themselves not free from faults. In His infinite wisdom the Lord has arranged it thus. Christ saved the world by His submission in the spirit of filial love, and we priests, in order to collaborate with the Lord in the redemption of souls, must unite ourselves to this obedience in our work. That is why we can say of any organization, whether it be a diocese or a religious community, that the measure of its strength is the obedience of its members.

In the words of the prophet Isaiah: "The Lord . . . hath made me as a chosen arrow; in His quiver He hath hidden me": *et*

---

[5] Rule, chap. 68.

posuit me sicut sagittam electam (Is 49:2). We may see here the figure of the obedient priest who has been duly prepared by his seminary and by his interior life to be employed wherever the glory of God and the defence of the Church require him. The arrow obeys the hand that casts it and, thanks to this docility, it acquires force and efficiency: of itself, however well made it may be, it can achieve nothing. Priests are like arrows in a hand full of power: *sicut sagittae in manu potentis* (Ps 127[126]:4). If they obey supernaturally in the exercise of their ministry, they will be, under the influence of the divine urge, instruments of grace and of victory: *Haec est victoria . . . fides nostra* (1 Jn 5:9).

The great enemy of the virtue of obedience is grumbling. Grumbling is the compensation which self-love resorts to in its powerlessness in the face of authority. It is a compensation which is often unworthy. I do not speak now of those complaints to which our poor nature sometimes gives expression when it is overwhelmed with suffering. Thus, when Our Lady said to Jesus: "Son, why hast Thou done so to us?" (Lk 2:48), she did not complain; it was merely the expression of the pain in her heart. The Saviour uttered this cry of anguish on the Cross: "My God . . . why hast Thou forsaken Me?" (Mt 27:46). Jesus did not complain; He merely revealed the immensity of His suffering.

Grumbling is always accompanied by the spirit of criticism and opposition, and it is in this that the evil lies. The priest who permits himself to grumble does not regard his superior as being invested with authority from God. If the bishop were not the representative of the Lord you would have no motive for submitting to him. As man, he has no right to give you orders; one man is good as another. But he derives his authority from his consecration. As the delegate of God, he has a share of His authority. The man who is truly obedient is submitting to God alone and this submission, rising above creatures, renders the homage of love to the Most High alone. The grumbler loses sight of all this.

In moments of difficulty, and they occur in every life, when we feel that obedience weighs heavy on us and when we long to enjoy more liberty and independence, we must fix our eyes on the divine Crucified One. He is our great model. In order to be really like Him we, too, must become victims with Him. I know that this life of oblation costs us dear; it may be very hard at times. But did Jesus find it agreeable to be given over to His enemies, to be insulted by the Pharisees and nailed to the Cross? No, all this filled Him with horror. And yet He accepted it from love and, by His sufferings, as St. Paul has so admirably expressed it, He served His apprenticeship in obedience: *Didicit ex iis, quae passus est obedientiam* (Heb 5:8).

After the mystery of the Trinity, what is the most fundamental dogma of Christianity, the dogma in accordance with which the priest must live his life in this world? It is the mystery of a God made man, Who redeemed humanity by His obedience and led it to the bosom of the Father.

Every time you celebrate Mass, cast a glance over the day that is before you; accept the aggregate of duties which await you. Say to the Lord: "You have loved me, O Jesus, and you have delivered yourself up for me": *dilexit me et tradidit semetipsum pro me* (Gal 2:20). "I also give up everything and deliver myself up for you": *Libentissime impendam et super-impendar pro te* (2 Cor 12:15).

This is the most practical way, the way most in harmony with his vocation and his ministry, for the priest to keep his soul open to the sanctifying influence of grace.

VIII.

THE VIRTUE OF RELIGION

EVERY practice of virtue in the Church is derived from the grace of Jesus Christ. He is the model, the meritorious cause, the living source of every spiritual perfection. The sanctity of the members is due to the fullness of grace of their head: *de plenitudine eius nos omnes accepimus* (Jn 1:16). Every virtue of Jesus, His love for the Father, His dedication to the service of man, His obedience, His chastity, His patience, lives on in the different vocations, both general and particular, which flourish in the Church. They are perpetuated in the hearts of His disciples, the imitators of the divine Master. This admirable multiplicity of graces constitutes the beauty of the mystical body. "The spouse of the Saviour," says Holy Scripture, "is decked out like a queen": *Astitit regina a dextris tuis in vestitu deaurato, circumdata varietate* (Ps 45[44]:10).

The *vestis deaurata* of the spouse symbolizes sanctifying grace diffused throughout the whole Church; the variety of adornments are the different virtues which shine forth from Jesus and are reflected in His members. The sanctity of Christ, therefore, remains ever living in His mystical body. Let us pause to consider one of these virtues which impregnated the whole life of Jesus and all His actions: an eager devotion to the Father.

This disposition of soul must live on in every minister of Christ. Is he not dedicated by his ordination, like Jesus Himself, "to the Father's business" (Lk 2:49), to the interests of the heavenly kingdom among men? This religious orientation must put the mark of its interior grace on his every movement; it must give sanctity to his life. and make him truly priestly.

It is essential for every Christian, and a fortiori for the priest, that his practice of religion should be supernatural. We must not misunderstand the moral character of this virtue; we know that it is derived primarily from right reason and the law of nature. Nevertheless, it is only by the light of faith that man can fully appreciate the sovereignty of God, the immensity of His bounty and the obligation to do Him homage. Religion finds its most solid support in faith. Moreover, for the Christian, the cult rendered to God must be dominated by charity. It is the queen of the virtues. It is the prerogative of charity to stimulate and inspire the activity of all the other virtues. In the soul blessed by God, love has always held the primacy. He reveals it to us Himself as He offers the act of religion par excellence, the sacrifice of the Cross: *ut cognoscat mundus quia diligo Patrem . . . sic facio*: "so that the world may know that I love the Father" (Jn 14:31). It must be so also with us; as grace is grafted on nature, sanctifies it and prevails over it, in like manner charity controls the practice of religion, and without affecting the character of the latter, it elevates it, gives new weight to its actions and supernaturalizes them. In Christianity the predominance of the theological virtues is at all times essential.

I. THE VIRTUE OF RELIGION IN THE CHRISTIAN ECONOMY

When Moses asked Yahweh what was His name, the Lord replied: "*Ego sum qui sum*" (Ex 3:14). It is the essence of God to be of Himself all that He is. We, on the other hand, exist only by participation: *In ipso . . . movemur et sumus* (Acts 17:28). As creatures we depend on Him absolutely: *Manus tuae fecerunt me et plasmaverunt me*: "Thy hands have made and fashioned me" (Ps 119[118]:73). He is our Lord and Master. The virtue of religion prostrates us before His infinite majesty. It makes us say: "You, my God, are everything, and I am nothing." Religion cannot be merely a passing sentiment: it must be a disposition fixed in the inmost depths of our souls; it must be a virtue inclining men to acknowledge by acts of worship the rights of God as the beginning and the final end of all things.

The concept of religion is dominated by the idea of rectitude or loyalty towards God. Knowing the absolute sovereignty of the Creator, we accept our dependence and proclaim it by humbling ourselves before Him.

Although it is calculated to unite man to God, this is not one of the theological virtues; it has not God Himself as its object. It is a moral virtue which makes us render homage to God, not for the formal motive of love or appreciation of His goodness, but because this submission is due to Him. In this way man fulfils a duty of justice which he recognizes as incumbent on him by the law of nature itself. The spirit of uprightness which urges us to discharge our obligation of justice towards God will always be reckoned as one of the most worthy motives of activity.

See how the Church proclaims this truth every day. In our liturgy, which is very restrained, every word must be weighed in order to extract from it its lesson. In the beginning of the *Preface* the Church insists on certain reasons for thanking God. She suggests the worthiness, the justice, and the equity of this act of religion: *Vere dignum, justum, aequum . . . Nos tibi semper et ubique.* Whatever the solemnity that is being celebrated, the same fundamental reason is always invoked to arouse the impulse of our soul.

Note also in the Ordinary of the Mass the expression used to describe our attitude towards the Lord. It is called "a service": *Hanc igitur oblationem servitutis nostrae,* and again, *Placeat tibi sancta Trinitas obsequium servitutis*: We are the servants of God. You will say: "Are we not also His children?" Yes, but our adoption does not prevent us from remaining what we are essentially: servants. Every man, but especially the priest, must have in his soul the firm resolution to devote himself always and with generosity to the accomplishment of those human acts which render homage to God. St. Thomas calls this eager desire to fulfil the duties of worship "devotion": *Voluntas quaedam prompte tradendi se ad ea quae pertinent ad Dei famulatum . . . ad opera divini cultus.*[1]

Charity towards God disposes Christians, His adoptive children, admirably to the practice of this "devotion", that is to say, to devote themselves, to give themselves up fervently, to the service of God.

By what acts do we practise this virtue of religion? The most

[1] *Summa* II-II, q. 82, a. 1.

fundamental is adoration: the entire submission of man, who thus acknowledges his nothingness before the absolute sovereignty of God. Adoration means looking at God and humbling oneself.

The offering of sacrifice is the supreme visible and social act of adoration. The immolation or destruction of a sensible thing as an act of homage to God is an attestation of the supreme dominion of the Lord over being, over life and death. This act, by its intrinsic meaning and by the intention which animates it, is essentially an act of *latria*, that is to say, of adoration, and is rendered to God alone. The exterior element of sacrifice has a symbolic value: "it is," says St. Augustine, "an outward sign which expresses the intimate sentiments of the heart of man when he renders worship to God"; *sacrificium visibile, invisibilis sacrificii sacramentum.*[2]

This spiritual and interior side will always be the most important element in the offering of sacrifice and of every act which springs directly from the virtue of religion. When we pronounce a vow, when we make an oath, whenever we give praise or recite vocal prayers, the words and gestures are intended to express the thought and the religious intentions of the soul. If they were not a true expression, these exterior acts would become a fiction and would be devoid of all virtue.

The better to appreciate the vital importance of the virtue of religion in the spiritual life, we must note that it is it which consecrates all the good actions of men—whatever the particular virtue from which they depend—to the worship of the Lord. And so St. James could say: "Religion, clean and undefiled before God and the Father, is this: to visit the fatherless and the widows in their tribulation and to keep oneself unspotted from the world" (Jas 1:27).

In the same way, the faithful observance of chastity, the accomplishment of the duties of our state, and indeed, all virtuous efforts are transformed into acts of worship when religion inspires the offering of them to God.

---

[2] *De Civitate Dei* 10, 5; PL 41, 282.

In the Old Testament, as you know, the virtue of religion was based, above all, on fear. It was only once a year and after many purifications that the High Priest entered into the sanctuary and tremblingly pronounced the name of God. It was the religion of subjects.

But Jesus has given us the privilege of being by grace what He is by nature: children. Our Creator has deigned to adopt His subjects as His children. That is the great wonder. For us, the virtue of religion is united with filial love without, however, excluding the spirit of profound respect. The great distinction between the two Testaments is the predominance of love in the one which Christ has sealed with His blood. Without losing its proper character, religion for the Christian is elevated by supernatural charity. It attains thus a new excellence: the added value which is conferred on it by love. What a happiness it is for us to know that God, our Master, is truly our Father! We have the Lord for Father. As such He merits our utmost respect and our utmost love.

II. THE RELIGION OF JESUS

By His Incarnation the Word, while remaining God, began to give glory to the Father under a new form, that of a creature. In His divine nature, in *forma Dei* (Phil 2:7), His whole being is directed towards the Father of Whom He is the splendour and the glory; in His humanity, in *forma servi* (Phil 2:7), His soul is, as it were, carried away in the movement of praise proper to the Second Divine Person. The life of the Word is directed wholly towards the Father, *est tota ad Patrem*; so also the human life of Jesus is constantly directed towards Him: *Ego vivo propter Patrem* (Jn 6:58). The Son pays honour to the Father by all His acts of humility. He practises in an eminent manner the virtue of religion.

In order to glorify the Father in the name of sinful humanity, He can not only adore, but expiate, suffer, be immolated, offered as a sacrifice. The virtue of religion in the Son of God is certainly unique, unparalleled.

Its first excellence is that it is sacerdotal. In each one of His actions the Saviour knew that He was the universal Pontiff of the glory of the Father, *catholicum Patris sacerdotem*; as Tertullian puts it so aptly.[3] The Incarnation had raised Christ to this dignity. When He said: "I honour My Father" (Jn 8:49), He meant, without any doubt, that He did so as a priest charged with the task of redeeming the world by the sacrifice of the Cross. The offering of this sacred immolation constituted an act of supreme religious homage. The redemption was certainly not, in the eyes of Jesus, a work which was exclusively His. It appeared to Him as the realization in time of a plan of eternal mercy conceived and willed in heaven. Christ recognized that He was the Pontiff of the New Testament. He accepted the will of the Father and carried out the programme planned in advance in the divine counsels. This is certainly the meaning of the words of Jesus: "I came not to do My own will but the will of of Him Who sent Me" (Jn 6:38). And again: "The chalice which My Father hath given Me, shall I not drink it?" (Jn 18:11). Since Christ was carrying out the will of His Father, was not His whole existence an incomparable act of religious homage? He says so Himself in His sacerdotal prayer after the Last Supper: "Father . . . I have glorified Thee on earth; I have finished the work which Thou gavest Me to do" (Jn 17:4).

Another characteristic of the virtue of religion in Jesus is that it takes its source in the intuitive vision of the Father which He alone enjoyed.

He comprehended the immensity of the divine sanctity and realized how incumbent it was on men to render honour and worship to God. "Just Father," said He, "the world hath not known Thee; but I have known Thee" (Jn 17:25); and again: "I know Him because I am from Him" (Jn 7:29).

This intimate contemplation produced in our divine Master the constant need to abase Himself before the infinite majesty. The activity of His soul consisted principally in ineffable adora-

[3] *Adversus Marcionem* 4, 9; PL 2, 406.

tion. "He that sent Me is with Me, and He hath not left Me alone" (Jn 8:29). These were the sentiments of Jesus, and this constant contact with the divinity not only maintained His soul in an attitude of profound abasement but served also to arouse in Him a thirst to sacrifice Himself for each one of us. The spirit of religion in Jesus proceeded wholly from this interior contemplation of the Father, and through it, it was elevated to heights beyond compare.

The virtue of religion in Jesus possessed a third excellence: the gift of self.

It is the fullness of His self-sacrifice in the carrying out of His acts of homage to God which makes His practice of the virtue perfect. This total gift of self made Jesus direct all the actions of His life to the service of the Father. "I seek not My own glory," said He, "there is one that seeketh and judgeth" (Jn 8:50). According to the divine plan, His whole existence, from the workshop at Nazareth to the Last Supper, was dedicated to the establishment among men of the cult and the love of the Father. The hour of His sacrifice was certainly the occasion of the supreme immolation but, while awaiting "His hour" Jesus was already offering Himself to the Father as a victim and an oblation. The virtue of religion was the constant inspiration of all the actions of His life.

Furthermore, the heart of Jesus was an ever-glowing focus of charity. If He wished that the name of the Father should be glorified, that His kingdom should come, that His will should be done on earth as it was in heaven, it was assuredly because this glorification was due in all justice to the Father, but He desired it also by reason of an intense movement of love for the infinite goodness.

In the harmony of interior activity in our divine Saviour, charity was predominant, and thus, under the inspiration of love, the virtue of religion attained in Jesus its highest perfection. When we read Holy Scripture we can remark that this eagerness to render to the Father the worship which was His due is characteristic of every stage in the life of Christ. Have we not seen it: from the moment of the Incarnation the whole activity of His soul was one sublime act of religion consisting in the total oblation of His life to God (Heb 10:5–7). The first words from His lips which the Gospels have preserved for us teach us this lesson that His whole life was consecrated to the work and to the rights of the Father: "Do you not know that I must be about my Father's business?" *In his quae Patris mei sunt oportet me esse* (Lk 2:49 Douay-Rheims). During all the years of His hidden life, Jesus—who can doubt it—was animated by the same spirit: He sought the glory of the Father. Then, as afterwards, at every moment, He was carrying out the divine will: *quae placita sunt ei, facio semper* (Jn 8:29).

In the course of His intimate colloquies with God did not Jesus practise, and with outstanding perfection, the virtue of religion? "The Father seeks adorers in spirit and in truth" said He, *in spiritu et veritate* (Jn 4:23). And was not He the first and most excellent of these? Who can ever envisage the mystery of those colloquies of the Saviour when He passed forty days in prayer in the desert or when, having retired unto the heights in the evening, He prolonged His prayer: *Erat pernoctans in oratione Dei* (Lk 6:12). Adoration was imposed on Him by an inner compulsion. When He preached at the lakeside, on the mountain or in the temple, when He cured the sick or confounded the Pharisees, everything was the expression of His inner consciousness that He is the Son of God. He came into this world to teach men to glorify the Father and to acknowledge His sovereignty. If He wishes that they render to Caesar the things that are Caesar's, it is in order to establish more forcibly the rights of the Most High: "Render to God the things that are God's" (Mk 7:17).

The supreme moment in the life of Jesus when He offered the sacrifice of the Cross was also the culmination of the virtue of religion in Him. As Pontiff of the New Testament, as Lamb of God, the Victim burdened with the sins of the world, His interior dispositions were divinely inspired: *Per Spiritum Sanctum semetipsum obtulit immaculatum Deo* (Heb 9:14). His immolation constituted the most complete act of homage, the most august act of worship that can ever be offered to the divinity.

Never forget that at every Mass the same sublime act of religion is continued when you present the sacred Victim to God; *hostiam puram, hostiam sanctam, hostiam immaculatam.* And there, as on the Cross, Jesus is not alone in His immolation. His Church is united to Him: she is His body and the fullness of Him: *est corpus ipsius et plenitudo eius* (Eph 1:23). As head of the mystical body, Jesus contains us within Himself and makes us participate in His ineffable devotion to the Father.

And now our Saviour is in heaven, *in gloria Dei Patris.* God be thanked for it! Jesus has entered into the glory which is His due. And yet the sacred humanity remains ever in profound adoration before the Father.

III. THE PRIEST PERPETUATES THE DEVOTION OF JESUS CHRIST

The great mission of the priest here below is to perpetuate that service of reverence, adoration and praise, that dedication of self to the work of the Father, which we see in the sacred soul of Jesus Christ. Thus, even in the most ordinary circumstances, his actions will bear the stamp of his priesthood.

The habit of keeping the soul in the presence of God by sentiments of devotion is of extreme importance in the exercise of sacerdotal functions. In this way, the minister of Christ establishes familiar relations with the divinity. If St. John was able to lean his head upon the heart of Jesus during the Last Supper, why should it not be the same for the priest during the sacred mysteries when his soul is filled with respectful love?

On the other hand, when the virtue of religion weakens in him, his heart becomes cold. He is distracted at the altar, without light, without enthusiasm. His quarter of an hour thanksgiving seems an eternity to him; he can find nothing to say to Jesus. In his relations with the faithful he has no real influence for good. Those who turn to him for spiritual encouragement come away disappointed. And why? The salt has lost its savour: *sal evanuit* (Mt 5:13). The grace of ordination is almost extinguished: *Lampades nostrae exstinguuntur* (Mt 25:8). As I have told you, to one deprived of the inner spirit, the most sacred

attitudes and gestures pass unnoticed, and the prescriptions of
the rubrics seem no more than a formality.

We must love the truth in everything: *veritatem facientes in
caritate* (Eph 4:15). We are pledged by our ordination in a very
special manner to practise the virtue of religion. It is for this
that the sacramental character has made its indelible stamp on
our souls: in the inner depths of our souls we are consecrated to
the worship of God. We must see ourselves honestly as we are,
and live our priestly life in the constant practice of the virtue of
religion.

The better to achieve this, I recommend to you two very
simple practices. The moral virtues are developed in us by the
repetition of those acts which they produce. The first good
habit which we must adopt is never to begin any sacred function without at least a moment of recollection. To recollect
oneself is to consider in the depth of one's soul the value of the
act which one is about to accomplish. Learn to pray before
hearing confessions, teaching catechism, or visiting the sick,
and weigh the consequences of your words and actions for the
eternal good of souls. Ask the Holy Spirit to enlighten your
intelligence and to inflame your heart. Unite yourself with
Christ; you are taking His place among men today in order to
be, in His name, the instrument of grace and salvation.

We must constantly renew this intention to act for God and
the good of souls alone, for we are very apt to be captured by
routine, and self-love under various disguises and divers pretexts
is quick to make its way into our hearts. An ejaculatory prayer, a
glance at the crucifix are matters of an instant, but by giving us
some measure of recollection, they will enable us to appreciate
better the supernatural significance of our actions. In the second place, we must take as the objective of our life the end
which the Father Himself adopted in the whole work of redemption; the glory of His Son. What was the great design of
God? Jesus has Himself given us the reply to this question: *Hoc
est opus Dei ut credatis in eum quem misit ille*: "This is the work of
God, that you believe in him whom he has sent" (Jn 6:29). The
Father wishes our lives to be consecrated to believing in His

Son, to venerating Him, to causing Him to be adored as the equal of Himself: "that all men may honour the Son as they honour the Father" (Jn 5:23) . . . "and that every tongue should confess that the Lord Jesus Christ is in the glory of God the Father" (Phil 2:11).

Is not this the finest ideal possible to encourage our daily effort? In the exercise of your priestly office you must have a very lively faith in the mystery of grace which Christ is operating through you in the souls of men, for you are acting *in persona Christi*. Be careful to remember this when you are baptizing, administering extreme unction, or receiving the mutual consent of husband and wife: this thought will serve to maintain the spirit of devotion in you. It is still more necessary when administering the sacrament of penance; then, through your mediation, the heart of Jesus is welcoming the contrite sinner and opens to him the treasures of His mercy.

It is, above all, at the altar that you must enter into the Father's design to glorify the Son. In the Eucharist, Jesus is hidden from our view, but if the heart of the priest is filled with the virtue of religion, he will show the same respect for Our Lord under the veil of the sacred species as if he beheld Him face to face. If you had the privilege of seeing Him in His glory as do the angels and the saints, would you not fall at His feet?

Consider the Church. What attitude of soul does the spouse of Christ wish above all to find in the ministers of the Eucharist? You need not be astonished: it is veneration: *Tantum ergo Sacramentum veneremur cernui*. If the virtue of religion makes us offer to God those acts of homage which are His due, has not Jesus Christ a right to our adoration and to our gratitude? Is He not our Saviour, the Jesus of the Last Supper, of the Passion, of the Resurrection, the supreme Pontiff from Whom our priesthood is derived? And His humanity is inseparable from the Word, which, eternally engendered by the Father, is ever consubstantial with Him, and is never separated from Him. And the Holy Spirit, Who proceeds from their mutual love, is a further bond of union between Them. Thus, the Blessed Trinity is present in the sacred Host.

Profound reverence amounting to adoration is the only attitude fitting for man in the presence of the divine sacrament. This religious veneration is a condition precedent for the communication to us by God of His graces through the Eucharist.

That is why the Church constantly makes us say this prayer: "Lord . . . grant us so to revere the sacred mysteries of Thy body and blood that we may ever feel in us the fruits of Thy redemption."

Outside Mass, the virtue of religion moves us to venerate Christ in the silence of the tabernacle; "Devoutly I adore Thee, O hidden divinity . . . it is to Thee that my heart submits itself completely": *Adoro te devote, latens Deitas . . . tibi se cor meum totum subjicit.* Jesus lives there amongst us in the plenitude of His divine power as formerly when He cured the sick and raised Lazarus from the dead. He is there a living and life-giving Victim filled with the power and the graces of each of His mysteries, and especially of the mysteries of His death and Resurrection. He is waiting for us in the immensity of His love, eager to communicate to us His gifts and to admit us to His friendship. There has been no change in those sentiments of merciful bounty towards men to which Christ gave expression while on earth. We must believe that Jesus, present under the sacred species, loves with the same love as at the Last Supper when He pronounced those solemn words: "with desire I have desired to eat this Pasch with you before I suffer": *Desiderio desideravi* (Lk 22:15).

The virtue of religion tends to confer on the priest a certain dignity in his exterior carriage.

We may note the recommendation of the Council of Trent: "It is fitting that clerics, being called to a complete consecration to the Lord, should regulate their conduct in such a way as to show themselves grave, moderate, and filled with the spirit of religion. This should appear in their bearing, their gestures, their gait, their conversation and, indeed, in everything.[4] This must all be unaffected and sincere."

---

[4] Sess. 22, *de reformatione*, 1.

As regards custody of the eyes, the priest must avoid all unseemly curiosity; in conversation with others the elevation and charity of his soul should exercise an encouraging and beneficial influence on those around him, even on the indifferent and unbelieving.

In the celebration of Mass we must be careful to conform to the rubrics. These are the rules of decorum or etiquette prescribed by the spouse of Christ for our relations with the King of Kings. Is it not only right that we should conform to the directions of the Church in the celebration of these mysteries which are so far above us? Obedience to the rubrics out of respect for the sacred character of the rites is a deliberate act of the virtue of religion even though there be question only of a simple bow.

Fidelity to this practice gives an increase of fervour and protects the priest from the very real danger of precipitation. Excessive haste in the gestures and formulas must be prejudicial to the piety of the minister. When you genuflect, let it be a conscious and sincere act of adoration of the Lord. When you make the sign of the Cross over the *oblata*, and especially over the body of Christ, let this gesture bear the mark of profound respect.

At times the attitude of some ministers at the altar makes one have doubts about their faith. On the other hand, the recitation of the liturgical prayers with recollection but without undue slowness, and the reverence which the priest shows for the holy Eucharist are more eloquent than the best sermon.

The same applies for other functions. For example, when the priest goes to a funeral, his bearing should display that dignity and gravity which will suggest to the other mourners that he has a living faith in the supernatural significance of the rites which he carries out and the formulas which he pronounces. We must spare no pains in our care of the ciborium and of the tabernacle, and we must be watchful for the cleanliness of the sacred buildings. A church may be bare of all riches and Jesus will not be offended; Bethlehem, Nazareth, the Cross were all poor in the extreme. But it must be properly kept. God cannot approve a want of respect towards His Son Who continues in the Eucharist the gift of Himself to men.

I do not wish to suggest that we should be too meticulous in our observance of all these rules and of every rubric. In case of doubt consult a priest or a prudent friend. If a colleague ventures to point out to you some fault or omission in the way you celebrate, accept his remark and, if it is well founded, pay attention to it. We should indeed be grateful for every suggestion calculated to enable us to carry out our liturgical duties more fittingly. Such gratitude will be a sign that the virtue of religion is a living force in your soul.

St. John Chrysostom[5] resorts to a comparison to suggest to the priest the attitude of religious respect which should be his in the exercise of his priestly functions. Taking an episode from the Old Testament, he recalls the memory of the prophet Elijah when he offered the sacrifice. Standing before the altar loaded with the victims, the man of God begs Him to send down fire from the heavens to consume them and to show in this manner that the oblation is pleasing to Him. The whole congregation is there, motionless, waiting. And suddenly, at the voice of the prophet, fire flashes from the clouds: "These things," says the saint, "are astonishing and an object of admiration, but turn now from these incidents to what happens in our days on our altars. Here you behold not merely wondrous incidents but a reality beyond admiration. The priest is standing there. It is not fire which he calls down but the Holy Spirit. He continues to pray for a long time, not that fire may come down from heaven and consume the victims which have been prepared, but that divine grace may be bestowed on the sacrifice and through it inflame the hearts of the faithful."

[5] *De sacerdotio* 3, 4; PG 48, 642. Cf. 1 Kings 18:36–38.

IX.

THE GREATEST OF THE COMMANDMENTS

On the day of our ordination the Church placed in our hands the chalice destined to contain the precious blood of our blessed Saviour. And, in return, she requires of us a sacrifice: that we should support the loneliness of the celibate state.

We need to have a great love of God to remain faithful to our mission and to the self-denial which it involves.

Our heart was made for love; we have an immense need to love; we cannot live without it. So powerful is the force of love that it can raise our poor nature to the point of overcoming monotony, suffering and even death: *Aquae multae non potuerunt exstinguere caritatem* (Song 8:7). The richer a nature is and the more capable of great things, the more it feels the need of a higher love. If we do not turn generously towards God we shall inevitably be drawn towards creatures. There can be no doubt about it: there can be nothing so fine, so potent and so profitable on this earth as a priestly heart completely dominated by the love of God. There are many such to be found. But again, there is nothing so deplorable as the heart of a priest profaned by an illicit satisfaction in creatures. Our hearts have been consecrated to God by our ordination. We have not the right to squander our affections.

It requires great virtue to live up to this vocation. To help us to do so, we must try to establish a loyal friendship with the divine Master and we may be assured that, if we love Him, He will be the most excellent of friends to us. Our defects are no obstacle to this. A true friend will not withdraw his friendship because he knows our defects, if he knows also that we regret them, and that we are seeking his help to fight against them.

Friendship consists in harmony between hearts; it is concord: *con-cordes*. That is what Our Lord asks of us: love, the union of our heart with His. Not to seek this intimacy constitutes for us priests a certain measure of infidelity, and this negligence will leave a great void in our souls.

I. THE SACRAMENTAL ORIGIN OF CHARITY

Christian spirituality, even in its highest form, is the flowering in us of the divine gifts which we received in baptism. I do not apologize for repeating this; it is a doctrine of capital importance.

By this sacrament there is established a mysterious but very real communion between the death and the Resurrection of Christ on the one hand and the soul of the baptized person on the other in which there is produced a spiritual death and resurrection. In fact, the grace proper to the sacrament not only purifies us of original sin, but creates in us a disposition to die to all exaggerated worldly affections and to all the human element in our life which is opposed to the divine. This death to sin is not an end to be pursued for itself; it is an indispensable condition for the full development of our new life in Christ: *viventes autem Deo in Christo Jesu* (Rom 6:11). The Apostle describes it in these terms: "Therefore, if you be risen with Christ, mind the things that are above, not the things that are upon the earth" (Col 3:1–2). In the mystery of Christ, first buried and then triumphantly emerging from the tomb, we have an expressive symbol of this double aspect of baptismal grace. But we must see in it something more than a symbol. Like the Apostle, we must always have faith in the *virtus resurrectionis*. By His Resurrection Christ enters into the fullness of His status as the giver of life: *Resurrexit propter justificationem nostram* (Rom 4:25). Glorified by virtue of the merits which He had acquired by His death, He became the efficient cause producing constantly in the mystical body all the grace of justification and of sanctity: "I am the true vine . . . you are the branches." *Ego sum vitis vera . . . vos palmites* (Jn 15:1, 5).

Although in many Christians baptismal grace may seem to have become inactive, by its very nature it possesses a wonderful dynamism: the power to regulate the whole inner life of man in accordance with God and justice, to orient the soul towards its final supernatural end, to lead it to a life dominated by love. Admittedly this work is not completed all at once and it requires the cooperation of man, but one fact is certain: it is by this gift of charity infused into our souls at baptism along with faith and hope that we are all enabled to love God above all things and to regulate all our actions according to the Gospel.

The little flame of love which lives in us is not born of our natural dispositions; to think so would be to lose sight of the fact that charity is a part of those excellent gifts granted by God to His children of adoption. Its entry into the soul is supernatural.

We must look at it in this perspective: it comes from God and it makes us like to Him. *Deus caritas est* (1 Jn 4:8). "The life of God is love." The Father engenders His Word and He contemplates Him in the spirit of love. The Son likewise contemplates the Father, and the Holy Spirit proceeds from Their mutual love.

By the exercise of charity our life here on earth reflects ever more faithfully the divine life; "the charity of God is poured forth in our hearts by the Holy Spirit Who is given to us": *Caritas Dei diffusa est in cordibus nostris per Spiritum Sanctum qui datus est nobis* (Rom 5:5).

In our priestly life, which is entirely consecrated to God and to souls, our hearts must be the focus of an immense love which will raise us above the passing influences of the impressions of our senses. Apart from the actual administration of the sacraments, we can only reach souls in so far as we love them supernaturally. How, indeed, could we communicate God to others if we did not ourselves participate in that which God is in His essence—love? Our charity must be derived from this divine source, it must be supernatural, virile, enlightened; it must be founded on faith and on the Scriptures and be as solid as they are.

II. THE PREEMINENCE OF CHARITY

In order to understand more fully the role of the love of God in the spiritual life we must ask ourselves the question: What is the rightful place of charity in the edifice of Christian and priestly perfection? As you know, the theological virtue of charity has as its object the supreme and infinite goodness existing in the Father, the Son and the Holy Spirit. In heaven this goodness constitutes the beatitude of the angels and the saints. Here on earth we must tend towards it by loving it for its own sake, above everything else without limit. It is revealed and communicated to the faithful by Jesus Christ. It is through Him, as head of the mystical body, that access to the bosom of the Father is granted to us. This charity is, therefore, the most excellent and the most valuable of the gifts which are derived from our divine adoption. How highly we should appreciate this capacity to love God with a filial love!

Consider Jesus: His interior life was animated by an overflowing love; the object of this charity was firstly His Father and then, in Him and for Him, all mankind. We know that His devotion and His life of obedience were wholly inspired by love. Has He not declared that He did always the things that pleased the Father? (Jn 8:29). Was not His Passion simply the supreme testimony to the world of His love of the Father? *Ut cognoscat mundus quia diligo Patrem* (Jn 14:31).

It is our destiny to imitate Christ by a complete consecration of ourselves to the glory of His Father. It is for this reason that St. Thomas, in his treatise *The perfection of the Christian life*, places sanctity, not in mortification nor in prayer, but in charity. Similarly, St. Francis de Sales writes: "Everyone conceives a perfection for himself according to his own idea; for some it consists in austerity of life, for others in the giving of alms, others again seek it in the frequentation of the sacraments. For my part, I know no perfection other than to love God with one's whole heart and one's neighbour as oneself." [1]

Why is it that charity possesses so eminent a dignity? First of all the act of charity is the movement of the will towards God to take its pleasure in Him and because of Him. This act is by its nature supremely unifying: *Amor est vis unitiva*. [2] It alone achieves

[1] André Hamon, *Vie* 7, 5.

[2] Pseudo-Dionysius, *Nomina Divina* 9.

the affective union of the soul with the infinite goodness. Moreover, as the will is the dominant faculty in man, it holds supremacy and sets the other faculties in motion. All our conscious and deliberate activity depends on its orders. When, in a transport of charity, the will gives itself to God, not only is it united to Him itself, but it brings to Him everything that is under its dominion. That is why it is the form of all the virtues: under its influence the exercise of them becomes an act of homage and love, and merits eternal life.

The first and the most important of all the precepts is that of charity: *Diliges Dominum Deum tuam ex toto corde . . . Hoc est maximum et primum mandatum* (Mt 22:37, 38).

So, by his consecration to love, the priest, like Jesus, dedicates all his energies, and all the movements of his soul and of his heart to the glory of the Father.

It is, therefore, the eminent prerogative of charity to elevate to God all the activity of the virtues.[3] However, it is worthy of note that, by a marvellous reciprocity, the other theological virtues and the moral virtues cooperate in the growth of charity and its domination within us. Were it not for the opposition exercised by the contrary virtues, the desires of the flesh, pride, vanity, and worldly affections, would not take long to check the impetus of charity and destroy its supremacy. It is important, therefore, that habits of prudence, of order, punctuality, justice, chastity, fortitude, patience, and perseverance, should assist in the maintenance and development of love.

If we allow defects of which we are conscious to remain in our hearts they will lead us into innumerable faults and by this they will restrict or even extinguish the radiation of charity in our lives.

We must carry out this work of interior reform much more for the love of God and of our neighbour than from any anxiety

---

[3] Religion refers to God the exercise of the other virtues as an act of homage of our servitude due to the Lord on account of His sovereignty; cf. above, p. 149. Charity refers this same exercise of the virtues to God, but as a tribute to love. So great is its joy in the supreme goodness and its desire to conform to the divine will that it stimulates man to practise all the virtues so as to find in their exercise a means of constant and disinterested union with God.

for our own perfection. We must correct our defects, not in the desire to carve out within ourselves a beautiful personality but, above all, to please God, to conform to His holy will, and to allow charity to have complete dominion in our hearts.

I have only one piece of advice to give to help you to increase your love for God: compel yourself, but in a spirit of peace and without any exhaustion of soul, to bring to every action as pure and as definite an intention as possible; "that the name of God may be sanctified, that His kingdom may come, that His will may be done". In this way, says the Apostle, your conduct will be worthy of the Lord and capable of pleasing Him in all things: all your good works will bear fruit (Col 1:10).

The capital importance of charity will appear still more clearly if we recall certain great theological truths the ensemble of which constitutes the essential doctrine of the supernatural life. Sanctifying grace exalts the soul; it makes it God-like, the habitation of the Blessed Trinity.

The theological virtues go with sanctifying grace, they enable the Christian to act in accordance with the supernatural state to which he has been raised; they establish an active and filial communion of the soul with God. By virtue of them, man assumes the correct attitude in the presence of the Lord when He reveals Himself (faith)—when He offers Himself as our eternal beatitude (hope)—and when He communicates Himself to us as the supreme Good which is loved for Itself (charity).

Moreover, charity contains in embryo, in a certain way, all the infused moral virtues: "Just as the many branches of a tree spring from the one root," says St. Gregory, "so the different virtues are born of charity": *Multae virtutes ex una caritate generantur.*[4]

With charity and the virtues God places in us also the gifts of the Holy Spirit. These are permanent dispositions which adapt the soul to answer readily to the inspirations of heaven. All this ensemble of grace finds its consummation in the fruits of the Holy Spirit. These appear in the soul when the habits of a holy

---

[4] *Homil. 27 in Evangel.*, PL 76, 1205.

life reach their maturity; they manifest the harmonious and perfect development of the different virtues now in their flood.
Outstanding among these fruits are peace and spiritual joy, condescension, and meekness.

This supernatural development is human in its expression but
divine in its origin. From within, grace exalts nature and its
activities. We must always see Jesus Christ as the source of this
divine life.

Finally, the degree of habitual charity acquired by the merit
of our whole life will determine, at the moment of our death,
our degree of heavenly glory. That same charity with which we
love God here on earth will be the inspiration of our eternal
union and our eternal beatitude. We must be watchful therefore
that the flame of love burns ever brightly in our hearts. In the
evening of our life it will be a bitter reflection for the Christian,
and especially for the priest, to think that he has possessed such
supernatural riches and has profited so little by them.

III. THE DOUBLE ASPECT OF CHARITY

(*Affective and Effective*)

We come now to the actual exercise of the virtue of charity. As
you know, there are two different ways of exercising charity; the
one is affective, the other effective. Far from being mutually
exclusive, these two forms of love are correlated, support and
complete each other. True charity, from which our merits
spring, includes both of them. Affective love is the first movement of the soul directed towards its own good.

When, through the eyes of faith, the divinity appears to us as
supremely worthy of our love, our latent charity is aroused towards God, and the soul embraces the desire of union. This supernatural charity is, in fact, a seed placed in the depths of the
Christian heart by baptism. Thanks to it, man finds his delight in
the Sovereign Goodness. He yearns towards it and seeks to please
it. These interior movements are the acts of affective love.

In his masterly treatise on the love of God, St. Francis de

Sales insists especially on three of these acts: delight in the divine perfections; warmth of heart which makes us wish to praise the Lord, to serve Him, and to work for His glory; and finally, the love of conformity which makes us accept in a spirit of perfect self-sacrifice all that God wishes or expects of us. These acts are essentially disinterested; we accomplish them without any thought of our own advantage "out of pure affection for God": *Caritas amicitia quaedam est hominis ad Deum,*[5] says St. Thomas. We have excellent examples of this kind of act of affective charity in the formula for an act of charity given in the Catechism, in the first petitions of the Our Father, in the preface of the Mass, the invocation *Deus meus et omnia* and in many ejaculatory prayers drawn from the Psalms or elsewhere. Remember, however, that while loving God by pure charity, we can and indeed must desire Him also by the theological virtue of hope inasmuch as God is our special good and inasmuch as He beatifies and fully satisfies the soul: *Tunc me de te satiabis satietate mirifica.*[6] In practice, we must express to God at one time our charity of pure love and at other times our love founded in hope; these sentiments are supremely pleasing to Him; they wipe out our venial faults, keep us united with the divinity and augment our merits.

Happy is the soul who, in time of recollection, feels these profound desires of love awakening in it.

Great as is the utility of our acts of affective love, we must couple with them acts of effective charity. These alone can guarantee the sincerity, the potency, the value, of the movements and the aspirations of our souls. St. Gregory expresses this concisely and strikingly: "The proof of our love is the evidence of our works": *Probatio dilectionis exhibitio est operis.*[7] In this, the great Doctor is merely echoing the lesson of the Gospel: "If anyone love Me, he will keep My word" (Jn 14:23). Let us consider the degrees of this effective charity. The first is to carry out the divine will as it is manifested in the ten command-

---

[5] *Summa*, II-II, q. 23, a. 1.
[6] Missal, preparation for Mass, Saturday.
[7] *Homil.* 30 *in Evangel.*, PL 76, 1220.

ments. The bishop asks this of us on the day of our ordination: *Decalogum legis custodientes.* This practical submission to the divine law is necessary in order to enter into the kingdom of heaven. Without it, our sentiments, our prayers, our pious exercises can avail nothing. Our Lord has stated it formally: "Not everyone that saith to me, Lord, Lord, shall enter into the kingdom of heaven, but he that doth the will of my Father Who is in heaven" (Mt 7:21). Now this will is manifested primarily by the ten commandments.

You will think, perhaps, that it is quite unnecessary to recall so elementary a truth. But no! You can see in the Gospel that the Pharisees observed the greater part of the prescriptions of the Mosaic Law, and yet their service was not pleasing to God because they neglected some of the fundamental precepts of the decalogue.

Allowing for the difference of circumstances, it may be the same for the Christian who carries out his exercises of piety with scrupulous exactitude but neglects his duties of justice. How can we be pleasing to the Lord if we are injuring the reputation of our neighbour, if we are getting involved in dishonourable money transactions, and even failing to pay our debts punctually, or if we are not working whole-heartedly at our daily task? It is a good thing to review these commandments from time to time during our period of prayer and to consider whether we are living in accordance with each one of them even in less grave matters, and then, in the spirit of love, to submit ourselves to the whole of the divine will of which they are the expression. This is an excellent exercise for our meditation.[8]

True love does not merely compel observance of the precepts of the decalogue and of the Church, which are binding under pain of sin; it urges us also to embrace the counsels. It would not have us follow them in the same way as religious, but according to our state in life. These counsels are matters of free choice; because they remove from our path the principal ob-

---

[8] As regards the avoidance of venial sin, see above, pp. 99–102.

stacles of the full development of charity they are of inestimable value for our spiritual progress. They tend to establish us in a higher degree of divine charity and to make us more pleasing to God.

At your ordination you accepted special obligations, you undertook great sacrifices, so that you might become, through your priestly consecration, perfect disciples of Christ. These renunciations which you have accepted can make you truly holy provided that you observe the obligations which they involve in a spirit of love, and not from mere routine. By your elevation to the priesthood you renounced first of all a great measure of your personal independence. You promised obedience to your bishop. You agreed to accept his orders and directions as manifesting the divine will in your regard. If you remain faithful to this attitude all your life; this submission will be a powerful means of sanctification for you personally and an important element in the fruitfulness of your ministry.

You freely accepted the obligations of chastity. You are therefore wholly consecrated to Jesus Christ. Did you not say to Him: "My Jesus, I want to love you with my whole heart, without any reservation, I renounce for my whole life all engrossing love but Yours. I shall love my neighbour for You and in You." This is a generous and an admirable sacrifice. A promise made to a fellow-man is a matter of grave importance, but an engagement undertaken to God is sacred. It is an act of worship, an inviolable religious act. Since we have renounced for the love of Jesus the legitimate joy of founding a home, we must not now think with regret of this form of life. Such regrets could be dangerous. It is a good practice to renew constantly before God this consecration of your chastity. When we do this in the midst of temptations and in face of the resistance to our nature, we give God a voluntary testimony of our fidelity and receive strength for the future.

You have made a vow of chastity, you have promised obedience; you have made neither vow nor promise of poverty. Still, one cannot entirely ignore this evangelical counsel. The material conditions of life differ from one district to another, and one cannot establish rules of general application. But, without any fear of going too far, I may remind you to be on your guard against two tendencies, both of which are inconsistent with our ideal.

First of all, we must not admit into our hearts an excessive or too constant preoccupation about the emoluments attached to our ministry; we must be strict in banishing from our souls every element of cupidity. Nothing is more calculated to sadden, even to shock, the faithful than the recognition of this spirit in their priest. We must be careful, too, not to be dominated by the desire for comfort and ease.

As for the great number of priests who live modestly, even austerely, their merit is great before God. Bethlehem, Nazareth, and Calvary furnish eloquent lessons in this regard and teach us that such priests are approximating more and more closely to the divine model.

The formula of St. Paul: "I know how to be brought low, and I know how to abound": *Scio . . . et satiari et esurire et abundare et penuriam pati* (Phil 4:12), expresses the attitude which the priest must be able to adopt according to circumstances. This practical knowledge of the Apostle was assuredly a virtue.

As I have already suggested, it is an excellent exercise of charity to obey the commandments for the sake of love and to practise the counsels. Still, if we wish to attain the perfection of this divine virtue, there remains a higher degree to which we must ascend: the state of holy abandonment. What do we mean by this?

A complete abandonment of oneself to God by the confident and loving acceptance of all His hidden designs in our regard; the surrender of oneself to the divine good pleasure, not merely as regards the pains of the moment, but for all the uncertainties of the future.

This state of soul—it is the culmination of love—supposes a lively faith and unlimited hope in the goodness of God, Whose wisdom arranges all the incidents of our life the better to lead us to Him.

For who is there who can know for certain what is to his best advantage in the supernatural sphere? Do we always appreciate the value of failure, of trials, of suffering, to purify us, to en-lighten us, to unite us to God? He alone can see the soul with a clearness which is incomparable; He alone knows how to heal it, to liberate it, to strengthen it, and to help it on its journey. By holy abandonment man accepts his daily life with its annoy-ances, its difficulties and its misfortune, *Dominus est*,[9] and also his future as Providence has arranged it; he embraces with the most complete confidence the unknown which awaits him, in-cluding the time and the circumstances of his death. By this, he glorifies God in His power, in His wisdom, and in His love; by this also, he draws closer the bonds which unite him to the heavenly Father. You understand, therefore, that in the spiritual life holy abandonment is the climax; without it, charity could not elevate us to the point of a complete and absolute gift of ourselves.

We should like to repeat with the Psalmist: "The Lord ruleth me and I shall want nothing . . . for though I should walk in the midst of the shadow of death, I will fear no evil, for Thou art with me" (Ps 23[22]:1, 4).

IV. OUR LOVE OF CHRIST

Our spirit of religion depends in great measure on the concept which we habitually form of God. This concept is the key of our spiritual life; it controls our attitude in all our relations with the supernatural. This is an ascetic principle of the greatest im-portance.

In the absolute transcendence of His unity, the divinity con-tains radically every perfection. But while in God all the gran-deurs exist, unified and in an infinite degree, it is not so in our

---

[9] In 1912, Dom Marmion was received in private audience by the Sovereign Pontiff, Pius X. At the end of the interview he asked the Holy Father to be good enough to give him, as he put it, "a text for his soul". Pius X thought for a moment; then, taking a picture, he wrote on the back of it: *In cunctis rerum angustiis, hoc cogita; Dominus est, et Deus erit tibi adjutor fortis*: "In all times of difficulty, think of this; it is the Lord, and the Lord will be your powerful helper." Dom Marmion often meditated on this text; we can perceive the echo of it in his spiritual notes and in his letters.

minds. We envisage God under different successive aspects. So, in the practice of religion, men, when considering God, confine themselves to one or other of His perfections.

Under the Old Law, God revealed Himself to the Israelites mainly in the thunder and the lightning of Sinai; He was a master to be feared, a Lord to be adored, prostrate on the ground, a dread Judge. "The Hebrews had received," as St. Paul says, "the spirit of bondage in fear" (Rom 8:15). Some Christians of little fervour may see in God only an Almighty Being able, now to punish them, now to fulfil all their desires. They serve Him, therefore, in the hope of avoiding hell or of receiving His gifts. This is an imperfect form of spiritual life.

One may also regard the Lord as being, above all, a God of love, and serve Him with a free heart from pure charity or friendship. So, in the New Testament, Christ leads us to consider God in His paternal goodness; the spirit which He communicates to us is not one of fear but "the spirit of adoption of sons, whereby we say: 'Abba, Father'": *Spiritum adoptionis in quo clamamus: Abba, Pater* (Rom 7:15). Whereas in the Old Testament they called God, the Lord, the God of Vengeance, the Christian calls Him, "Our Father, the good God, infinite Love".

However, this beauty, this goodness, so pure and so transcendent, which will ravish us for all eternity, are so far above our understanding that to many souls they seem incapable of arousing love: on these heights union with God seems to be something cold, and charity seems to have no warmth. One must have undergone those profound purifications of which St. John of the Cross speaks, and have lived with fidelity in the dark night of the senses and of the soul to be able to attain the repose of love in this divine mystery. In truth, the love of God is as incomprehensible as the divinity itself, for there are no limits to that truth: "God is charity": *Deus caritas est* (1 Jn 4:8). Our Lord, knowing us for what we are, came to us in His mercy; He came down into our valleys to meet us. The Word by His Incarnation assumed the capacity of human love. He took to Himself a human heart, He wished to love as we love. His heart was touched by the death of His friend, Lazarus; He felt broken by anguish before the Passion; the ingratitude of His disciples overwhelmed Him. On the Cross, pierced by the lance, He showed us the measure of His love. This heart wants our love just as we want to love and to be loved.

One does not need to be a great contemplative to be touched and strengthened by the sight of the love of Our Saviour as it is manifested at Bethlehem, on Calvary, in the Church, and in the sacraments, especially in the Eucharist.

While the charity of the Father appears to us wrapped in mystery, the love of the heart of Jesus manifests itself as something sensible, palpable, bringing comfort to all human miseries. The Lord has willed to give to our weak souls the support and the consolation which they need in order to make their way through the troubles of this life.

We can understand, therefore, why the Church, in order to awaken the love of Christ in the hearts of His children, has proposed to them in accordance with the wishes of her Spouse the devotion of the Sacred Heart.

This devotion is the worship of the Person of the Word Incarnate, considered under the aspect of human love, of which the heart of flesh is the living symbol. As you know, and, by the way, it is a point you should insist on in your preaching, all religious worship must be addressed to the Person. But the heart of Jesus may properly be an object of worship, and of the worship of *latria* which is due to God alone. Why is this? Because, as it is a part of the sacred humanity, it is always hypostatically united to the Word. It is, therefore, in the unity of the divine Person Incarnate that the heart of Christ must be honoured. It is certainly adorable, not for its own sake, but in as much as it is united to the Person of the Word Who has assumed it irrevocably as His own: *Adoratur in se, non tamen propter se, sed propter Personam Verbi*. This theological formula, the form of which is taken from St. John Damascene and St. Thomas,[10] expresses exactly the teaching of the Church on the adoration

[10] *Summa* III, q. 25, a. 2.

due to the humanity of Christ. It is in the same way that we must understand the devotion to the five wounds of Jesus. Our worship is directed to the Person of Our Blessed Saviour considered under the aspect of the sufferings and the love of His Passion. The sacred wounds bear testimony to these sufferings and to this love; they are the living expression of them; that is why we venerate them and why it is legitimate to adore them but always in the unity of the Person of the Son of God.

It is evident that devotion to the heart of Jesus understood in this way is most profitable. By it we are put in contact with a profound truth of our faith, the intimate mystery of the life of Jesus which is all love. The abjection of Bethlehem, the modesty of His public life, the opprobrium of Calvary, the death on the Cross, the gift of the Church and that of the Eucharist appear in us as ineffable marks of love. In the completeness of His mystery, in the plenitude of His perfections, in the whole of His mission, Christ is charity. Everything in His work flows from this charity and brings souls back to love.

We can readily understand, therefore, the cry of St. Paul in face of the revelation of these grandeurs: "The charity of Christ presseth us" (2 Cor 5:14): *Caritas Christi urget nos.* And again: "He loved me and delivered Himself up for me": *Dilexit me et tradidit semetipsum pro me* (Gal 2:20). And again we have this solemn declaration of his loyalty in reply to this gift: "Who then shall separate us from the love of Christ?" (Rom 8:35).

There is another aspect of this devotion to the Sacred Heart of Jesus which we priests must never neglect on account of our work for souls.

By the Incarnation of His Son the Father has manifested to us His merciful charity: *Deus . . . qui dives est in misericordia, propter nimiam caritatem suam qua dilexit nos . . . convivificavit nos in Christo* (Eph 2:4–5).

So subject are we to the world of the senses that we cannot grasp what is divine without seeking support from what is human. And so the Father has appointed that the visible love of Jesus should reveal to us in a perfect manner the depths of His mercy and goodness towards us. Jesus has said to us: "He who sees Me sees the Father": *qui videt me videt et Patrem* (Jn 14:9). He could have said: "He who sees My love sees the love of the Father."

Without losing sight of the immediate and sensible object of this devotion, let us try to discover through the veil of this heart which has been wounded and pierced, the incomprehensible charity of the Father for all mankind: "For God so loved the world as to give His only-begotten Son" (Jn 3:16). This charity of the Father exists also in the Son and in the Holy Spirit: *Ego et Pater unum sumus* (Jn 10:30). The Holy Trinity is an ocean of love of which the human love of the heart of Jesus is the faithful image, the manifestation of it adapted to our weakness.

And what is the reason of this complete conformity between the love which is in God Himself and the love in the heart of Jesus? It is the hypostatic union, that is, the unity of the Person of Our Saviour. By this, through the operation of the Holy Spirit, all the human activities of Christ, and first of all His love, were raised to a perfect conformity with the dignity of the Son of God.

If it is true that the goodness of Jesus towards us is an expression of the eternal divine charity, is it not necessary that this goodness of the Father, the Son and the Holy Spirit should become more and more the object of our love? While we render to Christ love for love, should we not learn also to ascend to the infinite Love, the source from which all the love of Jesus is derived?

It is God's design certainly that we should find our rest in the heart of Christ, but He would have us also go beyond this heart to reach through it and in it, the eternal mystery of love hidden in God Himself. Jesus never ceases to be the Mediator. That is why love for our Saviour teaches us to render homage to the infinite charity, the depths of which are revealed to us through the heart of flesh: "that the Father may be glorified in the Son": *ut glorificetur Pater in Filio* (Jn 14:13).

At Tabor the Father said of Jesus: "This is My beloved Son . . . hear ye Him": *ipsum audite* (Mt 17:5). By these words, the Father commanded us not only to listen with faith to the words of Jesus but also to appreciate the revelation of divine love contained in His gestures. "Whatever the Word Incarnate does," says St. Augustine, "is for us a message, a lesson ": *Factum Verbi verbum nobis est.*[11] In the love which Jesus manifests we must see the true reflection of the eternal charity: the love of Christ is the dazzling revelation of it to the world. It is only the contemplation of the love of Christ on the Cross that can furnish the answer to our disquiet in face of the problem of evil and of human suffering; in spite of all suggestions to the contrary, it alone demonstrates with absolute certitude that God's attitude towards us is one of fathomless love, of the purest mercy.

V. PER IPSUM, CUM IPSO, IN IPSO *

How are we to live united to Christ? The sublime words at the end of the Canon of the Mass suggest the answer.

Per Ipsum. We priests want to belong to God, body and soul, for time and for eternity. We have been consecrated to Him by the sacraments of baptism and holy orders; we are His for ever. But it is important for us to ratify this gift of ourselves every day by a free act of the will. The renewal of this consecration is a great act of love. The offertory of the Mass and our time of thanksgiving are the moments specially suited for the renewal of this act of oblation, for it is through Jesus Christ that it acquires all its value. It is the same for our desire to make reparation, by a life dedicated to the service of Christ, for all the offences committed against the divine goodness. Our love impels us to unite our present sacrifices and labours to the sufferings and expiations of Christ in the past, and it is in virtue of this union that our acts and our efforts satisfy our ingratitudes, for our sins and those of our fellow-men. Here again, it is the Mass which constitutes the most excellent reparation; "Christ is the propitiation for our sins; and not for ours only, but also for those of the whole world" (1 Jn 2:2).

[11] *Tractatus in Joannem* 24, PL 35, 1593.
* This is the doxology after the Eucharistic Prayer: "Through him, with him, in him. . . ."

We shall never fully understand to what an extent this mediation of Jesus supernaturalizes not only our prayer but also our work, our sufferings, and indeed our whole life. Jesus supplements with the immensity of His merits the poverty of ours. We must never lose sight of the fact that His merits are ours, in a much truer sense than those things which we possess in this world, for they are ours for eternity. We have constant access to the treasures of divine grace through the heart of Jesus. We can draw unceasingly upon His riches and receive from them enlightenment and strength. However great our wretchedness, we have always the right in Christ to approach God: *Adeamus ergo cum fiducia ad thronum gratiae ut misericordiam consequamur.* "Let us then with confidence draw near to the throne of grace, that we may receive mercy . . ." (Heb 4:16).

Cum ipso. Although we are full of imperfections and are often a burden to ourselves as well as to others, we are permitted to choose Christ as our friend. He permits it, He wishes it, He invites us to do so. This invitation to the friendship of Jesus comes to us through many channels: through our baptism, our priestly vocation, our daily Mass, the divine presence in the tabernacle. Every page of the Gospel repeats it to us, every liturgical feast renews it.

Did not Jesus walk along with the pilgrims to Emmaus and inflame their hearts? We must have faith that He is by our side as we walk the paths of life which are often so difficult. He is our travelling companion, the friend ever ready to pardon Whose friendship never wavers.

In ipso. These two words are the expression of our union with the mystical body. The whole life of love which is the priest's should be sustained by a very lively faith in this wondrous unity in Christ. When we celebrate our Mass we should remember that we are offering the sacrifice in the bosom of this tremendous unity which is the Church, and that we are praying in her name.

When we administer the sacraments, when we preach, when we carry out any work of charity, we accomplish our apostolic work in union with the chief of this body as faithful dispensers of grace for the benefit of its members.

But holy communion is the most excellent means of living *in Christo*. Through it, the priest unites himself in the full spirit of love to the Saviour: "He that eateth My flesh . . . abideth in Me and I in him" (Jn 6:57). Moreover, after holy communion he continues to live in the radiance of the heart of Jesus, enveloped, as it were, in the atmosphere of His love and of His grace. By remaining constantly united to the Saviour the priest makes the divine gift bear abundant fruit in his soul: "He that abideth in Me and I in him, the same beareth much fruit" (Jn 15:5).

The minister of Christ who has lived and suffered in these dispositions will view the approach of death without anxiety. Having lived in Christ, he will draw his last breath in the arms, on the bosom of Jesus. His death and his sufferings will be united to those of Christ and, as it were, taken up in them; the merits of Christ will be his riches and his hope. With Him he will say: "Father, into Thy hands I commend my spirit" (Lk 23:46). Our true joy lies therefore in the constant orientation of our soul towards the supernatural. Solomon, in the luxury of his palaces, had tasted every form of pleasure and had found in them nothing but weariness: "Vanity of vanities" (Eccles 1:2). When the soul yields to some passion for human satisfactions, it soon realizes their worthlessness. Pleasures taken outside of the divine plan produce a feeling of absolute emptiness in the heart. That is why it is in those cities which are called cities of pleasure that men feel most the futility of existence and it is in them that the number of suicides is the highest.

The one deep, durable joy of this life is to be found in union with God. This is true for all men, but it is a thousand times truer for the priest. It is in vain for him to try to quench his thirst for happiness by drinking at other springs; his heart has been consecrated to Christ and can find its rest only in charity. When we possess our Lord it is an affront to Him to regret the satisfactions of the world and to admit vain desires or sadness into our soul; it is as though we were to say to Him: "Lord, you are not enough for me." Jesus is everything for us.

As we were created for happiness, we tend towards it of necessity. We are not in error in seeking it. But we would be gravely in error if we thought to grasp it where we certainly cannot find it. God wishes to be our joy, even here below, and that by a free choice on our part, freely made and constantly renewed.

There are many degrees of love and of sanctity. We must not be content to live a mediocre life. On the contrary, under the influence of the Holy Spirit, may the flame of eternal charity burn ever brighter within us: *Accendat in nobis Dominus ignem sui amoris et flammam aeternae caritatis.*[12]

---

[12] See the personal notes of Dom Marmion, pp. 366–72.

X.

HOC EST PRAECEPTUM MEUM

I. THE ATTITUDE OF JESUS TOWARDS MANKIND:
THE GIFT OF HIMSELF

"From the moment of His birth He gave Himself to us as a friend; at the Last Supper He gave Himself as our food; by His death He ransomed us; in His kingdom He gives Himself as our reward": *Se nascens dedit socium, convescens in edulium, se moriens in pretium, se regnans dat in praemium.*[1] Note how the phrase, *se dedit—se dat,* recurs again and again, either expressed or understood, in this text of the liturgy. It is because this phrase expresses perfectly the whole attitude of Jesus towards mankind during His life on earth and even still at the present time from heaven. Jesus gives Himself and continues to give Himself unceasingly; He bestows Himself without reserve; He dedicates Himself to us; and always and at all times He does so in the fullness of love. From the moment of His entry into the world, the Shepherds, the Magi, the aged Simeon, understood that He was there for them. To His Apostles, to the sick, to the crowds in Galilee, Jesus appeared even more clearly as not belonging to Himself. Was He not sent among men in order to be the Shepherd Who gives His life for His sheep? Was not the baptism which He had come to receive amongst us and for which He longed, an absolute offering of Himself carried to the point of the shedding of the last drop of His blood? *Baptismo habeo baptizari, et quomodo coarctor usque dum perficiatur* (Lk 12:50). In his Passion Jesus delivered Himself up in a fervour of love. The *Crucifixus etiam pro nobis* of the Credo is the echo of a *pro nobis* in His heart which was unhesitating. St. Bernard, with divine enlightenment, sums up this mystery of the giving of Jesus to

---

[1] Hymn: *Verbum Supernum.*

mankind in these words: "He made an absolute total gift of Himself to me and spent Himself entirely for my good": *Totus siquidem mihi datus et totus in meos usus expensus.*[2]

But, as you know well, this communication of love is continued in the bosom of the Church. And it is you, as priests of Christ, who are the delegated ministers of this communication. You have been selected by your ordination to give Christ to the world. That is the purpose of your priesthood: *sacerdos* means "one who gives sacred things". And what is more sacred than Jesus Christ?

Our beloved Saviour had at all times a double love in His heart: the one was directed towards the Father Whose will He always did; the other embraced mankind. That is why Christ, in the Mass, first offers Himself for the glory of the Father; that is the primary object of the sacrifice. But then He gives Himself to all mankind as their food. He gives Himself to the good, to those who live in the rut of routine, to the tepid, even to the wicked: *sumunt boni, sumunt mali.*

He turns no one away; *accipite et comedite* (Mt 26:26). By this love He perpetuates in His mystical body this complete gift of self which is the consummation of His mission of redemption.

We are pleasing to God in proportion to our resemblance to His Son, Jesus. Christ offers Himself to His priests as a perfect model of charity, especially in His sacrifice. When the priest leaves the altar he should be ready to give himself unreservedly to men after the example of his divine Master. Please God, he will consecrate to their service his time, his strength, his life, and by the gift of himself allow himself also to be consumed by them.

As we are sharing with Christ the *cura animarum*, must we not develop a sense of our responsibility for the sheepfold of Christ? Whether you are a curate, a parish priest or a professor, a religious superior or a bishop, you must forget yourself and, like the good shepherd, give yourself unceasingly. In this way your life will be extremely agreeable to God.

---

[2] *Sermo* 3 *In Circumcisione*, PL 183, 138.

The zeal of St. Paul is an example for us. What is the source of the Apostle's ardour? It is Christ's love for him. "The charity of Christ presseth us": *Caritas Christi urget nos* (2 Cor 5:14).

The consideration of this giving of self by the Saviour made it impossible for him to go on living for his own selfish interests and compelled him, as it were, to live "not for himself but unto Him Who died for him and rose again" (2 Cor 5:15).

In a magnificent outburst he exclaims: *libentissime impendam et superimpendar ipse*: "I most gladly will spend and be spent myself for your souls" (2 Cor 12:15).

On the day of your ordination Christ chose you: *Ego elegi vos*, and for what? That you might bear fruit: *ut fructum afferatis* (Jn 15:16). If a priest is not filled with an ardent desire to draw souls to God, if he is busy only about his own affairs, he is not on the right path. Had he remained a layman, he could have devoted himself to learning, to public affairs, or to his private work without worrying about making his life useful to souls; but now that he is a priest, *pro hominibus constitutus in iis quae sunt ad Deum*: "appointed to act on behalf of men in relation to God" (Heb 5:1), he exists only to raise up men to God, to give Jesus Christ to them, and all his zeal must be directed to this end.

II. CHARITY IS BORN OF GOD

The love of one's neighbour as it appears in the New Testament springs from a virtue of the supernatural order—charity.

It has two important characteristics: firstly, it is a gift of God, a participation in His own charity towards us; secondly, in the practice of this love of our neighbour we do not stop at the man but attain to Christ through him: it is He Himself Who is the special object of our love in each of His members. The first of these characteristics is the theme of one of the most excellent passages in the teaching of St. John: "Dearly beloved, let us love one another, for charity is of God. And everyone that loveth is born of God and knoweth God" (1 Jn 4:7). According to the Apostle, charity is given to us by a divine communication;

when born in the soul, it unites it to God and renders it like to Him. He says again: "God is charity; and he that abideth in charity abideth in God, and God in him" (1 Jn 4:16).

So close is the connection between the love of God and the love of our neighbour that it is the same commandment which prescribes both: "and this commandment we have from God that He who loveth God, love also his brother": *Hoc mandatum habemus a Deo ut qui diligit Deum diligat et fratrem suum* (1 Jn 4:21). Love of one's neighbour forms therefore part of the very precept of charity.

Theology expresses this truth in technical language when it asserts that the one virtue of charity, *unico habitu*, is sufficient to make the Christian capable of exercising supernatural love towards God and towards his neighbour.

This is possible because, being united to God, the soul of necessity conforms to Him; it adopts therefore the same attitude towards its neighbour as He does. It will love others because God loves them and as God loves them, desiring to see them glorify the Lord and find in Him their beatitude according to the divine plan.

Christian charity differs profoundly from any form of natural philanthropy. The latter may undoubtedly be beneficial and worthy of praise, but it does not love its neighbour in order to lead him to God nor as God loves him: *sicut dilexi vos*. It is limited to this life, while charity looks to eternity.

Philanthropy does not go beyond the purely human point of view and motive. True charity, on the other hand, is entirely supernatural. Embracing in its scope God and our neighbours, the same movement which draws the soul towards the infinite Goodness inclines it also to generosity and loving devotion towards men. That is why St. John adds: "If any man say 'I love God' and he hateth his brother, he is a liar": *mendax est* (1 Jn 4:20).

As against the law of retaliation, Jesus inclines souls towards the fullness of kindness. "If one strike thee on thy right cheek, turn to him also the other; if a man take away thy coat, let go thy cloak also with him. And whosoever will force thee one mile, go with him another two" (Mt 5:39–42). This ideal is so exclusively characteristic of the New Law that Jesus calls charity towards one's neighbour "His commandment": *Hoc est praeceptum meum* (Jn 15:12). It is the sign by which His disciples will be clearly recognized: *in hoc cognoscent omnes quia discipuli mei estis, si dilectionem habueritis ad invicem* (Jn 13:35).

Where shall we seek the standard, the perfect model, of this love? In the heart of Christ. In Jesus the plenitude of His charity towards men was manifestly derived from His love of the Father: *quia tui sunt* (Jn 17:9). The human will of our beloved Saviour was perfectly united to the unchangeable act of eternal love by which God in His goodness loves men: "For God so loved the world as to give His only begotten Son" (Jn 3:16). The charity of the Heart of Jesus towards us has its source, its motive and its end in God himself.

Moreover, Jesus has carried His devotion even to excess. What excess? The giving of His life: "He hath laid down His life for us and we ought to lay down our lives for the brethren" (1 Jn 3:6).

Here again, the love of Christ for men is for us an example of the charity in our souls which is derived from God, and we may be quite sure that the heart of Jesus is burning with the desire to communicate a spark of His own love to the hearts of His priests.

It is only the heart which can touch hearts. We can influence souls in proportion to our love for them. This is the explanation of the astonishing fact that one sometimes meets priests who are scrupulous in carrying out their religious exercises but whose ministry remains more or less unfruitful. If one turns to them in moments of distress, one finds a brain and a way of life which are conscientious, but no greatness, no openness of heart. All souls, but especially those who are overwhelmed by suffering and by labour, have a right to expect in their priest an echo of their own grief. He must have, therefore, in his priestly heart this fire, this love, this zeal which brings souls to Jesus Christ. What is zeal? It is the movement of love but intensified to the point of making the soul capable of drawing others after it.

Such must be the ardour of our charity: we must eagerly desire to see the kingdom of God established in souls and in society: then we shall find the words which bring comfort, we shall combat sin, we shall accept trouble, weariness, and self-sacrifice.

III. THE LOVE OF CHRIST IN OUR NEIGHBOUR

The second characteristic of Christian charity is still more admirable; it arouses prodigies of devotion in the saints. Christ identifies Himself with our neighbours so that He is loved and served in them. This is the splendid truth proposed to our faith.

From the moment of the Incarnation, Christ identifies Himself with each one of us. St. Paul constantly repeats this truth: "you are the body of Christ, and members of member": *Vos estis corpus Christi et membra de membro*, and again: "For no man ever hated his own flesh; but nourisheth it and cherisheth it as also Christ doth the Church; because we are members of His body, of His flesh and of His bones" (Eph 5:29–30). If we are a part of His flesh and His bones does not this mean that we are truly one with Him? The Father sees us in His Son as members of His body; that is why He shows us mercy and bestows on us the riches of His grace. When God grants us pardon, draws us to Him, sanctifies us, it is really towards His Son that He is exercising His immeasurable goodness.

What is the practical effect for us of this identification with Christ? It is this: when we devote ourselves to the service of each other, it is Christ Whom we love and serve in His members. This is how we look on things in our daily life: whatever one does to a person's members one does to him; if I have a sore finger and you dress it, it is on me, on my person, that you bestow your care because my finger is part of my flesh. The same applies to the members of Christ; they are one with Him. Christ has united them to Himself and He says to us: "All that you do for your brethren you do for Me." God has established this law in His love for us and we cannot presume to change it. On the day of Judgement the final sentence will be pronounced in accordance with the manner in which we have observed or have not observed the precept of charity towards our neighbour. What will be the form of this solemn verdict, which will be pronounced by Christ Himself? "Come, ye blessed of my Father. . . . I was hungry and you gave me to eat." And the just will answer in surprise, "Lord, when did we see you in this need?" And He will answer: "As long as you did it to one of these my least brethren you did it to Me." To the wicked, the Judge will say: "Depart from Me, you cursed." "Why? Is it for not having prayed, for not having fasted? " "No, it is because I was hungry, I was thirsty, I was sorrowful and abandoned, and you did not come to My aid—as long as you did it not to one of these least, neither did you do it to Me" (Mt 25:34–45). You will ask perhaps: "Are there not other commandments to be observed in order to ensure our salvation? " Certainly, but their fulfilment will be of no avail if we have not accomplished the great precept of charity towards our neighbour. That is why St. Paul could write: "For all the law is fulfilled in one word: Thou shalt love thy neighbour as thyself": *Omnis lex in uno sermone impletur* (Gal 5:14).

We cannot regard as a mere empty formula this identification of Jesus with the suffering members of His mystical body. It expresses a reality which is full of meaning, pregnant with enthusiasm, creative of charity; it means that we must do everything for our neighbour as though he were Jesus Christ in person.

The saints filled their lives with love because they believed in the mystery of this sacred substitution. According to the mind of St. Benedict, for example, we obey Christ in the person of the Abbot; it is to Christ we give comfort by our care for the sick, it is Him we serve by devoting ourselves to others; the marks of respect shown in the reception of guests is an act of worship to Jesus as pilgrim.[3]

According to this same viewpoint of faith, we must be able to pardon our enemies. St. John Gualbert before his conversion was a proud knight from the neighbourhood of Florence. On

---

[3] Rule, *passim.*

Good Friday, he meets in a narrow path the murderer of his
brother. The first impulse of his heart is to fling himself on his
enemy and take vengeance. But the guilty one throws himself
on his knees in the middle of the path and, stretching out his
arms in the form of a cross, he implores pardon in the name of
the Crucified One. The future saint pauses; he sees the image of
Jesus Christ in this criminal. He is overcome by grace; getting
down from his horse he embraces his enemy and accepts him as
his brother for the love of Jesus. Deeply moved by his own
action, he goes into a neighbouring church and, while praying
at the feet of the crucifix, he sees Christ bow his head towards
him as a sign of great love.

It is therefore no fiction but a profound reality to say that
Christ identifies Himself with each of His members. He inspires them with supernatural life which is simply His own personal life, the life of sanctifying grace and charity. The members
of His body are united to Him like the branches to the vine in
one whole.

As priests, we enjoy the wonderful privilege of holding
Christ in our hands at the altar, but if we entertain feelings of
coldness or of rancour towards our neighbour is it not against
Christ Himself that our ill-feeling is directed? "How can you
avoid sinning against Christ," says St. Augustine, "you, who sin
against one of His members?" *Quomodo non peccas in Christum
qui peccas in membrum Christi.*[4] For the love of Christ we must,
before celebrating, forget all considerations of susceptibility and
self-love; we must put out of our hearts all deliberate animosity;
we must forgive everyone. Jesus Himself has given us the command: "If thou remember that thy brother hath anything
against thee, leave there thy offering before the altar and go first
to be reconciled to thy brother" (Mt 5:24). It is as though He
said: "First put your relations with your fellow-men in good
order, and then come and offer sacrifice to Me." On the other
hand, do not look for human gratitude; be good to others without expecting anything in return. If your charity extends to all

⁴ *Sermo* 83, 3; PL 38, 508.

men, Christ will be in your debt. He will give you credit for all that you do to His members as though it were done to Himself. And because He is infinite wealth, He will pay the debt munificently; He is not a haggler. He will overwhelm you with blessings. "Give," says the Gospel, "and it shall be given unto you, good measure and pressed down and shaken together and running over shall they give into your bosom": *Date et dabitur vobis; mensuram bonam et confertam et coagitatam et supereffluentem dabunt in sinum vestrum* (Lk 6:38).

IV. THE MARKS OF TRUE CHARITY

St. Paul describes the marks of true charity in these words: "Charity is patient, is kind; charity envieth not, dealeth not perversely, is not puffed up; is not ambitious, seeketh not her own, is not provoked to anger, thinketh not evil; rejoiceth not in iniquity, but rejoiceth with the truth, beareth all things, believeth all things, hopeth all things, endureth all things" (1 Cor 13:4–7).

Let us consider whether we can recognize these marks in ourselves. We receive at the altar Him Who is charity itself. This contact with the divine should free our souls, more and more every day, from all human egoism.

True charity, according to the Apostle, is patient: *caritas patiens est.*

The first natural inclination of man is to shake off everything which inconveniences him and, if he cannot rid himself of what is troublesome to him, he grumbles or gives way to anger. Charity endures tranquilly adversity, pain, injustice and insult. The greater it is, the greater is its power of endurance. Our beloved Saviour is the sublime model of this patience. When He delivers Himself up for us, they spit in His face, they strike Him, they accuse Him; but like a lamb led to the slaughter, He holds His peace: *Jesus autem tacebat* (Mt 26:63). On the Cross, in the anguish of death, He prays and does not complain.

True patience is accompanied by kindness and meekness of thought, of word, and even of action. Here, too, Jesus is the model. Judas came to betray Him and yet what gentleness in His words: "Friend, whereto art thou come" (Mt 26:50). The executioners crucify Him, and His prayer is one of pardon: "Father, forgive them, for they know not what they do" (Lk 23:34).

When people fail us, even in little things, what are our sentiments? Are we filled with indignation and bitterness? Do we harbour antipathy or rancour?

Patience is very necessary to us in our daily relations with neighbours. When we live together in close contact it is inevitable, even for priests, that often, and sometimes without realizing it, we annoy and irritate each other. St. Augustine has said: "We are mortal men, fragile, weak, bearers of earthen vessels; and these knock against each other." And he adds, "But if the vessels of flesh feel themselves constrained, the wide spaces of charity should put them at their ease": *Si angustiantur vasa carnis, dilatentur spatia caritatis.*[5]

If you were to bring together saints fit for canonization to collaborate in the same work, they would probably be a cause of suffering to each other. We must try therefore, each on his own account, to bear with the faults or even with the simple caprices of others. They, too, will have to bear with ours. Was not Jesus Christ, the most noble and the most sensitive of all men, often tried by these rough fishermen of Galilee during His public life when He was in constant contact, day and night, with the apostles? The disciples were very devoted to their Master but frequently they failed to understand the sense of His words or the sublimity of His actions.

In the exercise of the ministry, we require a great deal of patience: in the confessional, at catechism class, with our parishioners who may be indifferent, lukewarm or even sinners. But we must always have faith in the future, and sow the good seed with patience in the confidence that one day the hour of grace will come.

Benigna est. "If you are kind to those who love you," says

---

[5] *Homil.* 69, *De Verbis Domini*, PL 38, 440.

Jesus, "what reward do you deserve? Pagans also do this" (Lk 6:32). Charity is essentially a source of zeal, it engenders strong, generous action, it wishes to do good to all, even to enemies; it is obliging, benevolent, good towards all men. "The heavenly Father maketh His sun to rise upon the good and the bad" (Mt 5:45). We must act in the same way. To make the sun rise is to bring to all men comfort, efficacious help, and joy; it is to have as good a welcome for the sinner as for the fervent Christian, for the child as for the old man.

During His whole life Jesus showed Himself to be the perfect model of this kindness. Before giving His life for the salvation of men, He gave His heart to each individual. We see in the Gospel how He acted. Parents brought Him their children so that He might lay His hands on them and bless them. The disciples put them away. And Christ gives expression to the tenderness of His heart: "Suffer the little children to come unto me" (Mk 10:14).

Jesus was good to all those who suffered. How many miracles did He accomplish for them! We have not the power to cure the sick as He did, but we can visit them for His sake, we can console them in their suffering and encourage them to supernaturalize their ills.

The good Shepherd knows His flock. He carries the lost sheep on His shoulders. What an example this is to encourage us to know our flock well, to seek out and treat kindly all misery, every straying soul! Men must be able to say of us what St. Peter said of the divine Master: "He went about doing good" (Acts 10:38).

However, while the minister of Christ gives himself to the service of all, he must not forget the order dictated by Christian charity. If he has charge of souls, he will be solicitous firstly for those for whom he is immediately responsible, and among these his first care will be for those souls which are most abandoned and most in need of his help. The observance of this order in the exercise of charity in no way diminishes his true zeal. When Christians see this goodness radiating from the heart of a priest, they turn to him with complete confidence in all the trials of life. As it is popularly said: "One is not afraid to go to him; one can be sure of his complete devotion to duty." Believe me, if people are afraid to ask a service from a priest—faithful to his rule of life, to his meditation and examination of conscience— it is a sign that the great charity of Christ has not yet established its reign in his heart. If we do not open our hearts to our neighbours, we do not open them to Christ.

We practise charity in our works, but also in our thoughts and in our words. Some people are quick to pass an unfavourable judgement on the actions and even on the intentions of their neighbour. We must realize that when we act in this way we are going against the will of God and challenging the privilege of Christ; "The Father hath given all judgement to the Son" (Jn 5:22). It is only the eye of God that can penetrate into the inner depths of the conscience. He alone can judge the part which ignorance, weakness, heredity, sickness and nerves, play in the faults of others; He alone can see the chain of causes which predispose a soul to do wrong. What appears to us a great fault may sometimes, in view of all the circumstances, appear quite differently in the eyes of God.

Even though you may have great powers of perception, do not think that you are capable of forming a just estimate of another's conduct: *Nolite judicare ut non judicemini* (Mt 7:1).

If you wish to escape the severity of the Lord, show mercy to your neighbour. "If an action had a hundred aspects," said St. Francis de Sales, "we should always choose the best one to look at." We must be on our guard therefore not to offend against charity in our judgements.

It may happen, however, that a priest, outside the confessional, may be obliged, in virtue of his office, to express publicly an unfavourable opinion on the conduct of his neighbour. In this case he must do his duty boldly but refrain from judging the intentions of the wrong-doer.

Charity goes beyond human views and human thoughts; hence the excellent formulas of St. Paul: "Charity thinketh not evil, rejoiceth not in iniquity": *Non cogitat malum, non gaudet super iniquitate.* On the contrary, it rejoices in all the good which may befall a neighbour.

Caritas non aemulatur. Charity envieth not. When we see another enjoying some privilege, the natural instinct is to feel unhappy, as though by this we were deprived of something to which we were entitled. Jealousy can lead to the gravest disorders. It was from jealousy that Cain slew Abel, that the brothers of Joseph sold him to strangers. Never allow this vice to take root in your souls. Still, we must not be surprised if slight inclinations of this kind make themselves felt at times in the depths of our souls. It is human, but we must not yield to it. The apostles of Christ sometimes felt envious of each other. St. Luke tells us that before the Last Supper, *facta est contentio inter eos* (Lk 22:24), they were—we must face the word—quarrelling, as to which of them would seem to be the greater.

Charity arouses feelings which are directly contrary to envy; it is not saddened by the success of others, it does not belittle their merit, it does not employ underhand methods to injure them; it does not look on its neighbour as a rival, nor even as a stranger. In the unity of the body of Christ it holds its neighbour as a brother, as another self. That is why the Apostle says: "Who is weak and I am not weak? Who is scandalized and I am not on fire" (2 Cor 11:29). And again: "Rejoice with them that rejoice; weep with them that weep" (Rom 12:15). Such is the sublimity of heart produced by this most excellent of virtues.

Caritas non quaerit quae sua sunt. True charity is unselfish, forgetful of its own interests. The priest must know that he is chosen by God primarily to work for the supernatural interests of his neighbour. In this work he cannot be self-seeking. He must say, like St. Paul: "To the wise and to the unwise I am a debtor" (Rom 1:14).

The better to understand this viewpoint which is characteristic of charity, we may recall the theory of Hobbes. This English philosopher conceived a state of society in which everyone would claim his full rights. There results inevitably from this a state of perpetual war amongst men; everyone sees in his neighbour an enemy who is hindering him in the enjoyment of his desires. This theory is the apotheosis of egoism. It is, however, useful to understand it in order that we may appreciate more fully how charity raises men above the preoccupations of the ego. The queen of the virtues looks beyond the limits of personal interests; she forgets herself in order to think of the good of her neighbour.

When a man lives in this spirit he is not always standing on his rights. He puts in practice the precept of St. Benedict: "No one shall seek what he judges useful for himself but rather what he judges useful for others": *Nullus quod sibi utile judicat: sequatur, sed quod magis alii.* In Ireland, in moments of panic, they cry out as a joke: "Every man for himself and the devil take the hindmost!" We must prefer the saying of the Apostle: "For I wished myself to be an anathema from Christ for my brethren" (Rom 9:3). This saying, far removed from all egoism, expresses the immensity of Christian charity.

Charity is humble: *Non est ambitiosa, non inflatur.* Why? Because it gives itself without glorying in the giving, without drawing attention to it, without even claiming any great merit for it. This devotion, freed from the trammels of vain self-satisfaction, makes Christian charity conform closely to the charity of Jesus.

Right through the life of the divine Master we see His humility in the exercise of His love, but at no moment is it displayed in a more touching manner than before the Last Supper when, humbling Himself before the apostles, the Saviour willed to wash their feet. The priest who imitates this humility of Christ in his ministry does not break the bruised reed, nor quench the smoking flax (Is 42:3). Even when his duty requires him to contradict, to resist, to contest, he will act in a spirit of moderation which only the recollection of his own weakness and the virtue of charity can inspire.

All these tokens of goodness and of love are so many manifestations of a unique and supernatural virtue which Our Saviour introduced into the world. If we practise it as St. Paul has described it, we shall imitate beyond all doubt the pity of Jesus, and by this resemblance, remote as it is, we shall conform to the charity of Christ Himself. In all truth it is for

Him, it is like Him, it is by His grace, that we love our neighbour.

V. CHARITY IN THE MINISTRY OF THE WORD

The priest brings to men the grace of the sacraments and also the doctrine of Jesus Christ: he has received from the Lord the *ministerium verbi* (Acts 20:24), it is his duty to establish in the minds of the faithful the *verba Christi*. In the pulpit, in the confessional, in visiting the sick, in the catechism class, everywhere, even in private conversations, the words which fall from the lips of a priest are of great importance for the raising of the spiritual level of the faithful.

Revelation is a precious deposit of which every priest is in a certain sense in charge. "O Timothy," wrote St. Paul, "keep that which is committed to thy trust, avoiding the profane novelties of words" (1 Tim 6:20). It is incumbent on the minister of Christ to open the minds of the faithful to an understanding of the great and fruitful truths of revelation. *Sacerdotem*, says the Pontifical, *oportet praedicare*.

God has spoken to us through His Son: *Novissime, diebus istis locutus est nobis in Filio* (Heb 1:2). The Word, in Himself, expresses the infinite perfection of the Father, but as man, it is in human language adapted to our puny intelligence that He reveals to us the secrets of this divine life: *Unigenitus Filius qui est in sinu Patris ipse enarravit*: "The only Son, Who is in the bosom of the Father, He has made Him known" (Jn 1:18).

It is through Jesus that the thoughts of the eternal wisdom are made intelligible to our minds: they have been transmitted to the world through the Scriptures and tradition. These words, like the seed of the sower, are bearers of life: *Semen est verbum Dei* (Lk 8:11). "The words that I have spoken to you are spirit and life": *Verba quae ego locutus sum vobis, spiritus et vita sunt* (Jn 6:63).

When the priest proclaims these truths, he does not speak as a private individual. He is an ambassador speaking in the name of the Master: *Pro Christo legatione fungimur* (2 Cor 5:20). He is carrying out the order of Christ Who said: "Going therefore, teach ye all nations" (Mt 28:19). It is the Saviour Who speaks to the Christian people through his lips (Is 51:16). Christ prayed for those who will receive this word (Jn 17:20). Every priest must say with the apostles: "Woe is unto me if I preach not the Gospel": *Vae mihi si non evangelizavero* (1 Cor 9:16).

Protestant pastors preach sometimes with a conviction that is astonishing, but they have no mandate. For us, the duty of bringing the words of God to men is authoritatively imposed: *Deo exhortante per nos* (2 Cor 5:20). Your bishop receives his mandate from the Church; if he commissions you to teach the revealed truths to men, you speak as a divine legate: *Quomodo praedicabunt nisi mittantur?* says St. Paul (Rom 10:15). How can one preach without a supernatural mandate?

As regards the preaching itself, we must consider the brief but very pregnant directives of St. Paul: "Preach the word: be instant in season, out of season; reprove, entreat, rebuke in all patience and doctrine": *Praedica verbum; insta opportune, importune; argue, obsecra, increpa in omni patientia et doctrina* (2 Tim 4:2).

You will certainly not expect from me a detailed analysis of these directives, but let us single out a few points for brief consideration. First of all, the Apostle exclaims: "Preach!" The ministry of the word which the Lord has confided to His priests consists primarily in making known the gospel message and the value of Christian beliefs: *Testificari Evangelium gratiae Dei* (Acts 20:24). In order to fulfil his function the priest will rely on a doctrinal groundwork; this is indispensable. To preach well means at the same time enlightening the minds and touching the hearts of one's hearers.

With this end in view we must try to nourish our minds on Holy Scripture: "For what things soever were written, were written for our learning that through patience and the comfort of the Scriptures we might have hope" (Rom 15:4). I believe that every soul which is sincere in its search for God will find all that it needs in the teaching given by Jesus Christ and the apostles. To preach Christ and the immensity of His graces will always be effective.

Moreover, a solid theological formation is essential if we are to expose the revealed truths in language which is in harmony with the spirit of the Church.

I advise young priests, at least for the first three years, to go to the trouble of writing their sermons.

"Be instant in season and out of season." St. Paul is emphasizing here the unceasing zeal which is required in a true minister of Christ. His conscience must remind him everywhere and at all times of the mission which has been entrusted to him. His ardour must, however, always have the moderation of prudence; in his work for souls the priest must never ignore the dictates of common sense. In some cases it may be better to wait for years until the hour of grace will strike.

"Reprove, rebuke." We are not entitled to remain indifferent to the moral faults of the faithful or to their doctrinal errors. We have an obligation, on occasion, to reproach Christians for their bad conduct and to warn them against dangers to their faith. We must carry out this duty with vigilance, but we must not be one of those who spend the whole time in the pulpit giving voice to their displeasure and abusing everybody. Such men are quite wrong in thinking that they have announced the Gospel. It is the zeal of bitterness which inspires them, and it brings to mind the striking phrase of St. James: "The anger of man worketh not the justice of God" (Jas 1:20). Men who act in this manner are certainly not putting into practice the advice of the Apostle who warns us to preach *in omni patientia*.

"Exhort." The priest must encourage the faithful to do what is good. I cannot delay to describe the different forms which this exhortation may take. Each individual must adapt himself to his audience. We may remark, however, that it is often the personal religious conviction of the minister of Christ which will be the most effective argument with his audience: *Nos credidimus propter quod et loquimur.* "We too believe and so we speak" (2 Cor 4:13). Often it will be necessary for the priest to speak to the people and to beg them to improve their behaviour; it may happen that an urgent request will have more effect than reproaches, even though they be deserved. Finally, there are souls which only kindness can draw to Christ; we must appeal to their integrity of heart.

If the sacred ministry of the word is of such grandeur, we can understand how far removed from their ideal are those whose conversation is marked by bitterness, inclined always to criticism rather than to encouragement. In their zeal some priests devote a lot of time to looking at the black side of things; they are always dissatisfied with someone or something and are ever finding fault, even though it be the legitimate authority that is in question. There is no ill-will on their part, it is a kink, a mania which must be corrected.

The charity of Christ is quite foreign to this tendency, which compromises the supernatural influence of the priest. In the education of youth this spirit of sterile criticism operates to destroy or at least to prejudice that keen animation which is necessary to young people in their approach to life.

At every period of her history reforms have been admitted in the Church. They have been necessitated by the weakness of Christian morals, by errors concerning dogma, by the need of adaptation to new social requirements. In principle, these reorganizations must come from the head and not from the members. The members may suggest and ask for reforms, but it is not for them to take the initiative independently of the established authority. Remember what happened in the sixteenth century. The Church was manifestly in need of reform. Without having received any commission to do so, Luther, Zwingli, Calvin and Melanchthon wanted to change everything. These were not really bad men; Melanchthon, for example, detested the excesses of Luther, and his unquestionable loyalty commands respect. But these movements came from below, and they detached whole nations from the unity of the Church.

Reform was achieved by the Council of Trent. It came from above, proceeding from the head to the members. This is the way that God wants it, and, under the guidance of the Holy Spirit, it produced great fruits.

In our words and in our actions we must try to preserve unity in charity. Everything that causes division, be it in the Church, in the diocese, in the parish or in the community, everything which dissipates energy, should be avoided absolutely, as being opposed to that good zeal which is required of the priest.

Before I close, allow me to remind you of one point which is of the utmost importance. *Nemo dat quod non habet*: "You cannot give what you do not have"; the man who has not interior life himself can never exercise a beneficial influence on souls. We can give to others only the overflow of our own spiritual life, of the abundance of our own religious convictions which we have consolidated in our mental prayer: *Contemplata aliis tradere*, as St. Thomas so excellently expressed it.[6]

On the day of your ordination, the bishop said to you in the name of Christ: *Iam non dicam vos servos . . . vos autem dixi amicos*: "I do not call you servants . . . I have called you friends" (Jn 15:15). If you are the intimate friend of Jesus it must be a joy for you to increase the knowledge and love of Christ in every soul redeemed by His blood. True eloquence springs from truth vividly felt and vividly expressed. Without this profound conviction, without this union with Christ, a man can indulge in great flights of rhetoric: they will tickle the ears of the audience and flatter the vanity of the preacher, but that is all. And why? Because in order to have an effect on souls we must be united to Him Who is the source of all good, and we must work in dependence on Him. We cannot repeat it too often: we are the instrumental causes of grace, and the instrumental cause can only produce its effect in virtue of its union with the principal cause; the brush can produce marvellous results provided it is handled by an artist. The sacred humanity of Jesus was always united to the divinity. In theological language it is called *instrumentum conjunctum divinitati*; we are, of ourselves, instruments *non conjuncta*. That is why we must unite ourselves to Jesus Christ in the spirit of faith and of love so that He may deign to operate through our ministry.

Our mission is supernatural. Even the indifferent and the enemies of the Church cannot help venerating a priest who is

---

[6] *Summa* II-II, q. 188, a. 6. "To contemplate and give to others the fruits of contemplation" (the motto of the Dominican order).

entirely devoted to his work. Think of the Curé d'Ars. He drew thousands of men to him from all sides. Why? Because he was a saint. God chose him to show us how far this supernatural radiation can extend from a priest who is forgetful of himself and lives by divine love.

Finally, we must remember that the act par excellence of priestly charity is a Mass well said. When he is celebrating, the priest must not think of himself alone. He bears in his heart the responsibility of his charge of souls. He must pray for his flock, for his works; for his parish, for his diocese, for the whole Church and, from the chalice of benediction which he consecrates, he will pour out on souls, even those far distant, a flood of merciful grace. On Calvary, Jesus took upon Himself our anguish and our sufferings. He was the Good Shepherd Who gave His life for all His sheep.

At the altar, when he is offering the chalice, the minister of Christ, associated by Him in His work of salvation, must embrace in a great movement of charity the divers needs of the whole human race: *Offerimus tibi, Domine, calicem . . . ut pro nostra et totius mundi salute, cum odore suavitatis ascendat*: "We offer unto Thee, O Lord, the chalice . . . for our salvation and for that of the whole world, rising with a pleasing fragrance."

Part II

_____

THE PATH
TO PRIESTLY SANCTITY

B. *In iis quae sunt ad Deum*

XI.

DO THIS IN MEMORY OF ME

THE task of sanctification progresses in proportion to our application to those virtues which are especially ours. We achieve this application by carrying out the duty of our state as a mediator: by acts of worship and of the spiritual life. This is the teaching of the Apostle: "For every high-priest taken from among men is ordained for men in the things that appertain to God": *Constituitur in iis quae sunt ad Deum* (Heb 5:1).

There is no doubt that these acts are holy in themselves. Do we not say "Holy Mass", "Holy Communion"? And why? Because these actions put us in immediate contact with the source of all sanctity. The same may be said, though in a lesser degree, of the divine Office, of private prayer, and of our ordinary daily actions.

We shall see in the following chapters what are the principal actions which, as ministers of Christ, we are called on to renew every day. We shall be greatly helped in the work of our own perfection by having a deep understanding of their nature and of the supernatural benefit which they can bring us.

In the first rank of *Ea quae sunt ad Deum*, St. Paul places the offering of the sacrifice. And he is right.

The sacrament of holy orders was instituted in order to confer on men the power to consecrate the body and blood of Christ. The purpose of the imposition of hands is the communication of this power. When the priest celebrates the *mysterium fidei*, he is not merely carrying out one of the many functions attached to the high dignity of his state; he is accomplishing the one essential act of that state. This act involves an exercise of power far above that required for any other exercise of his ministry either ritual or pastoral. That is why the whole life of the priest should be an echo or a prolongation of his Mass.[1] It would require an

---

[1] Cf. in *Christ, the Life of the Soul* the chapter "The Eucharistic Sacrifice", and in *Christ in His Mysteries* the chapter "*In Mei memoriam*".

angel rather than a man to discuss the holy sacrifice worthily, and even an angel could not explain all the mysteries of the altar, for it is only God who can comprehend the full value of the immolation of a God. "If we understood what the Mass really is," said the Curé d'Ars, "we would die of love." [2]

Still, it is very useful for us to meditate on the greatness of the Mass: it is the centre of the whole life of the Church and the source of innumerable graces; it is the mystical fountain described by St. John in Revelation whose waters irrigate the heavenly city (Rev 22:1–2).

The effect which these divine mysteries produce in our souls depends in great measure on our faith and our devotion: *quorum tibi fides cognita est et nota devotio.*

In order to enlighten your faith, I shall put before you the Church's teaching, and I shall leave it to your piety to develop these thoughts in your prayer.

When dealing with the sacrifice of the Mass it is better to seek the pure doctrine from authoritative sources rather than to dwell on the personal opinions of theologians. We must never forget that in those matters which depend on His free will God might have conceived an entirely different plan. We must turn to revelation to find out what He has willed, for it alone can make known to us His thought and His designs. In these matters we cannot arrive at any certain knowledge by our own unaided efforts.

Where can we discover what God has revealed? There are two sources available: Scripture and Tradition. It is not always easy to interpret these sources; that is why the Protestants, who rely on private judgement, fall so easily into error. But if the sovereign pontiff or an ecumenical council defines something, we are sure of its truth, for the Church has the guidance of the Holy Spirit. Its teaching is the standard for our faith: *Regula proxima fidei.*

The liturgy also expresses the thought of the spouse of Christ. In her prayer the Church expresses her belief; she indi-

[2] The exact words of the saint are, it seems: "The priest will fully understand himself only when he reaches heaven. . . . If he understood while he was in this world, he would die, not of fear, but of love." *Esprit du Curé d'Ars*, p. 113, quoted by the Abbé Trochu, *Le Curé d'Ars*, p. 110.

cates the true sense of the words of the Scripture and the authentic tradition relating to the Eucharist. In the school of the liturgy we are like little children learning to pray by listening to their mother. This is especially true of the Mass; it is the sun of Christian worship. The formulas and rites in which the Church has enshrined the celebration of the divine sacrifice are supremely efficacious to make us understand its grandeur.

Of all the councils, it is the Council of Trent which established most fully and most precisely the traditional doctrine concerning the sacrifice.

The most important principles laid down by the Council are: The Mass is a true and real sacrifice: *verum et proprium sacrificium*.[3] As against the reformers of the sixteenth century, we must see in it more than a memorial of the Last Supper of Our Lord; nor is it a simple rite of the oblation of Christ hidden under the appearances of the sacred species, nor yet a mere symbolic representation of His death, but a true and real sacrifice.

In the second place, the Mass comprises the same oblation as that of Calvary. The only difference between the two sacrifices is the manner of offering them: "On our altars," the Council declares, "the same Christ becomes present and immolates Himself in an unbloody manner, Who, on the altar of the Cross, offered Himself in a unique sacrifice with the shedding of blood."[4]

The Mass is not a renewal of the redemption, but by this sacramental immolation it perpetuates for all time the offering of this unique sacrifice and applies to us the fruits of it superabundantly: *Oblationis cruentae fructus per hanc incruentam uberrime percipiuntur*.[5]

I. THE NATURE OF SACRIFICE

Sacrifice is an act of religion by which we acknowledge the infinite majesty of God and His supreme dominion over us. God is eternal, omnipotent, the sovereign Master. We are His

[3] Sess. 22, cap. 1.
[4] Sess. 22, cap. 2.
[5] Ibid.

creatures; He has created us out of nothing, and when the hour
of death strikes for us, we shall return to Him in spite of all our
resistance. Truth, order and justice require that we should acknowledge this power of God, the Lord of life and Master of
death, first Beginning and last End of everything.

It is true that the purely interior acts of adoration, of thanksgiving, and of contrition by which man acknowledges his absolute dependence are often, in the Scriptures, called sacrifices in
the wider sense of the term: "A sacrifice to God is an afflicted
spirit" (Ps 51[50]:17). But in the stricter sense, sacrifice is an
external religious act; it is the visible expression of that intimate
homage due to God alone; it is the revealing sign of it. Hence
its importance when worship is being offered to God in common. We may honour the Blessed Virgin, the angels, the saints,
even men, by certain marks of respect, by offerings and gifts.
But there is one supreme religious gesture which testifies the
nothingness of the creature before "Him Who is" (Ex 3:14). It
is the destruction of something in order to signify by this sacred
rite the absolute dominion of the divinity over man. Man, by
his very nature, is impelled to offer this homage to God. This
human act, though shrouded in mystery, symbolizes better than
any other the divine sovereignty. According to the natural law it
is the central act of worship.

In the Mosaic religion there were many different sacrifices
with the shedding of blood. All of them were directed to the
propitiation of God; some of them were expiatory, others were
sacrifices of adoration or of thanksgiving; but all of them were
figures of the sacrifice of the Cross; in themselves these rites
were, in the words of St. Paul, "weak and needy elements"
(Gal 4:9). Like the whole ensemble of the Old Testament, their
chief value lay in this figuration: *Haec omnia in figuris con-
tingebant illis* (1 Cor 10:11). They were only "a shadow of
things to come" (Col 2:17).[6] That is why, when the Hebrews
set out from Egypt, the doors of the houses of Israel had to be
marked with the blood of the paschal lamb and this sign pre-

---

[6] See the pages Dom Marmion has devoted to Symbolism of the two Testaments in
Présence de Dom Marmion (Paris: Desclée, 1948).

served the first-born from death. "Can the blood of an animal save man?" asks St. John Chrysostom. "Yes," he answers, "but only because it symbolizes the blood of Christ." *Valde, non eo quod sanguis est, sed quia Dominici sanguinis per eum monstratur exemplum.*[7]

The Mass also was announced and prefigured by these ancient sacrifices. "It is," says the Council, "their perfection and their consummation": *Velut illorum omnium consummatio et perfectio.*[8] This means that the power of adoration, of propitiation and of thanksgiving proper to the sacrifices of the patriarchs and to the rites of the Mosaic worship is contained in its entirety and in a supereminent way in the mystery of our altars.

II. PROPITIATORY CHARACTER OF THE SACRIFICE OF THE CROSS

In order to understand the grandeur of the Mass, let us take ourselves in spirit to Calvary and assist at the immolation of Jesus.

He is there, hanging on the Cross for love of us. Let us adore in Him the High Priest, holy, innocent, undefiled, separated from sinners (Heb 7:26). He is also the sacred Victim; having become our brother, He has taken our sins upon Himself.

Was this sacrifice truly propitiatory? There is not the least doubt about it. What does this word "propitiatory" mean? A sacrifice is called propitiatory when the attitude of the divinity towards man is changed in virtue of the sacred immolation: from being angry, it becomes favourable, disposed to clemency and to reconciliation.

Consider, for example, in the Old Testament, the description of a memorable sacrifice of propitiation: the sacrifice of Noah after the flood. Genesis tells us that on account of the iniquity of men the Lord had decided to destroy the human race. But Noah was spared with his family. When he came out of the

---

[7] *Homila ad neophytos, Edito Basiliensis,* 1539, V.r. 459.
[8] Sess. 22, cap. 1.

Ark, he constructed an altar of stone and, surrounded by his sons, he offered to the Lord a sacrifice of animals that were clean. And the Scripture tells us that the attitude of God was changed: The Lord smelled a sweet savour and said: "I will no more curse the earth for the sake of man" (Gen 8:21). As a sign of pardon, God made the sun shine, made the rainbow appear, and testified in this manner that He would once more admit His creatures to His friendship (Gen 9:13–20).

This sacrifice of Noah, like those of the Mosaic Law, was only a pale figure of the offering of Our Saviour on the Cross. This was preeminently a true sacrifice of propitiation. It was the immolation of God to God. St. Paul affirms it: "Who, being in the form of God, thought it not robbery to be equal with God but . . . He humbled Himself becoming obedient unto death" (Phil 2:6–8). By His submission and by His love, Christ presented to the Father an entirely adequate satisfaction for the offence caused to His majesty by the disorder of all the iniquities of the world.

This homage, worthy of God, was entirely acceptable, for it had been not only foreseen but planned by the Father in the merciful designs of His wisdom and His goodness. That is why the Apostle could say in all truth: "In Him it hath well pleased the Father that all fullness should dwell and through Him to reconcile all things unto Himself, making peace through the blood of His Cross" (Col 1:19–20). Elsewhere the Apostle says again: "For God indeed was in Christ reconciling the world to Himself": *Deus erat in Christo, mundum reconcilians sibi* (2 Cor 5:19). And: "We were reconciled to God by the death of His Son" (Rom 5:10). Did not Jesus declare at the Last Supper that the shedding of His blood would seal a new and eternal alliance? Thanks to Him, the attitude of God towards us has become, and for all time, one of pardon, of love and of mercy. The sacrifice of the Cross was, therefore, beyond all doubt, a propitiatory sacrifice.[9]

---

[9] See above, pp. 30–31.

III THE MASS—A PROPITIATORY SACRIFICE

The Eucharistic sacrifice is the sacramental continuation of the sacrifice of the Cross. Every time that we celebrate the divine mysteries, we announce the death of the Lord: *Mortem Domini annuntiabitis* (1 Cor 11:26). The Council brings out the full sense of the words of St. Paul: "It is the same Christ Who offers Himself now through the ministry of His priests and Who then offered Himself through His own ministry on the Cross": *Idem nunc offerens sacerdotum ministerio qui seipsum tunc in cruce obtulit.*[10]

If we can grasp the full significance of these words the propitiatory character of the Mass will be clearly manifest to us.

For God there is no past and no future. He possesses in an unchangeable present the whole infinity of His life of knowledge, and of love, and of beatitude. St. Thomas[11] has adopted the illuminating definition of the divine eternity given us by Boethius: *Interminabilis vitae tota simul et perfecta possessio.* This means that God in a *Nunc Stans*, that is to say, in a Now which is above all limits and all succession, possesses perfectly, totally and always "in act" (*tota simul*) the plenitude of a life which knows no beginning and no end. For us there is always a succession of time; existence is meted out to us instant by instant. That is why it is measured by time. But God, in His eternity, embraces in one glance the succession of events which constitute for man the past, the present and the future.

We must realize that, at the consecration, the whole drama of Calvary, with all the consequence of sufferings and humiliations which it involved for Jesus, is present before God. It may be said in all truth that we are displaying before the eyes of the Eternal One all this divine past; that is why the Apostle says so aptly that at every Mass "we announce to the Father the death of His Son".

You remember the story of the brothers of Joseph (Gen 37:31–32). After having plotted his destruction and sold him to

[10] Sess. 12, cap. 2.
[11] *Summa* I, q. 10, a. 1.

strangers, they soaked his cloak in blood and sent it to Jacob, so that it might be a sign to him of the death of his son.

Every time that a priest celebrates Mass, he is not displaying to the Father the garment of Jesus as a proof of His Passion, but presenting the Son Himself under the sacred species making, for love, a true immolation, though in sacramental form.

Let us dwell a little on this thought. What does the Father see on the altar stone on which the holy sacrifice is offered? He sees the body and blood of the Son of His love: *Filius dilectionis suae* (Col 1:13). And what is it that the Son is doing on the altar? *Annuntiat mortem*: He is placing before the eyes of the Father His love, His obedience, His suffering, the oblation of His life. And the Father casts on us a look of mercy.

There are many formulas in our liturgy which express the propitiatory character of the mysteries of the altar. At the offertory, the priest raises the chalice, and what does the prayer of the Church ask for in return for this offering? She asks that by it the Lord may be made favourable to the salvation of the whole world: *Pro nostra et totius mundi salute*. After the consecration, when the body and blood of Christ are on the altar, we beg the Father to deign to look on our sacrifice with a gracious and tranquil countenance: *Propitio ac sereno vultu respicere digneris*.

The whole doctrine is concisely expressed in the prayer *super oblata*: *Propitiare, Domine, populo tuo*: "Look with favour, O Lord, upon Thy people . . . and, appeased by this oblation, mercifully forgive our sins and graciously hear our prayers." [12]

So great was the sanctity of the sacrifice of the Son of God on Calvary and its propitiatory efficacy that the crime of the executioners, their hate and their blasphemies in no way detracted from the value of this sacred oblation, nor prevented the triumph of the redemption. This is true also for the sacrifice of our altars. The Council of Trent declares that no unworthiness, no stain of the ministers can affect it: *Nulla indignitate aut malitia offerentium inquinari potest*. [13]

We should constantly renew our faith in the grandeur of the

[12] Thirteenth Sunday after Pentecost. See also the Secret of the Mass of St. Cecilia.

[13] Sess. 22, cap. 1.

Mass. For many people the important things in this world are financial and industrial questions, matters of business, political events. These things have their value; they form part of our temporal destiny. To the eyes of faith, however, the Mass belongs to an order of values infinitely higher: it gives the fullest glory to God. There are many minds incapable of grasping this truth; they will consider what we say as being exaggerated, but in the next world, when they are face to face with reality, they will understand that the human actions which are truly great are those whose effect survives into eternity.

You hear people speak sometimes with a kind of thoughtless contempt of a priest who "says his little Mass" and can find hardly any useful work to do. And yet, in the eyes of the infallible Truth, this priest accomplishes a divine work simply by the pious celebration of his Mass, even though there be no congregation, for by it he honours the Sovereign Lord and renders Him propitious to the miseries of the whole world.

IV. THE MASS, A SACRIFICE OF PRAISE AND OF THANKSGIVING

As well as being a propitiatory sacrifice, the Mass is an act of praise and of thanksgiving: *Sacrificium laudis et gratiarum actionis.*[14]

The worship of pure praise rendered to God for His own sake involves different acts of homage. Why? Because the Lord is worthy of all adoration, of all benediction, of all thanksgiving. These acts of homage, united to the satisfaction offered by Jesus to the divine justice, constitute the primary object of the sacrifice. That is why, in the liturgy of the Mass, we have so often these acclamations: *Gloria Patri et Filio . . . Adoramus te, glorificamus te . . . Laus tibi, Christe, Deo Gratias.* The reply to the *Orate Fratres* is a clear expression of this object: "May the Lord receive this sacrifice to the praise and glory of His name." Our personal advantage, and that of the Church, takes only the second place.

---

[14] Sess. 22, can. 3.

In heaven, the liturgy will strike no note other than those of reverent praise, of love and of joy. The sacrifice of Jesus will certainly be ever present in its effect: it is He alone Who saves and beatifies the elect; but expiation, and the petition for pardon, as such, will no longer exist. In Revelation, St. John describes this glorious liturgy of heaven: he has seen the Lamb immolated, standing before the throne of God; it was surrounded by the ancients and the innumerable multitude of the elect redeemed by His precious blood, and they sang: "To Him that sitteth on the throne and to the Lamb benediction and honour and glory and power for ever and ever" (Rev. 5:13). Through the veil of these symbols we must try to catch a glimpse of the splendours of the reality that lies beyond.

Every Mass celebrated here on earth is united to the liturgy of heaven. In the silence of the Host, the Son of God, as the Word, renders to His Father boundless glory. It is beyond our understanding, it is inscrutable; but we can offer this praise, for the Father is pleased with it: Is not the Son the very splendour of His glory? *Splendor gloriae et figura substantiae eius* (Heb 1:3).

Still, our first duty at Mass is to unite ourselves to the praise offered by Jesus in His sacred humanity. This praise is the glorification of the Trinity by Him Who alone, by reason of the hypostatic union, can offer to It, in the name of the whole Church, a worship of infinite dignity.

You know the acts of homage which are essential for a sacrifice; adoration must be the foundation on which they are all based. Are we not poor creatures, wretched beings who need to receive everything from the hand of God? From Him we have our being and our life. We are founded on nothingness. If we are to remain in the way of truth, our praise, our admiration, our thanksgiving, must all partake of adoration. Thus it is with the blessed, as the liturgy tells us: *Laudant angeli, adorant dominationes, tremunt potestates.* They tremble, and yet these are angelic natures of the utmost purity who have never sinned; but they see the divine majesty and prostrate themselves before it.

If God were to raise the veil, if He were to show us the

grandeur of the mystery accomplished on our altars, like Moses, we would not dare to raise our eyes towards Him: *Non audebat aspicere contra Dominum* (Ex 3:6). But what does the Church teach us? *Praestet fides supplementum sensuum defectui.* Our faith must make the supernatural present to us as though we saw it. Some saints, like St. Philip Neri, had so lively a faith that it penetrated the mystery and enabled them to grasp the reality.

The Mass is furthermore, and par excellence, a "eucharist", that is to say, a splendid act of the homage of gratitude. It was by this name in preference to all others that the early Christians liked to designate it.

The Lord Himself has placed in the hands of His Church a divine gift: *Offerimus . . . de tuis donis ac datis.* In presenting to the Father the body and blood of His Son, we make to Him an offering of thanksgiving and this act of gratitude is always acceptable.

Noble souls feel the need to testify to their gratitude; there are other souls who can only think of themselves; they feel that they are entitled to everything and do not give thanks for anything. A character which is both great and humble may almost be said to suffer from this constant desire to express its gratitude. Consider St. Teresa: she had a heart as wide as the sands of the sea-shore, as the Introit of the Mass expresses it: *Dedit ei Dominus latitudinem cordis quasi arenam quae est in littore maris*; she experienced this thirst for thanksgiving; her heart was on the point of breaking under the strain of this torment. The writings of St. Gertrude, also, express this same greatness of soul. In her transport of gratitude, she liked to recall to the Holy Trinity all the favours which had been lavished on her from her childhood.[15] The whole of her magnificent book of exercises is simply a canticle of grateful praise. In this these great saints were only imitating their divine Spouse. The heart of Christ was the most noble that has ever existed. During the course of His mortal life He thanked the Father and even now

---

[15] *The Herald of Divine Love*, 2, 23.

He still offers Him thanks. He gives thanks first of all on His own behalf because His humanity has been assumed by the divine Person of the Word: because it belongs to the Word and shares His glory. On account of this grace of the hypostatic union it owes more to God than the whole of the human race.

Jesus thanked the Father also on our behalf in His capacity as Chief and Saviour: "He rejoiced in the Holy Spirit," St. Luke tells us "and said, 'I confess to Thee, O Father, Lord of heaven and earth, because Thou hast hidden these things from the wise and prudent and hast revealed them to little ones. Yes, Father, for so it hath seemed good in Thy sight'" (Lk 10:21–22). On the occasion of the miracle of the multiplication of the loaves, which was a figure of the superabundance of the gift of the Eucharist, and also before raising Lazarus from the dead, He gave thanks to the Father. When He was about to institute the ineffable sacrament, what does He do? *Gratias agens, fregit.* Here we have a glimpse of the interior life of His soul.

As for us, we owe everything to God: our existence, our divine adoption, our priesthood. When we recite the preface we should think of this ensemble of favours which comes to us through the Cross and which are for us a source of pride and of supernatural joy: *semper et ubique gratias agere.* The preface should always present before our eyes the wide horizons of the faith. Let us give thanks to Our Lord for having revealed to us the Holy Trinity, for having given us Christ in the different phases of His life, and for permitting us to honour Our Lady.

At this moment also we should unite ourselves with the angels: they, like us, offer their worship of praise and of thanksgiving only through Jesus Christ. *Per quem majestatem tuam laudant angeli.*

What thought should fill our hearts on the occasion of the liturgical feasts? Gratitude for the glories of Jesus and for the graces accorded to His mother, to the saints, to the Church and to ourselves. And for all this the Mass will be the best expression of our gratitude.

V. THE PARTICIPATION OF THE FAITHFUL
IN THE OFFERING OF CHRIST

Let us return once again to the source of all our privileges as Christians: baptism.

It is in virtue of his baptismal character that the Christian can take an active part in the worship of God as it is established in the Church. This worship—it is hardly necessary to say—is of the supernatural order: Christ is its sovereign Pontiff; and the Mass is its focus and its centre. That is why St. Peter gives to the assembly of the faithful the title of royal priesthood: *regale sacerdotium* (1 Pet 2:9). Not that the effect of baptism is to be confounded with that of holy orders, but, by virtue of his baptismal character, man becomes capable of uniting himself to the priest to offer with him and through him the body and blood of Christ and to offer in himself union with the divine Victim. It is important for us to understand this great privilege conferred by baptism and to instruct the faithful on it.

Let us examine these truths more closely. In every Mass the Supreme mystery is, beyond all doubt, the sacramental immolation of Jesus; but the offering presented by the Church comprises in its totality, with the oblation of Christ, the oblation of His members. On the altar as on the Cross, the Saviour is the one victim, holy, pure and immaculate, but it is His will that we should be associated with Him in His offering as being His complement.

Since the time of His Ascension, Christ has never been separated from His Church. In heaven He presents Himself before the Father with His mystical body brought to its perfection: "not having spot or wrinkle": *non habentem maculam aut rugam* (Eph 5:27). All the elect, united with Him and amongst themselves, live of the same life of praise in the light of the Word and in the charity of the Holy Spirit.

The mystery of unity and of glorification is prepared here on earth during Mass. The union of the members with the chief is still imperfect. It is ever growing and develops in faith, but on account of their offering with Christ, the faithful participate truly in His character of victim.

What do these words mean: "character of victim"? They mean that by uniting himself to Christ as He offers Himself, immolates Himself and gives Himself to be our food, the Christian wills to live in a state of total and constant dedication to the glory of the Father. It is thus that Jesus implants His life in the poverty of the human heart; He makes it like to His own, entirely devoted to God and to souls.

Among the faithful who assist at Mass some are inspired to a generous gesture; carried away by the example and by the grace of Jesus, they imitate Him unreservedly; they offer their being, their thought, their actions, and accept all the troubles, the contradictions and the labours which Providence disposes for them.

Others also participate in the oblation of Jesus but in varying degrees, without a complete abandonment of self; some souls are always bargaining. Nevertheless, Jesus accepts their offering. He never rejects one of His members, even the weakest. On the contrary, when they offer themselves with Him, He approves their good will; He vivifies them and sanctifies them.

This is the view of the Church.[16] The faithful by their baptism are delegates to the divine worship; they have a share, according to their condition, in the priesthood of Christ. They participate in the oblation not only because they offer the sacrifice by the hands of the priest but also because they offer it with him. Nevertheless, the unbloody immolation in the Mass is accomplished by the priest alone as representing the person of Christ and not as representing the person of the faithful.

The symbolism of her rites manifests in a very clear way how the faithful are invited to make of themselves one single oblation with Christ as Victim. As St. Augustine has explained, the

---

[16] In the thought of Dom Marmion, the union of the members to the offering of their Head does not in any way constitute the essential value of the Mass. [This thought of Blessed Columba was confirmed by Pius XII in *Mediator Dei* (1947) and by the fathers of Vatican II.] Dom Bernard Capelle very justly remarks that the oblation of themselves by the faithful, excellent in itself and entirely in accordance with the desire of the Church, can never constitute more than a complementary victim; "the hierarchy of values must be respected" ("*Le sens de la Messe*" in *Questions Liturgiques*, 1942, p. 22).

bread and the wine of the eucharistic sacrifice represent the union of the members of the Church among themselves and with their Head. "Is the bread made of one single grain?" asks the holy Doctor, "Is it not the product of the union of many grains of wheat? and the wine, likewise, is pressed from among many grapes . . . which, after being packed into the wine-press, form one single potion contained in the sweetness of the chalice"; consequently, it is you who are present on the altar, you who are there in the chalice: "*Ibi vos estis in mensa et ibi vos estis in calice.*" [17] The reality which faith perceives in the Mass is that the Church, from the offering of Christ immolated under the sacred species, learns every day to offer herself in Him and with Him. We quote again from St. Augustine: "*in ea re quam offert ipsa offeratur.*" [18] Our present-day liturgy faithfully reproduces the same teaching: "Grant, O Lord, those blessings of unity and peace which these offerings mystically represent": "*Unitatis et pacis propitius dona concede quae sub oblatis muneribus mystice designantur.*" [19] When, therefore, the bread and the wine are placed on the altar we are symbolically hidden in them, united to Jesus Christ and offered with Him.

The Council of Trent exposes the same mystery when it explains the significance of the mixing of the water and the wine in the chalice at the offertory. This rite expresses the mystical union of Christ with His members; *Ipsius populi fidelis cum capite Christo unio representatur.*[20] Then at the *suscipe sancta Trinitas*, after the oblation of the chalice, the priest recalls that the sacrifice is offered in honour of the Blessed Virgin, the apostles and all the saints of the Church triumphant. In her liturgy, the Church militant, oppressed by such great necessities and miseries, acknowledges that she is united in one single body under one single head and king to the liturgy of heaven—this belief is reiterated during the Canon at the *Communicantes* and the *Nobis quoque peccatoribus*.

---

[17] Sermons 227 and 229, PL 38, 1100 and 1103.
[18] *De Civitate Dei*, 10, 6; PL 41, 284.
[19] Secret of the Mass of Corpus Christi.
[20] Sess. 22, cap. 7.

After the consecration the Church makes us recite a prayer full of mystery. Bowing down in an attitude of humility the priest pronounces these words: "Humbly we beseech Thee, Almighty God, to command that by the hands of Thy holy Angel, this our sacrifice be uplifted to thine altar on high into the presence of Thy divine Majesty so that all of us who participate in the sacrifice of this altar by the reception of the most holy body and blood of Thy Son may be filled with all heavenly blessings and graces."

This prayer refers to us. It is we who must be brought before God. This *haec* means the *oblata*, that is to say, the members of Christ with their gifts, their desires and their prayers. It is on account of their union with their Head, Jesus, that the Church asks that they be transported to the altar on high, *in sublime altare tuum*. The Saviour entered with full right and once for all into the holy of holies: *Introivit semel in Sancta* (Heb 9:12), but every day at Mass, leaning humbly on our Mediator, we pass through the veil and enter after Him into the sanctuary of the divinity, in the bosom of the Father: *in sinu Patris*.

You will say, "Is Jesus not always face to face with His Father? Certainly. He is in His glorified humanity: *semper vivens ad interpellandum pro nobis* (Heb 7:25). Without leaving heaven, He comes down on our altars in order to raise us up to where He dwells Himself. In this liturgical supplication we express the desire to be carried away by Him so that God, in His great charity, may receive us and include us in the same look of love with which He beholds His Son.[21]

You remember what the Scripture says about the dedication of the temple of Solomon: *Maiestas Domini implevit domum*: "The majesty of the Lord filled the house" (1 Kings 8:11). The

---

[21] These views of Dom Marmion, which are the fruits of deep thought and mature experience, are inspired by the text of the liturgy, but they are not intended to be a literal explanation of it. The language of the prayer *Supplices* is partly figurative. The early Church, accustomed to the symbolism of Scripture, alludes here to the angel who, in Revelation, presides over the sacred offerings; in heaven he stands near the altar before the throne of God (Rev. 8:3). This angel, as Bossuet remarks, is not a mediator that we are providing for ourselves as though Christ were not sufficient; it is rather that the Church implores his cooperation so that, with her, he may present to God the gifts which are offered, but always through Jesus Christ (Bossuet, *Explication de la Messe*, chap. 38).

priests feared to enter; they were overwhelmed before the divine majesty. If that is true of the temple of the Old Law, what are we to say of our Churches where the divine mysteries are celebrated? By a prodigy of mercy God is present; Christ Jesus immolates Himself to the Father under the veil of the Eucharist; He offers Himself in union with all His members and thus prepares them for the unceasing praise of heaven. This is the thought of the Church which is expressed in her prayer: "Sanctify, O Lord . . . the sacrifice which is offered to Thee, and through it may we become an offering in Thy honour for evermore": *Nosmetipsos Tibi perfice munus aeternum.*[22]

VI. FRUITS OF THE MASS

By its divine institution the sacrifice of the Mass applies with the greatest abundance the graces and pardon which are the fruits of the sacrifice of the Cross. This is our faith: *Oblationis cruentae fructus, per hanc incruentam, uberrime percipiuntur.*[23]

St. Thomas had already given expression to this doctrine: "This sacrament produces for each individual all the salutary effect which flows from the Passion of Christ for the advantage of the whole world": *Effectum quem passio Christi fecit in mundo, hoc sacramentum facit in homine.*[24] Let us see what are these fruits intended for our advantage and for that of the Church and how we may understand their application to the faithful.

These fruits are, first of all, an increase of grace. If every good action obtains for us an increase of merit, of grace and of glory, the pious celebration of the holy sacrifice must undoubtedly bring down on us the same supernatural blessings. At Mass the priest is united with Jesus; through Him, he approaches very close to the majesty of God and is, as it were, enveloped in the divine charity. By all these ways grace visits his soul and abounds in him: *omni benedictione caelesti et gratia repleamur.*

---

[22] Secret of the Mass of Trinity Sunday; we have almost exactly the same formula in the secret of the Mass of Pentecost Monday.
[23] Council of Trent; Sess. 22, cap. 2.
[24] *Summa* III, q. 79, a. 1.

Then, because it is a sacrifice of propitiation, Mass satisfies for sin and disposes God to grant pardon and to extend His greatest mercies. Whatever our miseries, our weaknesses and our past may be, we must always have before our mind the declaration of the Council: "Rendered favourable by this oblation, the Lord, while bestowing His grace and the gift of repentance, grants pardon also for crimes and sins, however grave." [25]

According to the Council, the salutary force of the sacrifice applies to the whole world; it must be applied unceasingly in the Church in remission of the faults committed daily by men: *in remissionem eorum quae a nobis quotidie committuntur, peccatorum.*[26]

Not that the holy sacrifice remits of itself the offences committed against God as does the sacrament of penance, but it obtains for us abundant graces of contrition and true repentance. The Mass obtains for us also the remission of the temporal punishment due to sin. It is, therefore, a source of propitiation for the souls in purgatory as well as for us.

Finally, can our petitions ever find such powerful support as during the holy sacrifice? The Father no longer considers our unworthiness, but He hears the voice of His Son pleading on our behalf. The power of impetration in the Mass is immeasurable. The blood of Abel called down the divine vengeance, but the blood of Jesus Christ implores, not punishment, but mercy and grace. It is *melius loquentem quam Abel* (Heb 12:26).

How are these fruits of the sacrifice divided out? We may distinguish first of all the fruit reserved for the celebrant. As the minister of Jesus Christ, the priest receives a special communication of grace. This gift is so personal that, according to the general opinion of theologians, it is inalienable. The object of this divine favour is to transform the priest into Him whose place he holds. He is, in all truth, another Christ, and every grace which he receives tends to produce in him interior dispositions more and more in conformity with his priestly consecration.

[25] Sess. 22, cap. 2.
[26] Sess. 22, cap. 1.

Do those who are present at the sacrifice receive a special fruit? Undoubtedly they do; the *Orate fratres* and various other liturgical prayers allude to this application of grace to those who assist at Mass. First among these come the ministers and the server who cooperate with the priest in the carrying out of the rites.

Every Mass has always in the eyes of God and intrinsically, *ex opere operato*, its efficacy for propitiation and impetration. This efficacy is identical with that of the Cross. Nevertheless, the fervour of the priest and the care which he bestows to carry out worthily his sacred functions draw down without doubt additional graces on the faithful. We must think of this, we who have the charge of souls and who *ex officio* intercede with God for His people.

We can distinguish also another fruit which the theologians call "ministerial". This belongs in particular to the one or more for whom the priest has been asked to celebrate the holy sacrifice. This fruit assures for the beneficiaries a very special application of the merits and satisfactions of Jesus Christ. Masses offered in this way can produce great effects of mercy in the souls of sinners as also in those of the just and for the advantage of the members of the Church suffering.

Finally, there exists a universal fruit for the benefit of all the faithful. On many occasions during the Canon and elsewhere, the priest prays for the whole Church. He implores the Saviour to make His grace shine down on all living Christians, united in Christ by faith and by love. One of the dread effects of heresy and excommunication is to exclude souls from this source of divine favour.

The holy sacrifice which Our Lord gave to His Spouse is the most excellent expression of His worship and His prayer. "As often as the commemoration of this sacrifice is celebrated, so often is the work of our redemption accomplished": *quoties huius hostiae commemoratio celebratur opus nostrae redemptionis exercetur.*[27] We must have a high appreciation of our dignity as

---

[27] Secret of the Mass of the Ninth Sunday after Pentecost.

ministers of Christ. "Who can say," exclaims St. John Chrysostom, "what must be the hands which carry out such an office, what the tongue which pronounces such words and how much purer and holier still must be the soul which receives within itself the great breath of the Holy Spirit?"[28]

[28] *De Sacerdotio* 6, 4; PG 48, 681.

XII.

SANCTA SANCTE TRACTANDA

THE priest is raised to a dignity which is, in a certain sense, divine, for Jesus Christ identifies Himself with him. His role as mediator is the highest vocation in this world. It is worth repeating; if a priest did nothing during his whole life but offer the holy sacrifice piously every morning, or even if he were only to offer it once, he would have accomplished an act greater in the hierarchy of values than those events which convulse the world. For the effect of every Mass will endure for eternity, and nothing is eternal except the divine.

We must orient our whole day towards the Mass. It is the central point and the sun of the day. It is, as it were, the focus from which there comes to us light, fervour and supernatural joy.

We must hope that, little by little, our priesthood will take possession of our soul and our life so that it may be said of us: "he is always a priest." That is the effect of a eucharistic life, embalmed in the perfume of the sacrifice which makes us an *alter Christus*.

How good it is to see a priest after long years of fidelity, living with the true spirit of the divine oblation!

There are many priests entirely dedicated to Christ and to souls who realize this ideal fully; they are the glory of the Church and the joy of the divine Master.

If we also wish to rise to the heights of our priestly vocation, if we want it to impress its character on our whole existence so as to inflame us with love and zeal, we must prepare our souls to receive the graces of our Mass.

After years it may happen that some souls remark an habitual lack of fervour in the course of their lives. To what must we attribute this? Many reasons may be given. Remember that a radical death to sin, even to deliberate venial sin, is an indispensable condition for the definite triumph of charity in us.

Still, lack of effort to celebrate Mass every morning as well as possible is the most common explanation of a spiritual decline. In fact, by the checking up of conscience which it presupposes and by the atmosphere of grace with which it surrounds the sacred minister, the pious offering of the holy sacrifice affords the priest every day a providential opportunity to recollect himself, to humble himself, and to pull himself together. If we neglect this means, so well calculated to plunge us back into the supernatural current, we open the way more and more for the invasion of routine and mediocrity into our lives. On the other hand, as long as the anxiety to celebrate as well as possible remains in the soul, it will never be carried away in the drift.

I. THE IMPORTANCE OF THE DISPOSITIONS OF THE SOUL

It would be impossible to overestimate the importance of the interior disposition of the soul to enable us to receive abundantly of the fruits of the Mass.

Let us pause at Calvary.

Who were the witnesses of the drama of our redemption? We can divide them into three groups; the Blessed Virgin, John the beloved disciple, and the holy women form the first group; the Jews and the executioners of Jesus form the second. The third group cannot be seen by human eyes; it is the Blessed Trinity surrounded by myriads of heavenly spirits. The Father contemplated Christ immolating Himself on the Cross. He saw His Son, the brightness of His glory and the image of His substance (Heb 1:3), offering Him the sublime homage of justice and perfect charity. This sacrifice, foreseen and ordained by the divine Wisdom, rendered all glory to God and redeemed mankind. And the Father, the Word, and the Holy Spirit delighted in the supreme act of love which inspired the oblation of the Saviour. On the Cross, Christ offered Himself and died for all: *Pro omnibus mortuus est Christus* (2 Cor 5:15).

But how different is the spiritual benefit which each of the assistants receives from their presence at this divine sacrifice! Consider first of all the Blessed Virgin. She is the type of perfect sanctity; she accepts the will of the Father; she presents her Son to Him; she intercedes for us all. The grace which flowed from the Cross into her blessed soul surpasses all human understanding. Mary was sanctified by the Passion of Jesus more than any other being. The merits of her Son purchased all her privileges and the plentitude of the divine favours which had been showered upon her.

Perhaps we shall be tempted to say: "Lord, I can understand Your mother receiving such great gifts, but I am only a sinner." And Jesus replies to us: "See beside her Mary Magdalen; it was My will that a woman, a sinner—but a sinner filled now with penitential love, should be at the foot of My Cross." So great is the efficacy of this sacrifice that even the greatest sins are no obstacle to receiving the graces which flow from it, provided one has a repentant heart.

And was not the good thief also a sinner? But by the merits of Christ he received the gift of faith. He put his trust in Christ in all confidence and in that mysterious dialogue murmured from cross to cross he heard from the lips of the divine Master in His agony the words of final pardon: "This day thou shalt be with Me in Paradise" (Lk 23:43).

For all these, their presence at the death of Jesus was a source of sanctification.

If it had been granted to us to be present at this divine drama, it is by the side of His mother and the friends of Jesus that we would certainly have wished to stand.

The second group is that of the Pharisees, the priests, and the Jews, who had compelled Pilate to crucify Jesus. On the Cross the Saviour prayed for all of them: *Pater, dimitte illis, non enim sciunt quid faciunt*: "Father, forgive them; for they know not what they do" (Lk 23:34). No one was excluded from this prayer. It was certainly efficacious for some of them, though perhaps not at the moment. As for the Doctors of Law, they, according to the Scriptures, were actuated by a sacrilegious hate; they had blinded their souls and had hardened their hearts. Did they not cry out before Pilate: "His blood be on us"? *Sanguis eius super nos* (Mt 27:25).

Finally, there were the executioners; these were ignorant men and indifferent. Christ prayed also for them, but in this hour they have no interest in religion. They are not thinking of anything, or if they do think, their interest is in the lottery which will award to one of them the robe of Jesus, or perhaps they are enjoying the spectacle of a human being suffering.

The attitude of men in regard to Jesus is not dissimilar, though in varying degrees, even in our days, while He is perpetuating in our churches the mystery of His oblation. The Mass is the same sacrifice as that of the Cross. The Council of Trent has declared it: "It is one and the same Victim; the Offerer is still the same."[1] It is the sacrifice of the precious blood of Jesus Christ, one drop of which is sufficient to redeem the world. But those who assist at it with indifference draw little profit from it, while the fervent souls find in this contact of faith with Christ a light, a strength, and a heavenly joy which makes them triumph over the world and the flesh. If this be so for those who are merely assisting at Mass, how vital must be the interior disposition of the priest who is celebrating!

See these two priests coming down from the altar after the sacrifice; one has come close to God in prayer; he is full of zeal and holy joy: *ad Deum qui laetificat juventutem meam* (Ps. 43[42]:4). The other is distracted and uninterested; he could almost say like the Israelites: "Our soul now loatheth this very light food": *Anima nostra iam nauseat super cibo isto levissimo* (Num 21:5). The Mass, the Eucharist leave him indifferent. Is his sacrifice not the same as the other? It is the same, but the faith of this priest has not that vivacity which charity expects.

While we are carrying out the gestures of the ritual and pronouncing the sacred formulas, we must make the effort to awaken in ourselves these two theological virtues; it is they alone which, surmounting appearances, can attain to the supernatural reality.

If it should befall a minister of Christ to celebrate the holy mysteries with a conscience gravely burdened, would he have

---

[1] Sess. 22, cap. 2.

the right to count himself among the friends of Jesus? He would be committing a sacrilege. As a result of his obstinate attachment to sin, the terrible saying of the Apostle would be applicable to him also: "Crucifying again to themselves the Son of God": *rursum crucifigentes sibimetipsis Filium Dei* (Heb 6:6). I know, and it is an article of our faith, that there is pardon for every sin, but the experience of souls teaches us that this insult to the Son of God causes a terrible blindness. What will be the fate of such a soul if death befalls it unexpectedly? Before we celebrate, let us reflect that it will be for us as it was for those witnesses at the foot of the Cross: each one will receive grace or be hardened in sin according to his dispositions.

II. THE FUNDAMENTAL DISPOSITIONS TO UNITE OURSELVES TO JESUS CHRIST AS PRIEST AND VICTIM

By a unique privilege of His priesthood Christ is at the same time the Pontiff and the sacred Victim of the sacrifice of the New Testament. What is the fundamental disposition necessary for Christ's minister if he wishes to resemble as perfectly as possible his divine model? He must enter fully into the sentiments which actuated the heart of Jesus at the Last Supper, at Calvary and now in heaven. In this way he will comply with the exhortation of the Apostle: "Let this mind be in you, which was also in Christ Jesus" (Phil 2:5).

When Jesus was immolating Himself on the Cross under the inspiration of the Holy Spirit, it was love which reigned in Him: *ut cognoscat mundus quia diligo Patrem* (Jn 14:31). His soul was filled also with the spirit of adoration and of thanksgiving before the divine majesty; Jesus was burning with eagerness to sacrifice Himself in order to expiate the sins of the world and to merit the salvation of the whole human race. When we are celebrating, it is supremely desirable that we should share the views and the intentions of the unique Pontiff of all sacrifice. We must realize clearly that Christ has not ceased to love the Father now that He has entered into His glory, and it is with the same dispositions that we are called upon to perpetuate in the bosom of the Church the mystery of the Last Supper and of the Cross.

In the course of the sacred "action" let the priest, therefore, unite himself to the Saviour. Jesus is the perfect model of the sentiments of religion and love with which His minister must offer the sacrifice.

Christ is also our model in His capacity of victim. Here again we must make His sentiments our own. The ritual of ordination reminds us of this great obligation in expressive terms: "Imitate the sacrifice which you offer." That is to say that when celebrating the mystery of the death of the Lord, you will make die in your own members all vices and covetousness. Only then can you present to the Father your oblation in the most perfect way, the way chosen by Christ on the Cross.

Why, you may ask, did Jesus will to consecrate Himself to God for us as a victim?

One can make gifts to God in different ways: by alms, by pious foundations, by presenting precious objects, such as a chalice. All that is very good and agreeable to God, according to the motive of charity which inspires it.

But what is the difference between a victim and every other offering? There is a considerable difference. The presents are offered for a special purpose, which is indicated by their very nature or by the will of the donor. If I offer a chalice, it is certainly intended for a particular use and cannot serve any other purpose. Sacrifice, on the other hand, by its very essence is offered to God alone; it belongs wholly to Him; it is reserved exclusively for Him so that He can dispose of it as He pleases.

This is the profound reason why Jesus wished to be a sacrifice. We have spoken of this already, but the doctrine is of such capital importance that we may return to it. The first words of Christ when He came into the world were these: "Holocausts for sin did not please Thee; then said I, 'Behold I come . . . that I should do Thy will, O Lord'" (Heb 10:6, 7). And what was the will of God? It was the death of Calvary after a whole life of labour accomplished in the spirit of love. This is the offering of Christ. We too, in the Mass, like Christ and in imitation of His example, should offer ourselves as a sacrifice, so that God may do with us what He wills; we must abandon ourselves to our Creator and Saviour; we must give ourselves up to Him.

In union with the Word Incarnate we must accept ourselves with our failings, our wretchedness and our physical infirmities. We must habitually apply ourselves to dying to the solicitations and the attractions of the world whenever they are opposed to the reign of God within us. For the priest who is a religious, this fundamental disposition may be reduced to a spirit of absolute obedience.

We have here deep matter for meditation, grave cause for examination of conscience. Have we always allowed God to dispose of us as He pleases?

It is my earnest hope that you will take the resolution to imitate in all sincerity the mystery of the immolation of Christ which is perpetuated in your hands at our altars.

III. DISPOSITIONS SUGGESTED BY THE COUNCIL OF TRENT

The dispositions suggested by the Council are four in number: A true heart—an upright faith—fear and reverence—the spirit of compunction and repentance: *cum corde vero—et recta fide—cum metu et reverentia—contriti et poenitentes*.[2]

First of all, a heart which is entirely true. What does this mean? It means being perfectly loyal with oneself. This is a quality of great importance, and we must recognize the fact that it is rather rare. We believe sometimes that we are being entirely sincere in our conscience and yet there are recesses which we do not open even to the eyes of God.

In order to possess this true heart we must aspire ardently to know ourselves as the Lord knows us. In the recollection of prayer may the divine light penetrate into the last depths of our soul and show us ourselves as we really are. It is not enough to tell the truth when we speak to others; we must also be honest

---

[2] Sess. 22, cap. 2.

with ourselves: *qui loquitur veritatem in corde suo*: "he who speaks
the truth from his heart" (Ps 15[14]:2), and, above all, we must
be honest with God. If the priest at the altar wants to stand
worthily in the presence of God, he must have this *cor verum*.
Think of what will happen to us one day in heaven. Just as,
from the moment of the Incarnation, the soul of Jesus was
elevated to the vision of the Father and, as it were, enveloped in
glory, because it was the soul of the Son of God Incarnate, so
also by a wondrous condescension of love, the Lord will communicate Himself to the children of adoption. He will fill our
souls with His light and His happiness in proportion to the
degree of our charity at the moment of death. What is the
explanation of this generosity? The fact that He will see in us
the image of Jesus.

There is a little-known passage in the Scriptures which expresses very well what this beatitude will be: *denudabit absconsa
sua illi*: God will disclose his secrets to him.[3] Let us keep these
words in mind. God will show Himself to His elect as He is in
the unity of His Essence and the Trinity of His Persons; He will
reveal to them the *absconsa* of His eternal life; everything will be
unveiled to them in the full light of truth; "God is light and in
Him there is no darkness" (1 Jn 1:5).

For our part, we shall unite ourselves to the Lord and we
shall glorify Him in the full light of day. We shall see clearly all
the misery of our previous existence and the triumph of grace
in us. Then our heart will be perfectly humble; it will comprehend the depths of the divine mercy; it will be wholly true in its
praise of the Lord.

Believe me, it is God's will that, even in this life, we should
stand in His presence in the same attitude of absolute sincerity.

We often deceive ourselves. We have not always the strength
to meet the look of the divinity with the eyes of our soul, to
present ourselves before God as we are. We have defects, secret

---

[3] Sir 4:18. This revelation refers to Wisdom personified who, after having tested his
disciple, will fill him with joy by disclosing to him his secrets. *Sapientia laetificabit illum et
denudabit absconsa sua illi*. Dom Marmion applies the text to God when He introduces the
purified soul into the light of glory.

inclinations, attachments which we do not acknowledge; there are sacrifices which God asks of us and which we have not the courage to undertake.

We should meditate on these truths, and if God asks some act of self-denial from us, we should accept it. As we ascend the altar let us bring to God a heart which is true, open and loyal. In this way, the Council assures us, we shall receive abundantly of the fruits of the sacrifice.

The second disposition is an upright faith: *recta fide*. The Council draws its inspiration from the text of the Epistle to the Hebrews: "Having a confidence in the entering into the holies by the blood of Christ" . . . through the veil, that is to say, His flesh, *per velamen, id est carnem suam*, and since we have a high priest . . . let us draw near with a true heart in fullness of faith: *cum vero corde in plenitudine fidei* (Heb 10:19–22).

The figure of the Old Testament to which this passage of St. Paul alludes is splendidly realized in the holy sacrifice of the Mass. In it, Christ makes us enter with Him, not into the holy of holies of the temple of Jerusalem, but into the sanctuary of the divinity, that is to say, into the presence of the Father. He introduces us there by virtue of His Passion, the merits of which are applied to us by the offering of the altar. This faith will produce in us an unlimited confidence in the infinite value of the sacrifice.

The eucharistic mystery is in all truth the *Mysterium fidei*. The Church has introduced these two words into the formula of consecration of the precious blood. In this mystery everything is accomplished in the spirit of faith. The power of the words of the priest, the presence of Christ through the transubstantiation of the bread and wine, the fruits of salvation of which every Mass is the source; these are matters which only faith can grasp.

We have read of holy souls, who, as they assisted at Mass, saw Our Lord offering the sacrifice Himself; for them the priest disappeared; they saw only Christ. This is an extraordinary grace, but it is entirely in conformity with the teaching of the Church. What does the Council say to us in effect? It says that

Christ at the altar is the same Offerer of the sacrifice as on Calvary: *Idem nunc offerens.*[4]

This intervention of Christ as priest, *ut nunc offerens*, should not surprise us. Jesus has been appointed by the Father as judge of all men: *Neque enim Pater judicat quemquam, sed omne judicium dedit Filio*: "The Father judges no one, but has given all judgement to the Son" (Jn 5:22). Christ judges all those who die, and men die every second. Why then should he not be able also to cooperate actively and explicitly in every Mass with the priest who is perpetuating here on earth His sacrifice? Consider again what happens in the administration of the sacraments. St. Augustine expresses concisely the doctrine of the Church: "whether it be Peter, Paul or Judas who baptizes, it is always Christ Who regenerates the soul in the Holy Spirit". *Petrus baptizet? Hic (Christus) est qui baptizat . . . Judas baptizet? Hic est qui haptizat*: Christ baptizes of His own power; they baptize as instruments.[5] It is the same for the Eucharist; whatever the priest is who consecrates, whether he be a heretic or unworthy, it is always Christ Who, in a very real and sovereign manner, offers and consecrates, though He does so through the ministry of man.

Cum metu et reverentia: In the offering of His sacrifice, the heart of Jesus was overflowing with a profound reverence for the majesty of the Father. Did not Isaiah predict of Him that the spirit of the fear of the Lord would fill his soul? "And his delight shall be in the fear of the Lord": *et replebit eum spiritu timoris Domini* (Is 11:3).

When I was speaking of the virtue of religion I pointed out how the whole earthly life of Jesus was an act of religious homage. Even now in heaven, where He is *in gloria Patris*, Christ is still inspired by reverence and adoration; His human nature, being created, could not be established in truth if it did not recognize by its own abasement the perfections of God.

We, also, at the altar, should be filled with this reverential fear mingled with love and confidence. We must let it penetrate to

---

[4] Sess. 22, cap. 2.
[5] *Tractatus in Joannem* 6; PL 35, 1428.

our very marrow: "My flesh trembles for fear of Thee": *confige timore tuo carnes meas* (Ps 119[118]:120).

As for the last disposition mentioned by the Council, the spirit of contrition and repentance, I have already spoken of it in relation to compunction. I need not return to it here. But I cannot resist quoting here the words of St. Gregory which sum up the whole of Christian tradition: "It is necessary in the course of the sacred action to immolate ourselves to God with a contrite heart; when we celebrate the mysteries of the Passion of Our Lord we must imitate the sacrifice which we offer."[6]

IV. IMMEDIATE PREPARATION—CELEBRATION—THANKSGIVING

The dispositions of which we have just spoken should be ever alive in the soul of the minister of Christ, but such supernatural enthusiasm is beyond the possibilities of human weakness. For this reason it is very salutary before celebrating to try by our immediate preparation to make our faith more active and our heart more eager.

The missal contains excellent prayers in preparation for the holy sacrifice. We can recite them or meditate on them.

I shall confine myself to a few suggestions. All methods and all practices can be summed up in this proposition: the more we identify ourselves with Jesus Christ in the offering of the holy sacrifice, the more we are in harmony with the views of the Father, and the more fruitful in graces is our Mass. The secret of the Mass of Holy Thursday is an admirable expression of this truth of our faith; "we beseech thee, O Lord . . . that this our sacrifice may be made well pleasing to Thee, by Him Who this day commanded His disciples to celebrate it in memory of Him": *Ipse tibi sacrificium nostrum reddat acceptum*. Let the priest, therefore, clothe himself in the person of Jesus Christ as he is acting in His name. Before ascending the altar, let him say to

[6] *Necesse est, cum agimus, ut nosmetipsos Deo in cordis compunctione mactemus, quia qui passionis dominicae mysterii celebramus, debemus imitari quod agimus* (Dialog. 4, PL 7, 428.) This passage would seem to have inspired the present text of the Roman Pontifical: *Imitamini . . .* the whole of this allocution of the bishop only appears in the Pontifical of Durand de Mende (thirteenth century).

Jesus: "Lord, you have declared that *sine me nihil potestis facere* (Jn 15:5). I realize it; without You I can do nothing, and especially in this divine action of the holy sacrifice. I am quite incapable of being a worthy minister for You in this act of incomparable grandeur. Were I to pass my whole life in preparation, I would not be fit for such a ministry. But as I have received, through Your Holy Spirit, a participation in Your priesthood, I ask in all humility, that You communicate to me Your disposition as Pontiff and as Victim; the dispositions which were Yours at the Last Supper and those which You had on the Cross; graciously supply in Your mercy all that is wanting in me."

Is it right that the priest should perpetuate the sacrifice of the Cross without conforming himself, whole-heartedly, to the immolation which he carries out on the altar? When Christ speaks through his lips, when He offers Himself by his hands, can the heart of the priest remain cold and, as it were, a stranger to the intimate dispositions of the heart of the Saviour?

In His oblation, Christ bore in Himself the whole human race. Following His example, let us open our hearts wide to the necessities and sufferings of all men; let us think of sinners, of the poor, of the sick, of the dying, as though we were charged with presenting all their supplications to the Lord. In this way we shall each be the spokesman of the whole Church.

You should always put on the priestly vestments with dignity. We read a story in Genesis which may help us at this moment to raise our minds to the truths of faith. In order that Jacob might venture to approach Isaac and receive his blessing, he was clothed by Rebecca in the garments of Esau. Then he said boldly to his father: *Ego sum primogenitus tuus*: "I am your first-born son" (Gen 27:19). Our mother, the Church, says to us, "You are going to represent Jesus Christ, your elder brother": *Primogenitus in multis fratrius* (Rom 8:29), "clothe yourself in Him": *induimini Dominum Jesum Christum* (Rom 13:11–14). Then you can freely approach the Father. He will see in you, in spite of all your unworthiness, an *alter Christus*.

Another excellent way to prepare oneself to offer the sacrifice, for those to whom the Lord gives this attraction, is to unite oneself to the dispositions of the Blessed Virgin as she stood at the foot of the Cross, entering into the intimacy of the oblation which she made of her Son.[7]

During the celebration we must observe the rubrics exactly. It is a tribute of respect and of reverence. The priest who carries out the prescribed ceremonies in a spirit of devotion will become very pleasing to God. When we present the bread and wine at the offertory we must never fail to unite with the host on the paten and the wine in the chalice the offering of our actions and of ourselves. If Jesus sees us as victims, He will offer us to His Father with Himself. A whole day of fidelity will prolong the oblation which we have made in the morning, and the whole life of the priest will be passed in the radiancy of the Mass.

In the course of the celebration we must try to put ourselves in harmony with the formulas and gestures of the liturgy. The exhortation of St. Benedict: *Mens nostra concordat voci* is especially applicable to the prayers recited at the altar. There are many formulas in the missal which recall to us the work of glorification which is accomplished by our ministry. Is not the Mass the essential act of the worship of *latria*? The *Gloria Patri*, the *Suscipe*, *Sancte Pater*, the *Per Ipsum*, the *Placeat*, are constant reminders that we must fix our gaze on the Father and on the Holy Trinity: *Offerimus praeclarae majestati tuae*. But our thoughts should be fixed also, always in conformity with the liturgical texts, on the treasures of divine mercy and on the needs of men. Strengthened by the blood of Jesus, let us intercede for them all with many prayers. More even than the pontiff of the Old Testament who entered into the presence of God in the holy of holies, is it our function to plead the cause of the people prostrate at the foot of the altar.

The best possible thanksgiving is Jesus Christ Himself: *Quid retribuam Domino? . . . calicem salutaris accipiam.*

Still, whatever our sentiments of gratitude may be during the celebration, it is supremely desirable that, after the sacrifice, we

---

[7] See below, p. 344.

should give thanks to God from the bottom of our hearts. In the form of this everyone may follow his own inclination under the guidance of the Holy Spirit, but we must never leave ourselves open to the reproach of having received so much and given so little thanks. The customary prayers recommended after Mass suggest excellent acts of gratitude. By the canticle *Benedicite* we bring to life, so to speak, all creatures in our mind, so that they may praise God; man becomes the heart of all that which is naturally incapable of love, so as to bring all things to the Lord.

It is a good thing to add to these vocal prayers a period of more intimate personal prayer. This thanksgiving must comprise before all else an act of supreme adoration. The more Jesus humbles and conceals Himself, the more urgently our hearts should acknowledge His divine majesty: "You are Christ, the Son of the living God, in Whom the Father is well-pleased. And because I believe this, I surrender myself to You with my whole heart so that I may accomplish Your will in all things."

According to the general consensus of opinion, the principal effect of the sacrament is realized at the moment of reception. However, as long as the sacred species remain with us in their integrity, the Saviour, by His union with the soul, is a constant source of divine blessings for it; that is why the time of thanksgiving is so precious for learning to cling to Christ and to form with Him one single spirit in love. Prayer, which becomes more intense after holy communion, creates in the heart a precious habit of recollection. Did not Jesus say, when His disciples had just received holy communion after the Last Supper: "Father, I will that where I am, they also whom Thou hast given Me may be with Me" (Jn 17:24). By the grace of the sacrament, Christ draws us to Him to raise us in Him towards the Father.

The priest who, after Mass, has to hear confessions, attend funerals or give catechism class to children must not be discouraged if these functions prevent him from enjoying a period of recollection. He must be convinced of these two truths: these acts of his ministry are a prolongation of the holy sacrifice because they apply the fruits of the redemption to souls; are they not, in their own way, a worship of love for Christ in the person of His members? Then again, is it not a very real thanksgiving to have received the Eucharist with all respect and to have recited piously the prayers with which the Mass closes. It is true that the post-communions as a general rule do not contain any explicit expression of gratitude; we ask in them that we may share in the salutary fruits of the sacrament. Nevertheless, these prayers undoubtedly include an expression of our deep appreciation of the divine gift and bear testimony in this way to our profound gratitude for it.

Apart from the value of the thanksgiving involved in the Mass itself, let us repeat that it is important, even necessary, that, after the celebration, as soon as circumstances permit, the priest should turn to give thanks to the Lord, for—and we must never forget it—during these sacred moments the well-beloved Son Who dwells *in sinu Patris* is reposing *in sinu peccatoris.*

XIII.

THE EUCHARISTIC BANQUET

"BEHOLD," says St. John, "what manner of charity the Father hath bestowed upon us that we should be called and should be the sons of God": *Videte qualem caritatem dedit nobis Pater ut filii Dei nominemur et simus* (1 Jn 3:1). God is our Father. He loves us with a love which is incomprehensible. All the love which exists in the world comes from Him and is only a shadow of His charity which is without limit. "Can a woman forget her infant?" asks the Lord through the mouth of the prophet; "if she should forget, yet will not I forget thee" (Is 49:15).

Now, love inclines one to the giving of self; accordingly it seeks a closer union with its object. God is love itself: *Deus caritas est* (1 Jn 4:8); He is moved by a desire ever active and intense to communicate Himself to us. That is why St. John writes: "God so loved the world as to give His only begotten Son": *Sic Deus dilexit* (Jn 3:16).

This Son, Who shares the love of the Father, willed to accept the condition of a servant and to give Himself up on the Cross. *Maiorem hac dilectionem*: "Greater love has no man" (Jn 15:13).

And now, again, He hides Himself under the appearances of bread and wine, in order to enter into us and to unite us to Himself in the closest manner. The Holy Eucharist is the final effort of love which seeks to give itself; it is the prodigy of omnipotence in the service of infinite charity.

All the works of God are perfect (Deut 32:4). That is why the heavenly Father has prepared for His children a banquet worthy of himself. It is not material food which He serves to them nor manna from heaven; He gives them the body and blood, soul and divinity of His only-begotten Son, Jesus Christ. In this life we shall never fully comprehend all the grandeur of this gift; even in heaven we shall not entirely comprehend it, for in the

Eucharist God communicates Himself, and only God can fully comprehend Himself.

In this banquet we receive the Son of the Father, the beatitude of heaven; for all eternity the angels and the saints will find their refreshment in Him. Furthermore, the eternal Father Himself declares that He finds His delight in Him. "This is my beloved Son in Whom I am well pleased" (Mt 17:5). God could not bestow upon us anything more precious: "Do you not believe that I am in the Father and the Father in Me?" (Jn 14:10). He says again to Philip: "He that seeth Me seeth the Father also" (Jn 14:9). By holy communion we possess the Holy Trinity in our hearts, for the Father and the Holy Spirit are of necessity there where the Son is; they are Three in one and the same essence.

I. THE PARABLE OF THE BANQUET

It is not easy to say anything new about the Eucharist. It has occurred to me that meditation on one page of the Gospel would serve to enlighten our faith. This page casts a light on the nature of the union which the Eucharist produces between Christ and us.

You know the parable of the wedding banquet. Christ tells us: "The kingdom of heaven is likened to a king who made a marriage for his son": *Simile est regnum coelorum homini regi, qui fecit nuptias filio suo* (Mt 22:2; see also Lk 14:16). Who is represented by this king and his son? Who are the guests of this nuptial banquet? Is there a mystery concealed beneath this allegory?

According to the Doctors of the Church the king is the heavenly Father. When the Father decreed the Incarnation of the Word for the redemption of the world He prepared a wondrous nuptial feast by reason of the union of the human nature to the divine Person. The Incarnation of the Word is a marriage because the Son of God, in receiving the sacred humanity as His own, makes it His spouse.

In the most elevated sense, the "marriage of the Lamb", *nuptiae Agni* (Rev 19:7), was consummated then. As St. Gregory

remarks, this mystery was effected in Mary at the time of the
message of the angel: *uterus . . . genitricis Virginis huius sponsi
thalamus fuit.*[1] Two natures in one Person; what unity of being
and what a close embrace of love! "Who is that coming up from
the wilderness, leaning upon her beloved?": *quae est ista quae
ascendit de deserto deliciis affluens innixa super dilectum suum?* (Song
8:5). The humanity of the Saviour is that immaculate spouse
flowing with delights who rises out of the desert of this world
leaning on the Word, her beloved.

The liturgy chants the marvels of this union: *Mirabile mysterium . . . Deus homo factus est.* Without prejudicing the splendour of His eternal perfection, the Son of Man assumes a
human nature drawn from nothingness; *Id quod fuit permansit, et
quod non erat assumpsit.* And this union involves no fusion of
God and man; *non commixtionem passus*; on the contrary, it safe-
guards the absolute distinctness of the two natures now for ever
inseparable: *neque divisionem.*[2] We have here the whole doctrine
of the Incarnation.

According to the same Doctor: "By this mystery of the Incarnation the Father willed in His mysterious designs to realize
the mystical union of His Son with the Church": *In hoc Pater
Regi Filio nuptias fecit, quo ei per incarnationis mysterium, sanctam
Ecclesiam sociavit.*[3] To unite Himself to the Church meant for
Christ, as you know, above all to unite Himself to each individual soul by sanctifying grace and charity. Did not St. Paul
write to the Corinthians: "For I have espoused you to one
husband that I may present you as a chaste virgin to Christ"
(2 Cor 11:2). Note that the Apostle is not speaking to the virgins alone, but to all the baptized; by the grace of divine adoption every Christian, according to him, is called to unite himself
to Christ by love.

To return to the parable: the king had invited many guests to
take part in the banquet, and they all excused themselves. Then
he sent his servants out to the crossways to call in even the

---

[1] *Homil. 38 in Evangel.*, PL 76, 1283.
[2] Antiphon of the Mass of the Circumcision.
[3] Ibid.

poorest men to the abundant banquet which he had prepared. The banquet hall is opened thus to the humble, the feeble, and even to the lame.

What does this crowd represent? With Origen and St. Jerome, and in conformity with the liturgical use of certain texts of this parable, we may see in it the Christian people called by the divine munificence to the eucharistic banquet. Those who share in the sacred mysteries benefit of the union of love reserved to the guests of the banquet. Christ takes possession of their souls and they, for their part, possess Him, in faith and charity.

This union—and we should always keep this truth well before our minds—is an image in a certain sense of the union between the sacred humanity and the Word; it is the model for all the relations of intimacy and love between the creature and his God.

It is to these heights of the supernatural life that we are all invited.

II. THE MASS, THE BANQUET OF THE SON OF GOD

Every day this sumptuous banquet is prepared; the marriage feast of the Son of God is renewed every morning in the holy sacrifice; priests and faithful, we are all invited to take part in it.

The divine Wisdom conceived this mystery of union and entrusted the dispensation of it to the Church. In the bosom of the Church the Mass is the focus from which grace radiates on all the daily actions of the members of Christ. For the priest, in particular, the divine Office, his meditation, his ministry, his devotion to duty in all its forms, draw their supernatural impulse from the sanctifying power of this divine sacrifice. A prayer of the missal expresses this thought for us: "May these most sacred mysteries, which Thou hast ordained to be the fount of all holiness, in very truth sanctify us likewise."[4]

Now, how do these graces which flow from the Mass reach us? First of all, by holy communion. The Eucharist is, above all,

[4] Secret of the Mass of St. Ignatius of Loyola.

the sacrament which communicates to priests and congregation the fruits of the sacred immolation. The prayer, *Supplices*, of the Canon, asserts this very clearly. It asks "that as many of us as by partaking thereof from this altar, have received the adorable body and blood of Thy Son may from heaven be filled with all blessings and graces": *omni benedictione caelesti et gratia repleamur.* The gift of the Eucharist is the reply of the clemency of the Father to the offering which we make to Him of His Son. With supreme condescension the Father wills to feed the celebrant and the faithful with the actual victim of the sacrifice, and in this way to put them in possession of the immensity of super-natural benefits of which the Mass is the source. Thus Christ is united in love to all the members of His Church; He makes them "rich in all things in Him": *In omnibus divites facti estis in illo* (1 Cor 1:5). By the Eucharist, He makes them participate in the fruits of the redemption: *ut redemptionis tuae fructum in nobis jugiter sentiamus.*[5] At Mass, this *fructus redemptionis* is officially given to us by holy communion. Holy communion, therefore, may never be regarded as just one practice, a detail, nor even as an exercise of secondary importance, in the integration of our spirituality. In truth, when Jesus comes to us, He comes, according to the words of the Gospel, "that we may have life", and there is no parsimony in His gift; it is given with divine abundance: *Ego veni ut vitam habeant et abundantius habeant* (Jn 10:10). "If we knew the gift of God!" (Jn 4:10).

III. THE LEVEL OF LIFE
TO WHICH HOLY COMMUNION INVITES US

What is this supereminent life to which the eucharistic union invites the Christian and, above all, the priest? This teaching is so important that we must return to it constantly.

Christ is the perfect model of human sanctity which the Father wishes to see reproduced in His children of adoption: *Predestinavit nos conformes fieri imaginis Filii sui* (Rom 8:29). We

---

[5] Prayer of the Mass of Corpus Christi.

are all under obligation—though in varying degrees—to achieve this supernatural resemblance under pain of not participating in the banquet of heaven. Only this conformity with the Son Incarnate can assure us of the spiritual elevation, of that harmony between the human and the divine which the Father expects of us.

In what does the sanctity of Jesus consist? In the Holy Trinity, the Father is the source from which the Son receives all that He is. That is why Jesus has said: "As the Father hath life in Himself, so He hath given to the Son also to have life in Himself" (Jn 5:26). The humanity of Jesus also in its incomparable dignity receives from the Father all that it is; an inexhaustible effusion of divine life flowed constantly from the bosom of the Father to Jesus, by virtue of which He possessed in all plenitude sanctifying grace, infused charity, the virtues, and the gifts of the Holy Spirit.

The hypostatic union was already sanctifying by its own virtue the soul and the body of Christ; this grace of union with the eternal Son of God is at the root of all the other communications made to the sacred humanity for the divine accomplishment of its mission of redemption. Thus the soul of Jesus never ceased to contemplate the Father, the Word and the Holy Spirit. In the unity of the divine Person the two natures are certainly distinct, but in what an ineffable union are they united! Everything came to Jesus from the Father as from its unique source, and Jesus referred Himself entirely to the Father and glorified Him in every one of His actions.

Such is, in its most eminent perfection, the state of sanctity which Christ desires to establish in the soul of Him who receives holy communion.

In giving the Eucharist to the Church, God willed undoubtedly that Christ should be offered and immolated under the sacred species, that He should be adored, visited, loved in the tabernacle, but it was His will also that His Son should be our food so that we might be made participants in the divine life: "except you eat the flesh of the Son of man and drink His blood you shall not have life in you" (Jn 6:54).

Ordinary bread, without having life in itself, maintains the strength of our body but, when we receive the eucharistic bread and wine, it is a living being, it is Jesus Who enters into us, Who takes possession of us and, by this union, makes us like to Himself. Has He not said: "I am, *Ego sum*, the living bread which comes down from heaven" (Jn 4:51). In itself, the divine life is inaccessible, but through this sacrament, it is it which comes to us. All the increase of sanctity which the Father wills to grant to His children of adoption is there in Jesus, ready to be communicated to us. Consider this wonderful truth; the soul of the Saviour was in unbroken contact with the Word and was vivified by Him; our sacramental union with Christ lasts only a few moments each day, but short as it is, how immense is its power of sanctification! This union is certainly not as close as that of the Word with His human nature; and yet does not the author of grace take His repose in the soul? He clothes it with His merits; He enables it to live in the grace of adoption, and gives it access to the Holy Trinity; "If anyone love Me . . . My Father will love Him and We will come to Him and make our abode with Him" (Jn 14:23). The sacramental union prepared by the divine Wisdom is so true an imitation of the union between the Word and His human nature that Jesus expressly confirms it: "As the living Father hath sent Me and I live by the Father, so he that eateth Me the same also shall live by Me" (Jn 6:58).[6]

It is impossible to grasp the full depth of the mystery of the eucharistic union without considering this analogy willed by the divine Master Himself. Consider the astonishing eminence which this comparison reveals; allow your mind to be impregnated with the truth which it discloses. During your whole priestly life the respect and the expectation of grace which should accompany each of your communions will be strengthened and helped by it. St. Hilary sums up these elevated considerations in concise terms: "Christ has His life from the Father

---

[6] Lagrange, who admits that the choice is difficult, translates *for the Father*; Colmes, Crampton, Bězy and Osty translate *by the Father*; Dom Marmion has adopted the latter translation.

and, just as He lives by the Father, so we live by His flesh": *quo modo per Patrem vivit, eodem modo nos per carnem eius vivimus.*[7]

Among the principal glories of our Mass is that of being in all truth a nuptial banquet. At the moment of the Incarnation the Father presented to His Son a human nature destined to be united to Him like an immaculate spouse. At the altar the priest presents to Christ souls to be vivified: His own soul and those of the congregation, so that the Saviour, by the gift of Himself, may make them participate in His own life. We should realize to what heights holy communion invites us. For our progress in sanctity depends in a very large measure on the way in which we habitually participate in the eucharistic banquet.

IV. THE EFFECTS OF HOLY COMMUNION

The consideration of the nature of the divine union which the Eucharist establishes in us does not exhaust all that we would like to remind you of concerning this ineffable sacrament. Let us consider more precisely what graces each holy communion brings to the soul.

The sacraments produce the effect expressed by the sensible sign of each. As the holy Eucharist was instituted in the form of a banquet, it must produce in the supernatural order a mysterious nourishment of the life of the soul.

Corporal food is first absorbed; the organism then assimilates it to itself and in this way it conserves life and encourages growth. The eucharistic bread operates in us in an analogous manner. While we receive it with our mouths, *quod ore sumpsimus*, Christ unites Himself to the soul: *pura mente capiamus.* He fecundates and increases in the soul the divine life of which baptism has bestowed the seed.

The individual changes ordinary food into his own substance; but in receiving the Eucharist we do not change Jesus Christ into ourselves. On the contrary, it is He, the food of life, Who transforms us into Himself. In the mystery of this union,

---

[7] *De Trinitate* 8; PL 10, 248.

we see verified the mysterious words which St. Augustine put on the lips of the Lord: "I am the food of grown men; grow and you shall eat Me. And you shall not change Me into yourself as bodily food, but into Me you shall be changed." [8] This is the first sacramental effect, *ex opere operato*, of holy communion: the growth of sanctifying grace. By virtue of this increase we become, through every communion worthily received, more like to God, more deiform, by a supernatural participation in His nature: *efficiamini divinae consortes naturae* (2 Pet 1:4).

In order to achieve the fullness of union between man and Christ, the Father has willed also that the virtue proper to the sacrament should revitalize habitual charity in us, making it more fervent. This love which the Eucharist produces not only brings us closer to Christ but it unites us to Him in the bond of this union, it transforms us gradually into the object of our love: *in virtute huius sacramenti*, says St. Thomas, *fit quaedam transformatio hominis ad Christum per amorem*.[9] So great is the intimacy of the divine presence that Our Saviour could say: "He that eateth My flesh abideth in Me and I in Him" (Jn 6:57). The whole practice of the Christian virtues is vivified and strengthened by this voluntary loving adherence to Christ. The practice of charity is sovereignly efficacious in helping the priest to imitate the example of Jesus. In order that we may be saints, the Father requires us to reproduce in ourselves the characteristics of His Son Incarnate; we must become so like Christ that the Father will recognize us as His true children. The Eucharist is a potent support to us in this work of assimilation to Christ; it confers on us the necessary graces to conform in all things to Jesus by accepting the divine will, by giving ourselves to our neighbour, by patience and by pardon. We all want to be fervent priests. We may be weak by temperament, or perhaps energetic, but to all this sacrament communicates the strength which comes from God.

The bread given to Elijah to revive him in his discouragement was a figure of the Eucharist: *et ambulavit in fortitudine cib*

---

[8] *Confessions* 7, 10; PL, 742.
[9] *Sentiarum Distinctio* 12, q. 2, 2.

illius usque ad montem Dei: "And he arose . . . and went in the strength of that food . . . to the mount of God" (1 Kings 19:8). For us also, holy communion provides a remedy for our weakness. Is it not *fortitudo fragilium*?[10] By the love which it excites, it enables us to overcome weariness, lassitude, temptations; it helps us to bear our cross in the steps of the divine Master.

Does the Eucharist also effect the remission of venial sins? Undoubtedly. The fervour of love, which is the immediate effect of the grace of the sacrament, produces in the soul an aversion to every obstacle to union with Christ. This estrangement from sin obtains from God the pardon of venial sins to which we have no attachment. That is why the Eucharist purifies the soul of those stains which have been left in it by faults: *Ut in me non remaneant scelerum macula.*

Moreover, by the divine help which it assures us, it corrects our evil inclinations: *vitia nostra curentur.*[11] And do we not ask at every Mass to receive it as a salutary remedy? *Ad medelam percipiendam.*

An effect of holy communion to which we do not attach sufficient importance is spiritual joy. This grace means a great deal in our priestly life. Holy communion is an immense source of joy, of the purest, more intimate, most solid joy. God is beatitude itself. All the happiness that is to be found in creation is only a reflection, a shadow of this infinite felicity. So great is the joy of heaven that St. Paul tells us that: "it hath not entered into the heart of man what things God hath prepared for them that love Him" (1 Cor 2:9).

By the eucharistic union not only do we enjoy a flow of this heavenly beatitude but we receive the Author of it Himself with all the plentitude of His riches. St. Rose of Lima declared that at the moment of receiving holy communion it seemed to her as though she were taking the sun into her heart.[12] In fact, just as in creation the sun is the source of light, of vitality, and

---

[10] Third Post-Communion of the daily Mass in Lent.
[11] Post-Communion of the Seventeenth Sunday after Pentecost.
[12] *Acta sanctorum* 39, August 5, p. 958.

of cheerfulness, so Jesus, by holy communion, is the source of that contentment, ever new, of that courage, never disheartened, which constitute Christian strength.

I do not speak here of sensible consolation, but of that hope, of that enthusiasm which made St. Paul say: "I exceedingly abound with joy in all our tribulations" (2 Cor 7:4). This supernatural joy gave the martyrs the power to laugh and sing in the midst of their torments. They had been strengthened beforehand at the wedding banquet of the Lamb; they had received holy communion.

This happiness conferred by the Eucharist expresses itself in certain souls by a vivid sense of serenity and peace. General de Sonis, when in the field, received holy communion every time that he could. On the evening of the battle of Solferino he wrote: "During this terrible day I do not think that I was for one moment forgetful of the presence of God."[13] Is not the attitude of this soldier in the midst of tumult and dangers a striking example for us of the calm and tranquillity which a soul sanctified by the divine presence should possess?

It may happen that our faith is blind to the splendours of the Eucharist, but, as we receive holy communion, let us try to believe firmly in the reality, in the sublimity of the ineffable gift bestowed on our soul. Thanks to this lively faith a slow but sure transformation will be effected gradually in the inmost depths of our priestly life.

The fruits of this sacrament are so life-giving that it is impossible to exhaust their vitality. One cannot attempt to say everything; let me draw your attention at least to one last and supremely important effect: the Eucharist gives us a pledge of future beatitude: *et futurae gloriae nobis pignus datur.*[14] It prepares us for the heavenly banquet in the kingdom of the Father, a banquet promised on the occasion of the Last Supper by Christ Himself (Mt 16:29), a banquet at which He will satisfy the elect with His glory: *Satiabor cum apparuerit gloria tua:* "I shall be satisfied with beholding thy form" (Ps 17[16]:15). Do we con-

---

[13] Msgr. Baunard, *Vie*, p. 112.
[14] The Antiphon of Vespers of Corpus Christi.

sider this sufficiently when we say: "May the body . . . may the blood of our Lord preserve my soul to life everlasting"?

V. UNITY IN CHRIST

All the effects of which we have just spoken concern each one of us individually. But the Eucharist is also the sacrament of union with Christ as Head of the mystical body. It makes the faithful enter more fully into that plenitude of the supernatural order which makes Christ and us one incomparable unity.

We must develop in our hearts a living appreciation of the fact that we belong to the mystical body. For us priests this faith is indispensable to sustain our zeal in our work for those souls for which we are responsible.

Jesus desires ardently that this union of the faithful to their Head and between themselves should be realized in His Church. At the Last Supper, after having instituted the Blessed Sacrament, He speaks to the Father. And what does He ask of Him? The union of all in Himself: "Holy Father, keep them . . . that they may be one as Thou, Father, in Me and I in Thee . . . that they may be made perfect in one" (Jn 17:11, 21, 23). Mass and holy communion—the wedding banquet of the Son of God—are par excellence the sacred means destined to bring about this sublime union: "For we, being many, are one bread," says the Apostle, "one body all that partake of one bread": *Quoniam unus panis, unum corpus multi sumus, omnes qui de uno pane participamus* (1 Cor 10:17). The power of the sacrament makes souls enter into the mystery of the mystical body; it makes of them members more closely attached to the Lord, living more completely of His life, more devoted to His service.

In its full significance, the eucharistic union requires the faithful to love Christ and, with Him and for Him, His mystical body.

The grace of the sacrament makes us embrace in our love the whole Christ; the Head, the members and all the souls redeemed by His sacrifice; charity is therefore the powerful supernatural bond which, even in this world, effects, in the city

of God, a wondrous union of all the members among themselves. The reign of the charity of Christ in His Church should
become ever more the object of our desires, of our zeal and of
our preaching. We must work to realize it in the diocese, in the
parish, in our works, in our immediate surroundings. The
fervour of charity will move us to show respect and affection for
our neighbour, forgetfulness of ourselves and devotion to duty.
At the moment of holy communion it will banish from our
minds the memory of the wrongdoings of others; it will drive
from our hearts indifference, coldness, every thing that leads to
division. Thus, as one of the Post-Communions asks, the Eucharist—the sacrament of unity—will incorporate us ever more
fully in Christ: "Grant us, Almighty God, to be numbered
among the members of Him Whose body and blood we have
received." [15]

Does the sacred humanity of Christ dwell in the soul of
every member of the mystical body? By holy communion we
certainly enter into contact with Jesus, submitting ourselves to
His sovereign domination. As the Council of Ephesus says:
"the flesh of Christ is life-giving because it is the flesh of the
Word": *carnem Domini vivificatricem esse . . . quia facta est propria
Verbi.*[16] In the sacrament, Jesus touches, sanctifies, and takes
possession of the soul. He casts His rays upon it from the
glorious shelter of the Eucharist. As long as the sacred species
remain unaltered, the soul receives the benefit of this *contactus
virtutis*; it becomes more dependent on the action of the Lord,
more profoundly united to His mystical body. But when the
sacramental presence ceases, the faithful Christian, as a member
of the mystical body, remains still under the influence of the
Saviour. Christ assists him from without and from within; He
fecundates His supernatural life. He dwells, in a certain sense,
in His heart; *Christum habitare per fidem in cordibus vestris* (Eph
3:17). These words of the Apostle do not refer to the eucharistic presence, but to that efficacious, intimate and continuous
union, thanks to which Christ, the Word Incarnate, Head of

[15] Mass of the Saturday of third week of Lent.
[16] Canon 2.

the mystical body, dwells and operates permanently in the heart
of each one of us.

VI. OBSTACLES TO RECEIVING
THE FRUITS OF HOLY COMMUNION

It may happen sometimes that we are grieved because our holy
communions do not produce a great effect in us; we hear pious
souls making the same complaint. And yet this bread from
heaven contains all spiritual sweetness; *omne delectamentum* (Ver-
sicle of the Office of Corpus Christi). The lack of fervour of
our communions arises from many causes. Some of these may
be temporary: ill-health, environment, annoyances which arise
just as we are about to celebrate may prevent the soul from
savouring the divine presence in peace.

We may pass over these special reasons and consider two obstacles which everyone may encounter and to which we must
face up: a lack of vivacity in our faith and an inadequacy in our
giving of ourselves. The Eucharist is, supremely, the *mysterium
fidei.* When we contemplate the consecrated host there is nothing to reveal to our senses the presence of Our Saviour. Nevertheless, He is there in all His majesty and heavenly glory with
the same love which He had for us here on earth. It is only faith
which, surmounting the appearances of bread and wine, can
grasp this mystery.

If at the time of holy communion our faith is weak or dormant, or if it allows itself to be distracted by external things, it
cannot appreciate at their just value the gift of the Father nor
the merciful condescension of Jesus. For want of faith we remain, as it were, indifferent to the supernatural riches which are
brought to us by the Eucharist.

On the other hand, when our faith is alive and attentive, the
soul is struck with admiration; it knows how the gift of Christ
to the world and to each individual in particular is always
present, always active. By this sacrament in all truth we are
"filled unto all the fullness of God". This fullness comes to us *ut
impleamini in omnem plenitudinem Dei* (Eph 3:19). When, in spite

of your preparation, you suffer because you do not feel your heart thrilled by these wonders, you must not be distressed. God does not require us to enter into contact with the supernatural realities by means of sentiment; it is in the obscurity of faith and by your will that He asks you to love Him and serve Him. Sentiment is useful in so far as by it our faith is intensified. In your communions and in all your relations with the Eucharist try to unite yourself to the Lord by faith like St. Paul when he said: *in fide vivo Filii Dei*: "I live by faith in the Son of God" (Gal 2:20).

There is another interior disposition the absence of which is very prejudicial to the good effects of holy communion. That is the giving of self. As Christ is communicating Himself to us, is it not fitting that we should give ourselves to Him? This gift of self is a confiding of our whole life to the Lord, an accepting of His will for the present and for the future. This spirit of abandonment is the *dispositio unionis* par excellence. Thanks to it, Christ finds nothing in us to oppose His domination over the soul.

"Communion" means "union with" Jesus. We cannot realize this union unless we bring to the Saviour a soul such that He in His sanctity and love can be united with it. Christ cannot unite Himself to a soul which is not humble, to a heart which does not receive Him unreservedly, which neglects the duties of its state, or above all, which is closed to its neighbour for lack of charity or the spirit of forgiveness. Would it not be dishonest, in fact, to seek to be united to the Head at the same time as one was ignoring the needs of His members and their love? The things which create an obstacle to our union with Christ are our self-love, our susceptibilities, our plans for the future based on vanity, our egoistical aspirations, our worldly or unspiritual points of view; all these things are inconsistent with the full conformity of our will to the will of Jesus.

It is not therefore our weakness nor our moral wretchedness which constitutes an obstacle to our enjoying the fruits of the sacrament provided that, so far from being attached to them, we regret them. Jesus comes to us to give us the strength to combat our faults; "surely He hath borne our infirmities and carried our sorrows": *vere languores nostros ipse tulit et dolores nostros ipse portavit* (Is 53:4).

Where shall we find the most perfect model of this giving of self? In Christ Himself. According to the Fathers of the Church, the meeting of the two natures in Him was a nuptial union. When we receive holy communion our meeting with Christ is effected in love, and Christ draws us to Himself, unites us to Himself so that we may be His for ever. What was the primary disposition of the humanity of Jesus at the time of the Incarnation? It delivered itself, it gave itself in the spirit of abandonment like a bride to her husband. *Ecce venio . . . ut faciam voluntatem tuam*: "Behold I come to do your will" (Heb 10:7).

As for the Blessed Virgin Mary, what were her interior dispositions throughout her life? They were undoubtedly those manifested by her reply to the angel on the occasion of the Annunciation: "Behold the handmaid of the Lord." These two phrases: *Ecce venio . . . Ecce ancilla* are echoes of each other. Such should be the movement of our souls also when we receive holy communion. This disposition is essentially sacerdotal and in conformity with the mission of the priest in the Church; it corresponds with the *Imitamini quod tractatis* and assures great fruits of grace for our communions.

Apart from these two obstacles to the efficacy of the sacrament, zealous priests devoted to the care of souls are certainly familiar with another: the difficulty of conversing alone with the Lord both before and after holy communion. At this time when they would like to pray, they are constantly disturbed, pulled in all directions. Here is the advice which I think I may give them: let them try to compensate for this lack of recollection by a very great purity of intention; let them say to themselves: "I am serving Christ in His members, I am carrying out all my ministry for them and for love of Him."

The best immediate preparation for a good holy communion is the Mass itself, celebrated with a lively faith. In default of a thanksgiving immediately after the holy sacrifice, one can make up for it later on by some prayer or by a visit to the Blessed

Sacrament. Do not conclude from this, however, that it is justifiable to underestimate the importance of a devout and respectful thanksgiving. This is not at all what I mean to convey. I only want to remind you that if, despite your good intentions, you are called away by the urgent necessities of your ministry, you must not lose confidence on that account. The total gift of self is the *dispositio unionis* par excellence.

The habit of recalling during the day the splendid privilege of the communion of the morning and of looking forward to the communion of the following day is another excellent practice of piety to enable us to gain more benefit from the reception of the sacrament.

Every morning at the altar we meet a friend infinitely worthy of our love, Jesus, our God. Let us try to love Him humbly, to give ourselves to Him without reserve, for the present with all its vicissitudes, for the future with all its uncertainties. And in our desire to raise ourselves to this nobility of life, to this fullness of union, let us rely only on His merits and on His grace. This is what St. Augustine recommends: "Let us love God by the gift which God Himself bestows on us": *Amemus Deum de Deo.*[17] A soul who lives in these sentiments will always benefit from his Mass and his communion.

[17] *Sermo* 34; PL 38, 210.

XIV.

THE DIVINE OFFICE [1]

We do not cease to be priests when we come down from the altar. After the sacrifice of the Mass there remains another priestly activity which we must offer to God; we must offer praise to Him by the recitation of the divine Office. Was not the whole life of Jesus an act of priestly homage? From the time He came into the world, it was as a priest that the Word Incarnate presented Himself to the Father, and, during His whole life on earth the adoration and praise of Jesus was continuous.

Before the recitation of the Hours we allude to this constant sacerdotal prayer of the Saviour when we declare that we wish to recite these Hours in union with the divine intention which animated Him on earth in His praise of God.

By his daily recourse to the breviary; therefore, the priest intends to imitate Christ in His contemplation of the Father and in His perfect prayer. In this manner He gives to the Lord the glory which is His right.

From the time of his ordination to the sub-diaconate [currently the diaconate], the life of the minister of Christ is entirely devoted to the divine service. Worship is the first and principal purpose of his state. That is why the Church not merely urges him to be a man of prayer but prescribes the very form of his prayers. For the ordinary Catholic, apart from assistance at Mass and the reception of the sacraments, everything is left to his private devotion; but the supplication and praise of the priest are so important that the Church herself prescribes the order of them.

She imposes this prayer under grave obligation.* Why is the obligation grave?

[1] See, in *Christ, the Life of the Soul*, the chapter "*Vox Sponsae*" and, in *Christ, the Ideal of the Monk*, the two chapters "*Opus Dei*"—the Divine Praise—and "Means of Union with God".

* In 2002, the Congregation for the Clergy affirmed this obligation "sub grave" ("The Priest, Pastor and Leader of the Parish Community", 14).

First of all, because the canonical Hours constitute an act of religious homage which the Church considers herself bound to offer to God by the mouth of her ministers. Secondly, because the priest, if he is to avoid moral mediocrity and to maintain his fervour, must have recourse to this great instrument of prayer constantly renewed.

There are some who complain at times that the breviary means nothing to them, and that the recitation of it, instead of being a support and a consolation, is for them a heavy burden. I recognize the element of trouble which the daily application to the canonical Hours involves. Nevertheless, you may be quite sure that, if you grasp the great truths of faith which you are reminded of here, and if you follow the directions which I will suggest to you, you will discover to what an extent your priestly life can be supernaturalized by the worthy recitation of the breviary.

I. EXCELLENCE OF THE DIVINE OFFICE

How can we form for ourselves a true idea of the excellence of the official prayer of the Church?

In the adorable Trinity, God gives Himself a glory worthy of God, a praise which is perfect. We know this by revelation; it is the Word, the Second Person of the Blessed Trinity Who is the glory of the Father: *splendor gloriae et figura substantiae eius* (Heb 1:3). In the bosom of the Father, He is, of His own right, the sublime eternal canticle: *et Verbum erat apud Deum* (Jn 1:1), the infinite hymn of glory chanted *in sinu Patris*. We cannot form an adequate idea of this praise which the Son gives to the Father, as the subsisting Word, expressing all His perfection.

Moreover, being united with the Father and the Holy Spirit, the Word has created all things: *omnia per ipsum facta sunt*. The Father had conceived this creation in His wisdom: "in that which was made was the life" and it redounded to the glory of the Father: *quod factum est in ipso vita erat*. By the Incarnation the Son has not ceased to be the living Word, the Canticle which He was already; but, through the human nature which He assumed in His divine Person, He has praised the Father under a new form. And so, in the Word Incarnate, human praise acquired a new splendour. We can recognize in Christ, therefore, a divine paean of glorification—Which is of an order far above us and which we adore—and a human hymn of praise. As man, Jesus praised His Father and loved His Father in the joy of His participation in the eternal sonship. His soul contemplated, in the Word, the life of the Trinity.

But, furthermore, the whole of created nature took in Him a new impulse to bless the Father. Jesus was the mouth-piece of the whole of creation. This praise was still the praise of a God but it was expressed in human language in conformity with our nature, and varied in its expression.

What a subject for contemplation the prayer of Jesus during His life on earth affords us! *Erat pernoctans in oratione Dei*: "all night he continued in prayer to God" (Lk 6:12). And when Jesus sang in the synagogue or prayed in the temple with the Jewish community—as He did doubtless from the age of twelve—His prayer ascended to God like incense, like a sweet perfume, *in odorem suavitatis*. He knew the Psalms. All the religious attitudes evoked by these inspired canticles, took life in Him in a manner which was sublime: "All ye works of the Lord, bless ye the Lord"; "Yahweh, sovereign Master, how admirable is Thy Name in the whole earth": *quam admirable est nomen tuum* (Ps 8:1).

Jesus rendered in a perfect manner that worship of prayer which man owes to God in all justice. He honoured the Father by adoration, love, praise, thanksgiving and petition. And as a consequence of the union of the humanity with the Word these acts attained in Him a perfection and a value which were infinite.

Before ascending to heaven, Christ bequeathed to His Spouse, the Church, all the riches of His merits, of His graces, of His teaching, and also the power to continue on earth the work of the glorification of the Trinity which had been inaugurated by Him.

And the Church "leans on her beloved", *innixa super dilectum*

(Song 8:5), to make her prayer reach up to God. Jesus, in His glory, makes this praise His own: "By Him," says St. Paul, "let us offer the sacrifice of praise always to God, that is to say, the fruit of lips confessing to His name" (Heb 13:15). On the Cross, He gave Himself up completely for love of His Church, and He remains ever closely united to it. The canticle of his members mingles with that of their Head. Hence these amazing words of St. Augustine: "They are two in one flesh; why, then, should they not be two in one voice? . . . It is the Church which intercedes in Christ and Christ Who intercedes in the Church; the body is one with the Head and the Head is one with the body": *In Ecclesia loquitur Christus; et corpus in capite et caput in corpore.*[2]

A comparison will help you to grasp this mystery. The satisfaction of Christ for the expiation of the sins of the world was superabundant. This is the teaching of the Church. And yet, God willed to reserve a part of the suffering for the mystical body. The Apostle declares it: "I fill up those things that are wanting of the sufferings of Christ, in my flesh, for His body which is the Church": *Adimpleo ea quae desunt passionum Christi . . . pro corpore eius quod est Ecclesia* (Col 1:24). That which is true about expiation is also true about our obligation to adore God, to praise and thank Him. We must prolong and complete the homage which Christ rendered to the Father: *adimplere ea quae desunt laudationum Christi.* The Church has organized this prayer; she has done so in language and with gestures which are adapted to our human nature. Whatever be its manner of expression, the liturgy carries on the praise of the Saviour; it associates itself with the Canticle of the Word Incarnate and, through Him, its prayer ascends from the wilderness of this life to the bosom of the Father.

The sacrifice of the Mass is the *sacrificium laudis* par excellence, but the whole day long this sacrifice is prolonged by the divine Office of which the Hours constitute, as it were, a constant radiance of the sacred immolation. Our special mission as priests is to be the delegates to carry out these functions. On his

[2] *Enarratio super Psalmos* 11, 4; PL 36, 232.

ordination as deacon the priest received the privilege to speak to God in the name of all: *totius Ecclesiae sit quasi os* [that is, "the mouth of the whole Church"].[3] He prays for sinners and also for the souls united to Christ by charity. When he says his Office, he acts as an ambassador, as an accredited mediator, because he praises and intercedes for all in the name of the Church. This official prayer is always acceptable: *Sonet vox tua in auribus meis* (Song 2:14—"your voice is sweet"). At every moment the priest has free entry to audience with the divinity. Even if his own personal dispositions do not correspond to his mission, his delegation by the Church makes up in a sovereign manner for his deficiencies. That is why a missioner in the depths of the bush does not say *Orem* (I pray) but *Oremus* (Let us pray). It is in the name of the whole of Christendom that he sends up his prayer to God.*

This priestly work of praise and intercession is in the highest degree efficacious for the salvation of the world. "May the evening prayer ascend to you, O Lord, and may your mercy descend upon us."[4] The Lord could certainly sanctify souls without our help but, in His goodness, He wills to use our collaboration. The divine Office plays a great part in the order of Providence. Certainly the recitation of the Office is a great exercise of faith; we do not see the results of our efforts or of our prayers. God knows them and allots the merit due. We can understand, then, the value attached by the Church to the canonical Hours which St. Benedict calls by the splendid name *Opus Dei* and of which St. Alphonsus says that a hundred private prayers have not the value of a single prayer said in the divine Office.[5] It is a magnificent work which is entrusted to us. What does God expect of His priests? The generosity to spend

[3] St. Bernardinus of Siena: *Opera omnia, Venetiis, apud Juntas,* 1951. (I *Sermo* 20, p. 132.)

* In the aforementioned Congregation for the Clergy document of 2002, Blessed Columba Marmion is referenced from this section of *Christ—The Ideal of the Priest.* The document states in number 14: "In the Divine Office he supplies what is lacking in the praise of Christ and, as an accredited ambassador, his intercession for the salvation of the world is numbered among the most effective." The footnote references Dom Marmion, which is exciting for any Marmion devoté.

[4] Verse inspired by the Psalms of Vespers on Saturday in the Monastic Office.

[5] *Oeuvres Complètes* 11, p. 209, translated by Dujardin (Tournai: Casterman, 1882).

themselves for the salvation of souls certainly; but this giving of self must be made fruitful by the recitation of the breviary. You must be convinced of this.

II. PREPARATION

The divine Office is the official prayer of the Church. Hence its fundamental value.

But this prayer can only rise to heaven if it passes through our lips and through our heart. The personal piety of the priest, therefore, confers a very real value—though of another order—on the recitation of the canonical Hours. Thanks to the faith of the priest, to his love of Christ and his spirit of praise, the divine Office sanctifies him, gains him merit and makes his intercession more powerful in the eyes of God.

Before reading the breviary it is a good thing to prepare our hearts to read it well. The first and the most important point in this preparation is to spend a few moments in recollection. One cannot insist too much on this point. It is of capital importance.

Remember that without grace we are incapable of praying well: *sine Me nihil potestis facere* (Jn 15:5). The *Deus in adjutorium* ("God come to my assistance") at the beginning of every Hour is a constant reminder of this great truth.

However, here is what happens to us often enough: after having been busy with distracting or absorbing affairs, forthwith, without a moment's recollection, without asking God for grace, we take up the breviary and begin the recitation of the Office straightaway. We satisfy the strict canonical obligation, but this prayer will be gone through without unction and will bear little or no fruit.

I have been saying the divine Office for many years. I know by experience that unless one takes the trouble to make suitable preparation one prays distractedly. Holy Scripture is not deceiving us when it says: "Before prayer prepare thy soul and be not as a man that tempteth God" (Sir 18:23). What does it mean to "tempt God"? It means undertaking a work without doing all that depends on us to ensure its perfect accomplishment. It is certainly temerarious to presume to praise God in the name of the Church without recollecting oneself and without imploring His graces. Hear what St. Augustine says: "My lips could not praise you, Lord, if your mercy had not come to my aid. It is by virtue of your gift that I praise you": *Dono tuo te laudo*.[6]

And where are we to find the faith, the respect, and the love which we need for this task? Certainly not in ourselves. We must ask God for them. Without preparation, the breviary will inevitably be recited nonchalantly, mechanically. If we commence the Office in a state of distraction, we shall generally come away from it in the same state as we began. There is a danger then of the Hours becoming a burden for us instead of being a joy, a ray of sunshine in our interior life.

Let me quote a personal experience to confirm the necessity of this preparation. There were three of us friends at the Seminary. It was not a particular friendship. If it had been, it would not have lasted long. As it is, it has lasted for fifty years. We entered the Seminary together, and together we were sent to Rome. Later on, when I was curate near Dublin, one of these friends when visiting me noticed that I began to say the Hours without the few moments of recollection which had been recommended to us in college. He remarked it to me in a friendly way and I have always been grateful to him for it. When we met twenty years later I had an opportunity of remarking how my friend remained faithful to this practice and it was a source of edification for me.

What should we do during this pause for recollection? Firstly, make an effort of will to drive away all irrelevant thoughts. Say to Our Lord: "I want to think of nothing but You and holy Church. I am weak, my mind often wanders, but it is my desire, it is my wish to remain attentive, prostrate with the angels and the saints." This intention counts in the eyes of God during the whole Office in spite of any distractions that may come; we have disowned these in advance.

[6] *Enarratio super Psalmos* 52, 12; PL 37, 750.

Think of God and of your mission to render Him homage through Jesus Christ. At Patmos the veil which covers the heavenly realities was, so to speak, raised, and what did St. John see? He saw millions of angels around the Throne of God; they were singing the eternal *Sanctus*. And what were the twenty-four elders doing? They were throwing down their crowns before the Lord and proclaiming that He was worthy of glory, honour and power (Rev 4:11). This is the fundamental attitude of respect which is fitting when we propose to glorify God.

Others prefer to unite themselves to the Church militant. They call to mind the innumerable priests and religious, men and women, united all over the world in the same act of praise.

It is an excellent practice to form an intention which will serve as the motive for our recitation. It is easier to keep our minds alert when we have before our eyes the reasons which urge us to pray. Before we begin, let us think of the sufferings and dangers of so many souls; of the multitude of sinners, this immense mass of humanity harassed by demons and by vice. When we forget ourselves in this way, we can feel that we are the *os totius Ecclesiae* [mouth of the whole Church], and experience the inspiration of devotion.

An excellent means of recollection is to dwell on each word of the preparatory prayer, *Aperi*: "Open my lips, O Lord, to bless Thy Name, purify my heart of all thoughts which are vain, evil, or irrelevant, enlighten my intelligence, give me the spirit of love."

You may be quite sure that the time devoted to preparation is not lost; on the contrary, these are golden minutes. Even with the help of long-established habit—it is better to warn you of it—this recollection will always require a certain effort, but God Who witnesses it will reward you generously. In spite of all your good will it may happen on account of tiredness or some overwhelming preoccupation that you are troubled or distracted; that happens even to saints. But, here again, God, Who has seen the preparation of your heart, will accept your homage in spite of the weaknesses which accompany it.

III. THE RECITATION

We must consider now the recitation itself and the dispositions which it requires.

In the *Aperi* we ask to be able to say the Office in a worthy, attentive, and devout manner. These three dispositions are necessary if we wish to discharge our duty fittingly. What does "worthy" mean? It means reciting the divine Office with due regard for the majesty of God. We are mediators, ambassadors; an ambassador must observe the protocol which is recognized in the court of the king. Carelessness in this would constitute not merely a want of delicacy but a fault. The rubrics prescribed by the Church are the etiquette or external attitude required in the carrying out of the sacred functions. Open the Old Testament; the carrying of the ark of alliance and all the prescribed worship involved a good deal of ceremony. And yet this was only the figure. We have the reality of these symbols and rites.

We must be eager to render to God these external tributes of respect. These prescriptions may seem to you rather petty, but fidelity in their observance is always an act of virtue, and for three reasons. By it we are obeying rules prescribed by the Church herself for the common good—we are carrying out an act of external worship by means of which the body is united with the soul in the service of God; finally, and above all, our submission is the expression of our interior devotion to the King of kings. If we were to see God in the splendour of His majesty we would die; were He to allow us to see even some ray of the invisible world, we would fall on our knees. This was the effect on the three disciples on Mount Tabor: "They fell upon their face and were very much afraid" (Mt 17:6). What was the origin of this fear which prostrated them like this? It was the immediate effect of the keen realization of the presence of God. A glimpse of the brightness of the divine order sufficed to plunge their souls into adoration.

We, who live by faith, must speak to God with profound reverence. This will help us at all times to maintain an attitude of dignity during the recitation. There is nothing so helpful to piety, nothing which impresses the faithful more than this religious reverence of the priest in the practice of prayer.

If the word "worthily" applies chiefly to our external attitude, the word "attentive" refers exclusively to our application of soul. Why is it necessary to recite the Office with attention? Because all the enthusiasm and all the merit of praise spring primarily from love, and love requires knowledge.

St. Thomas distinguishes three kinds of attention: *ad verba, ad sensum, ad Deum.*[7] Attention to the words alone suffices to discharge the canonical obligation, but it is imperfect. Attention to the sense of the words, and especially attention to God, makes the prayer perfect. The latter is the most important. A nun who does not know Latin may fix her attention during the recitation on the mystery which is being celebrated, on God, on the Persons of the Holy Trinity, on the divine perfections. If she has a keen desire to pay homage to the Lord, she gives glory to Him and, with the help of the liturgy, she may attain to true contemplation.

For us priests this sense of the presence of God will normally be maintained by our understanding of the sacred text. The soul of the priest, attentive to the sense of the words he pronounces, will respond to the many suggestions of the liturgy. His religious conviction will gain in depth from his contact with the official prayer of the Church; so, likewise, will his confidence in the divine bounty, his gratitude, his humility and his love. What a spiritual elevation this daily prayer will give the priest if, to the tenets of faith which the text of his breviary recalls, he replies from the bottom of his heart: *Amen*; that is to say, "Yes, Lord, I believe all these sayings, I adopt them as my own."

In order to facilitate this effort of attention we should have a high appreciation of the Psalms. In the ages of faith, Christians made more use of the psalter; it was the chosen book of prayer. It was often the favourite book of the saints. "My psalter is my joy": *Psalterium meum gaudium meum,*[8] exclaimed St. Augustine.

[7] *Summa*, II-II, q. 83, a. 13.
[8] *Enarratiosuper Psalmos* 137; PL 37, 1775.

Admittedly we meet sacred canticles the subject matter of which is more or less foreign to us but, without attempting to conform to the suggestions of all the verses, it will suffice certainly, as we recite them, to establish a harmony between the soul and some of them in accordance with the saying of St. Bernard: "Food is savoured in the mouth; the psalm in the heart": *cibus in ore, psalmus in corde sapit.*[9]

The psalter is like a divine harp which the Church gives us that we may sing the praises of Him Whom we love. We find in it the perfect expression of those sentiments of faith, of hope, and of love which we should entertain in regard to Our Father in heaven. Only God knows Himself perfectly; only God knows how He should be praised. In the Psalms inspired by the Holy Spirit, He Himself dictates to us the terms in which He is pleased to be praised by us. These glorious formulas teach us how to bless the divine Majesty, to proclaim His infinite perfections, to acknowledge His merciful benefits, to tell Our Lord of our struggles, of our need of pardon, and of our joys.

How salutary it is for us to establish an interior harmony with those attitudes of soul to which the Psalms invite us! These attitudes are true, adapted to our human nature and eminently beneficial. See, for example, the expressions of love and appreciation which we meet in Psalm 110[109]: "The Lord says to my lord": *Dixit Dominus Domino meo.* We hear the Father glorifying the Son in His eternal generation and in His priesthood: "From the womb of the morning I have begotten you . . . I have sworn . . . You are a priest forever": *Ex utero ante luciferum genui te . . . juravit . . . tu es sacerdos in aeternum.* We cannot offer to Christ Jesus any higher or more acceptable praise than to associate ourselves with this testimony of the Father. What a revelation of the goodness of God in Psalm 89[88]: "The mercies of the Lord I will sing for ever." We see there the divine plan of the redemption unfolding itself. God chose for Himself a David in our race, He made Him His own Son and this Son looks on His Father and says to Him: *Pater meus es tu* ("You are my Father").

[9] *In Canticum* 7, 5; PL 183, 809.

In Psalm 104[103], after having gone through all the wonders of creation, we address the Lord, saying in the spirit of admiration: "How great are Thy works, O Lord! Thou hast made all things in wisdom."

We need not multiply examples, but we should realize that it is a good thing to choose from time to time, as a subject for meditation or study, a Psalm or some other part of the divine Office. Unless we do this, there is a risk that we shall pronounce these excellent prayers automatically like a gramophone. We should rather follow the advice of St. Jerome, who urges us to sing the Psalms "in the light of Holy Scripture": *in scientia Scripturarum*.[10] How far removed from this mentality was the good priest whom I knew when I was young and who used to say with a sigh after finishing his Office: "Now, I can say my prayers." Similar examples of piety gone astray could, I believe, be found in every country.

Attention to God must always be like the keynote which sustains the diversity of the movements of the soul. In this way the dictum of the Psalm: "Sing wisely", *psallite sapienter* (Ps 47[46]:7), will be realized in us. The more the soul is recollected, the more light it will receive to understand the texts: *Illuminans tu mirabiliter a montibus aeternis*: "Glorious art thou, more majestic than the everlasting mountains" (Ps 76[75]:4). This attention to God is made much easier when we have taken every care to prepare the Psalmody.

Devote. What is devotion? We often understand by devotion a certain sweetness experienced in prayer. This is a common belief, but it is an error. One may be in a state of spiritual barrenness and dryness and yet have perfect devotion. Speaking of St. Francis de Sales, St. Jane de Chantal tells us: "He told me on one occasion that he attached no importance to whether he was in consolation or in desolation; when the Lord gave him great consolations he received them in all simplicity; if He did not give them, he did not think of them."[11] Sensible sweetness is

---

[10] *Comment. ad Ephes.* 3, 5; PL 26, 562.
[11] *Lettres de Saint Chantal*, no. 121 in *Oeuvres Complètes de Saint François de Sales* (Lyons: Perisse, 1851), p. 118.

not, therefore, true devotion. When Christ said to His Father: "My God, why have You forsaken Me" (Mt 27:46), He was certainly praying in a perfect manner and yet He was experiencing no consolation. True devotion is disinterested. It delivers up the soul to God with all the force of love. The meaning of the Latin word *devotum* suggests the idea to us.

You know the words of Christ, "Thou shalt love the Lord thy God with thy whole heart . . . and with thy whole mind" (Mt 22:37). He does not say "with thy heart, with thy mind," but "with thy whole heart": *ex tota corde*. This word *totus*, repeated like this, is a true expression of devotion; devotion is love carried to its highest point.

During the recitation of the breviary, we must apply ourselves to the divine praise, not only by our intelligence, but also by all the fullness of our affections and especially by our charity. We must direct the forces of our soul towards God. This interior application constitutes the foundation of all good prayer, and it is quite compatible with spiritual dryness. It is very pleasing to the Lord. As God is love He is pleased by our effort.

In heaven you will appreciate the full utility, for the salvation of souls and for the Church, of the true devotion which you brought to the work of praise. The Hours are *Opus Dei*. To say them well is a work much more excellent than many others. If we devote ourselves with our whole heart to this task, a holy unction will be diffused through our souls; it will enable us to savour, in interior peace, the things of God. "Honey is found in wax," said St. Bernard, "and unction in the sacred writings": *Mel in cera, devotio in littera*.[12]

We must also keep our soul under the influence of the Holy Spirit. In a symphony, every member of the orchestra is careful to follow with perfect docility the direction of the conductor who now quickens, now moderates the movement. If the spirit of God found a like submissiveness in us, He would touch the most profound chords of our hearts and draw from them the praise which God expects of us. This is so true that, in the word

[12] *In Canticum* 7, 5; PL 183, 809.

of St. John Chrysostom, every time that the Christian people apply themselves to the recitation of the Psalms they become like a lyre ready to vibrate under the hand of the Spirit, their divine inspirer: *cithara fuistis Spiritus Sancti*.[13] How much greater is the obligation for us priests to be attentive during our Office, to the inspiration from on high!

IV. SPIRITUAL FRUITS OF THE DIVINE OFFICE; ASSIMILATION TO JESUS CHRIST

The primary object of the divine Office is to praise God, to pay Him homage. But, in His goodness, the Lord allows the soul who carries out this duty in faith and love to draw from it rich fruits of sanctification.

It is beyond all doubt, as experience teaches us, that. the pious recitation of the breviary has the most beneficial effects on the interior life of the priest.

The first and most striking of these is habitual union with Christ in His priesthood of eternal praise.

All the glory rendered to God on earth as in heaven ascends to Him only through Jesus Christ. We proclaim this great truth every morning at that solemn moment when we conclude the Canon of the Mass: *Per Ipsum, et cum Ipso et in Ipso.*

When we recite the Hours in communion with the whole Church, Christ, as Head of the mystical body and centre of the communion of saints, takes up and unites all our praise in Himself. Even the blessed in heaven must avail of His priestly mediation to sing their heavenly *Sanctus: Per quem maiestatem tuam laudant angeli.* How imperfect and deficient is our giving of glory! But Christ supplies for our weakness. "If you put in His hands your poor effort," says Blosius, "your lead will be changed into precious gold, your water into the finest wine." [14]

Remember always that no one in this world has ever appreciated the splendour of the Psalms like Jesus. When He was reciting them, He knew that many of them referred to Himself, to

[13] *De Lazaro*, PG 48, 963.
[14] *Miroir de l'Ame, traduction des Bénédictines, Collection* "Pax", t. ii, p. 44.

His mission and His glory. Has not He Himself declared that these canticles refer to His own Person? (Lk 24:44). Here, then, is our model. Let us invite Christ to stand close to us, let us share in the sublimity of His devotion, let us make our own His intention of blessing the name of the Father and of desiring His kingdom.

We must be firm in this belief: God gave to the sacred humanity of Jesus the power to raise us up to Him: "Father, I will that where I am they also whom Thou hast given Me may be with Me" (Jn 17:24). Relying on His merits we are introduced before the throne of God in an audience of mercy: *In sanctuarium exauditionis.* There, we are certain that the Father sees us, hears us, and loves us in His Son, and that, as the members of this Son, we can take our part in His praise.

When we have already formulated in our preparation this desire to remain united to Jesus, it is easier for us in the course of the Hours not to lose sight of the support and reinforcement which is afforded our prayer by the all powerful mediation of our sovereign Pontiff.

Furthermore, if the priest tries to live his liturgical year in the accomplishment of this task, he will find Christ there again.

The events of the worldly life of Jesus are not only holy in themselves, they are sanctifying. On the souls who meditate on them and wish to be associated with them they confer graces which increase their union with the life of the Saviour. Why is this? Everything which Christ did on earth was done certainly for the glory of the Father, but it was done for men and for their salvation: *propter nos homines et propter nostram salutem.* That is why each of His actions, each of His words, each of His states, is a constant source of grace for us. Bethlehem, Nazareth, Golgotha, the Resurrection, the Ascension, the sending of the Holy Spirit, constitute the principal phases in the drama of our redemption and of our supernatural adoption. On the day in our annual cycle on which the Church evokes again these different mysteries their sanctifying action operates on our souls. For all of us, but especially for the priest, these solemnities are not merely an occasion for admiration; they are, in the wider

sense of the word, sacraments or rather sacramentals which produce an increase of love and joy in hearts which are well
disposed.

Some people see in the feasts of the Church only the chant,
the beauty of the vestments, the brilliance of the lights. That is
the exterior side; it is the fringe of the garment of Christ. We
must seek in them, above all, a profound union with the divine
Master. He wishes that, as members of His body, we should live
over again in the spirit of faith the events of the great mystery
of redemption which He Himself lived for us, and that we
should associate ourselves with the sentiments of His Sacred
Heart. In this way, by His grace, our vital assimilation to Jesus
will become more and more effective. Have we not here our
whole predestination? [15]

You see, therefore, that through the liturgical cycle the Lord
manifests Himself to us in a light which is always new; He
reveals Himself as nearer to our hearts, He enlivens our faith,
revives our hope and sustains the enthusiasm of our love. In this
way, year by year, the soul becomes more receptive of the current of supernatural life derived from the constant succession of
liturgical feasts; their variety is the enemy of routine, and each
recitation of the office tends to become a *Cantate Domino
canticum novum* ("sing to the Lord a new song").

V. OTHER SPIRITUAL FRUITS OF THE DIVINE OFFICE

We have the charge of souls. The priest who recites his breviary
with fidelity and devotion will often find that he is helped in a
surprising way by the Lord in the works which he undertakes
for His glory. Far be it from me to depreciate in any way the
merit of exterior works; they are necessary, blessed by the
Church, and worthy of admiration. Nevertheless, the importance which we attach to them must not be allowed to prejudice one great and essential act of our priesthood: the act of

---

[15] Dom Marmion has developed these views at length in the chapters "The Mysteries of
Christ are our mysteries"; "How we may assimulate their fruit"; in the volume: *Christ in His
Mysteries*.

praising God in the divine Office and thus fulfilling all justice. While recognizing the absolute primacy of the Mass, we must believe with a lively faith that, by accomplishing our duty of praise, we redeem souls and make fruitful our efforts in preaching and in every other branch of our ministry. By the very fact that she imposes on us the obligation of the Office, the Church shows us the importance she attaches to it: she obliges us *sub gravi* to discharge this duty every day; we are not free, except in certain specified cases, to dispense ourselves from this task. We are bound to devote the necessary time to it. And certainly it is not time lost. The most efficacious prayer for the salvation and sanctification of souls is our breviary.

Let us imitate St. Francis de Sales. When he began to recite the divine Office he put out of his mind all thought of the administration of the diocese and gave his mind solely to the praise of God. And the Lord blessed his application to prayer. "On leaving choir," he wrote, "I often found that matters of great importance, which gave me much trouble, were dealt with in a moment." [16]

Another important fruit to be drawn from the pious recitation of the Hours is a more living knowledge of the Scriptures.

From the scientific point of view one may know a great deal about the sacred books, be familiar with the different versions, the history of the text, and the various interpretations. But to perceive the deeper sense of the sacred words, to be able to put them to personal use for our interior life and for our preaching, is a gift of the Holy Spirit. There are immense depths of splendour and of love in the Bible. Many priests do not even suspect their existence; they do not realize all the light that the inspired texts contain, well calculated to establish them in an atmosphere of supernatural truth and help them to influence souls. These sacred formulas have a sacramental power; they give force and ardour to your words, now to encourage those who are suffering, now to arouse others to serious thought.

Believe me, if you recite the breviary without rushing it, the

[16] André Hamon, *Vie* 2, p. 411.

phrases of Holy Scripture which you pronounce will finally become, as it were, a part of yourself. You will find that the ensemble of the texts of the Old and New Testaments in their setting in the *Temporale* and the *Sanctorale* form a *Promptuarium*, a treasure-chamber filled with graces and light. These illuminations will enlighten your faith in the mysteries of Christ, of the Church, and even in the mystery of the Holy Trinity.

Finally the Office, well-recited, is a source of great joy for the priest.

Why? Because the breviary makes him live every day in the hope and in the possession of the supernatural goods which God has given to His Church. The liturgy is filled with that fathomless joy conferred on the Spouse of Christ by the divine benefits which have been showered on her. The priest who recites this prayer in a worthy fashion shares in the current of joy which vivifies the holy city: *Fluminis impetus laetificat civitatem Dei* (Ps 46[45]:4).

God is infinite joy, to which nothing is lacking. When we speak of Him in accordance with our human way of thinking, we are always inclined to distinguish between what He is and what He has. In fact, God is His own joy.

What is joy? It is the sentiment aroused in us by the hope and, above all, by the possession of the Good. God is infinite Good Who knows Himself, possesses Himself, and is in full enjoyment of Himself. His beatitude is perfect. He could certainly have done without us, but in His goodness He has willed to surround Himself with a wondrous creation composed of a complete hierarchy of beings, multiple and diverse. This creation praises God and reflects His joy in its universality. That is why the Psalmist invites us so often to serve the Lord with gladness: *Jubilate Deo omnis terra, servite Domino in laetitia* (Ps 96[95]:1). Wherever God is, there His glory shines forth and His happiness reigns.

If we raise our eyes to the glorious Jerusalem of heaven what do we see? We see millions of angels surrounding the Lamb. And what are they doing? They are glorifying God in a spirit of universal joy: *Socia exultatione concelebrant*. They are living in such a transport of joy that they are, as it were, carried away: *exultant*. Above them, Our Lady is blessing God and giving Him thanks and her happiness is without end: *Gaudens gaudebo in Domino*.[17] All the blessed share, each according to the degree of his glory, in this praise and this rapture. "Let the children of Sion be joyful in their King": *Filii Sion exultent in Rege suo* (Ps 149:2).

Now, in virtue of the communion of saints we are "no more strangers and foreigners", *hospites et advenae*, but "the saints are your fellow-citizens: you belong to God's household," *cives sanctorum* (Eph 2:19). Every morning at the most solemn moment of the Mass we say *Communicantes* and, by this simple word, we enter into the society of the Virgin, of the apostles and all the elect; we participate in their hymn of gratitude and in their joy which is derived from the beatitude of God Himself. Every mystery of Christ, every feast of Our Lady or of any of the inhabitants of heaven has its own special joy. This joy, which we receive into our hearts during our prayer, will overflow into our whole lives; our preaching, our ministry and our devotion to good works will benefit largely by it.

Before closing, I would like to say a word to you about distractions. To priests who complain of them, the reply is often made that everybody has distractions. However, it must be noted that, if we neglect all preparation before prayer, the wandering of our minds during the Hours will be, generally speaking, imputable to us: the spirit in which we begin the Office will dominate the whole recitation. If we are at fault at the beginning, we are to a certain extent responsible for the imperfection of the whole.

Bearing this in mind, we must recognize the fact that the essential thing in the recitation of the breviary is the desire to render homage to God in union with Jesus Christ. Even though, for some reason independent of our will, our recitation is distracted, we succeed by virtue of the fact that we are trying to discharge devoutly an act of obedience, a duty. I readily endorse

---

[17] Introit of the Mass of the Immaculate Conception.

the direction given by Bossuet in one of his letters: "After distraction, one must return without strain and very gently to one's first design to praise God . . . without being precipitate in anything, one must nevertheless banish all scruple, carrying on boldly, honestly and simply as in any other prayer." [18]

We must intensify our enthusiasm as we begin the recitation. This zeal will deliver us from many distractions which are fostered by nonchalance. And by this daily effort to sanctify the name of God, we shall prepare ourselves for the praise of eternity. Tertullian gave expression to this encouraging thought when he wrote on the subject of the *Pater*: "We are serving our apprenticeship for the function which will be given us to accomplish in the glory to come: *Officium futurae claritatis ediscimus.*[19]

As we advance in age, we become more and more experienced in the breviary, and discover accordingly new depths in it. It is, as it were, a résumé or synthesis of the whole of Scripture and also of the life of the Church and of Christian sanctity.

Before beginning our Hours, let us say to God: "I believe that by this official prayer of which I am the minister, I can achieve much, in union with Thy Son Jesus, for the needs of the Church; to help those who are in suffering, who are in their death agony, who are about to appear before Thee; to cooperate in the conversion of sinners and of the indifferent, to unite myself to the holy souls on earth and to the blessed in heaven. May everything that is in me, Lord, confess and adore Thee": *Benedic, anima mea, Domino, et omnia quae intra me sunt nomini sancto eius* (Ps 103[102]:1).

---

[18] *Correspondance*, t. x, p. 22. Ed. *Les Grands Ecrivains de la France* (Paris: Hachette, 1916).
[19] *De Oratione* 3; PL 1, 1259.

XV.

THE PRIEST, A MAN OF PRAYER

THE modern world wants to do without God. This is the root of its ills. The great truth is, on the contrary, that we have an absolute need of God.

Without Him, we are, of our own nature, incapable of coming into existence or continuing to exist.

In the supernatural order our dependence is no less absolute. "Without Me you can do nothing" (Jn 15:5). St. Augustine[1] remarks that the Lord did not say: "Without Me you cannot do much": *Sine me parum potestis facere*, but He declares: "You can do nothing at all": *Sine me nihil potestis facere.* The great Doctor of grace says to us again: "Just as the soul is the principle of your bodily life, so the life of your soul is God": *Vita carnis tuae anima tua: vita animae tuae Deus tuus.*[2]

Our experience recalls this fact to us every day: without divine help our nature, of itself, cannot find its perfect moral equilibrium.

Now it is, above all, in our prayers that we acknowledge and proclaim the total subordination before God in which we pass our life: "In him we live and move and have our being": *In ipso enim vivimus et movemur et sumus* (Acts 17:28).

By a law of His Providence, God normally bestows His grace only in response to prayer. Since our need exists at all times, let us constantly raise our soul to Him. Has not Jesus said: "We ought always to pray and not to faint" (Lk 18:1)? The Gospels declare other means of salvation, like the sacraments, to be necessary or useful at times; it is only when speaking of prayer that they say "always". And we know that every word used by Christ is weighed and chosen.

The liturgy gives expression in its prayers to this humble

[1] *Tractatus in Joannem* 81, 3; PL 35, 1841.
[2] *Tractatus in Joannem* 97, 8; PL 35, 1737.

admission of absolute confidence in God alone: "May every prayer and work of ours begin always from Thee and through Thee be happily ended": *Cuncta nostra oratio et operatio a te semper incipiat et per te coepta finiatur.*[3] "Without Thy aid we cannot please Thee": *Tibi sine te placere non possumus.*[4] And again: "Human nature falls unless Thou support it": *Sine te labitur humana mortalitas.*[5]

More than others, the priest must be a man of prayer in order to live in truth. Every beat of his heart should be an act of love in reply to the charity of the Lord towards him.

I. NATURE OF PRAYER

Prayer, in which we turn to God as to a Father, whether it be vocal or interior silent prayer, is the privilege of those whom the Lord has adopted as sons. By His mercy, the "unsearchable riches of Christ" (Eph 3:8) of which St. Paul spoke so often, have become the possession of every baptized soul. It is not, therefore, as a mere creature that the Christian presents himself before God when he prays; it is rather as the adopted son or as the member of Christ. Without ceasing to be Creator and Master, the Lord has made Himself Father of mercies for the Christian: *Pater misericordiarum* (2 Cor 1:3). That is why the Christian, when he prays, must always say as Jesus taught him: "Our Father Who art in Heaven."

This communication between him and the heavenly Father must be based on faith. It is neither religious experience nor sensibility of heart which enables us really to find God. Art and poetry cannot give God to the soul any more than philosophical concepts. All these means may contribute to the search and the desire for God, but it is faith alone which introduces man into the supernatural sphere. Just as you are destined in your capacity of adopted children to contemplate God in heaven, so, even in this world, you address Him directly in prayer even though it be

[3] Prayer of the Litany of the Saints.
[4] Prayer of the Eighteenth Sunday after Pentecost.
[5] Prayer of the Fifteenth Sunday after Pentecost.

in the obscurity of faith. You display your wretchedness before the immensity of His goodness.

The true nature of Christian prayer is perfectly expressed in the following definition: Prayer is "an interview between the child of God and His heavenly Father".

Another excellent definition is given by St. John Damascene and St. Thomas: it stresses the elevation of the soul which prayer essentially involves: *Ascensus mentis in Deum.*[6] Prayer is "a raising of the mind and heart towards God" to offer Him our homage and to ask Him for all those things of which we stand in need. This is an accurate definition, but we must understand it as meaning a supernatural elevation of the soul.

We know as a certainty that since our baptism there are two lives in us: the one, which we have received from our parents, by virtue of which we are called children of Adam; the other which is supernatural. This latter life is a gift from on high, a grace which tends to make us like to Jesus Christ, the only-begotten Son of the Father. Just as existence according to nature supposes a birth, nourishment, and the need to breathe, so is it also with our supernatural life. Baptism is a second birth for the soul; the Eucharist is the food of this new life, and to the constant need of breathing in order to maintain life there corresponds in the Christian a sacred function—prayer. When the soul prays, it leaves behind the world of material and transitory things; it penetrates into the higher regions of invisible realities which God inhabits. Our worldly existence is enveloped, so to speak, in a supernatural atmosphere. By prayer, man rises up towards that kingdom which the senses cannot reach. Faith put him in immediate relations with the majesty of the heavenly Father, with Christ, the Blessed Virgin, the angels and the saints. He breathes in the atmosphere of God, and, however short-lived this ascension towards the Lord may be, it gives new life to the soul by putting it in contact with an element of eternity. If grace is the divine breath passing over the soul, it is prayer that inhales it, and

---

[6] *Summa* III, q. 21, a. 1 and 2.

lays open the inmost depths of the soul to its life-giving influence.

For the adopted sons of God, therefore, prayer in all its degrees, even the simple recitation of the *Pater*, is an interior elevation, a contact of faith with the supernatural world, an entry into the kingdom of the Father.

II. SOME DIRECTIVES FOR PRAYER

Three important directives will assist your elevation of soul to God; they are inspired by the definitions but, better than these, they will enable you to grasp what our attitude should be in the practice of prayer.

As prayer is an interview in the supernatural order, we must try to have a firm faith in the power of Jesus to introduce us into the presence of His Father. It is by virtue of this faith that the saints in their state of recollection are always near to the Lord.

When we consider God, so great and so holy, there is an inclination to be afraid to cast ourselves into His arms. This is natural, and that is why we must rely on Christ. You may say: "I am such a wretched creature." My reply is: "Has not Our Lord shown you mercy? Has He not enriched you with His Merits?" "I am so imperfect!" "Yes, but the blood of Christ has cleansed you of your sins." "I am so far-removed from God!" "No, thanks to your faith, distance does not exist; as you are united to Jesus, you are near to Him." Has not Christ said: "Father, I will that where I am, they also whom Thou has given Me may be with Me": *Ubi sum ego et illi sint mecum* (Jn 17:24). And where is Jesus? St. John reveals it to us: "The only-begotten son . . . is in the bosom of the Father": *Unigenitus qui est in sinu Patris* (Jn 1:18). At the beginning of your prayer turn always instinctively to Christ: as you share in His sonship and in His merits, you can claim to have access through Him to the divinity.

In a conversation, what do you expect first of all from your interlocutor? That he should speak the truth with due regard for your dignity and for his own status. When we pray, the Lord requires of us this same attitude of loyalty. We must express to Him our adoration, our thanksgiving, our confidence, our need of help, but our words, expressed in the secrecy of our soul, must be addressed to God in the full consciousness of His omnipotence and of our status. It is in this way that our prayers will be "true". It happens to some souls that when they have recited many formulas they realize they have said nothing to God from the bottom of their hearts. Our mind may be far distant from the words that fall from our lips.

In order that He may communicate Himself to us, the Lord requires of us this interior effort to maintain ourselves in His presence in all sincerity. The Psalmist says: "The Lord is nigh unto all them that call upon Him in truth" (Ps 145[144]:18). This pursuit of integrity is really humility. It is especially desired by God: "The true adorers shall adore the Father in spirit and in truth": *Veri adoratares adorabunt Patrem in spiritu et veritate* (Jn 4:23).

In our prayer we must like to give up to God our whole heart and our whole mind. In a sentence often borrowed by the liturgy, the Scripture recalls to our minds this great ideal of perfect prayer in which the soul is concentrated on God and given up to Him: "He will set his heart to rise early to seek the Lord who made him": *Justus cor suum tradidit ad vigilandum diluculo ad Dominum qui fecit illum* (Sir 39:5[6]).

Just as the sanctuary lamp burns itself out without reserving anything, so our soul in its conversation with God must be entirely dedicated to the Almighty.

It is the heart which prays. You may be quite sure of this. *Tibi dixit cor meum* (Ps 25[24]:1), says the Psalmist. And St. Augustine adds: "Your very desire is your prayer": *Ipsum enim desiderium tuum, oratio tua est.*[7]

Finally, the movement of ascending to God is possible only by virtue of interior liberty. We must be watchful therefore to free ourselves from preoccupations, from vain thoughts, and

---

[7] *Enarratio super Psalmos* 37, 14; PL 35, 404.

especially from covetousness, which tie the soul down to earth and prevent it from being entirely given over to the Lord.

Prayer always requires a certain effort, even from those who find in it their delight, because a certain strain is involved by its very nature in the concentration necessary to speak to God; it is always more or less difficult to maintain the soul in an atmosphere which is above its usual level. That is why, by the way, prayer can always serve as a sacramental penance. We must not be surprised at this difficulty in applying ourselves to prayer: to raise ourselves towards God, even in the smallest degree, is to exceed our natural powers.

III. IMPORTANCE OF THE SPIRIT OF PRAYER FOR THE PRIEST

Prayer in the life of the priest must not be limited to a number of isolated, passing incidents: the minister of Christ must cultivate the spirit of prayer.

What must we understand by this? An habitual disposition of soul whereby, in our troubles and discouragements, as in our joys and successes, our hearts turn towards Christ or towards our heavenly Father, as to our best friend, to the most intimate confidant of our feelings, the support of our weakness. And it is not only in the morning and in the evening that the soul should be raised to God, but always: *oculi mei semper ad Dominum* (Ps 25[24]:15).

By virtue of our grace of adoption, we must, in our relations with God, make ourselves simple like children: "Unless you become like little children, you will never enter the Kingdom of heaven": *Nisi efficiamini sicut parvuli, non intrabitis in regnum caelorum* (Mt 18:3). A son treats his father with all respect, but his reverence for him does not prevent him from relying on his goodness, or from pouring out his heart to him. And so it is for the priest: God must not be for him an unapproachable lord to whom one declaims every day certain formulas to be got through as quickly as possible. No, He is the father, the counsellor, the support. Even if you have the misfortune to incur His displeasure, your confidence in His goodness should not be shaken. Before every important undertaking we should formulate the desire in our heart to act for Him.

With time, this habit of raising our minds to God like this will become, as it were, natural, and our communications with the invisible world will be multiplied. Mass, the divine Office, and meditation, instead of being isolated acts wholly unconnected with the rest of our life, will be a more intense continuation of our friendship with God. The grace of filial union will become the centre of our whole existence.

Two reasons before all others require this spirit of prayer in the priest. On the one hand, there is the question of his own perseverance, of his fidelity to the love of Christ, and on the other, the necessity of ensuring the divine blessing on his ministry.

Is it possible for us priests, dedicated to the salvation of men, to live like Jesus after His Resurrection in the midst of the world without feeling the attraction of its constant appeal? In spite of the nobility of our vocation we remain weak and imperfect, we are at times harassed by temptation. Prayer is necessary for all if they are to persevere in the good life, but there are many for whom it should be almost continuous.

To remain constant until our last breath is a glorious gift of the Father: *Descendens a Patre luminum*: "Coming down from the Father of lights" (Jas 1:17). We cannot merit it strictly *de condigno* by our good actions. But we can hope with every confidence to obtain it from the divine goodness by virtue of humble and earnest prayer and of our efforts to be faithful to God. This capital gift: *Magnum illud usque in finem perseverantiae donum*, as the Council of Trent describes it,[8] does not make us incapable of sin; it does not free us from all temptation, but it does involve a providential aid and a series of graces which dispose the will to persevere in good until the end. The whole course of the life of the Christian is thus enveloped, as it were, in mercy until its final consummation.[9]

---

[8] Sess. 6, can. 16.
[9] *Summa* I-II, q. 114, a. 9.

Like beggars on the threshold of heaven, we must expose our infirmities before the Father without ever giving way to discouragement. Such was the conduct of the saints. Whatever the form of life of each individual, there was one feature common to all: constancy in their attachment to God, to His kingdom, to His good pleasure. All of them, having dedicated themselves to the Lord, persevered with remarkable stability of soul in this gift of self; they persevered until death. Their will was anchored in God, as the Church declares in the liturgy of confessors: *Voluntas eius permanet die ac nocte.*

Now, what is the secret of this firmness of union with God? It is within the reach of all; it is constant recourse to prayer. We can never plead that our passions are too intense, our temptations too strong. "My power is made perfect in weakness": *Virtus in infirmitate perficitur* (2 Cor 12:9). Look at St. Paul, who has been raised to the third heaven; he acknowledges his miseries; he deplores them, and in what striking terms! But, instead of giving way to discouragement, he exclaims in an admirable transport of confidence: *Libenter igitur gloriabor in infirmitatibus meis ut inhabitet in me virtus Christi*: "Gladly, therefore, will I glory in my infirmities that the power of Christ may dwell in me" (2 Cor 12:10). For us, also, temptations to evil, and sometimes even our very faults, play a providential role; instead of discouraging us, they should convince us that our souls, enriched as they are with the treasures of grace, remain always "earthen vessels" (2 Cor 4:7). Our weaknesses will teach us to pray in all humility and in all confidence; they will preserve us from pride and from presumption. God permits these weaknesses, the Apostle tells us, "that no flesh should glory in His sight": *ut non glorietur omnis caro in conspectu eius* (1 Cor 1:29).

Those priests whose studies are not directly connected with sacred matters, as, for example, those who are engrossed in administrative work, should be more solicitous even than others to maintain this spirit of prayer. They will be greatly helped by impulses of the heart in the form of ejaculatory prayers. They should choose from among the common formulas those which correspond best to their needs, or perhaps some text from the breviary or from the Scriptures, the full meaning of which has been made clear to them by the grace of God.

As ministers of Christ, how great is your interior happiness when, faithful to the spirit of prayer, you act in all things for God and for His Church under the inspiration of charity!

Prayer is of capital importance for your personal sanctification; it is no less so for drawing down the blessing of God on your works.

You may be quite sure that your influence on souls cannot be really beneficial unless it is made fruitful by God: *Ego plantavi, Apollo rigavit, sed Deus incrementum dedit*: "I planted, Apollos watered, but God gave the growth" (1 Cor 3:6). Certainly grace supposes nature, and we must not ignore the part played in supernatural works by the human intelligence and by human effort: "We plant, we water," this is our part and an indispensable part. But we must never forget that, if God does not give the increase, our work will be without fruit.

Believe me, whatever may be your talents, your knowledge, and your enthusiasm when you begin your ministry, unless you are men of prayer, you will do nothing worth while. In the life of grace, as St. Augustine teaches us, all growth exceeds human capacity, surpasses angelic excellence and may be attributed in its entirety to the Holy Trinity alone Who is the husbandman: *Excedit hoc humanam humilitatem, excedit angelicam sublimitatem, nec omnino pertinet nisi ad agricolam Trinitatem.*[10]

The saints who accomplished great things for love of God delighted certainly in devotedness and in action, but they were also men of prayer; look at St. Benedict, St. Francis Xavier, St. Charles Borromeo, St. Francis de Sales, St. Alphonsus Liguori, the Curé d'Ars; they all spent hours conversing with God.

Let us be, therefore, mediators conscious of our mission, men of prayer who, by virtue of our constant communion with the Lord, sanctify the souls of which we have charge, while at the same time sanctifying ourselves.

We priests cannot save ourselves alone. It is our sublime func-

---

[10] *Tractatus in Joannem* 80, 2; PL 35, 1840.

tion to draw souls to heaven. Let us thank God for this mission and be faithful to it so that our want of fervour may never be the occasion of apathy or ruin for any soul.

IV. THE SOURCES OF PRAYER: NATURE

In speaking of heaven, Jesus said: "In My Father's house there are many mansions" (Jn 14:2). The same may be said of the life of prayer: there are many stages in it. St. Teresa speaks of the seven principal ones in her admirable book, *The Interior Castle*. One cannot penetrate at one step into the inmost chamber.

To help you in this *ascensus ad Deum*, here are three different points of departure or three distinct kinds of supports from which the soul may ascend. All three lead to the Father's house.

We can ascend to the Lord either by contemplation of the created world, or by meditation on the revealed truths contained in Scripture, and on the life and mystery of Jesus, or finally, by attaching ourselves to Christ with a lively faith in His power to introduce us into the bosom of the Father. We are quite free to make use of any one of these manners of approach to God according to our personal disposition and to the circumstances. To make the matter clearer, I shall venture to compare them to the courtyards of the temple of Jerusalem. You must not be confused by this: it is only a way of putting the matter.

What do we see in the temple of Jerusalem? The most sacred place was the holy of holies. In front of it were courtyards. The dignity of each of these depended on its proximity to the chief sanctuary.

The courtyard of the Gentiles was a very broad, open space, unroofed. Everyone could enter it. From this courtyard one entered into that of the Jews through doors by which the uncircumcized could not pass. In this vast enclosure, the chosen people assisted at the sacrifices, heard the reading of the Law, and sang Psalms. From here they could see, behind the altar of holocausts, that part of the sanctuary which was reserved for the ministers of religion.

At the end of that place which was called holy, behind the sacred veil of the temple, *post velamentum*, came the mysterious holy of holies. There, according to the Epistle to the Hebrews (9:3–4), beside the altar of incense, was the ark of the testament, covered with gold, which contained the tables of the Law, the manna, and the rod of Aaron.[11] Once a year, after many purifications, the high priest entered this sanctuary alone.

To return to the degrees of prayer. The first court, that of the Gentiles, symbolizes the prayer in which the soul is raised to God without recourse to revelation by considering the order and beauty of nature. Does not St. Paul invite us to admire these created things when he says: "The invisible things of Him . . . are clearly seen, being understood by the things that are made"? (Rom 1:20).

You may ask: "Can one pray by considering the beauties of nature?"—And why not? God is the supreme artist. Everything that has been made by Him has been conceived in His Word. Creation bears the mark of its Author. Some souls find their satisfaction in contemplating the great spectacles of the work of God: the immensity of the ocean, the peaks of the mountains, the majesty of the landscape, move them to pray. Why? Because, behind the curtain of nature, they divine the hidden presence of God. The whole universe cries out to them: *Ipse fecit nos et non ipsi nos* (Ps 100[99]:3). The prophet Baruch wrote: "The stars have given light in their watches and rejoiced: they were called and they said: 'Here we are', and with cheerfulness they have shined forth to Him that made them" (Bar 3:34–35). You also can look on the starry sky and by this spectacle raise your soul to the love of Him Who has created the space of the worlds.

V. THE GOSPEL

In the court of the Jews everything is of the order of revelation and consequently supernatural. The form of this Mosaic worship with its rites and its multiple sacrifices has been prescribed

---

[11] The Ark and the other sacred objects were lost at the time of the destruction of the temple of Solomon and the captivity of Babylon about 598 B.C.

to Moses by God Himself: "Look and make it according to the pattern that was shown thee in the mount" (Ex 21:40).

We should like to reflect on the fact that Mary, during her life on earth, when she came into the court of women and watched the sacred ceremonies, was filled with admiration and love. And Christ Jesus! He entered into the temple as into the house of His Father. He knew that this temple represented Himself. "Destroy this temple," He said, "and I shall rebuild it in three days" (Jn 2:19).

In the court, He was witness of the holocausts and of the Judaic worship; He, the true Lamb of God, understood how all this represented His mission and foretold His role.

When the priest sprinkled the people with the blood of the victims and entered alone into the holy of holies, Jesus thought of the redemption of the world by His precious blood, and His soul was exalted to the ineffable realities of which these Jewish rites were only the shadow, *umbrae futurorum* (Heb 10:1).

What does this court signify for us in our relations with God? Here there is no longer question of an elevation of soul provoked by the marvels of nature, but of prayer arising out of revelation. God has deigned to speak to us, and His words are contained in the inspired books. Prayer is inspired primarily by the texts of Holy Scripture. Hear the words of St. Paul: "Let the word of Christ dwell in you abundantly in all wisdom; teaching and admonishing one another in psalms, hymns and spiritual canticles, singing in grace in your hearts to God" (Col 3:16).

It is possible to read Holy Scripture and find nothing in it to arouse one to prayer, but it is possible also to read it humbly as a child of God in such a way that the prayer of our soul, enlightened by the divine words, becomes truly fervent.

In this courtyard, we must apply ourselves especially to considering Jesus Christ and the mysteries of His life. The liturgy will be of great assistance in this.[12] In fact, when we take the trouble to meditate on the words and actions of Jesus, we give

---

[12] Compare what has been said above (p. 268) about the divine Office. This form of prayer will be greatly helped by the collection *Words of Life on the Margin of the Missal*, which is composed exclusively of extracts from Dom Marmion's works. These extracts have been chosen for each day in accordance with the mystery, the solemnity or the saint which the

God the opportunity to communicate Himself to us. The mere recollection of Jesus is sanctifying. You can meditate on the Gospel scenes as if you were by the side of Jesus, as if you were listening to His words with your own ears or seeing Him with your eyes. You can kneel down before the crib with the shepherds; at Nazareth, with Mary and Joseph, you can adore Him in His hidden life; with His disciples you can accompany Him on His journeys; you will receive His sacred words and prostrate yourself before Him at the washing of the feet and during the Last Supper. Consider Christ in the garden of Olives, in His Passion and, above all, on the Cross. He is God. Hear His last words . . . did He not say to each one: "It is for you, for love of you, that I am offering My life"? St. Paul was carried away by this thought to the point of exclaiming: "He loved me and delivered Himself up for me" (Gal 2:20). As we contemplate Jesus in all the stages of His life from His childhood to His Resurrection and Ascension, there emanates from Him a constant force of sanctification: "Power came forth from him and healed them all": *Virtus de illo exibat et sanabat omnes* (Lk 6:19).

Let us fix our eyes on Him with faith so that we may imitate His virtues, not externally but from within: *ut per eum quem similem nobis foris agnovimus intus reformari mereamur.*[13]

As regards the manner of meditating, here are some brief considerations.

Many priests employ a method; if they find it satisfactory, they would be very wrong to abandon it. The Church has freely proclaimed the usefulness of many of these methods. Still, it would be a mistake to identify the method with prayer itself, as though prayer could not exist outside such a framework. Methods are only means to an end.

In early times, learning mental prayer meant, primarily, acquiring the habit of pausing in the course of one's reading of the Holy Scripture or of a pious work. During these pauses, the

---

Church is celebrating. In this way the Gospel of the Mass and the lessons of the breviary with the comments of Dom Marmion furnish the soul with matter for its prayer. This results in a great unity in the spiritual life of the priest.

[13] Prayer of the octave of the Epiphany.

soul meditated, reflected, convinced itself of the truths proposed, realized its duties, made acts of conformity to the divine will, and gave expression to its hopes and its petitions. When these sentiments of faith, confidence and love were exhausted, one resumed quite simply the reading of the sacred text.

This was the approach to mental prayer as the fathers of the desert, those great masters of holiness, understood it. With St. Benedict, the monks of the West simply carried on this tradition. St. Teresa of Avila also recommends this method.[14] It is a very simple method, but it has the great advantage of being within the capacity of everyone, and it lessens distractions. Considering that so many souls have been introduced to contemplation in the past by this way, why should it not lead us to this same grace?

Everyone must consider for himself how he can meditate. Be careful that your meditation is adapted to your spiritual needs, to the weaknesses you have to surmount, the duties which you have to accomplish, and make sure that it develops an ever-growing loyalty to God in your soul. In the beginning a certain amount of groping is inevitable; that is why you must not hesitate to seek the aid of a book. In an antiphon for the feast of St. Cecilia we read: *Evangelium Christi gerebat in pectore suo, et a colloquis divinis et ab oratione non cessabat.* She bore the Gospel of Christ, not in her pocket, but *in pectore*, in her heart. It is in the humble and affectionate meditation of the Gospels, the Epistles and other books of Holy Scripture that you too will find, little by little, the spirit of prayer. After having made an act of contrition and having put yourself in the presence of God, expose yourself fully to the sanctifying influence of Jesus and to the action of the Holy Spirit, then read a little, making pauses during the reading, and in this way your soul will learn unconsciously to speak with its Lord.

Do not forget that the great revelation of the second courtyard is the knowledge of Jesus Christ and of His mysteries; we cannot aspire to know the ways and the will of God, nor God

---

[14] Teresa of Avila, *Life*, chaps. 11 and 12.

Himself, except by contemplating and listening to His Word Incarnate.

VI. THE CONTEMPLATION OF FAITH

We come now to the third enclosure.

Once a year the high priest entered alone into the holy of holies, beyond the sacred curtain. He uttered the name of Yahweh and, in the presence of God, spoke to Him in an attitude of profound adoration.

This symbolizes the entry of the soul into the contemplation of pure faith, beyond the veil of the sacred humanity of Jesus: *per velamen, id est carnem eius* (Heb 10:20).

Everything that has been said about the nature of prayer is realized in the most perfect way in this prayer of faith: it is supereminently the interview to which the children of God are invited in virtue of their baptismal grace. Being united to Christ and sharing in His filiation, they can, together with Him, have access to the bosom of the Father. You will have some idea of this prayer if you recall to mind the good countryman whom the Curé d'Ars used to see every evening in the church, with his eyes fixed on the tabernacle, saying nothing. He asked him what he was doing, and the countryman replied: "I am looking at God and He is looking at me." That is the prayer of simple consideration: one looks, loves, and is silent. Every faithful soul should attain to this form of prayer after a certain time. In its initial stages it is still dependent on acquired prayer, that is to say, prayer in which our own effort enables us, with the help of grace, to find our repose in God.

What is it that prevents souls consecrated to God from attaining to this prayer? Trifles—it is sad to have to admit it, but we spend hours on matters which are of no importance, we think a lot about ourselves, we become attached to all sorts of trifles, and time passes. Never forget that our prayer is the reflection or the expression of the true state of the soul.

Both for his own sanctification and for the direction of fervent souls it is essential for the priest to realize that God chooses for Himself in this life faithful servants with a view to raising them to a specially intimate union with Him. He is King; as sovereign Master He issues His commands; it is for them to answer the call, to follow the divine attraction, and try to live in all things according to love. This repose in the bosom of the Father is that which is best of all in this world: it is the *optima pars* (Lk 10:42).

How can we comprehend the splendour of this prayer? The beatific vision is, as it were, the transcendent model of it. How shall we see God face to face in heaven? By the light of glory. This light strengthens and enlarges the capacity of the created intelligence, so as to enable it to achieve intuitive vision.

And according to what measure is this light granted to the elect? According to the measure of their love. Our degree of glory in heaven will correspond to the degree of charity which we shall have attained at the hour of our death.

To return now to contemplation in this world. What is it that corresponds here on earth to the light of glory? Faith. Faith is a certitude, light in the darkness; the greater perfection it attains, the nearer it approaches to God in the reality of His mystery.

Just as the degree of beatific vision accorded to each one of us depends on our degree of charity, so it is with this prayer of faith; that knowledge, confused indeed, but of a higher order, which is accorded to the soul, gushes forth in it as a consequence of its union of love with God. Hence this marvellous truth: the prayer which elevates souls to the holy of holies makes them like to the Lord, enabling them to know Him and to love Him in faith, just as God in the Holy Trinity knows and loves Himself.[15]

A phrase of Scripture: "For our God is a consuming fire": *Deus noster ignis consumens est* (Heb 12:29), helps us to understand the splendour of the prayer of faith. If God is a consuming fire, the closer we approach Him the more we are enkindled. Now, it is in the course of prayer that the spark falls on us; the

[15] See *L'enseignement de Dom Marmion sur La Mystique*, in the *Vie Spirituelle*, January 1948, pp. 100–115.

fire lights up, and the soul is wholly captured by love for the supreme good; it desires ardently to be united to the Father through the Son Incarnate and to be drawn into their mutual and eternal love, the Holy Spirit. Let us take our place at the feet of Jesus, let us sit down under the shadow of the Well-Beloved: "With great delight I sat in his shadow": *Sub umbra illius quem desideraveram sedi* (Song 2:3). What is this shadow? It is the sacred humanity of Christ. The light in which the Father dwells is inaccessible to us: *Lucem inhabitat inaccessibilem* (1 Tim 6:16). The Word is the infinite brightness of this eternal light. *Candor est lucis aeternae* (Wis 7:26). He is the brilliant sun whose rays dazzle us, the furnace whose heat we cannot bear. And so, in order to approach the Word, the soul rests in the love and in the shadow of the sacred humanity.

When it rejoices in this union, the world and all its attractions mean nothing to the soul; it understands that God alone is the "one thing necessary": *unum est necessarium* (Lk 10:42). United to Jesus, hidden in Him, the soul says to Him: "You see the Father, I am in the darkness, but I contemplate Him through Your eyes."

How good it is to live there on the other side of the veil of the sacred humanity, under the eyes of the Father: "Neither doth anyone know the Father, but the Son and he to whom it shall please the Son to reveal Him" (Mt 11:27).

In the prayer of faith, our love is not directed towards a mere concept or an intellectual representation of God; it seeks rather to possess Him and likewise to be possessed by Him. We cannot receive the Lord in this way by means of any created idea. It is in the obscurity of the complete acceptance of faith that this union is consummated.

Ordinarily, even for very holy souls, prayer begins on the outer threshold. There, our work, helped by grace, disposes us to make of Christ our all.

When God invites man to enter further into the contemplation of pure faith, he lets him experience his absolute incapacity to raise himself by his own resources. At this time our confidence must not fail, even though the wait seems long. The soul must be resigned to remaining in the darkness, praying Christ to imprint on it His divine characteristics.

We would only spoil His work if we tried to achieve by ourselves this resemblance to the Son of God. It is only according as we die to self that the Lord acts on us. We must learn to say: "Lord, if this powerlessness, if this darkness is for Thy glory, I accept it all; if I must remain 'as earth without water unto Thee', *sicut terra sine aqua tibi* (Ps 143[142]:6), may Thy Name be ever blessed." However imperfect our manner of praying, we priests cannot attach enough importance to the frequent raising of our soul to God. The Father is constantly regarding us with a look which penetrates to the very depths of our priestly souls. He loves us in His Son, Jesus: *Ipse Pater amat vos, quia vos me amastis* (Jn 16:27). Our reply to His look, so full of mercy, must be to pour out before Him with generous fidelity our humble attempt at prayer.

VII. THE PRAYER OF JESUS [16]

Let us ask Christ to teach us to pray: Domine, *doce nos orare.* By His example as well as by His words and also by the Holy Spirit, Whom He sends into our hearts, He is the great teacher of prayer.

In Nazareth, His hidden life was devoted to silence and recollection. During His public life He gave Himself without reserve to the crowds and to individuals alike, but His thoughts were ever fixed on the Father. He lived in a state of continuous prayer. The Gospels tell us that He prayed, sometimes alone on the mountain, at other times in public, as when He recited the *Pater* in the presence of His disciples, or when He gave thanks before the multiplication of the loaves (Jn 4:11).

Is it possible for us to get some idea of the mystery of these sublime elevations of the soul of Jesus? We are here on the threshold of a holy of holies, the mystery of which is beyond us. It seems, however, that we can form some idea of it if we

---

[16] See what has been said above concerning the devotion of Jesus, pp. 151–55.

consider the three forms of knowledge proper to Christ in His human nature. Theologians have called them the three *scientiae* of Christ. Each of them illuminated the intelligence of Christ with its own special light, and on account of these different illuminations the three *scientiae* were distinct sources of prayer in Him.

By virtue of the hypostatic union, Jesus enjoyed the vision of the divinity. He had hidden in Himself a sanctuary that was sacrosanct, as it were, a pinnacle of His soul which He alone could reach. In the presence of the Father He is at all times the only-begotten Son.

When we, on our part, invoke God, we call Him "Our Father" in the sense that all the children of adoption call Him Father. But Jesus looked on the Father and found His repose in Him because He was His Son by a filiation which belonged to Him alone. He was the only-begotten Son because the human nature of Jesus is the human nature of the Word.

Jesus surmounted as it were with one stride the distance which separates the created from the uncreated. His union with the Father was continuous. Jesus could say in all truth: "He that hath sent Me is with Me and He hath not left Me alone" (Jn 8:29). By reason of the beatific vision, the contemplation of Jesus surpassed the most sublime prayer. It was a function of the very highest faculty of His soul. His solemn prayer after the Last Supper, which St. John has preserved for us, tells something of this converse of the Saviour with the Father: "Father . . . glorify Thy Son, that Thy Son may glorify Thee" (Jn 17:1). This vision was entirely spiritual and supernatural; the imagination had no part in it; neither had flesh and blood. Even the sufferings of the Passion could not obstruct it.

Apart from this intuitive knowledge—that is to say, knowledge which operated without the help of ideas—there existed besides, in the soul of Our Lord, another form of *scientia*, the object of which was not God in Himself. This is *scientia infusa*. By virtue of this, Jesus knew, and in a different manner from us, the truths which He was bringing to the world and the whole work of redemption. He knew it by a radiation of supernatural light. This knowledge was not acquired, it was received from on high. It enabled Jesus to comprehend the decrees of the divine wisdom concerning the salvation of humanity and the mystical body, the Church. The full gravity of sin, the love and the ingratitude of men were made clear to Him.

It is thanks to these lights that Jesus, as soon as He came into the world, made Himself, as St. Paul puts it, a prayer of oblation: "Behold I come, *Ecce venio*, that I should do Thy Will, O Lord" (Heb 10:7). During His earthly life, this *scientia* served Him to glorify the Father and to thank Him for the benefit of the Gospel teaching: "I confess to Thee, O Father, Lord of heaven and earth, because Thou hast hid these things from the wise and the prudent, and hast revealed them to little ones" (Mt 11:25).

It is likewise this illumination which made the chalice of the Passion acceptable to Him and inspired that prayer of supreme abandonment and love: "Father . . . not My will, but Thy will be done" (Lk 22:42).

Finally, we must never forget that Christ was a man as we are, like us in all things except sin. There was in Him a third kind of knowledge, a knowledge which was human, natural, acquired, experimental, such as we all have. This also was a source of prayer for Him. As He travelled over the mountains and plains of Galilee, as He looked at the vines, the harvests and the flowers of which He had spoken in the Gospel, all the beauties of creation appeared to Him as reflections of the divine splendour and roused His soul to acts of praise. Penetrating the veil of creatures, He ascended without effort to the divine perfections of which these creatures were the remote expression.

The great contemplatives, such as St. John of the Cross or St. Angela of Foligno, tell us that after ecstasy there remains in the soul a supernatural light which makes it discover, to its indescribable joy, the signs of God in nature. This reflection of the divine light existed certainly in Jesus also, but supereminently. The glory of the direct vision of the divinity is extended—as we can well understand—to all His knowledge, infused or acquired.

Let me repeat before I finish that, however poor our prayer may be, it is very useful for us—and more so for us priests than for the ordinary Christian—to think of the ineffable discourses of Christ with the Father. The Apostle has not hesitated to say to us that Jesus is the ideal towards which our weakness must raise its eyes without ever giving way to discouragement: "Looking to Jesus the pioneer and perfecter of our faith . . . so that you may not grow weary or fainthearted": *Aspicientes in auctorem fidei et consummatorem Jesum . . . ne fatigemini, animis vestris deficientes* (Heb 12:2–3).

XVI.

THE FAITH OF THE PRIEST IN THE HOLY SPIRIT

THE Holy Spirit is the agent of all sanctification in the Church. The supernatural activity of the children of God in its different degrees depends on His vivifying influence: "For all who are led by the Spirit of God are sons of God": *qui Spiritu Dei aguntur, ii sunt filii Dei* (Rom 8:14). This is our faith.

It is incumbent on all, but especially on priests, to establish as perfect a harmony as possible between their personal spirituality and their faith. Let us consider, therefore, whether we allow the Holy Spirit to play a sufficient part in our interior life. Are we convinced of the absolute necessity for our sanctification of exposing our soul fully to His salutary influence?

It is beyond doubt that Jesus came into the world to reveal the Father: *Pater . . . manifestavi Nomen tuum hominibus* (Jn 17:6). But, in the divine economy, this was not the sole object of His coming. It was ordained also that man should learn from the sacred lips of the Saviour to know the Holy Spirit and to venerate Him as the equal of the Father and of the Son.

Hence this astonishing saying of Jesus to His disciples: "It is expedient for you that I go." What does this mean? Christ came to save us, to guide us, to be everything to us, and now He declares that it is expedient that He should go. The reason given by Our Lord is still more astonishing: "If I go not, the Paraclete will not come to you" (Jn 16:7). Had we been present, we would perhaps have replied: "Master, we have no need of the Paraclete; You are sufficient for us; stay with us; why should you send us a substitute?" And yet Jesus declares clearly: "It is expedient for you that I go."

According to the designs of the Father, it is by faith alone that the children of adoption must enter into contact with the supernatural world: with Christ, the Church, the sacraments and, above all, with the Eucharist; it is by faith that they must hope in God, love Him and serve Him. This doctrine supposes the disappearance of the visible Jesus from amongst us, and the invisible but vivifying influence of the Holy Spirit. It is for Him to guide the Church and each individual soul to its eternal destiny.

I. THE HOLY SPIRIT VIVIFIES THE CHURCH

The mission of the Holy Spirit is revealed to us by the Gospel as being ordained to complete the work of Christ. When Jesus had pronounced the *consummatum est* ["it is finished"] on Calvary, what evidence had we of the efficacy of His precious blood to sanctify us? Jesus had preached certainly; He had trained His apostles; He had given them their first holy communion a few hours before; He had ordained them priests. Yet with the Passion of the Lord everything seemed to be lost; the disciples were terror-stricken; Peter denied his Master.

But at Pentecost, the disciples were filled with the Holy Spirit and the face of the world was renewed: *Emittes spiritum tuum et renovabis faciem terrae* (Ps 104[103]:30). Peter no longer fears anyone; he appears in the middle of Jerusalem; he preaches Christ.

The voice of the twelve is borne to the ends of the world, and in a few years the Christians are numbered in thousands. How has this prodigy been brought about? We find the answer in the Preface of Pentecost; "Christ . . . ascending over all the heavens and sitting at the right hand of the Father, according to His word, sent down the Holy Spirit upon the children of His adoption."

From this moment, the Church, in spite of persecutions, of disputes about doctrine, in spite of the faithlessness of her own children, has lived and triumphed in a wondrous manner. She advances through the centuries, strong in her prerogatives which are the unmistakable marks of her divine institution; she is always one in her faith and in her allegiance to the See of Peter; at all times she produces sanctity in her members by virtue of her own sanctifying power; she includes, as of right, the whole human race in her sheep-fold; finally, based on the foundation of the apostles, she remains indefectible. The Church, one, holy, catholic, apostolic and Roman is at the same time divine and of this world; she is assailed and surrounded by perils, but she holds out and advances, always unchanged in her divine constitution, indefectible in her faith and continuously vivified by the Holy Spirit: *Spiritum vivificantem.*

What do we know of this Holy Spirit? Let us raise our eyes to the Holy Trinity.

The Son, begotten from all eternity, is the perfect image of the Father: *Deus de Deo, lumen de lumine* [God from God, light from light]. But He is reflected back into the bosom of the Father and this union of the Father and the Son is fruitful. Proceeding from the unique breath of their mutual love, the Holy Spirit is infinite love and refers Himself entirely, as such, to His principle of origin.

Sanctity consists in dedicating oneself to God in charity. The third Person of the Blessed Trinity, because He is entirely oriented to the Father and the Son by an eternal reflection of love, is supremely worthy to be called holy; the Holy Spirit is His proper name.

The Holy Spirit, proceeding from the love of the Father and the Son is, furthermore, the infinite gift which seals their union. He is the consummation, the final achievement, of the communication of life in God.

As the gift of love in the bosom of the Trinity, He is for us the supreme gift of the Almighty, *Altissimi donum Dei.* With the Church, and in the same sense as she does, we venerate in Him the guest of our souls; He dwells in them and makes of them the temples of the Lord: *Templum enim Dei sanctum est quod estis vos* (1 Cor 3:17).

The Holy Spirit descends upon the whole Church and upon each Christian with all the riches of grace: *Fons vivus, ignis, caritas.*[1] He is the life-giving fountain of supernatural inspiration, the fire which gives ardour, the charity from which springs the sanctification and the union of hearts.

---

[1] Hymn *Veni Creator Spiritus.*

Coming to us, He brings His gifts. The liturgy recognizes seven, *Sacrum septenarium*; this number is traditional in the Church. It signifies the plenitude of the operation of the Holy Spirit in our souls.

The gifts are accessory to the state of grace. They are infused permanent dispositions, distinct from the virtues and conferring on the Christian a special aptitude for receiving light and impulses from on high. By this influence of the Holy Spirit it becomes possible for the children of God to act under the movement of superior instinct and in a manner which excels the rational exercise which is normal for the virtues.[2] The exercise of these gifts establishes the Christian in an atmosphere which is entirely supernatural. In this way the resemblance to the Son of God is perfected in Him in the most exalted manner.

In practice, the activities of the virtues and the gifts are interwoven, and the more closely the soul is united to Christ, the more it is subject to the influences of the Holy Spirit. This fact stands out in the lives of the saints.

II. THE NECESSITY OF HAVING RECOURSE
TO THE HOLY SPIRIT

While our whole existence is dedicated to things holy and eternal, it must be passed amidst the vicissitudes of this earthly life. Under the influence of our environment there is a danger that we may discharge our ministry in too human a manner, and restrict ourselves to the mere material carrying out of the prescribed work without rising to its supernatural significance. Moreover, however holy the sacred rites may be, repetition tends to introduce into them a certain routine by force of habit.

[2] Although this cannot be accomplished without supernatural inspiration, our acts of faith, hope and charity as well as our acts of the infused moral virtues are exercised by us according to the rational procedure proper to all the superior activity of man; we move ourselves to act by weighing the motives and reasons. On the other hand, when a man acts by virtue of the gifts of the Holy Spirit, the sentiments which he experiences and the acts which he exercises are the product of a divine impulse. While not opposed to reason, they are not determined by it: the psychological process is supradiscursive; it is the outcome of a superior divine motion, and is carried out in a manner which theologians call superhuman, or divine.

As a protection against this all-pervading naturalism and indifference, it is indispensable that the life-giving breath of the Holy Spirit should fructify each one of our actions.

It is this Spirit which will light in our hearts the flame of love: *tui amoris in eis ignem accende.* In spiritual matters it is He alone who gives full rectitude to judgement: *recta sapere.* He also it is Who inspires the filial attitude which permits us in all truth to invoke the Lord as a Father; He it is Who inspires our prayer: "The Spirit helps us in our weakness . . . [and] intercedes for us with sighs too deep for words": *Spiritus adjuvat infirmitatem nostram . . . postulat pro nobis gemitibus inerrabilibus* (Rom 8:26).

These are some of the forms of the action of the Holy Spirit in us. Whoever wishes to live as a child of God must try to keep his soul under this influence. How many, even among priests, know this spirit of love? And yet He alone is the source of their whole interior life. He alone fructifies their whole priestly activity.[3]

How is an Ecumenical Council opened? By the *Veni Creator.* If this is the rule for the great official assemblies of the Church, let it be your rule also never to undertake any action of importance in the course of your priestly life without first invoking the Holy Spirit. In the exercise of your sacred ministry, be it confessions, preaching, visiting the sick, you will never call on the Spirit of God in vain. It is on Him that the government of hearts depends. In the direction of consciences—and this is a truth you should never forget—the role of the pastor is, above all, to prepare the soul for the action of the Holy Spirit. I may mention in passing that, as a general rule, the priest must not allow his penitents to write pages on pages to him, and that he

[3] Categorical as is this statement of Dom Marmion, it is not inconsistent with his teaching on Christ, our life and the universal efficient cause of grace in each of the members of His mystical body. We have here two aspects of a unique supernatural reality which are perfectly reconcilable. According to St. Thomas, we must acknowledge that God alone communicates to man the gifts of His grace. As it is only fire which can spread fire, so it is only God Who can make creatures participate in His own nature. He deifies them. This birth of grace in us proceeds from the Holy Trinity but, as it is an operation of love, it is appropriated to the Person of the Holy Spirit. This same communication of the divine life can, however, quite properly be envisaged as the work of Christ, Whose sacred humanity is the efficient cause—not the principal but the instrumental efficient cause—of all grace bestowed on men. Cf. *Summa* I-II, q. 112, art. 1; III, q. 64, a. 1.

must normally confine himself to directions which are short and precise; they are often all the better for being short.

There is no question of denying the importance of human effort, or of minimizing the part played by generosity, constancy and prudence in our work for souls. I am fully persuaded of the value of all these elements, but they must not make us lose sight of the supernatural side.

This point is of such capital importance that I would like to insist on it. There is a striking text in the Epistles of St. Paul: "No one can say 'Jesus is Lord' except by the Holy Spirit": *Nemo potest dicere Domine Jesu, nisi in Spiritu Sancto* (1 Cor 12:3). Do these words mean that we are incapable of pronouncing with our lips the words "Lord Jesus", or that we cannot understand their literal sense? Certainly not. We are all able to do this. But in order to pronounce this sacred name and to attain to the Person of Jesus in a salutary manner with Christian hope and charity, we must be moved from on high. The Council of Orange has defined that without the illumination and inspiration of the Holy Spirit we can do nothing which is efficacious for our salvation.[4] This is our faith.

When Our Lord was living on earth, all could certainly approach Him. Had He not come down to us for the salvation of all? And yet, what a difference of attitude was there among those who approached Him! Some, like the Pharisees, had their hearts hardened and closed to Him; others perceived something of the mystery of His Person and of His mission; they believed in Him and attached themselves to Him. What is the explanation of this difference? There are many incidents in the Scriptures which make it clear, commencing with the very start of Jesus' life on earth. Mary visits her cousin Elizabeth and the latter exclaims: "Blessed art thou . . . and blessed is the fruit of thy womb." Who gave to Elizabeth this penetrating insight? The Holy Spirit had filled her soul (Lk 1:41). At the time of the presentation of Jesus in the temple in Jerusalem, the old man Simeon recognizes the Messiah in the child of the Virgin.

---

[4] Can. 7.

Under what inspiration is he acting? He had come to the temple moved by the Holy Spirit: *venit in Spiritu Sancto in Templum* (Lk 2:27). There can be little doubt that the sick, who went with such confidence to the Lord to be cured, were also under the influence of this hidden but efficacious impulse of this same Holy Spirit. It was He Who led Magdalen to repentance when she bathed the feet of Christ with her tears. He inspired St. Peter and the other disciples to leave the nets to follow Jesus; it was He again Who invited John to lay his head on the bosom of the Master, and to accompany Him to the foot of the Cross.

We must realize that there exists for us a contact with Jesus which is as intimate, as immediate, as fruitful, as the one of which we have been speaking. It is the contact of faith. It is the Holy Spirit alone Who can cause this salutary contact in us. How does He do it? He does it when by efficacious grace He makes the soul capable of believing, hoping, and loving supernaturally.

As long as Christ lived on this earth His divinity remained hidden but His humanity was visible; it exercised of itself a certain attraction; it was not an object of faith. At present we cannot reach Jesus in His human nature or in His divine nature except by faith alone. This is the divine plan. All our relations with Christ must he founded on this adherence of faith. This contact of faith is a necessary condition if the divine gifts are to descend upon us. "He that believeth in Me," Jesus declared, "out of his belly shall flow rivers of living water." And it is noteworthy that the Evangelist adds that the Saviour "said this of the Spirit Which they should receive who believed in Him" (Jn 7:39). That vivifying contact with Jesus in faith is only effected by the gift of the Holy Spirit. It is possible to approach very close to the tabernacle of the altar and yet remain very far away from Christ; on the other hand, if the influence of the Holy Spirit embraces our lives, contact is established, and we are near to Jesus.

The Holy Spirit is the bond between the Father and the Son. He is also the bond between Christ and us. We can understand therefore how important it is that we should at all times be subject to His sanctifying action in our sacred ministry.

III. HOW TO INVOKE THE HOLY SPIRIT

You remember the indelible mark graven on your soul by the sacraments of baptism, confirmation and holy orders. These characters are permanent in you. They are permanent testimonies of your dependence on Christ which you can at all times, when you will, present before God. Thanks to them you can recall within you the Holy Spirit and thus revive the supernatural effects proper to each of the sacraments. St. Paul teaches this formally for holy orders: "I admonish thee," he writes to Timothy, "that thou stir up the grace of God which is in thee by the imposition of my hands" (2 Tim 1:6).

At baptism, said Jesus, man is born to a new life by virtue of water and the Holy Spirit: *ex aqua et Spiritu Sancto* (Jn 3:5). From that time the Spirit of Christ dwells in the baptized soul; it preserves it: "because you are sons, God has sent the Spirit of his Son into our hearts": *quoniam estis filii, misit Deus Spiritum Filii sui in corda vestra* (Gal 4:6).

Of its own accord our baptismal character is already crying out to heaven; it is pleading for us. Let us rely on it in our invocation of the Holy Spirit, asking Him to teach us to pray as children of God, to treat with our Sovereign Lord as with a father; asking Him to inspire us to live in all things in accordance with the fullness of our baptismal grace, according to the example of Jesus, the one Son by nature.

What is it that Christ does at confirmation by the ministry of His bishop? He extends his hand over the heads of those to be confirmed, and then anoints them with the chrism; making the sign of the Cross on their foreheads, he says: *Signo te signo crucis.* This visible sign of the Cross represents the invisible character imprinted on the soul. The imprint of Christ, glorious in the sight of the angels and saints, is graven on the soul. This imprint attests His domination and His love. The bishop continues the ceremony: *Confirmo te chrismate salutis. . . .* That is to say, I make you strong, I complete the effect of baptism, I make you a perfect Christian, a soldier of Christ, ready to defend His cause. The holy chrism spread on the forehead represents the unction of the Holy Spirit which enters into souls and extends itself in them to give them strength.

Invoking this character, we must pray to the Holy Spirit that in all the struggles and difficulties of life, He may give us the strength to be faithful soldiers of Christ, proud to serve Him and zealous to defend and to extend His kingdom.

In your case, as priests, there is a third sacred mark, that of your ordination, always present in the depths of your being, as a constant invocation of the Holy Spirit. Every morning, strong in your faith, *fortes in fide*, raising your hands towards heaven, you can exhibit to the Lord your soul marked with the seal of Christ. The priesthood of Christ, His blood and His death are engraved on your souls. When you present your soul before God with this mark upon it, you invoke the Holy Spirit and ask Him to revive in you the grace received at your ordination.

We must have a vivid appreciation of the characters of these sacraments. Take full advantage of them, for your whole supernatural life consists in the persevering development in yourself of the graces proper to your vocation as one baptized, confirmed, and ordained a priest of Christ.

This invocation can find its expression in a simple movement of the heart, in prayer to the Holy Spirit or in one of those burning aspirations in which the liturgy of Pentecost is so rich: "Come, Father of the poor . . . source of graces . . . sweet guest of our souls . . . heal our wounds." It is an excellent practice in the course of the day to renew our fervour by means of these ejaculatory prayers. The blessed Peter Fabre of the Society of Jesus carried this practice so far that even during the divine Office between the Psalms he used to address himself mentally to the Father, saying: "Heavenly Father, give me Your Spirit." [5]

[5] *Monumenta Historica Societatis Jesu. Monumenta Fabri* (Madrid: 1914), p. 505. From the time of his novitiate (1887) Dom Marmion had adopted this practice. See *A Master of the Spiritual Life*, pp. 453 and 985.

IV. THE GIFTS OF THE HOLY SPIRIT
IN THE CELEBRATION OF THE MASS:
GIFTS OF FEAR, OF PIETY AND OF FORTITUDE

Right through our life, in every action of our sacred ministry, we can thus invoke the sanctifying intervention of the Holy Spirit. Let us pause to consider more attentively His activity at the most sublime moment of our whole priestly day: our Holy Mass.

It is in all truth a very great honour for us to be associated with the sacrifice of Jesus Christ, to be employed as minister by the Son of God in this most sacred priestly act. It is the Holy Spirit alone who can give us that inner elevation of soul to fit us for such a function.

Speaking of the oblation of Christ on Calvary, St. Paul is careful to note that it was carried out under the influence of the Holy Spirit: "who through the eternal Spirit offered himself without blemish to God": *Per Spiritum Sanctum semetipsum obtulit immaculatum Deo* (Heb 9:14). Let it be the same for us: let us offer this unique sacrifice with our souls adapted to receive the impulse of this Spirit of love.

I would like to suggest to you how the Holy Spirit can exercise a most salutary influence on us by means of His gifts while we are celebrating. I do not propose to deal here with the whole doctrine of the gifts,[6] but only to call your attention by a brief outline to the riches of grace which they bring us.

First of all, have the gifts of fear of the Lord and piety any significance for the celebration of Mass? Undoubtedly they have. It is their part to inspire the most fundamental attitudes in the priest's soul.

We must never forget at the altar the immense, fathomless, infinite majesty of the most holy God to whom the sacrifice is offered: *Suscipe, sancte Pater . . . Suscipe sancta Trinitas.*

As creatures, we must stand before God in an attitude of

---

[6] Dom Marmion has done so in *Christ, the Life of the Soul*, in the chapter "The Holy Spirit, the Spirit of Jesus"; see also *Christ in His Mysteries*, the chapter "The Mission of the Holy Ghost".

adoration and self-effacement under the pain of failing in truth, and it is at the Mass especially that we must be possessed by these sentiments. As I have already pointed out to you frequently, the divine sacrifice requires to be celebrated *cum metu et reverentia* [with fear and reverence]. It is essentially an act of worship which acknowledges the absolute rights of God, an act of homage to His supreme sovereignty. Christ offered His sacrifice on the Cross in that spirit of intimate reverence and religious respect towards the Father which was fitting in the pontiff as well as in the victim of so sacred an act. When we approach so close to the divinity, we must make these sentiments of the heart of Jesus our own.

Let us conceive also, like the Saviour, a keen aversion for all the sins of the world, for all the offences against the supreme Goodness, and let us foster in our souls the eager desire to make reparation for them.

Through the secret impulse of the Holy Spirit attributable to the gift of piety, the priest will come to appreciate that the spirit in which the sacrifice is offered must be one of filial love. By what name does the liturgy address the Lord? By the name of Father. And our access to the divine Majesty is free, assured and confident *per Jesum Christum, Filium tuum, Dominum nostrum*. So intimate is our communion with the Father that we can venture to associate ourselves with His loving delight in His Son and to share in it: *Ut nobis corpus et sanguis fiat dilectissimi Filii tui*. The priest on the altar identifies himself with Jesus: how fully then must this filial spirit be manifest in him!

Let us ask the Holy Spirit to inspire us with a lively faith in God's love for us and with absolute confidence in our heavenly Father.

Under the influence of the divine Spirit we shall feel ourselves impelled at the altar to take upon ourselves all the needs of the human race for, by the gift of piety, we are associated interiorly with the charity which filled the heart of Jesus Christ. As we consider the multifarious sorrows of this world, we shall think of the sinners for whom Christ shed His blood; we shall think of the afflicted, of the sick, of the dying, and in face of this immense chorus of unhappiness which rises from this vale of tears we shall implore the divine mercy for all. Or rather, it is Christ Who, through our lips, will ask His Father to have pity on them. Jesus has willed to assume all our infirmities: "Surely he has borne our griefs": *Vere languores nostros ipse tulit* (Is 53:4); let us believe this firmly. When we offer Jesus to the heavenly Father, it is Jesus Himself, clothed, as it were, in all the ills of His members, Who implores the divine clemency. These dispositions of piety are perfectly consistent with reverential fear, as one of the liturgical prayers asserts so admirably: "Bestow on us, O Lord, both an abiding fear and an abiding love of Thy Holy Name": *Sancti nominis tui, Domine, timorem pariter et amorem fac nos habere perpetuum.*[7]

Instead of approaching the holy sacrifice with a cold heart we can enkindle it with these burning truths. Then the Holy Spirit will inspire us and make us pray with more fervour.

You may wonder perhaps what spiritual help the gift of fortitude can confer on the celebrant.

This gift is necessary on account of the great faith which is required of him and on account of the temptations against this virtue which he may have to undergo. All men are exposed to temptations against faith, but the priest is particularly liable to them. Does that astonish you? Well, here is the reason: when the faithful look on the sacred host, it is either at the solemn moment of the elevation when the whole congregation bows down to adore it, or it is in the monstrance, surrounded with light and incense, or finally it is in the recollection of holy communion. But the faithful can never touch the sacred species; they are never in close personal contact with it.*

The priest is always in immediate contact with the appearances under which Christ is hiding as under a veil. He pronounces the words which Christ pronounced at the Last Supper; he touches the sacred host, he breaks it, he moves it about: it is at his mercy.

[7] Second Sunday after Pentecost.

* This was written before the Second Vatican Council permitted the reception of Communion in the hand.

The devil can avail of this ineffable condescension of Jesus to tempt His minister, and the minister will need the gift of fortitude to maintain his faith at the level of the act which he is accomplishing, to triumph over all temptation, and to convince himself that in all truth he is in the presence of his Saviour, as though he saw Him with his own eyes.

It is this same gift which gives us the courage to offer ourselves each day to God as victims dedicated to all the desires of His will, even the most crucifying. When our cross seems too heavy to accept or to bear, let us ask the Holy Spirit to inspire us with something of that supernatural fortitude which filled Jesus at the moment of His sacrifice.

V. THE GIFTS OF KNOWLEDGE, UNDERSTANDING AND COUNSEL

We come now to the three intellectual gifts of knowledge, understanding and counsel. You must not be confused by the fact that I have changed the customary order; when we are celebrating, the important thing is not so much to know whether the Lord is directing us by this gift or by that, as to have an active faith in the influences from on high and a soul fully disposed to receive them.

You may be quite sure that the most sublime ideas about the Mass will be quite incapable of bringing us close to God unless they are illuminated by the Holy Spirit. It is an excellent thing certainly to know one's theology and especially all that it teaches about the holy sacrifice, but you might read the most learned writings on the subject and yet feel as cold and uninspired as before. Why? Because it is the brain which has done all the work. We must have a supernatural sense of the divine mysteries to complement our studies; there must be something to complete the letter of our reading. Now, it is only the Spirit of love that can give us a deep, living knowledge of the eucharistic offering and immolation.

By the gift of knowledge, the Holy Spirit inspires in us a supernatural appreciation of created things, that is to say, He makes us judge of their importance or unimportance according to the judgement of God. Scripture calls this kind of knowledge the knowledge of the holy things (Wis 10:10). By virtue of this higher rectitude of judgement the saints emancipated themselves from the fascination of the world and exclaimed with the Apostle: "I count all things but as dung that I may gain Christ": *Omnia arbitror ut stercora ut Christum lucrifaciam* (Phil 3:8).

This gift enables us also to understand the incomparable value of the realities of faith and of the sacred acts of worship. That is why, before celebrating, we should implore the Holy Spirit to give us a true understanding of the value of the Mass in accordance with the outlook of God Himself on the august sacrifice.

This understanding will not be the fruit of reasoning. It is intuitive, but the intimate conviction which it gives us is most fruitful for the priest.

May the Holy Spirit graciously grant us the grace in silence and prayer to appreciate, as God appreciates them, the mysteries which are renewed each day by our hands.

By the gift of understanding, the Holy Spirit casts light on the truths of faith in themselves in the depths of our souls. "The spirit searcheth all things," says St. Paul, "yea, the deep things of God"; it is He also Who makes us know "the things that are given us from God": *Ut sciamus quae a Deo donata sunt nobis* (1 Cor 2:10, 12).

In our ordinary life, when we read something, our understanding, by its own light, extracts the meaning which the words express. This is why St. Thomas writes: *Intelligere quasi intus legere.*[8]

Something analogous occurs in the supernatural order; a secret light enables our soul to enter in some small measure into the truth which God illuminates. It is true certainly that the Christian already accepted this truth by a simple act of faith; he held it as true but as something outside of himself; by the gift of understanding the truth is fully revealed.

The Church affirms the reality of these interior lights in

[8] *Summa* II-II, q. 8, a. 1.

many of her prayers: May the Spirit, O Lord, Who proceedeth from Thee enlighten our understanding and may He, even as Thy Son hath promised, lead us into all truth: *Et inducat in omnem sicut tuus promisit Filius veritatem.*[9] In this way, we enter, in a certain manner, into the very sanctuary of the divinity.

You will very readily understand the value of this gift for those who offer the holy sacrifice or participate in it. A divine act is accomplished on the altar; neither man nor angels can grasp the full significance of it, or measure its amplitude; it is ineffable. The Son of God is there; He offers Himself; He immolates Himself under the sacred species; He gives Himself. The Father looks on the Son. . . . It is only a ray of light from on high that can enable us to understand something of these mysteries and to adapt our souls to them. When we read the texts of Scripture and the liturgy, we must have faith that for us, as for the disciples after the Resurrection, the Holy Spirit can make clear their sense: "Then he opened their minds to understand the scriptures": *Aperuit eis sensum ut intelligerent scripturas* (Lk 24:45). These sacred words conserved religiously in our hearts will become more and more soul-stirring to awaken in us the love of God.

The gift of counsel disposes us to recognize, as though by a superior instinct, what actions are useful to guide us and others to our supernatural destiny. "For whosoever are led by the Spirit of God, they are the sons of God," says St. Paul (Rom 8:14). By virtue of this gift, in the ordinary course of life, the Holy Spirit protects us from the impulsiveness of our nature, from our pride, or self-opinionatedness. These defects are sources of illusion and error in the spiritual domain: they incline us to act without giving due consideration to the views of God on the individual souls.

The gift of counsel does not seem to have any great part to play in the celebration of the holy sacrifice. Yet, for the priest, the Mass is the supreme moment for him to ask for those lights of which he stands in such great need. How indispensable these

---

[9] Collect of Wednesday of Pentecost Ember Week.

lights are to him in his words, in his decisions, in all his pastoral activity!

Still, it is important to realize that the priest's faith in the intervention of the Holy Spirit does not justify him, in the carrying out of his duties, in neglecting wise judgement and human means. The gift of counsel was not given by God to His children to replace the virtue of prudence, but on the contrary to assist it and perfect its activity: *Ipsam (prudentiam) adjuvans et perficiens.*[10]

VI. GIFT OF WISDOM

The most eminent of the gifts is that of wisdom. It is a knowledge of God and of things divine gained in the actual exercise of the life of union with the Lord. This wisdom is a fruit of charity; it is therefore of quite another order to theoretic or reasoned knowledge. It is sweet: *sapida cognitio*; it establishes an intimate living contact between the soul and God.

How are these things possible? They are possible through the secret action of the Holy Spirit. When the Christian prays and serves God with great fidelity and love, the Holy Spirit gives him this supernatural wisdom while his soul is concentrated on the Lord. The soul savours the presence of God; it experiences in a certain manner, in its inner being, His merciful goodness and the communication of His life which He makes to the children of adoption. By this gift, the Holy Spirit inspires the human heart to prefer unhesitatingly the beatitude of union with God to all the joys of this world and to say with the Psalmist: "How lovely are Thy tabernacles, O Lord! Far better is one day in Thy courts above thousands" (Ps 84[83]:1, 10). However, we can only dispose ourselves to enjoy this spiritual savour if we put out of our life the desires and indulgences of the world. "The sensual man perceiveth not these things that are of the spirit of God," says St. Paul (1 Cor 2:14).

In holy Mass, the priest gets quite a different understanding

---

[10] *Summa* II-II, q. 52, a. 2.

of the eucharistic mysteries from that given by a reasoned study. A supernatural attraction establishes in his heart the true spirit of oblation. *Imitamini quod tractatis.*

Besides, have we not immense need of divine help to enable us to savour the eucharistic bread spiritually? We frequently repeat the phrase: "Bread from heaven . . . containing all happiness": *Panem de cœlo . . . omne delectamentum in se habentem.* And yet, when we are about to receive holy communion, it may happen that we feel no desire for this bread of life.

The gift of wisdom produces also in the heart an inner peace which supports the soul in the midst of the difficulties and sorrows of life. That is why the liturgy likes to see in the Holy Spirit the supreme consoler; frequently it makes us ask that we may at all times enjoy His consolations. How desirable for the priest is this peace coming from God! Thanks to it, during the sacred sacrifice, he will feel in the depths of his heart the effects of the eternal goodness.

Incomplete as this outline is, it may serve to enliven our faith and our hope in the action of the Holy Spirit during the sacred mysteries and thus help us to overcome the spirit of routine.

Before Mass, we can draw inspiration from that prayer in the missal: "May Thy good Spirit enter into my heart; there in silence to cry aloud to me; there to give wordless utterance to all truth. For exceeding deep are the secrets of God and over them He has cast a sacred veil." [11]

Liturgical tradition proclaims the faith of the Church in the intervention of the Holy Spirit during the sacrifice. Without entering into the problem of the ancient formulas of the *epiclesis*, we may consider the prayers of the offertory as we have them today. When the bread and wine have been prepared on the altar, the congregation is offered in union with it: *Suscipiamur a Te.* What does the priest do then? He raises his hands over the whole oblation and invokes the coming of the Holy Spirit: *Veni sanctificator omnipotens aeterne Deus.*

We may consider also the ceremony of consecration of an

---

[11] Preparation for Mass on Sunday.

altar, one of the most beautiful ceremonies in the whole liturgy. After the table of sacrifice has been purified by aspersions and consecrated by anointings, they place on the five crosses, which represent the five wounds of Jesus, grains of incense which are burnt, and, as the incense burns, the pontiff, with all his clergy, sends up to heaven the prayer: *Veni Sancte Spiritus*. . . . It is one of the most solemn moments in this admirable ceremony. They implore the Holy Spirit, the fire of love, to come down on to this altar where Jesus is to offer Himself *per Spiritum Sanctum* as He did on the Cross; they ask Him to sanctify all the oblations that will be placed upon it and, above all, by the fullness of the power of holy communion to unite the holocaust of the whole Christian assembly to the divine Victim.

By virtue of the imposition of hands by the bishop, we have received the Holy Spirit in a very special way. This same Spirit has imprinted on our souls an indelible character and has filled them with priestly grace. His mission in us is invisible, but by it we are assured of heavenly aid through the whole course of our life: help to celebrate the sacred mysteries, to preach, to direct souls wisely and to console the afflicted. Let us honour the Holy Spirit equally with the Father and the Son by a worship of adoration, by a homage of profound gratitude and of total abandonment to God's will, and by constant fidelity to His inspirations. In this manner we shall be led to serve God as St. Paul recommends: "With the joy of the Holy Spirit": *cum gaudio Sancti Spiritus* (1 Thess 1:6). "O Holy Spirit, love of the Father and the Son, take up your abode in the centre of our hearts and, like a burning flame, bear on high our thoughts, our affections and our actions even to the bosom of the Father, so that our whole life may constitute one *Gloria Patri et Filio et Spiritui Sancto*." [12]

---

[12] This invocation forms part of a consecration to the Blessed Trinity written by Dom Marmion in 1908. The act, which was the climax of an important period in his spiritual life, became for him a point of departure for a further interior ascent. See the complete text, pp. 383–84. We have given a commentary on this consecration formed entirely of extracts from the writings of Dom Marmion.

XVII.

SANCTIFICATION BY MEANS OF
ORDINARY ACTIONS

MANY people think that sanctity consists in spending long hours in prayer. Others conceive it as a series of renouncements and sufferings endured for love's sake: to their mind the function of sanctity is to mortify all tendencies of nature in man.

As against these one-sided points of view, St. Benedict has laid down his ascetic principle: "At all times we must serve God by means of those gifts which He Himself has placed in us." [1] This is a very healthy standard in the spiritual life. Its aim is to produce in us submission to God and a harmony between the human and the divine. Progress is achieved by the exercise of our human faculties in the accomplishment of our duties in the state in which Providence has placed us.

Many of you have your days crowded with divers occupations, and these seem to combine to impede any effort to achieve an interior life. All the same you must not lose heart: you can sanctify yourself by all your activities, even the most commonplace. This is the teaching of the Epistles of St. Paul and St. John.

Certain conditions are necessary to ensure the sanctifying effect of these actions: they must be—true—inspired by the idea of supernatural love—united to the merits of the actions of Jesus—and through them our priestly sanctification must be dedicated to the good of the Church.

It is not necessary that we should have these conditions always in mind; it is sufficient if we think of them from time to time in order to revive our faith and to help us to refer all the glory to the Lord. You may be quite sure that the spiritual life should be a life, not of anxiety or rush, but of peace; it looks on

[1] Prologue to the Rule.

God as a Father and with holy hope it looks for union with Him less as a result of our own thoughts than from the power of grace and our fidelity.

This application to the task of raising our hearts to God during the day certainly requires an effort; but nothing lasting in this world can be achieved without some trouble.

We must hear in mind also the dogma of the communion of saints. In many convents there are numbers of souls consecrated to God who offer daily their sacrifices and their prayers for the sanctification of priests. We should appreciate the value and the beauty of this gesture and find support in their generosity.

I. TO WALK IN TRUTH

This expression comes from St. John. It occurs in many places in his Epistles (2 Jn 1:4; 3 Jn 1:3.) What do these words mean according to the mind of the Apostle? To walk in truth means to regulate all our conduct in accordance with the views and intentions of God, in conformity with our state in life.[2]

As author of our nature and of the order of grace, the Lord desires in us a rectitude of conduct in perfect accord with our condition as created beings and with our twofold dignity as adoptive children of God and priests of Christ. It is for us, therefore, to accomplish at all times the duties imposed on our conscience both by the natural law and by the requirements of baptism and the priesthood. Such is God's idea in relation to us. When our manner of acting is in conformity with this divine will, we are performing a work of righteousness; we are walking in truth.

The Lord is pleased to find in us this perfect correspondence between our actions and the laws of our life. Without this harmony, our works, however fine they may appear to be, do not fulfil the divine expectations.

A first consequence of this doctrine for us priests may be expressed thus: on account of our special vocation to sanctity

[2] See in *Christ, the Life of the Soul* the chapters "Truth in Charity" and "Our Supernatural Growth", where Dom Marmion has developed at length the ideas touched on here.

we are bound, more strictly than the laity, to cultivate the natural virtues. We must be perfectly just and equitable in our judgements, truthful in our words. We must never admit in our conduct any breach of natural fairness. On no account, not even on the pretext of serving the cause of religion, may we lose sight of the obligations which probity of conscience imposes on every man. Our priestly activity necessarily presupposes this moral basis. Further, the effort to harmonize in ourselves the gifts of nature and the gifts of grace, certainly means striving towards a noble ideal. But in practice this ideal can only be realized by the mortification of many tendencies and many desires inherent in our nature: these, in fact, are not always compatible with our state in life. Certain sacrifices prove indispensable, either as a safeguard for the elevation of soul proper in a priest, or in view of his mission to the faithful. That is why, although the support of human love is perfectly legitimate in marriage, the plenitude of priestly devotion and the balance of the interior life require a generous renouncement in this regard on the part of the minister of Christ.

If grace does not destroy nature, neither does it overwhelm our personality. It assails, certainly, pride, hardness of heart, and many other defects natural to certain vigorous characters; but it accepts, when it meets them, the great natural qualities of soul, of heart, and of will which constitute the best groundwork of the true human personality. Consider the saints of all times. By the gifts of grace they have excelled the common mediocrity; they were, most often, superior personalities, courageous, and radiant. Far from smothering their natural gifts, grace exalted them and supernaturalized them by the most entire submission to God according to the order and plenitude of charity.

In every circumstance we are faced with a choice. We must never give in to negligence, or to anxiety about our comfort, but prefer the joy of living according to the rectitude proper to our condition as human beings and according to the sanctity of our priestly vocation. Does not the Psalmist invite us to strive towards this great ideal when he makes us say: "I have chosen the way of truth": *Viam veritatis elegi*? (Ps 119[118]:30).

II. OMNIA COOPERANTUR IN BONUM

We know that in all things God collaborates for the good of those who love Him, of those who have been chosen as the elect according to His free purpose (Rom 8:28). And have we not been chosen by Jesus? (Jn 15:16).

Some souls are inclined to believe that the Mass, the breviary and pious exercises alone can unite a soul to God. This view is incorrect. Certainly these acts of piety develop and maintain our interior life; by them our conviction of the primacy of the supernatural and of purity of intention in zeal for souls is strengthened. By virtue of these dispositions the heart of a holy priest raises up towards God, fortifies and consoles, all who approach Him.

These acts, it must be admitted, are the soul of every apostolate. Still, it is true to say, with St. Paul, that every action of a disciple of Christ, even the most commonplace, contributes to the good of his soul and to his sanctification.

Let us examine from this point of view the make-up of our day. The duties of our ministry fill up a great part of it. Is it possible to sanctify ourselves by them? Certainly. The acts of our ministry in themselves are ordained, not for our personal sanctification, but for the spiritual utility of our neighbour. While we should see in them above all an occasion to devote ourselves to others, they can become indirectly a means of purifying, enlightening or elevating our souls.

But this devotion to others is undoubtedly a source of merit and of grace for us.

Hearing confessions, and administering the other sacraments, teaching catechism, and visiting the sick, are acts of charity towards our neighbour. By this very fact they increase in us the flow of divine life. This is true also when we attend funerals or take part in parochial and social activities.

All these duties, if carried out in a supernatural spirit, are sanctifying. For many of us this giving of self in acts of charity is repeated every hour of the day and sometimes of the night also. The faithful of all ages expect many services from our zeal. This generosity certainly brings us nearer to God.

To this tireless devotion we must add another virtue, that of patience. It alone, according to St. James, makes our works perfect: *Patientia opus perfectum habet* (Jas 1:4). This disposition is especially necessary to us in our divers relations with souls. It contributes a great deal to the supernaturalization of our lives. Here, we meet indifference or stubbornness, there, hostility or hate. Yet, we must never abandon the meekness of Christ. In our immediate circle there exist often views opposed to ours; we come up against misunderstanding. How often do we find our good will and our ardour thwarted! Are we to be discouraged by this? Certainly not. We must rather seek in the patience of Our Saviour strength to maintain our own. The virtues are strengthened by this fidelity in using all occasions, great and small, to practise them. We do not rise to God by fruitless complaints about the past nor by fine projects for the future, but by accomplishing every hour of the day the duty of the moment.

In order to attain this end it is of great profit to adopt a rule of life, and to keep to it, while avoiding all suggestion of scruple.

There are many advantages in a wise arrangement of the day: we save time; we carry out our duties in a spirit of obedience to the will of God: this is of capital importance; finally, this is a very efficacious weapon against our tendency to negligence and indolence. Let us pause to consider this last point.

Some priests, as we know, are overburdened with work; others have a good deal of leisure. My experience is that at all times everyone needs a serious occupation to which he may apply himself with a full realization of his responsibility.

There is no greater danger for the priest than idleness: *Multam enim malitiam docuit otiositas*: "idleness teaches much evil" (Sir 33:27). A really idle priest has neither rule nor order in his day. As he is incapable of fixing his mind on any subject worthy of attention, he wastes his time; often he is behindhand in his recitation of the breviary. In this state he can become an easy prey for the enemy of his salvation. In a remarkable sermon attributed to St. Augustine we read: "It was not during work but during their hours of leisure that Samson, David and Solomon yielded to the solicitations of the senses. We must not think that we are holier, or stronger, or wiser than they": *Nec sanctiores David, nec fortiores Samsone, nec sapientiores Solomoni.*[3]

The spirit of work plays a great part in the sanctification of the priest. Without it, the most excellent qualities, the richest talents, bear no fruit. The good of his neighbour and the dignity of his own life require of every minister of Christ constant attention to making good use of his time.

The law of work is universal. The words of the Lord addressed to Adam apply to us all: "In the sweat of thy brow thou shalt eat thy bread" (Gen 3:19).

The new Adam, Jesus, our model, willed to experience Himself all the burdensome conditions of our life, excepting sin: *Tentatus autem per omnia, pro similitudine, absque peccato* (Heb 4:15).

The stern necessity of work has pressed on Him just as it presses on us all. He submitted Himself in the spirit of love to this decree of the Father. Was He not, during His life, taken for the son of a workman? *Nonne hic est fabri filius* (Mt 13:55).

Let us willingly imitate the work of Jesus, Mary and Joseph in the house at Nazareth. We should not scorn to add to the normal occupation of the priestly life humble manual labour when occasion requires it. Let us remember the example of St. Paul: "Such things as were needful for me . . . these hands have furnished" (Acts 20:34). Again he writes: "In labour and toil we worked night and day, lest we should be chargeable to any of you" (2 Thess 3:8). How many saints from the time of the apostles until now have sanctified themselves by the most ordinary manual work!

According to the idea of some people, it is only the man who handles a spade or a trowel that is really working. The architect who draws the plans, the employer who looks after the running

[3] *Sermo* 17 in *Append. St. Augustini*; PL 40, 1264.

of the factory and the distribution of the products are only idlers in their eyes. In these times many people have the same idea about the spiritual order. They are quite certainly mistaken. We know by experience that work of the mind and of our holy ministry is often more laborious and more exhausting than manual labour.

Among the different forms of intellectual work, we should have a preference for the study of theology and holy Scripture. *Nostrae divitiae sint, in lege Domini nostri meditari, die ac nocte,* writes St. Jerome. And again: *Ama scientiam Scripturarum et carnis vitia non amabis.*[4]

The most serious preparation we can make for the ministry of the Word is to keep up the knowledge of the Scriptures and theology which we acquired at the seminary. But apart from its advantages for preaching, competence in the sacred sciences or, indeed, in the profane ones, raises your level of life and increases the measure of your influence over many souls.

It is quite normal in your priestly life to make provision for recreations in order to help you to practise the virtues and to give you some relaxation after your work. The wise choice of these is important for our sanctification; there are amusements which may be permissible for laymen which are not compatible with our obligations as priests. We should indulge freely in the companionship and friendship of our confrères in the priesthood: *Frater qui adiuvatur a fratre quasi civitas firma*: "A brother helped is like a strong city" (Prov 18:19). At those times especially, when we feel our loneliness weighing heavily on us, we should not hesitate to turn to a confrère to whom we can speak freely. Did not Jesus Himself speak of His anguish to His disciples in the garden of Olives? It may be a great help to us to open our heart to a faithful friend; at times it may be a necessary consolation. Still, we must not depend too much on human consolation. We must seek our strength and our joy primarily in God.

---

[4] *Epistolae* 30 and 125; PL 22, 442 and 1078.

III. ROOTED IN CHARITY

In the order of Providence man has only one final end: heaven and the beatific vision. It is, therefore, of supreme importance for him to direct all the free activity of his life towards this beatitude. It is charity alone which makes us love God as the Supreme Good, and which gives a supernatural value to every one of our actions. That is why St. Paul said: "If I should have all faith so that I could remove mountains . . . and if I should distribute all my goods to feed the poor and if I should deliver my body to be burned and have not charity, it profiteth me nothing" (1 Cor 13:2–3). St. Francis de Sales expresses the same truth in his own inimitable style: "A flick of the finger borne with two ounces of love is worth more than martyrdom borne with one ounce." [5]

It is not enough, therefore, for man to serve the Lord and do his duty from a mere sense of human decency or natural punctiliousness, but in the most commonplace actions as well as in the greatest, he should have his eyes fixed on God, with the intention of doing His will and pleasing Him. It is not possible to have the intention of referring ourselves to God ever actively present in our minds, but if our souls rise up to God from time to time by an act of love, then the words of St. John will be realized in us: "He that abideth in charity abideth in God and God in him" (1 Jn 4:16).

The marvellous consequence of this doctrine may be expressed thus: when charity is firmly planted in our hearts, the nature of our actions is of relatively minor importance for our sanctification. Let me explain my meaning.

What is the difference between the saints and imperfect souls? Is it in the nature of the work to which they devote themselves? Evidently not. During the whole of our lives we are performing actions which are sublime, and at the end of a long career we may be far from being saints. On the other hand, we see simple Christians—such as Marie Taigi or Matt Talbot, a

---

[5] André Hamon, *Vie* 2, 360.

Dublin docker—whose whole day is taken up with commonplace occupations, and they are saints. How does the difference arise? From love. Charity, more and more detached from all that is not God, has made of these apparently humdrum lives an unbroken canticle of praise, an unceasing prayer.

Consider the life at Nazareth. The occupations of Mary and Joseph were for the most part merely those of ordinary working people. Yet the least of them gave incomparable glory to the Trinity. Why? Not only on account of the eminent dignity of the Virgin and her spouse, but also because each one of these actions was accomplished under an impulse of perfect love.

So, in the spiritual life, it is evident that charity is of capital importance.

Yet we are sometimes tempted to believe that if we were entrusted with this duty or if we could be relieved of that employment, or could be freed from the company of some irritating person, we should make more rapid progress in the way of perfection. This is a great illusion. In principle these imagined obstacles are intended to be transformed into ladders to lead us up to God for, as we pointed out, our perfection depends neither on the form of our work, nor on our environment, but on the charity which inspires our activity.

Experience teaches us, however, that there are few souls sufficiently advanced in the ways of love to draw their inspiration on every occasion from supernatural charity alone. The need of human support is nearly always present. Contradictions, difficulties, and crosses are not in themselves infallible means of sanctification. The soul of the disciple of Christ must be sufficiently enlightened, sufficiently strong, and sufficiently generous, to receive them from the hand of God and to endure the trial without yielding to discouragement.

Generally speaking, a director of conscience cannot invariably require of the faithful soul all the acts which he may judge useful for its advancement. Without losing sight of the perfection which is his aim, it is prudent to make allowances for the weaknesses of each individual and for the time required for spiritual growth. Charity, as we all know, comes to us from

God; it is the splendid prerogative of the children of adoption. Did not Jesus, our divine model, live by love? In all His human activity His eyes were fixed on the Father, so that He might act in full conformity of love with Him: *quae placita sunt ei facio semper* (Jn 8:29). We also, following the advice of St. Paul, must have our souls "rooted in charity": *in caritate radicati* (Eph 3:17); we must do all things in charity: *omnia vestra in caritate fiant* (1 Cor 16:14). The holy bishop of Geneva prescribed in the most imperative manner this domination of divine charity over our entire lives: "We must," said he, "have no other law or compulsion than that of charity."[6] In order to attain this high ideal here is my advice: during the day you should renew frequently, but without wearying your mind, your intention to carry out all your actions from love. Formulate this intention in a prayer. You can use, for example, a verse of the Psalm: "I love thee, O Lord, my strength": *Diligam te, Domine, fortitudo mea* (Ps 18[17]:1); or the aspiration of St. Augustine: *Fac me, Pater, quaerere te.*[7] In this matter everyone can choose as the Holy Spirit inspires him. But of one thing you may be sure: in the spiritual life nothing is achieved without perseverance.

Perhaps you are still wondering what, in the final analysis, is the reason of the primary importance of charity?

The answer is that, in His intimate life, God is love: *Deus caritas est* (1 Jn 4:8). The Father engenders His Word and finds in Him His delight. The Son, likewise, contemplates the Father and is attracted to Him irresistibly. The Holy Spirit proceeds from their mutual love. The more that our existence here on earth reflects the life of the Holy Trinity by virtue of charity, the more closely it approaches the fullness of perfection.

IV. IN NOMINE DOMINI JESU CHRISTI

In a life which seeks to be entirely dominated by charity, progress is possible only through union with Jesus Christ. This is the teaching of St. Paul: "That we may in all things grow up

---

[6] *Oeuvres de St. François de Sales* 13 (vol. III, *Lettres*), ed. d'Annecy, p. 184.

[7] *Soliloquia*, 1, 6; PL 32, 872, or the prayer of Prime: *dirigere et sanctificare*.

in Him" (Eph 4:15). And again: "All whatsoever you do in word or in work, do all in the name of the Lord Jesus Christ giving thanks to God and the Father by Him" (Col 3:17).

We must try to get a clear understanding of the Apostle's thought.

Take an ambassador, for example. He can act in his own name, as a private individual, like any other man, or he can act in his capacity of envoy. In the latter case he will rely, not on his own merits or personal talents, but on the authority of the sovereign whose credentials he bears. This identification with the head of his government is extrinsic and temporary.

Our union with Christ is quite different. He has made us His own for ever. We bear our credentials in our souls; they are valid for eternity. They are sanctifying grace and the characters conferred by baptism and ordination. These divine gifts bear permanent and explicit testimony that we belong to Jesus Christ.

The words of the Apostle, "Whatsoever you do", have a profound significance. They do not merely give us the counsel to pronounce the formula: "In the name of Christ, Our Lord" before acting; they mean that in prayer, in work and, above all in our ministry, we have the right to present ourselves habitually before God in the strength of our dignity as members of Christ and ministers of His priesthood. This is the secret which assures us of access to the Father, and guarantees the fruitfulness of our work for souls.

Every priest has the immense privilege of speaking to God and treating with Him in the name of Jesus Christ, and relying on Him; but there are some who forget their privilege on account of their lack of faith. The more we practise self-effacement when we present ourselves before the Lord, the more fully we understand the mystery of Christ. Why is this? Because our unlimited confidence in the merits of the Saviour bears witness to the firmness of our faith in His divinity.

In one of his Epistles, St. John says to us in this regard: "If we receive the testimony of men, the testimony of God is greater." Now, what is the testimony which the Father gives about Jesus? That Jesus is His Son; "He who believes in the Son of God has the testimony in himself": *qui credit in filium Dei habet testimo-nium Dei in se* (1 Jn 5:10). That means that faith in the divinity of Jesus makes us participate in the personal knowledge of the Father; in the generation of the Word, He contemplates Him from all eternity as His consubstantial Son, as His equal. Our faith in Christ as true God is therefore an echo of the very life of the Father. Believe, therefore, with your whole heart that the Son of God belongs to you; you possess Him as your own with all His merits, with all the dignity of His divine Person. St. Paul exulted in the fullness of this gift: *quommodo non etiam cum illo omnia nobis donavit*: "will He not give us all things with Him?" (Rom 8:32). He cannot find expressions strong enough to proclaim the "unsearchable riches of Christ" (Eph 3:8); He sees us so over-whelmed with benefits in Christ that no grace is wanting to us: *Ita ut nihil vobis desit in ulla gratia* (1 Cor 1:5 and 7). Is not our life of faith, when understood in this light, something magnificent?

In many Christians this lively hope in the Person and in the merits of the Man God has become apathetic; the idea of pre-senting themselves before the Father in the name of Jesus Christ, or of relying on their baptism or their status as children of God through Jesus is in practice unknown to them. For our part, in spite of our miseries and our unworthiness, let us go to the Lord in a spirit of holy daring.

A simple and efficacious way to guard against the danger of naturalism in our lives is to recall how Jesus in His Person sanc-tified all the actions which make up the pattern of our poor earthly existence. He prayed and worked like us; like us He conversed with His contemporaries; He sat at table with them. On His apostolic journeys He felt tired after a long walk: *Fati-gatus ex itinere sedebat sic supra fontem*: "wearied as He was with His journey, He sat down beside the well" (Jn 4:6). He slept in the boat and had to be awakened by the cries of His disciples who were in fear of the tempest. The feelings of His heart were similar to our own: He really loved His own people; His soul was filled with sadness and anguish; He suffered from ingrati-tude and, especially at the hour of His Passion, He was over-whelmed beyond all measure by His sorrows.

Jesus carried out these human actions with ineffable love for the Father and for us; by each one of them He merited to produce in us the necessary graces to imitate Him and to love Him. We may be quite sure that the divine Master wishes to communicate to His members, and especially to His priests, the strength to follow His example.

In our priestly life we are called to continue, in a certain way, His virtues. Like Him, we have dedicated our lives to the defence of the rights of God among men and to the glorification of His name. In our submission to the obligations of our circumstances we imitate the obedience of the Saviour to the will of His Father. In our life of dedication, of patience and of chastity we are certainly reproducing His examples.

In our work, in our troubles, and in our difficulties, we are never alone. Jesus assists us from without as the model of all sanctity, but more than this, He strengthens us from within as the source of life. Are we not the authorized dispensers of His grace, His legates among men? (2 Cor 5:20.) In all our activities of the ministry, we act by the power of God Himself! *Tamquam ex virtute quam ministrat Deus*: "as one who renders it by the strength which God supplies" (1 Pet 4:11). Because He has chosen us, Christ regards each one of us as another self. He is pleased to see us enter ever deeper into the mystery of this resemblance to Him and of this union with Him. We should have this thought frequently in our minds; it is a source of lively joy and zeal.

Let us place Jesus in the centre of our heart. Every morning we celebrate the sacred mysteries; we receive His body and blood; may this divine contact be the centre of our day, inspiring all our activity and elevating it to the supernatural plane.

V. CHRISTUS DILEXIT ECCLESIAM

We are called to sanctity, not as individuals, but in the unity of the mystical body of Christ.

While we are members of this body as Christians, it is further incumbent on us as priests to vivify it by the grace of the sacraments and by the ministry of the word. Our personal sanctification achieved in the bosom of the Church is intended for the good of the Church itself. Sanctity is diffused in the mystical body; from Christ it descends on all the members and it is reflected from the minister of Christ on all the faithful who are entrusted to his care. The priest, therefore, sanctifies himself for the benefit of souls.

In this way he imitates more and more the divine Master of Whom St. Paul says: "Christ loved the Church," *dilexit Ecclesiam*, "and delivered Himself up for it," *tradidit semetipsum pro ea*. Why did He deliver Himself up even to the sacrifice of the Cross? "That he might present it to Himself a glorious Church not having spot or wrinkle . . . but that it should be holy and without blemish" (Eph 5:25 and 27).

This sanctification of the priest for the benefit of others presupposes in him a firm faith in the Church itself. The foundation of our whole spiritual edifice is certainly faith in the divinity of Jesus Christ; but if it is to be perfect, this faith must extend from the Person of the Saviour to the visible society instituted by Him and destined to lead men to their eternal happiness.

As we believe in Christ, true God, so the divine reality of His Church is equally an object of our faith.

This faith reminds us how intimate and vital is the bond between Christ and the Church. St. Paul compares this union to that which exists between the head and the members, between husband and wife (Eph 5:30–32). The Church prolongs the mission of the Saviour here on earth; it completes His work of redemption. In fact, Jesus Himself does not cease to operate in it. Before ascending into heaven, He proclaimed in the clearest manner the indissolubility of His union with it: "Behold I am with you all days even to the consummation of the world" (Mt 28:20).

Our faith in the supernatural character of the Church involves, besides, a complete acceptance of its divine institution. The hierarchy, the power of orders and of jurisdiction, the infallibility of the Roman Pontiff, the eucharistic sacrifice, the sacraments, all these are not born of a human concept nor of fortuitous circumstances, but constitute a realization in time of a design which was preconceived and determined by the eternal Wisdom. Admittedly the Lord made use of the cooperation of men in the phases of the organic development of the Church and in the elaboration of its doctrinal formulas. He wished them to play their part. But He alone remained at all times the sovereign master of this evolution through the constant action of His Spirit which vivifies the mystical body: *spiritum vivificantem.*

When we believe firmly in the divine origin of the Church, it is easy for us to think, to judge, to will and to act as she thinks, judges, wills, and acts *sentire cum Ecclesia.* This is the homage and obedience of faith which is highly recommended by the Apostle: *obsequium fidei: obeditio fidei* (Phil 2:16; Rom 16:26).

God requires this submission from every Christian, but it is especially necessary in the priest. Protestants, as you know, do not accept this renunciation of liberty of mind which is asked of believers. They profess, on the contrary, the doctrine of private judgement. They are like a navigator who wants to steer his course on the ocean without a compass; he is free to go where he likes and to safeguard his full autonomy. The Catholic may be compared to the pilot who plots his course with the aid of this instrument; the infallible compass which is his guide is the authority of the Church. She controls his convictions and directs his thoughts and his actions.

Thanks to this directive, the disciple of Christ can advance boldly; he will not strike against the reefs of error. The Protestant has complete liberty but it is a liberty to lose his way and be shipwrecked.

Living faith is a source of action. Consequently we priests should spare no effort to extend the kingdom of God, and of the Church. We must know how to devote ourselves to that portion of the fold of which we have charge. The Church is a Mother, *Mater Ecclesia.* She is destined by God to engender mankind to the supernatural life and to make that life increase in them. She cannot accomplish this work of wondrous fruitfulness without the devotion of her priests. It is for you to effect this new birth of souls and to transform them into the image of Jesus Christ, by the administration of the sacraments, by the ministry of the Word, and by the radiation of your charity. By virtue of this work carried out in the name of the Church, you can repeat to your flock the words of St. Paul: "In Christ Jesus . . . I have begotten you" (1 Cor 4:15). And again: "My little children, of whom I am in labour again, until Christ be formed in you" (Gal 4:19).

Confidence in the final triumph is the greatest encouragement that we can have for this gift of self. If the Church is divine, let our hearts be filled with great hope. Christ has said of His Church: "The gates of hell shall not prevail against it" (Mt 16:18).

Relying on this divine promise, we must cherish in our hearts the certainty of victory. In our days there are perhaps some who are sceptical about the power of the Spouse of Christ to achieve the redemption of mankind; they think that she is not adapted to present-day aspirations. But we priests must never cease to hope in the Church; the message of the Gospel, of which we are the bearers in her name, contains for all men the chief hope of salvation. We should be proud to make our own the words of St. Paul in his Epistle to the Romans: "I am not ashamed of the Gospel. For it is the power of God unto salvation to everyone that believeth": *Non erubesco Evangelium, virtus enim Dei est in salutem omni credenti* (Rom 1:16). At the Last Supper, after the institution of the priesthood, Jesus said: "Father . . . for them do I sanctify Myself"—that is to say, that for them I separate Myself from the world in order to offer Myself as a sacrifice and to unite Myself fully to You, "that they also may be sanctified in truth" (Jn 17:19). This prayer was uttered in the presence of the apostles, but Jesus was thinking of us, His future priests, as well as of the twelve. He saw the whole Church before Him. He offered Himself as a consecrated victim for all so as to make every soul, and the whole Church, share in His sanctity.

By a special choice Jesus has invited us to participate in His great mission of sanctifying the Church by sanctifying ourselves. Let us make every effort to reply with love to this invitation. It is our most noble mission; it is also the most certain means of drawing down on our work the divine benediction.

XVIII.

THE BLESSED VIRGIN MARY AND THE PRIEST

MARY is Queen and Mother of all Christians. She is in a special manner Queen and Mother of priests. Because of their resemblance to her divine Son, Our Lady sees Jesus in each one of them. She loves them, not only as members of the mystical body, but on account of the priestly character imprinted on their souls, and for the sacred mysteries which they celebrate *in persona Christi.*

No one has understood as well as she the role of the priest in the Church. The priest carries on the work of her Son by the ministry of the Word, by the administration of the sacraments, and especially by perpetuating the divine immolation under the veil of the sacred species. It is the desire of Mary to come to the aid of each one of us on all occasions: to support our weakness, to elevate our souls. At the altar and all during life it is supremely useful to invoke frequently the powerful intercession of our heavenly mother. She knows the greatness of our dignity and how much we stand in need of heavenly grace.

Exempt from sin, she does not know within herself human misery* [translation from French original]. Yet, of all His creatures, Mary has been, in a certain sense, the object of the greatest mercies of God. The divine goodness has operated in her regard, not to pardon, but to preserve her from all stain. We cannot doubt that Mary, for her part, will be full of commiseration for us: *Salve Regina, Mater misericordiae.*

It is difficult to speak of the Blessed Virgin. Everything that one can say falls so far below what one would like to be able to express and what one would like to convey to others. Let us try, however, to consider briefly the theological basis for our

* Because of her Immaculate Conception, Mary is ontologically free from the human experience of sin (concupiscence); however, it does not exclude her existential experience of fallen humanity. In other words, though she is sinless, Mary remains close to us and our experience of suffering in the world.—ED.

devotion to Mary and the practical manner in which we can offer her our filial devotion.

In its primary sense the term "devotion" means the gift, total or partial, of oneself and one's activities to a person or to a work. For us priests it is to God and His cause that we dedicate ourselves and all the resources of our activity. But if God, in His goodness, loves and overwhelms with honour one of His creatures, our devotion to the supreme Majesty makes it incumbent on us to imitate His attitude and render to this privileged creature the homage of our profound veneration.

Now the Blessed Virgin has been overwhelmed with graces by the Holy Trinity. Her privileges have raised her above all creatures, and now she reigns triumphant in heaven, on the right hand of Jesus, as Queen of the angels and of the saints. In order to understand fully the veneration due to Mary we must go back to the free act of the divine will by which the Father "so loved the world as to give His only begotten Son" (Jn 3:16). In His eternal predestination He willed that this Incarnate Son should satisfy in a perfect manner the exigencies of His justice, and that in this way, thanks to Him, the divine mercies might be extended to the whole of humanity.

The Son of God might have appeared among us as a grown man; by a simple act of His will He could have clothed Himself with a nature like ours without having ever known a mother's womb, and realized here on earth the programme of His whole life. Admittedly, in that event the Saviour would not have been truly the "Son of Man", but was not God free to grant His pardon in consideration of any form of reparation? In His wisdom the Father preferred another plan; the Redeemer of men would be "formed of a woman", *factum ex muliere* (Gal 4:4) like them. Consequently, in the decree of the Incarnation, God included the choice of a woman, blessed amongst all women, who would be the mother of the Saviour, the mother of God.

The incomparable dignity of Mary can only be measured in

the light of her predestination. The Virgin was present to the
divine thought before every other creature. That is why the
Church says of her: "The Lord possessed me in the beginning
of His ways (Prov 8:22). Is there not an indissoluble bond between the Word made flesh and her? In the eternal designs, the
same divine will effected the maternity of Mary and the whole
work of the redemption.

St. Bede gives concise expression to this unique and glorious
dignity of the motherhood. "Christ," he writes, "received His
flesh neither from nothing nor from any other source, but from
the Virgin. If it had not been so, one could not in all truth call
Him the Son of Man whose origin had not been human." [1] It
was not without reason, therefore, that the angel said to Mary:
"Thou shalt bring forth a Son": *Paries filium* (Lk 1:12), and that
later we hear Mary say to Jesus when she had found Him in the
temple: "Son, why hast thou done so to us?" (Lk 2:48). She
calls Jesus her Son. And Christ Himself on account of His birth
"in the likeness of sinful flesh" (Rom 8:3) is not ashamed to call
them brethren: *non confunditur eos fratres appellare* (Heb 2:1).

How inexpressible is the exaltation of the Virgin! The child
born of her is a divine person; He is her Creator: *Genuisti qui te
fecit.*

Here is a fact which is a further demonstration of how much
honour God willed to bestow on Mary. The angel announces
her marvellous destiny but, according to the divine plan, the
dignity of being the Mother of God will not be bestowed on
her without her consent. The Lord makes the redemptive Incarnation subject, so to speak, to the *Fiat* of the Virgin. When
this was pronounced, then, and only then, with an unspeakable
condescension of love, the Son of God became man. [2]

---

[1] *In Lucam* iv:ii; PL 92, 480.

[2] In his theological teaching Dom Marmion liked to stress the point that in Jesus the
double birth, divine and human, did not connote a double filiation. The term *filiation* is
understood to mean the origin of the complete subsisting being, that is to say, of the person.
In Jesus, the divine Person preceded the Incarnation. When Mary calls Jesus her Son, she
does not claim to have been the fountainhead of His Person as our mothers were for us, but
only to have borne Him in the womb, formed Him of her flesh and brought Him into the
world. *Christus dicitur realiter filius Virginis matris ex relatione reali maternitatis ad Christum*
(Thomas Aquinas, *Summa* III, q. 35, a. 5).

In this admirable manner the Father made of Mary a creature singularly privileged. At this moment everything depended on her, everything came to us from her.

The divine maternity of Our Lady is the reason for her singular prerogatives. It is to this dignity that she owes her Immaculate Conception, her preservation from all sin, her sanctification. Her sanctification like the rising dawn: *velut aurora consurgens*,[3] developed from the childhood of Mary until the day when, having been assumed into heaven, she was crowned in glory and power on the right hand of Jesus.

You can see that devotion to the Blessed Virgin is not an accidental matter; it belongs to the very essence of Christianity. One would cease to be a true disciple of Christ if one did not give His mother the respectful homage which the Incarnation imposes on us. The Church recognizes her incomparable excellence by a form of veneration superior to that offered to all other saints: the veneration of *hyperdulia*.

In the chant of the *Te Deum*, the monks of Cluny in former times used to bow deeply when they came to the words: "for our salvation . . . didst not disdain the Virgin's womb": *non horruisti Virginis uterum*. Even though we do not imitate this gesture, let us preserve in our hearts a very deep veneration for the blessed mystery of love which Mary bore in her womb.

II. MARY OUR MOTHER

Firm as is this first basis for our devotion to her, we have another powerful motive for honouring Our Lady: she is our mother. By the veneration which we offer her as sons are we not still more like Jesus Who loved and venerated His mother?

We are the children of God, not merely in name but in truth (1 Jn 3:1); so also we are truly the children of the Virgin Mary. This is not a mere figure or metaphor, but the teaching of our faith.

What is the foundation for this happy certainty that we are

---

[3] Antiphon of the Assumption.

the children of the Queen of heaven? First of all it is founded on the dogma of our incorporation with Christ as members of His body. Is not a woman a mother when she is the source of life for others—when she communicates to another the life which she enjoys herself. Now, in the supernatural order, whence comes to us this divine life which is destined not to end with death like our corporal life, but to bloom into glory in eternity? Eve gave us life according to nature and to sin; but life and grace have come down to us through Mary. Mary is the new Eve associated by her predestination to the new Adam. How efficacious her cooperation has been for the work of redemption! At the time of the Annunciation, as we have already said, God willed to make the coming of His Son subject in a certain way to her consent. Henceforth the Virgin was to be the privileged creature who communicated to all the gift of God, supernatural life; she accepted her motherhood in all the fullness of the divine intentions. Now, it was in the designs of God that she should be mother not only of Christ but of all His members.

That is why the liturgy sings with exultation: "Acclaim, O redeemed peoples, the life which the Virgin has bestowed on you": *Vitam datam per Virginem, gentes redemptae plaudite.*

St. Augustine expresses the same thought: "Mary, who is mother of Christ in the natural sense of the word, has become spiritually the mother of all the members of the body of her Son": *Plane Mater membrorum eius, quod nos sumus.* And what is the reason? Because, by her love, she has cooperated (with her Son) so that the faithful who are His members might be born into the Church: *quia cooperata est caritate, ut fideles in Ecclesia nascerentur qui illius membra sunt.*[4]

However, it was at the foot of the Cross in the grief of her compassion that Mary was finally declared mother of the human race. Had she not at this moment reached the culmination of her life here on earth? She had accomplished to the full the *fiat* of the Incarnation and fulfilled the role which had been

---

[4] *De sancta virginitate* 6; PL 40, 399.

ordained for her by the sovereign Wisdom. A partner in the immolation of her Son, she was, as it were, transfused into Him by love and had with Him the one will of submission to the Father, the one intention to suffer and to carry out the eternal designs. By virtue of this moral union and in complete subordination to the one true Mediator, Mary was a co-redeemer. In this way she engendered us to supernatural life, and became in a true sense our mother.

Jesus willed that we should hear these great truths from His own lips. Let us go in spirit to Calvary. From the height of the Cross where He is in His agony, Jesus utters those sublime words, the full profound sense of which has been only gradually revealed in the Church. The last words spoken by a son at the hour of death are sacred to the heart of a mother. Mary loved Jesus more than any other creature ever loved Him. As a mother, and as a mother endowed with all the gifts of grace, she cherished her Son with all the intensity of her affection. Now, what were the last words of Jesus to His mother? Mary was standing close to Him at the foot of the Cross; her eyes were fixed on the countenance of Her Son and she treasured every word that He spoke: "Father, forgive them" (Lk 23:34). "This day you will be with me in paradise " (Lk 23:43). Then Jesus lowered His eyes towards her and His well-beloved disciple. What is He going to say? In a voice which is failing, He pronounces these words: "Woman, behold thy son" (Jn 19:26). These last words of Jesus are for Mary a testament of incomprehensible value.

We may see in St. John all the faithful souls to whom Mary became a mother, but we must not forget the fact that he had been ordained priest the evening before. On this account, he represents especially all priests. We like to think that at the hour of His death, at that moment of supreme solemnity, Jesus turned to us; in the person of the apostle whom He loved, He entrusted us to His mother.

By accepting Mary as our mother, we enter fully into the merciful designs of the Lord. Has not the Father predestined us to be made conformable to the image of His Son? *Praedestinavit nos conformes fieri imaginis Filii sui* (Rom 8:29).

These words embrace all Christians, but especially priests. In virtue of our ordination, our priestly perfection consists in reproducing, in our personal life, more perfectly than the rest of the faithful, the image of Jesus Christ.

Christ is essentially the Son of God and the Son of Mary. If He was not in all truth the Word, consubstantial with the Father, He would not be God; if He was not the fruit of the womb of Mary, *consubstantialis matri*, as St. Bede puts it,[5] He would not be the Mediator Who, in the name of His brethren, satisfied for sin and merited all grace. In order to imitate Christ fully we must be, like Him, children of God, though by adoption, and children of Mary. Jesus wishes to share with us without reserve all His most precious possessions, all that He is.

As we are assimilated to Christ by our baptism and still more by our ordination, let us confirm this grace by filling our hearts with respect, with confidence and with devotion in regard to Our Lady; let us strive to have for her the most perfect filial dispositions. We have the perfect model in the dispositions of Jesus towards His mother.

What a consolation to reflect that by our veneration and love for Mary we are gradually perfecting our resemblance to the Saviour!

III. MEDIATRIX OF GRACES

The power of Mary to dispense graces is another ground for our devotion to her.

Beyond all doubt, as St. Paul teaches us: "There is one mediator of God and men, the man 'Christ Jesus'" (1 Tim 2:5). This is the established order. But, in order to facilitate our access to the supernatural, the Lord has willed to establish for our benefit other mediators who are, however, entirely subordinated to Christ, to His merits, and to His efficacious influence on souls. Thus we have the role of intermediary which belongs to the visible Church; so, too, we have the privilege of media-

---

[5] *In Lucam* iv:ii; PL 92, 486.

tion bestowed on the Virgin Mary and likewise the intercessory power of the saints.

Mary was the Queen of martyrs; she shared, more than any other creature, in the sufferings and humiliations of Jesus. That is why, *mutatis mutandis*, we may apply to her the words of St. Paul about Jesus: "God hath exalted her, *exaltavit illam*, and hath given her a name which is above all names" (Phil 2:9). He has glorified her more than the angels and the saints, He has made her Queen of heaven and dispenser of the treasures of grace.

According to the opinion of many theologians, she is the mediatrix of all graces. God willed to give His Son to men only through her; so, likewise, He wills that all graces should come to them through Mary. As Bossuet puts it very effectively: "As God once willed to give us Jesus Christ through the Blessed Virgin, and as the gifts of God are irrevocable, there will be no change in this order. It is and always will be true that, having received, through the charity of Mary, the universal principle of all grace, we shall continue to receive through her mediation the various applications of that grace in all the divers circumstances which make up the Christian life." [6]

The Lord is therefore pleased when we invoke Our Lady as mediatrix of His pardon and of His benefits. She is our advocate for His mercy. Her prayers and her merits constitute an intercession for us which is unceasing, so that for centuries Christian piety has proclaimed her "The all-powerful suppliant": *Omnipotentia supplex*.

When we cast ourselves at the feet of Our Lady, we can say to her: "I am a priest . . . turn towards me your merciful countenance"; Mary sees in us, not only a member of the mystical body of her Son, but a minister of Jesus who shares in His priesthood. She sees her divine Son in us and cannot reject us; it would be to reject Jesus Himself. The priest can repeat, with even more confidence than the simple Christian, those beautiful words: "It is a thing unheard of that anyone who had recourse to thy protection and implored thy assistance was left forsaken." [7]

---

[6] *Oeuvres Oratoires*, ed. Lebarq, 5, 609.
[7] *Memorare*.

When you feel that you are plunged into an abyss of misery, recall to mind the words of St. Bernard: "When you feel the breath of temptation passing over your soul . . . invoke Mary . . . if you are troubled by the remorse of conscience, frightened by the thought of the judgement, if you are sinking into the depths of sorrow or discouragement, think of Mary: *Mariam cogita*." [8]

Our Lady knows well that she has received all things by grace and privilege. She owes to the supreme goodness the ensemble of favours attached to the splendour of her predestination. The Holy Trinity chose her to be the mother of the Word Incarnate. Her Immaculate Conception is like a diadem which she found awaiting her on her entry into the world. She owes it to the fore-ordination in the divine dispensation of the Passion and death of her Son: *Ex morte Filii sui praevisa*, as the Church proclaims it in the prayer for the feast on the eighth of December. If the Virgin was not touched by sin, if the tide of evil which has defiled us all did not reach her, it is by the free disposition of divine mercy.

Our Lady knew that she was the object of immense divine love: *Benedicta inter mulieres*, and she offered thanks without ceasing to the Lord for having "regarded the humility of His handmaid" and for having accomplished great things in her (Lk 1:48–49).

That is why our mother knows how necessary it is for us poor sinners, weak as we are by nature, to have recourse to grace. Without its aid how could our souls, in frequent contact with the world, preserve that supernatural atmosphere which is indispensable for a minister of Jesus Christ?

We must have, therefore, an immense filial confidence in the mediation of the Blessed Virgin. We should present our prayers and good actions to God under her patronage. When, in the course of your ministry, you meet souls which are hardened, full of pride or despair, souls for which it seems that you can do nothing, then, as a last resort, recommend them to Mary.

---

[8] *Homil. 2 super missus est*; PL 183, 70.

IV. OUR DEVOTION TO MARY

In a general way it may be said that devotion to the Blessed Virgin for the priest consists in acting towards her as Jesus Himself acted.

What will be the first act of our devotion?

The Blessed Trinity freely chose Our Lady to be the mother of Christ. We can imitate this divine choice by the consecration of ourselves. Deliberately and freely, each one of us should dedicate to Mary his person and his life. This is a fundamental act of devotion which we should renew frequently, for example, after our Mass. Let us offer ourselves then to our mother and ask her to watch over us as her children.

Furthermore, let us honour the Blessed Virgin by some special pious practices. I do not want to load you with exercises of all kinds. Devotions are like flowers in a garden; it is sufficient to choose one or other of them. Would it not be very pleasing to Our Lady if every day we observed with particular care one liturgical prescription in her honour? In the Mass, an inclination of the head is prescribed at the *Communicantes* when we pronounce her name. Let us make this inclination with all respect and love. In the divine Office we recite the *Pater* and the *Ave* frequently; let us say the *Ave* with special devotion. The antiphon of the Blessed Virgin at the end of each canonical hour is another excellent occasion for practising devotion to Mary.

When the liturgy celebrates the feasts of the Blessed Mother of Jesus, we should have the explicit intention of offering the divine Office and the Mass for the glory of Mary; we should thank the Lord for having done great things in her (Lk 1:49). To admire the perfections of God, to rejoice in them, to exalt them, is a very high form of divine love. So, likewise, in regard to Our Lady, it is an act of homage and of love to rejoice in her privileges, in her fullness of grace, in the beauty of her sacred actions, and to bless the Lord for them. Now, every liturgical feast of Our Lady is a marvellous canticle of this kind.

As for the Rosary, we sometimes meet people who despise it,

considering it a devotion fit for children and pious women. Yet, did not Jesus say that we must recapture the humility of little children if we are to enter into the kingdom of heaven? (Mt 18:3).

Here is an example to help you to understand the efficacy of the Rosary. You remember the story of David who vanquished Goliath. What steps did the young Israelite take to overthrow the giant? He struck him in the middle of the forehead with a pebble from his sling. If we regard the Philistine as representing evil and all its powers: heresy, impurity, pride, we can consider the little stones from the sling capable of overthrowing the enemy as symbolizing the *Aves* of the Rosary. The ways of God are entirely different from our ways. To us it seems necessary to employ powerful means in order to produce great effects. This is not God's method; quite the contrary. He likes to choose the weakest instruments that He may confound the strong: "God chose what is weak in the world to shame the strong": *infirma mundi elegit ut confundat fortia* (1 Cor 1:27).

Now, why is the Rosary so efficacious? First of all, on account of the sublimity of the prayers which make it up. The *Pater* comes to us directly from the love and sanctity of the eternal Father by the lips of His Son Jesus; the *Ave* was brought down from heaven with the salutation of the angel Gabriel. The Church, as the interpreter of the needs of her children, has added a petition to this salutation: she makes us repeat to Mary one hundred and fifty times the request that she may be with us now and at the hour of our death. Could there by any request more opportune even for the priest?

Then again, the recitation of the Rosary makes us relive the different stages of the redemption. I have said it already, but it is not out of place to repeat it here, that each event in the life of Christ gives forth, as it were, a divine power, and this power operates on us when we meditate on the scenes of the Gospel. Through the Rosary, we render to the Saviour, by the mediation of Mary, the worship of our thought and of our love, in His childhood, in His suffering and in His glory, and in virtue of this contact of faith many divine aids are accorded to us.

Besides, in the actions of the Virgin, all so simple and at the same time so generous, we find many examples of virtues to imitate, many inspirations of hope, of charity, and of joy.

Consider, for example, the first mystery: the Annunciation. What can be more salutary than to contemplate the Virgin speaking with the Angel? With him, we salute Mary, full of grace . . . blessed amongst women. St. John, speaking of the Incarnation, says: "the Word dwelt *amongst us*: *in nobis*". But in all truth one might adapt the text of the Gospel and say: "*Verbum habitat in illa.*" "The Word dwells in Mary." He dwells in her as the Son conceived of the Holy Spirit in the virginal womb.

It is a great consolation to reflect that Our Saviour on His entry into this world met one heart, that of His mother Mary, all of whose love was consecrated to Him. Jesus lives without doubt in each one of us, but it is a life curbed by our sins. Even in saintly souls, His reign is often fettered by their imperfections; He finds Himself, in a certain sense, confined. But in Mary, Jesus is not confined; everything in her belongs to Him; His love is the vitality of her existence. Is she not *gratia plena*? Let us beg her therefore to communicate to us this Christ Whom she has conceived for love of us.

Consider the charity of the Virgin in the mystery of the Visitation. The age of Elizabeth and the impending birth of John the Baptist required that Mary should be with her cousin. Our Lady hastened. *Abiit . . . cum festinatione* (Lk 1:39). Hardly had she entered the house of Elizabeth than the latter, moved by the Holy Spirit, exclaimed: "Blessed art thou among women!" And she added: "Blessed art thou that hast believed." Why? Because unlike my husband who hesitated to give faith to the word of the angel, you accepted immediately the wondrous announcement of Gabriel.

Then the Virgin offered to the Lord the canticle of her gratitude: "He hath regarded the humility of His handmaid . . . He hath done great things to me." The formulas of the Magnificat are borrowed from the Bible, but the Virgin made them her own to express the transport of gratitude and of joy with which her heart overflowed. The inner life of Mary—her humility, her holy wonder, her love, are revealed in these magnificent verses. The soul of Jesus dwelt in her and these words are inspired by Him.

The Church, unerring in its discernment, makes us chant these verses every day at Vespers. She teaches us in this way to magnify the Lord in union with His mother. In the same way, we can meditate on the other events recalled by the Rosary. What a help it would be for our prayer if our minds and our hearts were filled with the great memories which the different mysteries evoke so vividly!

You hear people complain sometimes of having their minds empty at the time of meditation. Small wonder, if the soul is not fed on pious considerations!

When someone cannot appreciate the Rosary, it is often a sign that he has never made a determined effort to recite it with devotion.

There are those who think that they can tell their beads without giving it any attention. This is a mistake; in prayer, it is important to apply ourselves to the sense of the words which we pronounce, or at least to think of Him to Whom we are addressing them.

When a soul enters into the spirit of the devotion of the Rosary, it finds great joy in it. In his last sickness St. Alphonsus Liguori had his rosary constantly in his hand. He was being looked after by a brother of his congregation who was not always considerate. One day, the last *Aves* of the decade were not finished and the brother wanted to move the old man to the table so that he might take his meal. "Wait a moment," said the saint, "is not one *Ave* worth more than all the dinners in the world?" On another occasion the brother said, "But, Monsignor, you have already said your Rosary, there is no need to repeat it ten times." And the saint replied: "You do not realize that on this devotion depends my salvation."[9]

Have you not often met poor old women who are most faithful to the pious recitation of the Rosary? You also must do

[9] P. Berthe, *St. Alphonsus de Liguori*, 2:579.

all that you can to recite it with fervour. Get right down, at the feet of Jesus: it is a good thing to make oneself small in the presence of so great a God.[10]

Apart from the Rosary, we should at all times pay to Our Lady the tribute of our filial thoughts. Do not children like to remember all that their mother did for them formerly and how even now she comes to their help in times of difficulty? When we are preaching to the people we should like to speak of the Virgin, the mother of Jesus and our mother.

As well as our practices of devotion towards her, each one of us as a son has a duty to obey Our Lady in the practical side of life. In what are we to obey her? Has she given us any command? We find the answer to this question in the Gospel. At the marriage feast of Cana, pointing out Jesus, Mary said to the waiters: "Whatsoever He shall say to you, do ye" (Jn 2:5). Does she not say the same thing to us? If we wish to please Our Lady, we must imitate the waiters at Cana. Jesus speaks to them; they listen. Jesus tells them to fill with water the urns intended for the purifications of the Jews; they carry out the order in spite of its apparent futility. For us also, obeying Mary means submitting ourselves in all things to Jesus; it means being attentive to His words and His examples; it means making our conduct conform to the directions of those who take His place amongst us. The great desire of her heart is to find in us faithful disciples and zealous ministers of Christ; it is to see us animated by the interior dispositions of Christ Himself towards the Father, towards men, and towards herself. This is the most excellent form that our devotion to our heavenly mother can take.

We should rely also on the help of the Blessed Virgin to celebrate Mass well. At the foot of the Cross she took a part, and a unique part, in the sacrifice of her Son, although she was in no way qualified to share in His priesthood. By all the affection of her soul she was united to Him. So close was her adher-

---

[10] A booklet called *Les Mystères du Rosaire* (*éditions de Maredsous*) gives the substance of Dom Marmion's doctrine on this devotion; there is one page to each mystery to help us to meditate on them, and the matter is all taken from the writings of Dom Marmion.

ence to Him that her sorrow, her offering, her submission and her immolation were indistinguishable from those of Jesus.

May we not apply to her "compassion" on Calvary what Jesus said of His own Passion: that it was "her hour" par excellence?

Who better than she can teach us the sentiments that Jesus Christ wishes to find in the heart of His priest during the sacred mysteries? We must not expect, apart from a special call of grace, to enjoy a continuous and sensible union with the Virgin during our Mass. This is an exceptional favour which God does not intend for all His priests. But for our part, before ascending the altar, we should always put ourselves under the protection of Mary. This is a filial practice highly to be recommended. With this intention we may recite the prayer approved by Leo XIII: "Mother of goodness and mercy, just as you stood by the side of your Son when He hung on the Cross, so likewise in your clemency graciously stand beside me, poor sinner that I am, and by the side of all the priests who offer the divine sacrifice today here and throughout the Church; so that with your help we may be able to offer an oblation worthy and acceptable in the eyes of the sovereign and undivided Trinity."

In closing I would like to make this final point. Before drawing His last breath, Jesus entrusted His mother to St. John. In this moment of unique solemnity He gave His disciple a legacy which was supremely precious. And what was the reaction of the apostle, the priest to whom Jesus confided the care of His mother? As a son, "he took her for his own": *Accepit eam in sua* (Jn 19:27).

Let us also take Mary for our own, as a son full of affection receives his mother; let us dwell with her, that is to say, let us associate her in our works, in our troubles, in our joys.

Does not she desire, more than anyone else, to help each one of us to become a holy priest and to reproduce in himself the virtues of Jesus?

XIX.

THE TRANSFIGURATION

THE spiritual life of the priest has Jesus Christ as its foundation; it is entirely oriented towards Him, and in Him it finds its perfection. This life is a grace and a work of transfiguration. These words express a complete concept which sums up the sequence of thought of our conferences and I would like you to retain it in mind.

St. Paul tells us that, according to the designs of divine pre-destination, sanctity for all men consists in becoming like to the image of the Son of God: *praedestinavit nos* (Rom 8:29).

The gift of sanctifying grace at baptism inaugurates our conformity to Christ. This resemblance must be perfected day by day. The development of our life as children of God requires by its very nature a double transfiguration, if one may use the term: it requires a transfiguration of Christ, Who makes Himself progressively known to the soul as the source of all sanctity, and a transfiguration of the soul, which tends by reason of its fidelity to grace to be gradually transformed into a living image of the divine model.

This is true of the simple Christian; it is particularly true of us priests on account of the nobility of our vocation and of the priestly character.

There is an admirable passage in the Gospel which throws a light on this teaching. In the evangelist's account of the public life of Christ, miracles abound; the accounts of them succeed and closely resemble each other. But there is one episode which stands alone, which is unique—the Transfiguration. There is no similar incident in the life of Christ.

You remember the facts. Taking with Him Peter, James and John, Jesus brings them up to a high mountain to pray. They arrive at the summit, and while He is praying, *dum oraret*, suddenly His appearance changes; He is transfigured, His countenance shines like the sun, His clothing becomes as white as snow. In this splendour, the disciples see Moses and Elijah talking with their Master. An indescribable joy fills their hearts. "Lord, it is good for us to be here," exclaims St. Peter, in a transport. And behold, a cloud covers them with its shadow, and from the cloud a voice is heard. Full of majesty it gives testimony to Jesus: "This is My beloved Son in Whom I am well pleased; hear ye Him" (Mt 17:1).

This transfiguration of Jesus, which was wholly unexpected by the disciples and full of mystery, was beyond all doubt the source of a very special grace for them: the strengthening of their faith in the divinity of Jesus. From now on they knew with absolute certainty that under the appearance of the man with whom they spoke every day: *habitu inventus ut homo* (Phil 2:7), the veritable Son of God veiled His supreme dignity. This faith was confirmed by the coming of the Holy Spirit at Pentecost.

But the words of the Father which the disciples heard did not descend from the clouds for them alone. They are addressed to all the succeeding generations of Christians. As St. Leo says: "The three disciples represented the whole Church eager to receive the testimony of the Father": *In illis tribus apostolis universa Ecclesia didiscit quidquid eorum . . . auditus suscepit.*[1]

Later, Peter himself, now established as prince of pastors, will recall with enthusiasm to the first Christians the vision of magnificent glory on the holy mountain (2 Pet 1:18).

That is why the liturgy evokes the memory of this incident on divers occasions. It does so in particular on the Saturday of Quarter Tense [the Ember days] of Lent, a day appointed for ordinations.[2] It does so again the following day, the second Sunday of

[1] *Sermo* 51, PL 54, 313.

[2] It was on this day, 12 March 1881, that Fr. Marmion was ordained sub-deacon at Rome in the Basilica of St. John Lateran. The first office which he recited was that of the Transfiguration. He must have received from it a strong impression of grace. When preaching retreats, he frequently began with a lecture on this mystery. It seemed to us that the profound significance of this discourse would emerge more clearly at the end of this book and would serve to sum up and, so to speak, crown the whole doctrine of Dom Marmion on the sanctification of the priest by Christ. The chapter which he devotes to this episode in his work *Christ in His Mysteries* is one of outstanding beauty.

Lent; it celebrates it finally in a special feast on the sixth of August.

What object has the Church in view in recalling this mystery? Doubtless she wishes to fix the attention of her children, and especially of her priests, on the grandeur and on the final end of their vocation.

Christ is at all times ready to transfigure Himself for each one of us, and the voice of the Father proclaims unceasingly through the teaching of the Church the divine Sonship of Jesus. Certainly Christ is not subject to change, He remains ever the same: *Christus hodie, heri et in saecula* (Heb 13:8). He presents Himself always before us as one "Who of God is made unto us wisdom, and justice, and sanctification and redemption" (1 Cor 1:30).

But we only realize gradually the divinity of His Person, the incomparable value of His redemption, the immensity of His merits, the gift of love which His coming constituted for mankind.

Thus we are initiated into this "excellent knowledge of Jesus Christ my Lord" (Phil 3:8) of which the apostle speaks. You must understand, however, that this knowledge is not purely intellectual; it consists rather in an interior illumination of faith.

In face of this intimate and supernatural revelation, the Christian feels arising within him the desire to bring his soul and his life more and more into conformity with the soul and life of Jesus Christ.

This desire must be particularly keen in the heart of the priest. Was it not in order to reveal Himself more fully to us that the Saviour called us by a special vocation like Peter, James, and John? Is it not in order that we may penetrate more deeply into His ineffable mystery that He invites us to ascend every morning the steps of the altar?

St. Paul liked to extol this transfiguration which is operated in the ministers of Christ even in this world. He tells the Corinthians how Moses came down from Mt. Sinai from his conversations with Yahweh all radiant with glory. Moses was the bearer of the tables of the Law graven on stone but, before announcing to the people the alliance of the Lord, he had to veil his face because the children of Israel could not support its radiance. "If there is a splendour in the proclamation of our guilt", adds the Apostle, "there must be more splendour yet in the proclamation of our acquittal; and indeed, what once seemed resplendent seems by comparison resplendent no longer, so much does the greater splendour outshine it" (2 Cor 3:9–10).

In what does this excelling glory, which St. Paul attributes to our priestly ministry, consist? Is it merely that we announce with face unveiled the gift of Christ and the New Testament? No, it is chiefly the fact that our priesthood is a participation in the priesthood of the Son of God and that we are called, as the Apostle says, to reflect, like a mirror, the perfection of the Lord Himself. In this way, we are transformed into a splendid image of Him. This is the work of the Holy Spirit in us: "changed into his likeness from one degree of glory to another; for this comes from the Lord who is the Spirit": *in eandem imaginem transformamur a claritate in claritatem, tamquam a Domini Spiritu* (2 Cor 3:18).

These words of St. Paul indicate clearly that in this mortal life our transfiguration in Christ is subject to a law of growth under the influence of the Holy Spirit.

The object of our conferences has been to help you to appreciate better the value of this grace so that you may cooperate with it faithfully.

Following the example of the Apostle, I have tried to show you the sublime grandeur and the Sovereign prerogatives of the priesthood of Christ.

The Son of God, the Word made flesh, appeared to us as the supreme Mediator Who was at the same time Pontiff and Victim of His own sacrifice. This sacrifice was inaugurated at the moment of the Incarnation, was mystically accomplished at the Last Supper, and consummated with the shedding of blood on the Cross. It attains its full perfection in heaven in the praise of eternity.

Christ willed to perpetuate here on earth His unique priesthood and His unique sacrifice through the medium of chosen men to whom he imparted a share in His power. All our priestly power is derived from His. Through a call from on high, and in virtue of the *spiritualis potestas* with which he is clothed by the sacramental character, the priest carries on among men the mystery and the work of the Incarnation of redemption. In all truth he is *alter Christus*.

By the very fact that we participate in the power of Jesus Christ, we are required to aspire to a sanctity worthy of such a dignity.

This sanctity, of which Christ is the model and the source, will serve to reproduce in us the characteristics and the actions of the Saviour, Son of the Father, and supreme Pontiff.

We shall realize this sanctity by imitating the virtues of Jesus and by uniting ourselves to Him, as far as the conditions of our life permit.

Of all the virtues, faith is, for us priests, of supreme importance.

There is one truth so essential for our sanctification and for the fruitfulness of our ministry that I shall make bold to repeat it to you here: the object of this faith is centred in the divinity of Jesus: the divinity of His Person, of His mission, of His sacrifice and of His merits. This is a point on which we must be absolutely clear and definite. You have noticed in the Gospel that the voice of the Father was heard only three times, and, each time, and especially on Mt. Tabor, it made itself heard to proclaim solemnly that Jesus is His beloved Son and that we must listen to Him. This testimony is the most exalted and the most precious revelation which God Himself has made to the world. And all sanctity may be reduced to receiving this testimony and conforming to it.

Faith in the divinity of Christ, moreover, is the light which must shed its rays on our whole priestly life.

It is this faith which, by placing before our eyes the divine figure of Christ, shows us the malice of sin, the grandeur of humility, and the strength of obedience; which imposes on us in our relations with God the tribute of worship and the primacy of love; which makes us see Christ in our neighbour. Every day it reminds us of the sublimity of the Mass, the nobility of the life to which the eucharistic feast invites us, and the value of our breviary.

It is the light of this faith alone which makes possible our life of prayer and union with the Holy Spirit, and our sanctification by the most ordinary actions of our day. And because our resemblance to Jesus is perfect only if, in imitation of Him, we are true children of Mary, faith makes us turn to the Virgin who was predestined to give us Jesus in the Incarnation and to become our mother at the foot of the Cross.

Christ and His mysteries are gradually revealed to us by the ever-growing light of this lively faith. And we for our part, by the constant practice of the virtues, by our daily contact at Mass, and in our prayer, with the very source of our sanctity, by our docility to the inspiration of the Holy Spirit, continue the work of conforming ourselves to the image of our High Priest; day by day—due allowance being made for time and for our weakness—we get closer to Him Who is the ideal of our perfection. The generosity of the love which we bring to this work becomes itself a source of new light: "he that loveth Me," said Jesus, "I will manifest Myself to him" (Jn 14:21).

So it will be until the time when, having arrived, as St. Paul puts it, "unto a perfect man" (Eph 4:13), we shall enter into eternal life.

Will this twofold grace of transfiguration play a part in the perfecting of our sanctity in heaven? Assuredly it will.

On the one hand, by virtue of the effect of the light of glory in us, Christ will appear to us face to face in the infinite splendour of His divinity. In the radiance of the Word, His sacred humanity will manifest itself, shining with the glory proper to the only-begotten Son of the Father, "filled with grace and truth". Filled with wonder, we shall contemplate this plenitude of which we have all received. More perfectly than to the apostles on Mt. Tabor, the majesty of Christ, the eternal Pontiff, to Whom "the Father has given a name which is above all names" shall be revealed to us; we shall understand then the profound truth of those words of the *Gloria in excelsis* which we have so often repeated: "Thou only art holy, Thou only art

Lord, Thou only art Most High, Jesus Christ with the Holy Spirit in the glory of God the Father."

On the other hand, from the moment that he enters the heavenly city, each one of the elect is transformed into the perfect resemblance of the Son of God. So great is the power of our grace of adoption that it is destined in its final development to transfigure us into the image of God Himself. Has not St. John said to us, "When He shall appear, we shall be like Him, because we shall see Him as He is"? (1 Jn 3:2). Why shall the fact of seeing God transfigure our souls in this way? Because our souls are like mirrors and when they contemplate the ineffable Beauty, they will become, and for ever, pure images of this beauty.

This is true for every Christian, but a special additional grace is reserved for us priests on account of our sacramental character. Though invisible in this world, this character, which establishes our resemblance to Christ, will appear then in glorious splendour. The truth of the words: "thou art a priest for ever" will be revealed to our souls in all its depth. Our dignity as ministers of Christ will be for us an eternal source of incomparable honour, an eternal cause for thanksgiving, for praise and for pure and indescribable joy.

When Jesus had just instituted the priesthood and ordained His apostles priests, He prayed for them and for all the priests who would be called to carry on His work of redemption: "Holy Father . . . I pray for them . . . for them whom Thou hast given Me because they are Thine. . . . I pray not that Thou shouldst take them out of the world, but that Thou shouldst keep them from evil. . . . As Thou hast sent Me into the world, I also have sent them into the world . . . that they also may be one in Us . . . as We are one . . . that the world may believe that Thou hast sent Me and hast loved them as Thou hast loved Me. Father, I will that where I am, they also whom Thou hast given Me may be with Me that they may be My glory which Thou hast given Me because Thou hast loved Me before the creation of the world" (Jn 17:19–24).

❈ ❈ ❈

DOM MARMION'S LIFE
AS A PRIEST

DOM MARMION's doctrine is the expression of an intense interior life; it is a doctrine which has been lived; and which has been developed by this life.

Many have testified to the fact that by simply reading his works one gets the impression of a doctrine springing from experience rather than mere theory.

The publication of his biography, *A Master of the Spiritual Life*, brings out very clearly, by virtue of the intimate personal notes and letters on which the work is based, the interrelation between his life and his doctrine. It reveals to what degree the man has become, under the influence of grace, identified with the doctrine: we have there the clearest proof of this identity and it is particularly evident in his priestly life.

We have thought it useful to give a few illustrative extracts here which, coming from the pen of Dom Marmion himself, will give a clear idea of the confident certitude of his preaching. These pages cannot fail to augment the satisfaction of our priestly readers as they discover in the text the vital quality of Dom Marmion's teaching on the priesthood.

We have arranged these extracts according to the order of the chapters in this book. We have given no extracts for the first three chapters as they are of a more strictly didactic nature. In each chapter we have adopted a chronological order to enable the reader to follow the trend of development of the spiritual life of the master.

> NOTE. Dom Marmion was in the habit of underlining certain words to stress his thought or to draw special attention to it. We have recognized this procedure by printing in italics the words which he underlined once, and in small capitals the words underlined twice. This applies to the English text; the Latin quotations are always in italics.

IV. EX FIDE VIVIT

1896. I am reading the works of St. John of the Cross. This reading floods my soul with abundant light. I am beginning to understand what the life of faith is, and what it is to pray the prayer of faith irrespective of changes of time and of temperament. At the same time, I perceive more clearly than ever what a danger they run who trust their own judgement and are guided by a light other than that of the doctrine of the Church and the revealed word.

During the Octave of the Epiphany (1897) I realized that the great fact, the great truth, the one outstanding truth is that Jesus Christ is the Son of God.

1. God the Father Himself proclaimed this truth solemnly on two occasions: at the baptism of Jesus and at the Transfiguration. *Hic est Filius meus dilectus in quo complacui. Clarificavi et adhuc clarificabo. Ut in nomine eius omne genu flectatur.* The glory of His Son (Who humbled Himself unto death for love of the Father: *ut cognoscat mundus quia diligo Patrem*) seems to be the great preoccupation of the Father.

2. Jesus Christ Himself proclaimed it solemnly before His judges, and it was for this declaration that He was crucified. *Adjuro te per Deum vivum ut dicas nobis si tu es Christus, Filius Dei benedicti? Tu dixisti . . . Debet mori quia Filium Dei se fecit.*

On this day (middle of December 1899, the Octave of the Feast of the Immaculate Conception), God made me see that the great object of my life must be the glory of Jesus as it is His object; it is also the object of all Mary's desires. I have been very much struck by the words: "God so loved the world as to give His only begotten Son." God's gift is worthy of Him: it is His own Son. Oh, if you knew the gift of God! From all eternity the Father has found His delight in His Son, the only-begotten Son, Who lives always in the bosom of the Father.

This same Son is in our bosom by holy communion and by faith. "Christ", says St. Paul, "dwells in our hearts by faith." Through faith we must find all our joy in Jesus as the Father finds His delight in Him: "This is my beloved Son in Whom I am well pleased." But it is faith which realizes all this: "be it done to you according to your faith."

25 February, 1900. As I was meditating to-day on the faith of Abraham, I felt a strong movement of grace urging me to consecrate my whole life and all my energies to the glorification of Jesus Christ in myself and in others, imitating in this the Father Who gives us His Son: He tells us to hear Him.

I realized that by faith we identify ourselves in a certain manner in the Holy Spirit with Jesus Christ so that we may obtain all that we ask. This is His promise. But, as we see from the story of Abraham, we may have to wait a long time for the realization of this promise.

Dominica in Albis, 1900. Everything to-day speaks to us of faith: "Blessed are those who have not seen and have believed." It is the basis and the root of all "justification". It is by a living faith, the conviction of the divinity of Jesus Christ, that we live of the divine life.

1. It is by faith that this divine life begins: Those who believe in His name *are born of God*. "All that which is born of God overcometh the world. . . . Who is he who overcomes the world but he who believes that Jesus is the Son of God?" This intimate conviction of the divinity of Jesus Christ prostrates us at His feet like the man born blind: "The just man lives by faith"; "He who believes in Me, though he be dead, he shall live."

2. By this *faith* we identify ourselves in a certain sense with Jesus Christ:

(*a*) In *our thoughts*: "He who believes in the Son of God has the testimony of God in himself." Our thoughts are the same as those of Jesus Christ: "the man who unites himself to the Lord forms one spirit with Him."

(*b*) In *our desires*: "Have in your heart the same sentiments as those which animated Jesus Christ."

(*c*) In *our words*: "If any man speak, let him speak in the words of God." Christ becomes the inspiration of all our words: "In order that Christ may dwell BY FAITH in your hearts."

(*d*) In our actions: "Whatsoever you do in word or in deed, do all in the name of Our Lord Jesus, giving thanks through Him to God the Father."

Then we achieve the "I live; now not I, but Christ liveth in me. . . . I live in the faith of the Son of God Who has loved me and has delivered Himself up for me" [cf. Gal 2:19–20].

February, 1906. Our Lord's words: "This is the service which God requires, that you believe in Him Whom He has sent" have made me realize still more clearly that we possess all things in Jesus Christ. He who has given himself up without reserve to Jesus Christ by faith is carrying out, in a perfect manner, with Him and in Him and through Him, all his duties to the Father.

Jesus is *one* with His Father: "The Father and I are one." He is in the bosom of the Father, and he who is united by faith to Jesus achieves in that unity the same service as that which Jesus renders to the Father. The member performs in its own way the same function as the person: "You are the body of Christ and members one of the other."

When we are united by faith to Jesus Christ and when, in the obscurity of this faith, we lay our intelligence at His feet, accepting in the spirit of love all that Jesus does in our name in the full sight of His Father, this is a very exalted form of prayer, and it is offered in spirit and in truth.

December 15th, 1916. I have just finished this morning preaching a retreat at ———. The theme was this: the life and all the activity of Jesus considered as flowing from the contemplation of His soul, which constantly looked on the face of the Father—as the model of our life *of faith*, drawing all its inspiration from the constant contemplation of God in union with the soul of Jesus Christ.

V. "DEATH TO SIN"

Easter, 1900. I was greatly moved by grace as I meditated on the words of St Paul: "Jesus Christ was delivered up for our souls and rose again for our justification." Jesus Christ is eternal and infinite wisdom and He has chosen His agony and death as the means of expiating our sins. Though exempt from death *by right* (because sin, by which alone death came into the world, *per peccatum mors*, had no part in Him) He *freely* accepted death for us, in our stead. I appreciated the supreme efficacy of that death, and I united myself to Jesus in His death, so that with Him I might die to sin. I experienced intense sentiments of abandonment to God's will, gratitude, etc.

Resurrexit propter justificationem nostram—The object of the risen life of Jesus is our justification. I understand very clearly how much importance Jesus attached to this sanctity, and how efficacious the union of our life with His is for our sanctification: "If, when we were enemies, we were reconciled with God by the death of His Son, much more now, being reconciled, shall we be saved by His life!"

January 14th, 1908. Every morning I offer myself to God and I accept in advance the kind of death He wills to send me and the time when He wills to send it.

1915. I cannot describe to you what it means to find oneself in such a situation: only the actual experience can give you an idea of what one feels when one sees oneself on the point of appearing before God. When I saw myself on the threshold of eternity I felt overwhelmed by fear and I made up my mind that if God spared my life, I would be in such a state when death came as to have no occasion for fear.

1917. Death is a great thing. It is a solemn moment. St. Benedict tells us that we should always have it before our eyes: *Mortem cotidie ante oculos suspectam habere.* For myself, I confess that it is constantly in my thoughts.

Beginning of 1919. God is very good to me. He sends me all kinds of trials, but at the same time He unites me more and more to Himself. Thoughts of God, of eternity, of death, are hardly ever absent from my mind, but they leave me in joy and in a great peace. I have a great fear of the majesty, the sanctity, and the justice of God, and at the same time a great confidence based on love that our heavenly Father will arrange everything *for the best*.

January 1st, 1920. I, too, have a great fear of death. This is the *divine* punishment for sin: *merces peccati mors*, and this fear . . . if it is accompanied by hope, honours God greatly. As I make my stations of the Cross every day, I recommend myself to Jesus and to Mary for the moment of my agony and judgement, and I am convinced that they will come to my aid.

February 20th, 1920. I feel a great and ardent desire for heaven. I am afraid of the judgement, but I cast myself on the bosom of God with all my wretchedness and all my responsibilities, and I put my hope in His mercy. Nothing else can save us, for our poor works are not worthy to be presented to God, and it is only His paternal love which deigns to accept them: *Non aestimator meriti sed veniae quaesumus largitor admitte*, as we say during the Mass.

December 17th, 1922. According as we acknowledge our own wretchedness or accept a share in the Passion of Jesus, in the weakness in which He was pleased to clothe Himself, in like measure shall we share in His divine strength: *Gloriabor in infirmitatibus meis . . . cum infirmor tunc potens sum.* We become then the object of the divine mercy and of the delight of the Father Who sees us in His Son.

It is at the hour of death especially that we shall experience this mystery and benefit by it. Christ has abolished the punishment of death. Our death has been buried in His. Henceforth it is His death which pleads for mercy for us, and the Father sees in our death the reproduction of the death of His Son. That is why "the death of the just is precious in the eyes of the Lord": *Pretiosa in conspectu Domini mors sanctorum eius.* For some time I have been imploring Christ every morning at Mass to lend to all the dying the merits of His own death. In making this prayer we may be confident that Christ will do for us in the hour of our agony and death what we have asked Him to do for others.[1]

VI. PENANCE AND COMPUNCTION

1917. During Mass, as I say: *ab aeterna damnatione nos eripe,* it often occurs to me that we have a special motive for our hope of salvation in that we are called by God every day to recite this prayer just as we are about to substitute for our own wretchedness and unworthiness a Victim Who is infinitely worthy and perfect.

I take a special pleasure in meditating on those episodes in the life of Jesus in which we see His moving tenderness for poor sinners, for the Samaritan and Mary Magdalen. The more I read and meditate on the Scriptures, the more I pray, the more clearly do I see that God's treatment of us is all mercy: *non volentis, neque currentis sed miserentis est Dei.* This mercy of God is the infinite goodness diffusing itself into the hearts of us wretched ones.

We find constant confirmation that this is God's way in our regard. Now, when I am reciting the divine Office, I seem to see in almost every verse of the Psalms a beam of light which speaks to us of the divine mercy.

September, 1918. My interior life is very simple. During my stay here at B., our Lord has granted me great union with Him, but it is a union in *simple faith.* I am convinced that this is the way by which He wishes to lead me. I never experience any sensible consolations; nor do I desire them. I have moments of enlightenment, sudden perceptions of the profundities of truth. I am particularly attracted by compunction: the thought of the father of the prodigal son, of the Good Samaritan, of Jesus with Mary Magdalen at His feet, fills me with compunction and with confidence.

[1] Dom Marmion died on the following 30th January.

December 13th, 1919. As I was making the stations of the Cross this morning I realized that Jesus has done for us all that the justice and the sanctity of the Father required, but that He invites us to take our little part as He invited Simon the Cyrenean. That is why I bear my cross joyfully. When I have annoyances, when things go against me, when I suffer from spiritual aridity, I have only to meditate on the Passion of Jesus as I make the stations of the Cross to be comforted: it is like plunging my soul into a refreshing bath from which it always emerges with its strength and joy renewed: it acts on my soul like a sacrament.

November 1st, 1921. Jesus has made me understand that when He said: *Corpus autem aptasti mihi*, His Father had not given Him a body which was glorified or free from all weakness. "He experienced all the infirmities," says St. John Damascene, "which were not unworthy of His divine Person": *Vere languores nostros ipse tulit.* That is why He invites us to share in them. He *assumes* them; He divinizes them and they become the fountain of that *virtus Christi* of which St. Paul speaks.

December 29th, 1922. (To one of his sisters who was a nun). Every morning at Mass I place you in the heart of our dear Lord. Christ died for us all, says St. Paul, so that He might present us to His Father, He, the just One, dying in the flesh for us sinners so that we might be filled with the strength and the power of His Spirit. It matters not how wretched we may be, anything that He presents to the Father is always most pleasing to Him. Every morning I present you to the Lord.

I can see that our dear Lord is about to introduce you into that last stage through which your soul must pass before it reaches Him. Our Lord has taken upon Himself all our sins and has made the fullest expiation for them, and this expiation is applied to us individually by compunction and absolution. Subject to this reservation, He has taken on Himself all the infirmities and weaknesses of His spouse. Before she comes to Him, she must *see*, she must *feel*, she must *know* that everything comes from Him and that our wretchedness, our poverty, our infirmities, having been assumed by His sacred humanity, have been exalted in Him to possess a divine value. This is a great secret which few really understand. St. Paul expresses it in this way: "Gladly will I rejoice in my infirmities."

Every day when I make the stations of the Cross and contemplate God, the Infinite, the Omnipotent succumbing to weakness and trembling in Gethsemane, I realize that instead of assuming a glorified body in the Incarnation, He took a weak body like ours *in order to make our weakness divine in His own Person.*

VII. HUMILIAVIT SEMETIPSUM FACTUS OBEDIENS

April 8th, 1887, Good Friday. (To one of his sisters who was a nun.) I have had the happiness of spending almost three hours before the Blessed Sacrament. I felt a great desire to love God with my whole heart. The thoughts which came to me yesterday during the *Mandatum* have made a great impression on me and they are still present to my mind. They gave me a great insight into the love which inspired Jesus during His Passion and into the inexpressible love and humility which were His when He washed the feet of His disciples. When the Abbot approached to wash my feet I realized how fully he represented Jesus Christ. Our Lord wishes that this ceremony, instituted by Him, should be renewed by us; He shows us in this way that He is ready to perform it for each one of us in the person of His priests. As Jesus delights in humility, I felt that He would give me a special grace in this washing of my feet. I felt as though I were Judas and that Christ was saying to me: "If you wish to arrive at a great love for Me, you must imitate My example and become the servant of all; humble yourself in all things, submitting to be trodden on by all men and you will become great in love."

October 5th, 1887. I have been given the grace to see that a great means to achieve true humility is to love my superiors and my confrères *humili caritate.*

Above all, humility is careful never to act on its own initiative, but to be obedient in all things to the impulse of grace, that is to say to leave the initiative to God and to grace in accordance with the words of Jesus: "I can do nothing of myself, but I do what the Father tells me to do."

Humility sees the divine in everything; hence the inclination which it inspires to be submissive to all superiors, but especially to spiritual superiors. There is no authority but that which comes from God. Whatever their personal character may be, superiors, *as superiors*, participate in the divinity, and humility is naturally submissive to them. This is the basis of all these texts relating to authority: "I have said: Ye are gods"; "he who hears you, hears Me"; "all power comes from God", etc.

This applies equally to all men, and humility sees in others that which there is in them of the divine so that it can venerate it, and sees in itself only its own works. In this way it finds no difficulty in holding others in higher esteem than itself.

September 11th, 1895. (To one of his sisters who was a nun.) Your letter caused me great joy, for I see that, in spite of your unworthiness, God is guiding you and is full of loving mercy towards you. Your chief aim should be to achieve a high degree of humility. This is the way which leads most surely to the love of God. For such is the power of God that He can change our very corruption into the pure gold of love, provided that He does not meet any obstacle: now, the great obstacle is pride. Believe me, if you are sincerely humble, God will do the rest.

There is one little practice, *which I observe myself*, which may help you to become humble. It is to make three stations every day. *The first station.* Consider what you *were*. If you have fallen into mortal sin even once in your life, you have merited to be accursed for all eternity by Him Who is infinite Truth and infinite Goodness. And this malediction would have resulted: (*a*) in eternal separation from God; in eternal hatred of God and of all that is good, right and beautiful; (*b*) in living trodden under the feet of demons for all eternity. And this judgement, pronounced by Him Who is Goodness itself, would have been just. Oh, my dear child, we have perhaps deserved all this, and if we are not now enduring this condemnation it is because of the divine mercy and the sufferings of Jesus Christ. In view of this, can anything be burdensome to us? Can we be afflicted when we are despised by others?

Second station. What we *are*. We cannot take a single step to bring us closer to God without His help. Then our daily infidelities, our sins, our ingratitudes, even our best actions, all these make up a very wretched reality.

Third station. What we are capable of becoming. If God removed His supporting hand, we would be quite capable of becoming what we once were and even worse. God sees that. He knows the depths of perfidy of which we are capable. How, then, can we be proud?

But after these stations there is another which we must not forget. We are *infinitely* rich in Jesus Christ and, when compared with our miseries, the mercy of God is like an ocean compared to a drop of water. There is no better way of giving glory to God than by having such confidence in His mercy and in the infinite merits of Jesus Christ that, in spite of the realization of our sins and our unworthiness, we cast ourselves on His bosom in the spirit of abandonment and love with the conviction that He cannot reject us: "O Lord, You will not despise a humble and contrite heart."

April 1st, 1918. I am sixty years old to-day. The multitude of my sins and ingratitudes has been lost in the infinite multitude of the mercies of the heavenly Father.

1920. The liturgy tells us that God manifests His omnipotence *maxime miserando et parcendo.* Be a monument of His mercy for all eternity. The greater the wretchedness and the unworthiness, the greater and the more adorable His mercy: *Abyssus abyssum invocat*: the abyss of our wretchedness invokes the abyss of His mercy. It is an immense consolation for me to see that you are travelling by this road which is so sure, which leads to such heights, and which glorifies the precious blood of

Jesus Christ and the mercy of God. It is the way I have chosen too. Help me by your prayers.

December 29th, 1922. I am never so happy as when, prostrating myself before the infinite mercy of the Father and exhibiting to Him my wretchedness and my unworthiness, I seem all the time to behold His unlimited mercy rather than my own wretchedness.

VIII. THE VIRTUE OF RELIGION

1897. In the exercise of the sacred ministry to souls, in order to be a true representative of Jesus Christ, I shall be careful to keep at an infinite distance from all that is natural. Jesus cites what He undertook for men as a proof of His love for His Father: *Ut cognoscat mundus quia diligo Patrem et sicut mandatum dedit mihi Pater sic facio.* And what is this commandment? To shed His blood for men. So, I shall carry out my ministry solely for the love of God, and in order to co-operate with Him in His loving designs towards men; for each one of them He has given His Son, and Jesus has given the greatest proof of His love: *Majorem hac dilectionem nemo habet.*

January 4th, 1900. At the beginning of this year, I felt a strong attraction of grace to take as the object of my life, that which God has appointed as His object: the glory of His Son Jesus. I have offered myself to the Father and to Mary in that intention.

1902. In the confessional the priest is the minister of Jesus Christ, and the more closely he identifies Himself with His divine Master, the more fully he will enter into His dispositions towards the Father and towards souls—the more also will his ministry be blessed. It is very important:

1. Before beginning to hear confessions to humble oneself profoundly before God, acknowledging one's inability to do the least good for souls without Him: *sine me nihil potestis facere.*

2. To offer this holy action as an act of love to Our Lord Who has said: "As long as you did it to one of these My least brethren you did it to Me" (Mt 25:40).

3. To efface oneself as much as possible so that Christ alone may act: *Illum oportet crescere, me autem minui*. To talk and act in the name of Jesus Christ and in great dependence on His Spirit: *Si quis loquitur quasi sermones Dei; si quis ministrat, quasi ex virtute quam administrat Deus ut in omnibus glorificetur Deus per Jesum Christum*.

4. Not to want to make penitents attached to us but to direct them towards God in a spirit of great detachment.

February 1st, 1906. For some time, our Lord has given me a very clear perception of the following truth: He said of Himself: "I am the beginning Who also speak unto you" (Jn 8:25). He must become the beginning of all my activity. To achieve this, I must renounce all to follow Christ. This continuous immolation of self before Christ is the fulfilment of the great desire of the Father: "Thou hast subjected all things under His feet" (Ps 8:6). All His Angels adore Him (Ps 97[96]:7). "This is the work of God, that you believe in Him Whom He hath sent" (Jn 6:29). Our Lord said: "If any man minister to Me, him will My Father honour" (Jn 12:26). The essence of ministry lies in placing all one's faculties at the feet of one's master so that they can be employed in accordance with his judgement and will. My divine Master has said: "All power is given Me in heaven and in earth" (Mt 28:18). My part is to carry out His order, to accomplish His designs. He is wisdom, power and love; without Him I am foolishness, weakness, egoism. "Without Me you can do *nothing*."

I have realized that this is only made possible by a life of recollection and by constant recourse to the divine Master.

November 1st, 1908. Pray for me that Jesus may become the absolute *Master* of my interior life and that there may be no activity in me which is not inspired by Him. This is the object of all my desires, but I am still *very far away* from it.

December 2nd, 1908. Jesus is *everything* for me. I can neither pray, nor celebrate Mass, nor exercise my ministry except in complete dependence on His influence and His Spirit. God inspires me with a great desire to establish Jesus as the supreme Master of my interior life and as the unique source of my activity. I am undoubtedly *very far* from this ideal on account of my self-love and my innumerable infidelities. Still, I have great confidence that one day I shall be able to say truthfully: "I live, now not I but Christ liveth in me." Then, in accordance with His promise, He will reveal to me the secrets of His divinity: "If anyone loves me," He has said, "I will manifest Myself to him" (Jn 14:21).

December 15th, 1908. Pray well for me that Jesus may become the supreme Master of my inner life and that I may live in ever greater dependence on His Spirit. I see that this is my way and that, in spite of my great misery, if I attain this, Jesus will employ me for His glory.

December 21st, 1908. Pray for me that I may become a humble and faithful servant of Jesus; that everything in me may be subject to Him: *Omnia subjecisti sub pedibus eius*, and that He will bring me to where He is: *in sinu Patris.*

December 13, 1913. For some time the Lord has been drawing me strongly towards a life of closer union with Him. My great desire is to see Jesus reigning and living in my interior life so that all my powers, all my faculties, and all my desires may be perfectly subject to Him. Pray for this intention.

IX. THE GREATEST COMMANDMENT

October 5th, 1887. When I am tempted to discouragement, as I read the lives of the saints, by the realization of my inability to practice their austerities, I am consoled by one thought, and that is: *Plenitudo legis dilectio.* Love can be perfect without these austerities, but these austerities without love are *aes sonans aut cymbalum tinniens.* If I could renounce my own will entirely in all my actions, and perform them solely for the love of God, I would soon be astonished at my own progress. And after all, why have I left everything, and why did I enter this monastery if it was not to attain to the love of God?

April 18th, Easter Tuesday, 1900. Received many lights in reflecting on these words: "Christ lives for God." I felt the intensity of this life of Jesus *all for God*. The union of our life with that life is the highest form of perfection. Without Him we can do nothing, but it was just in order to communicate that life to us that He came: "For as the Father hath life in Himself, so He hath given to the Son also to have life in Himself" (Jn 5:26). "I am come that they may have life, and may have it more abundantly" (Jn 10:10). The Resurrection is the mystery of that life, and Jesus communicates it to us especially in holy communion: "Except you eat the flesh of the Son of man and drink His blood, you shall not have life in you" (Jn 6:64). This bread gives life to the world. I have felt more and more keenly the desire to associate myself with this divine life so that Jesus may be glorified in me. For that is the object of His *glorified* life. "He rose again for our justification" (Rom 4:25), and He continues this action all the time: "Always living to make intercession for us" (Heb 7:25). This life of Jesus is the love of His Father producing the flowering of all the *human virtues* which are divinized in Him. Here is our model. I have made a resolution to try to unite my poor life to this life, intense and divine.

June 1st, 1901. As a practice of the interior life, I feel more and more drawn to *lose myself in Jesus Christ*. May He make His thought mine, His will mine, and may He bring me to His Father. In the *Pater* the only petition for our souls which He teaches us to make is: *fiat voluntas tua sicut in caelo*. I am trying to love His holy will in the thousand little annoyances and interruptions of every day.

November 4th, 1903. Once we have fully understood that the will of God is the same thing as God Himself, we can see that this adorable will must be preferred to all other things and must be accepted in what it causes, in what it prescribes and in what it *permits* as the sole standard for our will. We must keep our eyes fixed on this holy will and not on those things which pain and trouble us.

April 18th, 1906. When we are united to Jesus we are *in sinu Patris*. This is the life of *pure love* which presupposes the effort to do always what is most agreeable to the Father: "He hath not left me alone: for I do always the things that please Him" (Jn 8:28). Our weakness and our wretchedness do not prevent us from being *in sinu Patris*, for it is the bosom of love and of infinite mercy, but it presupposes a profound self-abasement and self-contempt and these must be all the greater because we are so close to this infinite sanctity. It is necessary too that we rely on Jesus "Who of God is made unto us wisdom, and justice and sanctification and redemption" (1 Cor 1:30).

Everything that is done *in the bosom of the Father in the filial spirit of adoption* is of immense value. But this state presupposes freedom from all deliberate fault and from all refusal to follow the inspirations of the Holy Spirit. For though Jesus takes upon Himself our infirmities and miseries, He will not accept the least deliberate sin.

Retreat at Paray-le-Monial, March 20th, 1909. During a meditation to-day on the text of St. Paul (Eph 1:11), I realized that Jesus is our *all*. My heart being united to His becomes the object of the delights of the Father. His heart is the *human heart of God*. This heart, as heart of the Word (to Whom He is hypostatically united), is entirely dedicated to the Father and *being created, acts in absolute dependence on Him*.

I saw very clearly that this dependence gives a divine value to our activity. I realized that we must cultivate this dependence and ask for it.

I have resolved to read the Scriptures, as a general rule one epistle of St. Paul at a sitting, if possible; it will be for me a source of light and peace.

August 14th, 1912. I shall sing the Mass for both of us, that the heavenly Father may unite us more and more in His holy love and lead us to Jesus. "No man can come to Me, except the Father Who hath sent Me, draw him; and I will raise him up on the last day" (Jn 6:44). Yes, every best gift and every perfect gift (Jesus, Mary, grace, holy friendships), comes down from the *Father.*

Oh, let us love Him with our *whole* heart! "For whosoever shall do the will of God," said Jesus, "he is My brother and My sister, and mother." We can do nothing which will be more pleasing to the heart of Jesus than to unite ourselves to Him in His love for His Father and in His carrying out of His holy will.

February 16th, 1913. It is my earnest hope that I may be able for the future to live for God *alone.* I feel that Our Lord wishes me to live as He did *propter Patrem,* and to do so in two ways: (1) by drawing all my inspiration from Him; (2) by employing all my activity for Him.

December 4th, 1917. Let us remain closely united in the heart of Jesus. Let us unite our soul and our heart to His so that we may see through His eyes and love through His heart.

The Word proceeds *entirely* from the Father. That is why the Father finds in Him His glory and His infinite joy. The Word returns *entirely* into the bosom of the Father and does so with a love that is infinite; Jesus expresses this mystery in His humanity: (*a*) by His absolute dependence on the Father. He has no doctrine, no design, no work which He does not see in the Father. That is the absolute divine perfection: (*b*) by doing all things for love of the Father: *quae placita sunt Patri facio semper.*

And for our part: the Father has engendered us *voluntarie* in the Word. In Him and with Him we must return in the spirit of love *in sinum Patris.* (a) It must be our joy: *facere voluntatem eius qui misit me.* Projects and ambitious dreams are inconsistent with this love; (b) we must do everything for the sake of this love: *ambulate in dilectione sicut filii carissimi.*

March 19th, 1918. I am asking our Lord fervently on your behalf: *Sanctifica eam in veritate.* We should have an ardent desire to be exactly what our heavenly Father wants us to be and nothing more—or less. I said to Him a few days ago: "Father, do Thou be my director; make me to be just what Thou wishest: very feeble, very wretched in myself, but very strong and very faithful in Thee and in Thy Spirit."

I *believe* in the love of the Father for us, and I want Him to see in return my love for Him in Jesus Christ.

March 9th, 1922. I am getting on well, *Deo gratias.* God is helping me. In spite of great temptations and interior trials I remain closely united to His holy will. At times it seems that He is rejecting me, and that is what I deserve, but I persist in hoping in Him. I realize that the true way to go to God is to prostrate oneself frequently before Him with a profound sentiment of our unworthiness, and then, *believing* in His goodness: *nos credidimus caritati Dei,* to cast ourselves in His arms, to seek rest on his paternal heart.

X. HOC EST PRAECEPTUM MEUM

May, 1889. I have been greatly impressed by the thought that God accepts as if it were done to Himself everything that I do for *my brethren.* Jesus gives Himself to me without reserve every morning in the blessed sacrament, and He asks me to give testimony during the day of my love for Him in the person of my brethren.

Resolution: Habitually to venerate Jesus Christ in the person of my brethren, often casting myself in spirit beneath their feet, and reminding myself frequently that whatever I think of them or do to them may be applied to Jesus Christ.

The more I reflect on this charity towards my brethren, the more I realize its importance, and the better I understand why the Apostle St. John never tired of urging it on us. As I meditated on Jesus appearing to the disciples of Emmaus, the thought that they were not content to offer Him hospitality but forced Him to come in, gave me a clear light on the way in which I should practise charity, seeking occasions to help my brethren at the expense of my own convenience.

June 1st, 1901. During prayer our Lord invites me to identify myself with Him, to live, "He in me and I in Him." Then He urges me: (1) to make acts of love to the Father in union with Him; (2) for my own part, to abandon myself entirely to Him; (3) to love my neighbour as He has loved him. It is this last point especially which has attracted me for some time. I feel a *great increase* of my love for the Church, the Spouse of Christ. I have come to regard my neighbour habitually as Jesus Christ, and I feel urged to exercise great charity towards everyone. I realize very clearly that true charity includes all the virtues and imposes a constant renouncement.

February 23rd, 1903. Our Lord gives me an ever-increasing confidence in the holy sacrifice and in the divine Office. It seems to me that when I celebrate or when I recite the Office, I am carrying the whole world with me: the afflicted, the suffering, the poor, and all the interests of Jesus Christ. When I give myself to Jesus Christ, it almost always seems to me that He is uniting Himself to me and to all His members, and that He is asking me to do as He does, of Whom it has been said: "Truly He has taken on Himself all our languors and borne all our sufferings."

January 20th, 1904. (To his superior.) For some time our Lord has kept me in much closer union with Himself, and I see more clearly the nothingness of creatures . . . it is curious, but since I have been giving myself more fully to God in prayer, I have received a very keen sense of my union with all the members of the Church and with *certain individuals* in particular. It seems to me that I am carrying the whole Church in my heart, especially at Mass and during the Office, and in this way I no longer have distractions as before.

January 19th, 1905. You cannot imagine how all my time is eaten up. I say *eaten* because every morning I place myself on the paten with the host which is to become Jesus Christ; and just as Jesus is there to be eaten by all sorts of people—*sumunt boni sumunt mali, sorte tamen inaequali*—so am I eaten all the day by all sorts of persons. May our beloved Saviour be glorified by my destruction as He is by His own immolation.

February, 1906. Jesus is at all times united to His Church and . . . this union is the type of every other union . . . Jesus loves His Church and is united to her because He contemplates her in the love of His Father: "I pray for them because they are Thine" (Jn 17:9). He who is united to Jesus in truth is united also to all the members of His Church and carries out all His duties in Him and through Him. Jesus presents Himself to us in the name of His Church, bearing all her weaknesses and all her sufferings *as though they were His own*: *vere languores nostros ipse tulit et dolores ipse portavit.*

December 16th, 1917. I thank you from the bottom of my heart for this splendid book (the *Life of St. Dominic*) which you have sent me. There is in the preface a reference to our holy founder which finds an echo in my own heart: "He passes through the world . . . like the Word of God . . . he speaks, he preaches, the word always in action." What a magnificent ideal! Samson (the figure of Christ Who is the wisdom and the strength of God) crushes the Philistines with the jawbone of an ass. Samson is more powerful, more formidable with this rude weapon than any other person would be with the most perfect weapon. My desire is to be this weapon in the hands of the Word, for the instrumental cause always acts in virtue of the power of the principal cause. Let us pray for each other that we may attain this divine, sublime ideal.

XI–XII. THE SACRIFICE OF THE MASS

Pentecost, 1907. I have realized that Jesus, Who is, by His very essence, entirely consecrated TO THE FATHER, has chosen the most perfect manner in which to give Himself to the Father in His human nature, that is, as *Victim*. That is why, at the moment of His Incarnation, He became a "priest for ever". St. Paul reveals to us His first gesture at the moment of His Incarnation: as He enters the world, Christ considers the sacrifices of the Old Law and sees that they are only poor and feeble beginnings which cannot give due glory to the Father: "Sacrifice and oblation thou wouldest not, but a body Thou hast fitted to Me" (Ps 40[39]:6). At this moment He offers Himself as Victim: "then said I: 'Behold I come'" (Ps 40[39]:7). From this moment Christ is a priest; He has offered Himself: "Who by the Holy Spirit offered Himself unspotted to God" (Heb 9:14). He offers Himself from *love*: "that the world may know that I love the Father" (Jn 14:31).

The Apostle urges us to imitate Christ in this oblation: "I beseech you therefore, brethren, by the mercy of God, that you present your bodies a living sacrifice, holy, pleasing unto God, your reasonable service" (Rom 12:1). We share in the priesthood of Christ and in His state of victim. For He said: "offer up your body". That is the function of the priest; but it is ourselves that we offer, *corpora vestra*, and as a living holocaust. As priests, we must imitate the reverence of Christ for His Father: "He was heard for His reverence" (Heb 5:7), and this especially because we are so unworthy, whereas He is a "high priest, holy, innocent, undefiled, separated from sinners, and made higher than the heavens" (Heb 7:26). As intermediaries between men and God, our attitude must be one of adoration, of self-abasement before the majesty of God. As victims, we must deliver ourselves up to God and to all the manifestations of His will like the immolated Lamb Who lies submissively before the sovereign Creator and yields Himself up without reserve to the sovereign Goodness.

This sacrifice of Jesus Christ never ceases, for He is ever

being immolated on the altar, and He is ever a Victim in the tabernacle. Our life should constantly be united to this life of Jesus Christ as Priest and Victim.

September, 1910. I have understood more clearly than ever that: (1) the Church is *Israel quem coaequasti Unigenito tuo*, and when we associate ourselves with her, we benefit by all the merits of Jesus Christ in spite of our wretchedness and our unworthiness.

(2) On Calvary Jesus merited everything and even applied those merits. On the altar He no longer merits, but He applies all His merits according to our faith and our union with Him.

(3) One can die of thirst beside a fountain of pure water. One must take the trouble to put oneself in contact with it. So, likewise, at the altar: *Sicut credidisti fiat tibi.* During the *conventual Mass* which we sing every day, I am at leisure to meditate on the *great action* which is being accomplished, and generally I feel my heart overflowing with joy and gratitude at the reflection that I possess in Jesus, present on the altar, an offering of reparation to the Father worthy of Him, a satisfaction of infinite value. What an abundance of graces are contained in the Mass!

1910. I have meditated a great deal on God's love for us in giving us His Son: *Sic Deus dilexit mundum ut Filium suum uni-genitum daret.* I asked myself what I could give Him in return and He has made me understand that I give Him this same Son. At the moment of the consecration, I adore this Son of His delight and I offer Him to the Father, and all the day long I try to maintain in myself this attitude of adoration and oblation which was that of Our Lord to His Father. Do this and you will be lost in Him. While God the Father is the object of many affronts, He is also the object of a love than which there could be no greater: *Majorem hac dilectionem. . . .* Our Lord applied this primarily for the glory of the Father: *sicut mandatum dedit mihi Pater.* That is why I experience a sense of keen consolation when I reflect that I hold in my hands and offer to the heavenly Father this Son Who loves Him infinitely.

April 4th, 1917. As I put on the vestments before celebrating Mass, I feel that, through the Church, I am entering into an intimate union with the High Priest Jesus and that, with her and through her, I am sharing in the dispositions of Jesus Christ.

September 4th, 1918. My usual preparation for Mass is to enter into intimate union with Jesus the Priest and the Victim. After Mass, I seem to hear Jesus say to me: *Ego et Pater unum sumus.* Then I lay at His feet my soul, my heart, and all my strength and I say to Him: "My Jesus, You are one with the Father, I am one with You, and I ask only one thing: that I may do all things for You, with You and in You."

When I possess Jesus in my heart after Mass, I am united to Him. Faith tells me that He is in me and that I am in Him. Jesus is in the bosom of the Father, and I, poor sinner that I am, I am there with Him.

Then I say to the Father: "I am the *Amen* of Jesus. Amen! May your well-beloved Son, the Word, say for me all that has to be said; He knows me; He knows all my wretchedness, my needs, my aspirations, my desires." What confidence springs from this thought!

1921. When I celebrate Mass, it seems to me that the heavenly Father is in front of me and that the weaknesses and wretchedness of my soul and of the souls of all those for whom I pray become the weaknesses and wretchedness of Christ because He identifies Himself with His members: *vere languores nostros ipse tulit.* Every day at Mass I think of all those who are in trouble or affliction and I ask Christ to pray through my lips for all those miseries; in this way the priest is truly *os totius Ecclesiae* [mouth of the whole Church].

XIII. THE EUCHARISTIC FEAST

Feast of the Sacred Heart, 1888. I am very much struck by certain thoughts about the blessed Eucharist which come into my mind. I see clearly that it is the great fountain of grace. Jesus brings with Him the Holy Spirit and graces and favours of all kinds.

I have been greatly struck also by the thought that in giving us Jesus Christ in holy communion, the Father gives us all things, and the surest pledge of all that we ask, so that, *for His part*, there is not the least doubt that He is disposed to grant us all things: "with Him has He not bestowed on us all gifts?" The fault is, therefore, mine, if I receive little.

1888. It is my custom—every day at midday—while making a short visit to the Blessed Sacrament, to recollect myself and say to Our Lord: "My Jesus, I shall receive Thee to-morrow into my heart, and it is my desire to receive Thee perfectly. But I am quite incapable of doing so. Thou Thyself hast said: 'Without Me you can do nothing.' Do Thou, O eternal Wisdom, dispose my soul that it may become Thy temple. I offer to Thee for this intention my actions and sufferings of this day so that Thou mayest make them agreeable in Thy sight and implement Thy words: *sanctificavit tabernaculum suum Altissimus.*"

Holy Thursday, 1901. I have just made my Easter communion. In the silence of prayer, I realize ever more clearly, and especially to-day, that the great object which Our Lord had in view in giving Himself to us in the holy Eucharist was to incorporate us in Him as in His mystical body, so that with Him and in Him we might perfect the great enterprise of the Father: our sanctification and the salvation of the world: *Opus consummavi quod dedisti mihi ut faciam.* I am conscious of the ever more pressing invitation of Our Lord to give myself up to Him without reserve and without any plan or desire other than that of carrying out His will according as it is manifested to me.

1904. Holy Communion unites us through Jesus Christ to the three divine Persons. When I possess Jesus in my heart, I say to the Father: "Heavenly Father, I adore Thee, I give Thee thanks, I unite myself to Thy divine Son and, with Him, I acknowledge that all I have, all that I am, comes from Thee": *omne datum optimum . . . manus tuae fecerunt me.*

Then I unite myself to the Word and I say to Him: "O eternal Word, of myself I know nothing, I am nothing; but I know by faith what Thou knowest and I can do all things in Thee." Finally, I unite myself to the Holy Spirit: "O substantial Love of the Father and the Son, I unite myself to Thee; I want to love as Thou lovest; I am a worthless creature, but graciously permit me to unite myself to Thee with my whole heart and transport me to the bosom of God."

Sometimes, after holy communion, having Our Lord within me, I run over in my mind the succession of His states of life: I adore Him in the bosom of the Father, in the most pure womb of the Virgin which He chose as His dwelling; I go to Bethlehem, to Nazareth, to the desert, to Calvary. I unite myself thus with Jesus at each stage of His life, and in this contact with Him I receive the grace of all His mysteries.

1918. To sing, in union with the Word, the canticle of the Universe to the Father. In the *Benedicite* every creature receives life in our intelligence, just as it exists as an archtype in the intelligence of the Word *in quo omnia constant, per quem omnia facta sunt.* In this way man becomes the eye of all that is without vision, the ear of all that has no hearing, the heart of all that cannot love. That is why the Church would have this canticle recited after Mass by the priest who is representing Christ: *Verbum caro factum est et habitavit in nobis.*

The God of revelation is the Father of Our Lord Jesus Christ, the Father of mercies and the God of all consolation. Silent adoration of the divine majesty hidden in Christ. (This will vary according to the liturgy of the day and the movement of grace.)

1920. I cannot express to you the divine joy of the heavenly Father, and especially after holy communion when He sees a soul buried in His Word, living His life and gazing on Him with humility and love. This is the moment of the day when I am at peace and when I *see* God in the darkness.

April 21st, 1922. God is so good to me. I live now by my daily communion. All the morning I carry on by the strength of this divine food, and in the afternoon I live in the thought of the communion of the following day, for we are strengthened by it in the measure of our desire and our preparation. Our Lord has promised that he who eats Him will live by Him. His life becomes the source of all our activity.

XIV. THE DIVINE OFFICE

May 1st, 1887. I find that I am greatly helped in the recitation of the divine Office by the thought that I am really an ambassador sent by the Church many times each day to bear a message to the throne of the Most High. This message must be presented in the terms and according to the ceremonial prescribed by the Church.

1888. In prayer, and particularly in the divine Office, I find it a great help to unite myself to Jesus in His capacity as Head of the Church and advocate before the Father. Jesus exercises His eternal priesthood by standing before the throne of the adorable Trinity in heaven and by displaying His sacred wounds. God *cannot* reject His prayer: *exauditus est pro sua reverentia.* I unite myself therefore to Jesus Christ *as a member of His mystical body.* I experience great consolation in this and receive many lights.

1914. I am firmly convinced that the more one advances in life, the more one has relations with God, the better one understands the grandeur of the divine praise in the Office. There is no other work which approaches even remotely this praise. Built up around the holy sacrifice which is its centre, it constitutes the purest form of glory which man can give to God, because it is the most intimate association of the soul with the canticle which the Word Incarnate renders to the adorable Trinity.

1921. Here is a thought which I find a great help in the recitation of the divine Office: The Holy Spirit is the sovereign director, the Doctor of perfection Whom the Father and the

Son give to us. I frequently experience great joy during the divine Office when I feel that the Holy Spirit is praying in us "with unspeakable groanings" (Rom 8:26), and that in the Psalms I have the consolation of saying to the heavenly Father all that I have to say to Him. The Psalms are so full! When we recite them under the guidance of the Holy Spirit Who composed them, we are really setting before God all our troubles, our needs, our joys, our praise, and our love. I make it a practice also to say with each Psalm: *Pater caritatis, da mihi spiritum tuum.*

Before the divine Office, after making an act of faith to Christ present in my heart by grace, I unite myself to Him in the praise which He gives to His Father; I ask Him to glorify His blessed mother, and the saints, particularly the saints of the day and my patron saints. Then I unite myself to Him as Head of the Church and as supreme Pontiff to plead the cause of the whole Church. In this intention I cast a glance on all the miseries and needs of the world: the sick, the dying, the tempted, the despairing, the sinners, the afflicted; I take into my own heart all the sorrows, the anxieties and the hopes of every soul. . . . I apply my intention also to the works of zeal undertaken for the glory of God and the salvation of the world: missions and preaching. Finally, I take the intentions of those souls who are closely united to me, and thus I prepare myself to intercede for all together with Christ: *qui est semper vivens ad interpellandum pro nobis.* Then I pray to the heavenly Father: "Father, I am unworthy to appear before Thee, but I have absolute confidence in the sacred humanity of Thy Son which is united to His divinity. Relying on Thy Son I venture to present myself before Thee, to penetrate into the splendours of Thy bosom and, in union with the Word, to chant Thy praises."

XV. THE PRIEST, A MAN OF PRAYER [2]

Feast of the Sacred Heart, 1887. I felt to-day that we are agreeable to God in proportion to our conformity to Jesus Christ,

---

[2] The texts on this subject are very numerous; we give only a very small selection.

especially in His interior dispositions. That is why a *child-like* confidence in prayer, in spite of our sins, is so agreeable to God. "I know that Thou hearest Me always" (Jn 11:42), said Jesus to His Father. We are the adopted children of God, and we must, in all humility and simplicity, treat God as a Father.

After September, 1893. JESUS. I see more and more clearly that Jesus is everything for us and that His riches are inexpressible, unspeakable. He is true God and true man. As God, He is the Word, "the brightness of His glory and the figure of His substance" (Heb 1:3), containing in Himself all the life of the Father. He lives in us by faith, and when we pray and act, being united in this manner to Jesus, our prayers become this canticle which the Word chants continuously to the Father and by which the hymn of creation is offered to God. Jesus has said: "If you abide in Me, and My words abide in you, you shall ask whatever you will, and it shall be done unto you" (Jn 15:7). I like, therefore, in the light of this promise to set before my eyes some saying of Our Lord and to present my request, "strong in faith". I find this method of *prayer* very easy and efficacious. Take for example this saying of Jesus: "Ask, and it shall be given you" (Mt 7:7). I cast myself then in spirit on my knees before Jesus, meditating on these words which come from the mouth of the Word, and I adore the infinite Truth, *fortis in fide* by His grace.

1894. If our sins make us unworthy of being heard, the sanctity of Jesus and the fervour with which He prays for us make the Father forget our unworthiness, and He considers only Him Whom He has appointed to be our advocate. Moreover, by our baptism we have become the members of Jesus Christ; as a consequence of this union, our needs are in a certain sense the needs of Jesus Christ Himself; we cannot ask for anything relating to our salvation or the perfection of our souls without asking it also for Jesus Christ Himself, for the honour and the glory of the members are the honour and glory of their Head.

The second Sunday of Lent, 1896. I have understood that all the promises made to Jesus Christ as the only begotten Son of God are made also to the adoptive sons.

The more closely one is united to Jesus Christ by faith and love, the more one is a child of God: "As many as received Him, He gave them power to be made the sons of God" (Jn 1:12). This "receiving" of Jesus comprises different degrees—the more fully the promises of God are realized in us. When we present ourselves before the heavenly Father in the name of Jesus Christ and firm in our faith in Him, the Father says: *vox quidem est vox Jacob, manus autem sunt manus Esau.* That is to say that we are so fully "clothed in Jesus Christ" that the Father sees only His merits and, charmed "by the fragrance of His virtues": *fragrantiam vestimentorum ejus,* He forgets our unworthiness: *ecce odor filii mei sicut agri pleni cui benedixit Dominus,* and He overwhelms us with His blessings, not with the blessings of this earth such as the Patriarch Isaac called down on Jacob, but with heavenly blessings.

February 28th, 1902. I pass nearly all my time of prayer in contemplating and adoring the will of the Father as it appears in the wisdom of His Word, with Whom I identify myself in the same love for the Father.

September, 1906. During prayer I like to prostrate myself at the feet of Jesus and say to Him: "I am a very wretched creature, I am nothing, but Thou canst do all things; Thou art my wisdom and my sanctity. Thou seest Thy Father. Thou adorest Him, Thou sayest to Him things which are ineffable, O My Jesus! Whatever Thou sayest to Him, I wish to say to Him also; say it to Him on my behalf. Thou seest in Thy Father all that He desires of me, all that He desires for me; Thou seest in Him whether I shall have sickness or health, consolation or suffering; Thou seest when and how I am to die. Thou dost accept it all for me and for my part I wish it also, because Thou wishest it."

Christmas, 1908. Consecration to the Holy Trinity. O Eternal Father, prostrate in humble adoration at Thy feet, we consecrate our whole being to the glory of Thy Son, Jesus, the Word Incarnate. Thou hast established Him as King of our souls; submit to Him our souls, our hearts, our bodies; let nothing in us move except by His orders, except by His inspiration. United with Him may we be borne into Thy bosom and consummated in the unity of Thy love. O Jesus, unite us to Thee in Thy life of perfect sanctity, wholly consecrated to Thy Father and to souls. Be unto us our wisdom, our justice, our sanctification, our redemption, our *all*. Sanctify us in truth.

O Holy Spirit, love of the Father and the Son, establish Thyself as a furnace of love in the centre of our hearts and bear constantly upwards, like eager flames, our thoughts, our affections and our actions even to the bosom of the Father. May our entire life be a *Gloria Patri et Filio et Spiritui Sancto*.

O Mary, Mother of Christ, Mother of fair love, do Thou form us according to the heart of Thy Son.

This act of consecration, the climax of a period of generous fidelity, became the point of departure for new interior progress.

December, 10th, 1911. A form of prayer which helps me a great deal in the midst of my weaknesses and my cares is to cast myself at the feet of the eternal Father *in the name* of Jesus Christ, saying to Him: "Father, Jesus has said that anything that is done to the least of His little ones is done to Himself; and I am one of the members of Thy Son, *concorporei et consanguinei Christi*; and all that Thou doest for me Thou doest for Him. He has never refused Thee anything; my miseries are His: *Vere languores nostros ipse tulit.*" I feel that this prayer moves the Father of mercies.

February 28th, 1916. Our Lord attracts me more and more to a *life of prayer in naked faith*, without consolation, but grounded in truth.

August 22nd, 1916. Caro et sanguis non revelavit tibi sed Pater meus qui in coelis est. I try to live in this light from on high for it is, according to Ruysbroeck, the point of contact in which the soul meets the Word. *Erat* LUX VERA *quae illuminat omnem hominem venientem in hunc mundum.* The *oratio fidei* alone can lead us to this light. It purifies, divinizes, and transforms us in ever-increasing light.

December 12th, 1916. For my part, I must say with St. John Perboyre: "My crucifix takes the place of all books for my prayer, for Christ is the way and it is by Him that God wills to reveal Himself to us: *Illuxit nobis in facie Christi Jesu*: He enlightens us in the countenance of Jesus Christ." When I contemplate Christ on the Cross I pass through the veil of His humanity into the holy of holies of the divine secrets.

April 4th, 1917. It seems to me that my soul remains constantly at the same point, that is to say a good deal of light and facility when I have to speak of God or exercise an act of ministry, but in the ordinary course of life a confused feeling that I am united to Christ and that, through Him, *I remain under the eye* of God and that this eye is normally hidden in deep obscurity: *Nubes et caligo in circuitu eius.*

May 9th, 1917. I experience powerful graces and great lights in the depth of my soul; it seems to me, not only that Christ dwells within me, but that I am, as it were, buried in Him, *spiritually surrounded* by His sacred presence. I adore Him in response to the Father Who reveals His divinity to me, and I do so tranquilly, without effort, and more and more as a matter of habit. From this springs a great faith and unlimited confidence in the goodness of the heavenly Father in spite of the constant realization which He gives me of my wretchedness, of my faults, and of my unworthiness.

February 24th, 1921. Never forget that prayer is a state and that, in souls which are seeking God, it persists, often unconsciously, in the spiritual depths of the soul. These silent desires, these sighs, are the true voice of the Holy Spirit in us and they move the heart of God: *Desiderium pauperum exaudivit auris tua.*

XVI. THE FAITH OF THE PRIEST IN THE HOLY SPIRIT

March 3rd, 1900. When the Word espoused His humanity, He brought it a dowry. As the Spouse was God the dowry was necessarily divine.

According to the Fathers and Doctors of the Church, the dowry which the Word presented to His humanity was the Holy Spirit, Who proceeds from Him as from the Father and Who is the substantial plenitude of sanctity. . . . For some time I have felt a special and ever increasing attraction to the Holy Spirit. I have a great desire to be guided, led, moved in all things by the Spirit of Jesus. Our Lord as man did nothing except under the impulse of the Holy Spirit and in dependence on Him. Thus it is that while, in virtue of the hypostatic union, it was the Word and the Word alone Who possessed the sacred humanity, He never acted in it or made it accomplish anything except through the Holy Spirit.

We have received the same Spirit in baptism and in the sacrament of confirmation: *quoniam estis filii, misit Spiritum Filii sui in corda vestra. Qui adhaeret Domino, unus Spiritus est.* St. Paul speaks constantly of the Spirit of Jesus which guided and enlightened him in all things.

Everything in our activity which comes from this Holy Spirit is itself holy: *quod natum est ex Spiritu, Spiritus est . . . Spiritus est qui vivificat.* The man who delivers himself up without reserve or resistance to this Spirit, which is *Pater pauperum . . . Dator munerum*, will be infallibly led by the same road as Jesus, and in the manner which Jesus wills for each individual. This Spirit impelled Elizabeth to praise Mary, and Mary is impelled by the same Spirit of Jesus to proclaim the glory of the Lord.

The Holy Spirit impels us to approach the Father as Jesus approaches Him: *Spiritus adoptionis in quo clamamus: Abba, Pater*; to glorify Jesus: *ipse testimonium perhibebit de me*; to pray as one should, forming our requests in our hearts *gemitibus inenarrabilibus*; He impels us to humility and to compunction: *quia ipse est remissio omnium peccatorum.* It is through Him that we do good to souls (the apostles accomplished so little before Pentecost). It is He Who renders all our activity fruitful: *Nemo potest dicere*: *Domine Jesu nisi in Spiritu Sancto.*

I shall try to live in this Holy Spirit.

October 5th, 1906. God seeks those who seek Him in spirit and in truth. The Holy Spirit is the Spirit of the Father and the Son, and those who allow themselves to be guided by Him are seeking the Father and the Son in truth. He is the Holy Spirit because all His inspirations are infinitely holy; He is the same Spirit Who inspired Jesus in all His actions and all His thoughts. It is by union with Him that the interior life of Jesus is formed in our hearts. He is the "Father of the poor", and He unites himself constantly to those who live *in adoration and in the spirit of self-abasement* in His presence. He is the Spirit of holy charity, and, being the same in all men, He unites us in holy love.

Pentecost, 1907. It is by the Holy Spirit that Jesus united Himself to His Father. This same Spirit dwells in our hearts: "He dwells amongst you and He will be in you." He is entirely dedicated to the Father and the Son, and He carries with Himself into the bosom of the Father and the Son all creation (which He loves in His "procession").

The more we abandon ourselves to this Holy Spirit of love, the more are all the tendencies of our being directed towards God. There are three spirits which are liable to take possession of us: the spirit of darkness, the human spirit, and the Holy Spirit. It is very important to distinguish the action of these spirits so that we may deliver ourselves up only to the Spirit of God.[3]

November 15th, 1908. It seems to me that the more intimately I am united to our divine Lord, the more He attracts me to His Father—the more also He seeks to fill me with His own filial spirit. This is the whole spirit of the new law: *Non enim accepistis spiritum servitutis in timore sed accepistis Spiritum adoptionis filiorum in quo clamamus Abba, Pater.*

---

[3] See in *Union with God* the fine commentary which Dom Marmion gives on this final stage.

Letter of April 9th, 1917. During this paschal season, the Church invites us to revive in ourselves the grace of our baptism (as St. Paul exhorts Timothy to "revive the grace" of his ordination to the priesthood). The three sacraments: baptism, confirmation and holy orders, leave us the *pignus Spiritus*, the pledge of the Spirit, a pledge which always calls down on us the grace of the sacrament. Baptism contains all *sanctity in embryo*. (1) Grace: participation in the divine nature, residing in the *essence of the soul*; (2) Theological virtues: faith, hope and charity in the *powers of the soul*; (3) Gifts of the Holy Spirit; (4) Infused moral virtues. All these gifts are the equipment of the child of the heavenly Father redeemed by Jesus Christ.

Confirmation strengthens and perfects this seed of life; the Eucharist provides its nourishment; faith is its root and its life: JUSTUS EX FIDE VIVIT.

All the rites and prayers employed in the administration of these sacraments have lasting effects which we can revive by faith and in the Holy Spirit. I frequently make my mental prayer by contemplating the heavenly Father in Jesus Christ in order to beg Him to renew in me all that the Church has asked for me and effected in me on the occasion of the reception of these sacraments. This is my refuge unless the Spirit of Christ attracts me to other activities.

XVII. SANCTIFICATION THROUGH OUR ORDINARY ACTIONS

1888. As I am convinced that my works can only be satisfactory and meritorious according to the degree of their union with the merits of Jesus Christ, it follows that my great aim must be to unite myself as *intimately as possible* to Jesus Christ and to His sufferings in all my actions—in this way it will matter little what is the nature of my occupation.

January 1st, 1899. The Church begins the year with the name of Jesus. Let us keep this name on our lips and in our heart. Our efforts are feeble, but, united with Him and with His merits, they are of great value in the eyes of the Lord. "Through Him and with Him and in Him all honour and glory to the Father." In the business world men strike a balance at the end of the year in order to determine their line of conduct for the future. Let us do the same. *Expenditure*: Three hundred and sixty-five days, physical and moral energy, sufferings. *Gain*: God, and all that is done for God: "their works follow them." All the rest perishes.

This year, let us do everything for God. Yet, how imperfect are even our best works! In the eyes of God, says the Scripture, all our justice is like soiled linen. The more we know, the better we can see our imperfections in the light: "we all fall in many things", but Jesus is our help. He is for us. He came down from heaven for us and for our salvation. His riches are ineffable and inestimable. He dwells in our hearts. Let us do all things in union with Him. He has sanctified all our actions. That is why St. Paul tells us to do all things in His name: "Do all things in the name of Our Lord Jesus Christ."

October 28th, 1902. I feel myself more and more drawn to lose myself, to hide myself in Jesus Christ: *vivens Deo in Christo Jesu*. He becomes, as it seems to me, the eye of my soul, and my will is merged with His. I feel myself drawn to desire nothing *outside* of Him, to remain lost *in Him*.

January 1st, 1906. The Church imprints the adorable name of Jesus on the whole year: "and thou shalt call His name Jesus" (Lk 1:31). I feel a great desire to imprint this sacred name on my whole being, on all my actions, in order "to abound to every good work" (2 Cor 9:8). I realize more and more clearly that the Father sees all things in His Son, loves all things in His Son; for He is entirely dedicated to Him. We are pleasing in His eyes according as He sees us in His Son: "He that abideth in Me and I in him, the same beareth much fruit" (Jn 15:5).

A little thing done in the name of Jesus is greater in the eyes of God than the most remarkable actions carried out in our own name.

I shall try to disappear so that Jesus may live and act in me: "He must increase, but I must decrease" (Jn 3:30). St. Paul was filled with this spirit: "I wished to lose all things, counting all things [actions performed in our own name] but as dung that I may gain Christ, not having my own justice which is of the law, but according to that which is of the faith of Christ." That is why he says to us: "All whatsoever you do in word or in work; do all in the name of Our Lord Jesus Christ" (Col 3:17). That is to say that we should act in our quality as members of Christ, in His dispositions and according to His designs.

January 20th, 1906. Jesus has accepted all the will of the Father for Himself and for His members, and we honour Him by uniting ourselves with this acceptance and by asking Him to take from our hearts all desire or inclination to do anything at all which is not within the framework of this will. (We can meditate on the life of Jesus Christ in the light of this thought, and such meditation is a source of great peace and great union with Him.) It is in this way that we fulfil perfectly the precept of St. Paul: "All whatsoever you do in word or in work, do all in the name of Our Lord Jesus Christ" (Col 3:17).

For we can do in His name only that which He sees to be the will of His Father in our regard. It is thus that the saying is realized: "He must increase, but I must decrease" (Jn 3:30). Then we become the object of the complacency of the Father from Whom come down all excellent gifts and all perfect graces: "Every best gift and every perfect gift" (Jas 1:17). The smallest actions become great because they are accomplished in God.

Letter of November 9th, 1910. Our Lord gives me a great attraction for this way: the laying of my whole being completely and constantly at the feet of the Word Incarnate. My desire is to imitate the sacred humanity of Jesus in His unity (with the Word), in His submission, and in His absolute dependence on the Word. Help me to realize this ideal, for everything is contained in it. There are no graces or favours which the Father will not grant to a soul which He sees united like this to His Word.

The sacred humanity of Jesus is the way. He is infinitely powerful to unite us to the Word. Let us then be saints for His glory: *In hoc clarificatus est Pater meus ut fructum plurimum afferatis.*

XVIII. THE VIRGIN MARY AND THE PRIEST

Feast of the Seven Dolours of Our Lady and Feast of Our Lady of Mercy, 1888. I have experienced a great increase of devotion to the Blessed Virgin Mary. Our perfection is in proportion to our resemblance to Jesus Christ: "This is my beloved Son in Whom I am well pleased." The love and reverence of Jesus for His blessed mother was immense. Therefore, I must try to imitate Him in that. This imitation must appear in a special manner in the priest who is *alter Christus.* On the feast of Our Lady of Mercy, I experienced great devotion in reciting the divine Office *in persona beatae Mariae Virginis*, offering my praise and my prayers *in her name*, as she must have offered them to the eternal Father through Jesus Christ—trying to enter into her sentiments of profound adoration and humility, of confidence and joy, at the thought of the triumph of her Son.

I have received a light which made it clear to me that all praise addressed to Mary is rendered in its entirety to the adorable Trinity (for example the Magnificat); so when I consecrate myself to her, she receives this gift simply in order to offer it immediately to God.

1888. I derive great help from the thought of the heroic confidence of the Blessed Virgin Mary in the truth of the Word made flesh, at Cana, on Calvary, and while the body of Our Lord was lying in the sepulchre. Confidence is a virile virtue which should be frequently stirred up and defended against the attacks of the demons.

March 25th, 1900. On the feast of the Annunciation I received a great light on the significance of these words: "Be it done to me according to Thy word." The whole life of Mary has been *secundum Verbum*, which is the infinite Wisdom. I felt a strong impulse to abandon myself to this Wisdom, to substitute this Wisdom for my own; Christ has become our wisdom through God, under the guidance of His Spirit: "Who of God is made unto us wisdom" (1 Cor 1:30). Jesus, the infinite Wisdom, has done all things under the guidance of this life-giving (*vivificans*) Spirit, and we have this same Spirit through grace, "the Spirit of adoption of sons whereby we cry Abba, Father!" (Rom 8:15).

March 22nd, 1918. I realized to-day (Good Friday) that Mary WAS PERFECT in her sublime faith at the foot of the Cross. O that she may obtain for us this signal grace of perfect faith, even in the desolation of trial! Nothing can glorify the Father like this unshakable faith in Christ in the drama of Calvary.

1920. In the morning, after Mass, when I possess Jesus in my heart, I present myself before the Blessed Virgin to consecrate myself to her and I say to her: *Ecce Filius tuus*: "Behold thy Son", O Virgin Mary, I am thy child; moreover I am a sharer in the priesthood of Jesus; accept me for thy son as thou accepted Jesus. I am unworthy of thy gifts, but I am a member of the mystical body of thy divine Son. And He has said Himself: "As long as you did it to one of these My least brethren you did it to Me" (Mt 25:40). I am one of these *minimis meis*; to refuse me would be to refuse Jesus Himself.

XIX. TRANSFIGURATION

Letter of December 13th, 1919. What a magnificent thing it is that, being founded and rooted in Christ, we can unceasingly contemplate with eyes of faith the countenance of the Father Whom we shall contemplate in heaven for all eternity! And, just as in heaven, *similes ei erimus quia videbimus eum sicuti est*, this vision being the source of our sanctity, so, here on earth, this vision of faith is a fountain of life: *quoniam apud te est fons vitae.* Pray a great deal for me that in the midst of so much bustle I may not cease to contemplate the face of the heavenly Father.

BEATIFICATION HOMILY
BY
JOHN PAUL II
(Exerpt)

Today the Benedictine Order rejoices at the beatification of one of its most distinguished sons, Dom Columba Marmion, a monk and Abbot of Maredsous. Dom Marmion left us an authentic treasure of spiritual teaching for the Church of our time. In his writings he teaches a simple yet demanding way of holiness for all the faithful, whom God has destined in love to be his adopted children through Jesus Christ (cf. Eph 1:5). Jesus Christ, our Redeemer and the source of all grace, is the center of our spiritual life, our model of holiness.

Before entering the Benedictine Order, Columba Marmion spent some years in the pastoral care of souls as a priest of his native Archdiocese of Dublin. Throughout his life Blessed Columba was an outstanding spiritual director, having particular care for the interior life of priests and religious. To a young man preparing for ordination he once wrote: "The best of all preparations for the priesthood is to live each day with love, wherever obedience and Providence place us" (Letter, December 27, 1915). May a widespread rediscovery of the spiritual writings of Blessed Columba Marmion help priests, religious and laity to grow in union with Christ and bear faithful witness to him through ardent love of God and generous service of their brothers and sisters.

SEPTEMBER 3, 2000

INDEX